AMERICAN SECULARISM

RELIGION AND SOCIAL TRANSFORMATION
General Editors: Anthony B. Pinn and Stacey M. Floyd-Thomas

Prophetic Activism: Progressive Religious Justice Movements in Contemporary America
Helene Slessarev-Jamir

All You That Labor: Religion and Ethics in the Living Wage Movement
C. Melissa Snarr

Blacks and Whites in Christian America: How Racial Discrimination Shapes Religious Convictions
James E. Shelton and Michael O. Emerson

Pillars of Cloud and Fire: The Politics of Exodus in African American Biblical Interpretation
Herbert Robinson Marbury

American Secularism: Cultural Contours of Nonreligious Belief Systems
Joseph O. Baker and Buster G. Smith

American Secularism

Cultural Contours of Nonreligious Belief Systems

Joseph O. Baker and Buster G. Smith

NEW YORK UNIVERSITY PRESS
New York and London

NEW YORK UNIVERSITY PRESS
New York and London
www.nyupress.org

References to Internet websites (URLs) were accurate at the time of writing. Neither the author nor New York University Press is responsible for URLs that may have expired or changed since the manuscript was prepared.

Library of Congress Cataloging-in-Publication Data
Baker, Joseph O., 1938–
American secularism : cultural contours of nonreligious belief systems /
Joseph O. Baker and Buster G. Smith.
pages cm. — (Religion and social transformation)
Includes bibliographical references and index.
ISBN 978-1-4798-6741-7 (cl : alk. paper) — ISBN 978-1-4798-7372-2 (pb : alk. paper)
1. Secularism—United States. I. Title.
BL2747.8.B285 2015
211'.60973—dc23 2015012227

New York University Press books are printed on acid-free paper, and their binding materials are chosen for strength and durability. We strive to use environmentally responsible suppliers and materials to the greatest extent possible in publishing our books.

Manufactured in the United States of America

10 9 8 7 6 5 4 3 2 1

Also available as an ebook

For Amy, Hazel, and Ingrid

CONTENTS

Acknowledgments ix

Introduction: A Nation of Nonbelievers 1

1. Classifying Secularities 13
2. A Cultural View of Secularities 25
3. Historical Foundations 45
4. The Great Abdicating 66
5. Nonreligious Belief Systems 89
6. Ethnicity, Assimilation, and Secularity 106
7. Gender and Secularity 133
8. Marriage, Family, and Social Networks 151
9. The (Explicit) Politics of Secularity 167

Conclusion: A Secular, Cosmical Movement? 201

Data Sources Appendix 219

Notes 223

Bibliography 271

Index 283

About the Authors 293

ACKNOWLEDGMENTS

Although books are credited to their authors, behind any creative endeavor are numerous people supporting, contributing to, and enhancing the project who do not receive their due credit. Numerous scholars generously lent their time and talent to offer feedback on parts of this manuscript, including Zach Dresser, Amy Edmonds, Penny Edgell, Stephen LeDrew, Jerry Park, Kelli Smith, Sam Stroope, and Andrew Whitehead, as well as helpful anonymous reviewers. Special thanks go to Tony Pinn. Without his generosity and encouragement, a book-length project on secularity in the U.S. would not have materialized.

Both East Tennessee State University and Catawba College have been very supportive of this project at all stages. At ETSU, colleagues in the department of sociology and anthropology have been immensely supportive. In particular, Bill Duncan and Melissa Schrift have listened to more than their fair share of questions and musings about all things secular. Tony Cavender, Paul Kamolnick, and Martha Copp have been consistently encouraging and engaged senior faculty. The College of Arts and Sciences at ETSU also supported this research with a Summer Research Fellowship in 2013. Thanks to Gordon Anderson in particular for his support of this valuable resource. The faculty at Catawba College was remarkably encouraging throughout this process, particularly Maria Vandergriff-Avery. In addition, repeated faculty development funding made it possible to collaborate on and continue this project.

We also want to express our gratitude for the vast data resources available through the Association of Religion Data Archives, directed by Roger Finke and Chris Bader. Nearly all of the array of datasets we use in this book are publically available through the ARDA (www.thearda.com). The open access to quality data on religion (and secularism!) is revolutionizing our field, for the better.

We are also grateful to Cecil Bothwell, Lori Lipman Brown, and David Tamayo for sharing their time and experiences with us. All are gracious, affable, and positive examples of secularity. The book is far more interesting because of their contributions. Thanks to Roy Speckhardt and August Brunsman IV for providing information on the American Humanist Association and Secular Student Alliance, respectively.

Finally, thanks to those whose love and support makes our work possible. Carmen Arendt, as well as Joanna and John Baker provided superb care for Hazel Baker-Edmonds, sometimes in difficult circumstances. Most of all, thanks to Amy Edmonds and Ingrid Erickson, who have tirelessly supported this project, even as it meant working long hours away from the ones we love. It is to them we dedicate this book.

Introduction

A Nation of Nonbelievers

There are more individuals who consider themselves "not religious" living in the United States than in any other nation in the world except China. This fact stands in stark contrast to declarations that America is a fervently religious or Christian nation. The numeric magnitude of secularity in the U.S. is generally overlooked because there are many countries, particularly in Western Europe and East Asia, where the *proportion* of secularists in the population is higher. For instance, in 2011, 28% of American respondents to the World Values Survey (WVS) said that they were "not . . . religious person[s]" or were atheists, and also that they attended religious services infrequently or not at all.[1] Many other countries included in the same wave of the WVS had a higher proportion of respondents who said they were not religious or were atheists, including Australia (56%), China (87%), Germany (47%), Japan (70%), the Netherlands (54%), New Zealand (51%), Russia (38%), South Korea (57%), Spain (58%), and Sweden (66%). Earlier waves of the survey also found a higher proportion of secular individuals in locations such as France (52%) and Great Britain (49%). Such comparative analyses have led many scholars to designate the U.S. as "exceptionally" religious relative to other postindustrial nations.[2]

There is certainly some validity to this claim, proportionally speaking. At the same time, portraying the U.S. as exceptionally religious obscures the many millions of Americans who are not religious. In recent years, however, secularism in the U.S. has been making headlines and receiving more attention due to a rapid increase in the number *and* proportion of Americans who are secular. For example, in the first wave of the WVS, collected in the U.S. in 1981, 8% of respondents answered that they were not religious persons or were atheists, and also that they infrequently attended religious services. The 1995 (15%) and 1999 waves

(13%) showed a substantial increase in secularity. In the 2006 wave, the percentage jumped to 22%, then rose again to 28% in 2011. Figure I.1 shows this increase of 3.5 times in the proportion of the population that is secular over a thirty-year span.[3]

Reflecting the rising numeric prominence and cultural awareness of secular Americans, Barack Obama declared during his first inaugural address that the United States is "a nation of Christians and Muslims, Jews and Hindus, and non-believers."[4] The rhetorical apex of Obama's speech was an effort to recast the civil religious nationalism of the U.S. as a more inclusive, cosmopolitan national identity.[5] In the period between 1980 and 2008, American presidential rhetoric had moved away from cosmopolitanism and toward particularistic religious nationalism, culminating in the explicitly religious post-9/11 rhetoric of George W. Bush, which emphasized America's exceptional, God-ordained role and destiny in global affairs using dualisms such as freedom/tyranny, good/evil, and us/them.[6] In contrast with his predecessor, Obama dissociated such dualisms—one of his primary rhetorical techniques.

The inaugural mention of nonbelievers was a remarkable moment.[7] Not that the politics of secularism are new. Quite the contrary. For example, the list of Americans who have used some variety of secular philosophy as a foundation from which to build lasting political and cultural legacies is long and distinguished—from Thomas Jefferson and Thomas Paine, through Thomas Edison and Mark Twain, to A. Philip Randolph and Carl Sagan.[8] Indeed, historians and philosophers have recently reemphasized the influence of freethought traditions on the foundational ideas of the American republic, as well as on globalized ideas about democracy and civil liberties.[9] Yet, in spite of the influence of secular traditions on American culture, widespread public recognition of the importance of such traditions remained elusive, particularly in the post–World War II era.

In national communications by American presidents to the public from Franklin Roosevelt to George W. Bush, secularists were rarely mentioned. Further, Gerald Ford's mention of atheists in a 1974 speech to Congress in the immediate wake of assuming the presidency after the Watergate scandal was the only instance where secularists were not discussed in a context of condemnation. Ford said of atheists at the close of his speech:

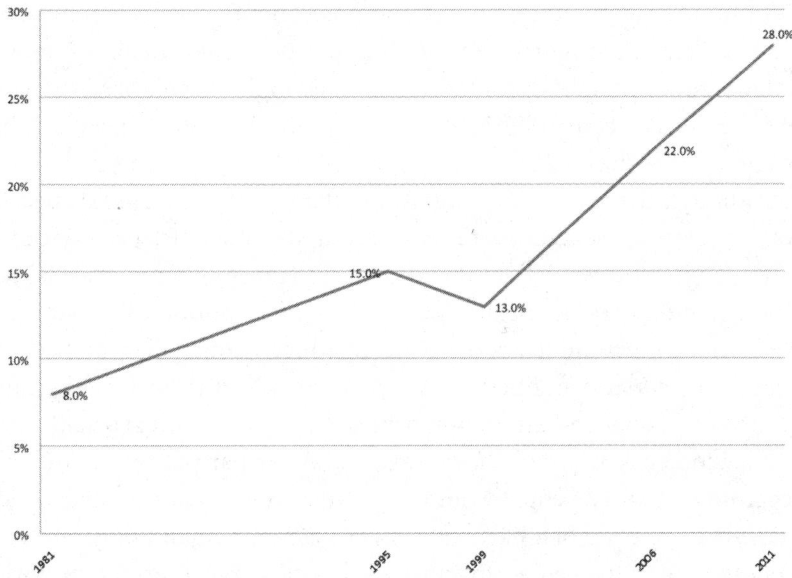

Figure I.1. Percentage of Americans "Not Religious" or "Atheist" Who Also Rarely Attend Religious Services, World Values Surveys 1981–2011

> To the limits of my strength and ability, I will be the President of black, brown, red, and white Americans, of old and young, of women's liberationists and male chauvinists—and all the rest of us in-between, of the poor and the rich, of native sons and new refugees, of those who work at lathes or at desks or in mines or in the fields, of Christians, Jews, Moslems, Buddhists, and atheists, if there really are any atheists after what we have all been through. Fellow Americans, one final word: I want to be a good President. I need your help. We all need God's sure guidance. With it, nothing can stop the United States of America. Thank you very much.[10]

This qualified, begrudging acknowledgment that secularists were indeed American citizens (but also at the outer limits of tolerance), followed by a reminder to listeners that we "all need God's sure guidance," was hardly a ringing endorsement of secularity. Yet this was still the most positive mention of secularity in presidential rhetoric in the twentieth century. Acknowledging secularists as worthy of respect in one of the most highly anticipated and watched presidential speeches in history made Obama's inaugural comments about nonbelievers all the more noteworthy, especially considering that even highly secularized threads of nationalist discourse still reference generalized theism, particularly in inaugural speeches.[11]

Although the symbolic recognition offered in the inaugural speech was a milestone, secularists remain among the most distrusted groups in the United States. When the 2003 American Mosaic Survey asked whether members of specific groups shared respondents' "vision of America," a much higher proportion answered "not at all" when asked about atheists and nonbelievers (37%) compared to other religious groups and racial and ethnic minorities. By comparison, 21% said "not at all" when asked about "homosexuals." A similar pattern is present regarding whether people would approve or disapprove of their child marrying someone of a particular social category. Again, nonbelievers were the most disliked, outpacing Muslims and racial/ethnic minorities. Over half (51%) of religiously affiliated Americans reported that they would disapprove of their child marrying an atheist or nonbeliever, compared to roughly one third of non-Muslims disapproving of their child marrying a Muslim. Acceptance for the nonreligious remains rare, even relative to other "othered" groups in American society.[12]

At the same time, the rhetorical inclusion of secularity in a list of the world's most prominent religious traditions marks a dramatic shift in the religious composition of the U.S. (and the Western world more generally) over the past half century. Although secularism remains strongly othered, recent generations of Americans are more accepting of, and more likely to be, secular. What is the meaning of this transformation? Naturally, the answer depends on whom you ask. Many religious believers see the trend as evidence that America has fallen away from its moral values, while many secularists see it as evidence of increasing enlightenment and rationality.[13] Meanwhile, some social scientists have claimed that the trend reflects measurement error rather than an actual increase in secularity.[14] We see it as none of these things. Instead, we view changes to American secularism as reflective of a shift in the political meanings of "religion" in American culture.

Our goal is to provide an empirically rigorous, interpretively meaningful, and ethically evenhanded portrait of secular individuals.

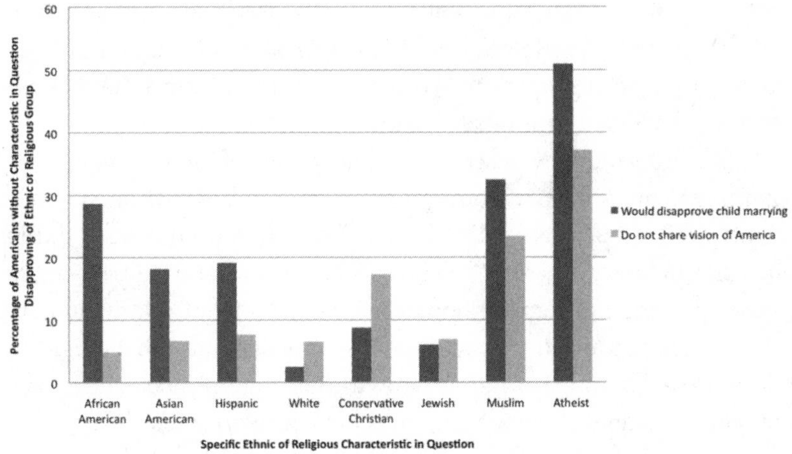

Figure I.2. Percentage "Othering" Individuals with Specific Ethnic or Religious Characteristics, 2003

Although the trope of "objectivity" is common enough in official presentations of methodology by social scientists, the implementation of these ideals is often lacking in practice, particularly in studies of both religion and secularism. As we will see, the acuity of this problem inheres in our intellectual origins. Developing better frameworks for understanding religion and secularism can be achieved only by a thoroughgoing commitment to presenting social phenomena *as they are*. This is no simple dictate or easy task. It requires sustained effort and attention to detail. As much as possible, we attempt to make our primary bias that of empiricists. Fully aware of the potential pitfalls and blind spots that accompany the rhetoric of neutral inquiry, we have nonetheless set out in this book to create an objective portrait of American secularism(s).

Background and Goals of the Study

While changing cultural responses to, and rates of, secularity have recently made high-profile headlines, the social and cultural dimensions of these consequential changes often remain poorly understood, particularly in four key areas: (1) the variety and complexity of expressions of secularity; (2) the implications of secularism for explanatory and interpretive theories "of religion"; (3) the historical, cultural, and political dimensions of secularities; and (4) the sociological patterns and consequences of various forms of secularity.[15]

On the first count, even scholarly conceptions of secularism are only beginning to move beyond homogeneity, while public views often remain stereotypical and pejorative. Rather than being simply an issue of the absence of religious belief or affiliation, there are wide varieties of secular expression, ranging from passionate antipathy to tepid apathy, and also including the privatization of spiritual concerns and nominal religiosity. Indeed, there are as many "atheologies as theologies."[16] Cultural expressions at the borders of binary thinking about religion and secularity such as "implicit religion," "believing but not belonging," "spiritual but not religious," and the like complicate these issues further. Mapping the diversity of secular expressions and conceptualizing secularisms as assertive worldviews in their own right, rather than merely negated reflections of religion, stands as a crucial challenge for better understanding secularity, and religiosity. Although criticism of religion is central to understanding secularism, restricting secularity solely to opposition to religion denies secularists' potential for edifying identities and positive values, furthering the polemical claim that to be secular is necessarily to be immoral.[17]

On the second count, a conceptual framework capable of integrating investigations of both religiosity and secularity is needed to advance theoretical and empirical knowledge in the multidisciplinary study of religion. Instead of a binary distinction, religiosity and secularity should be understood as poles of a continuum, ranging from thorough irreligion to zealotry. In order to conceptualize religiosity and secularity in this way, a broader organizing concept capable of housing each is required. We propose *cosmic belief systems* as a concept capable of usefully integrating studies of religiosity and secularity. Further, we use the idea of relational social status—where and how a person is "positioned" relative to others she interacts with—as the basis from which to understand both religiosity and secularity. Rich traditions of interactionist and cultural sociology provide a ready-made platform for such work, along with related work in political science, anthropology, communications, psychology, and other disciplines.[18] The key is to connect these pursuits to empirical studies of religion and secularism.

These conceptual reformations provide the groundwork for the third theme, connecting contemporary secularities to history, politics, and culture more broadly. As we noted, wide recognition of the historical realities of secular traditions is often surface at best, even among secularists. Tracing the history and influence of secular organizations and individuals not only enriches our understanding of the past, it illuminates many of the contemporary issues involving secularism. Even scant engagements with histories of secularism reveal the importance of interactive connections to both organized religion and politics. While the specifics of these dynamics change over time and place, a full understanding of secularism requires viewing it in relation to religion and in political context. While this assertion is unlikely to provoke strong intellectual resistance, the corollary of understanding religion through its relation to secularism has, as far as we can see, few current advocates; but it is an important consideration that can open studies of religion to new insights.[19] In essence, we advocate and practice approaching religion and secularism from a cultural perspective that foregrounds issues of politics and social context, regardless of the methods of inquiry used.

These considerations provide the foundation for our final theme: advancing an empirical understanding of secularism and secularities. Clarifying and classifying common forms of secularity is a primary step toward this goal, so in this book we outline a basic typology of secularities found in the contemporary U.S.: atheism, agnosticism, nonaffiliated belief, and cultural religion. Using this categorization scheme, we provide detailed, empirical information about different expressions of secularity. We also dissect the increase in secularity in the U.S. over the last forty years, providing explanations for these changes that are grounded in empirical data. We draw on multiple data sources collected with the intent of representing the general population of American adults. Most centrally we use the General Social Surveys (1972–2012) and the Pew Religious Landscape Survey (2007), but we also use a variety of other data sources where needed.[20] Further information on our central data sources is available in the appendix at the end of the book, and tabled results of analyses supporting the information presented in the text of chapters can be found in the Data Analyses Appendix, available at http://nyupress.org/americansecularism-appendix.pdf.

While important, analyses of general patterns and themes of secularity can go only so far.[21] Like religion, at root secularity boils down to the narratives people tell about how we got here, who we are, "how the world works," and what, if anything, lies beyond what we can directly observe. To bring out the narrative dimensions of secularities, we listen to and retell the stories of Lester Ward, W. E. B. Du Bois, and Frances Wright, as well as contemporary Americans openly engaged in matters of secularism in the public sphere. We also pay close attention to how secularity is understood and discussed in public discourse, particularly in relation to political dimensions of inclusion and exclusion.

To avoid the confusion that surrounds the multiplicity of uses for many of the terms we use throughout the book, some basic clarification on terminology is necessary. Below is a list of terms we use, along with the intended meaning we assign to them. We outline the definition of specific views such as atheism and agnosticism in the next chapter.

Secular—a general designation for people, organizations, or institutions that are *not* religious.[22]

Nonreligion—a general term that incorporates multiple expressions of secularism and secularity under a broader concept. Nonreligion is "anything which is *primarily* defined by a relationship of difference to religion."[23]

Secularity—social status or personal identity built on nonreligious assumptions.

Belief system—a constellation of interrelated beliefs. We use "belief system" and "ideology" interchangeably, but prefer "belief system" because "ideology" often carries negative connotations, which we do not intend. We also make the distinction of "cosmic" for belief systems concerned with basic facts about the nature of the universe and "how the world works."

Secularism—cosmic belief system that is explicitly nonreligious in orientation.

Secularization—a process of change from religious to secular that can occur at individual, organizational, or institutional levels.

Irreligious—strongly, vocally opposed to religion; essentially a synonym for "anti-religious." We avoid using this term except where directly applicable.

Regarding references, we have included a bibliography of theoretical, historical, and empirical work on secularism directly related to our study. Sources listed in the bibliography are cited in the endnotes by author name and year of publication. Other sources not listed in the bibliography are cited with complete information in the endnotes.

Outline of the Book

Chapter 1 lays out some of the basic methodological considerations for our study, including a mutually exclusive typology of secular individuals: atheists, agnostics, nonaffiliated believers, and the culturally (nonpracticing) religious. We also distinguish between those raised in religious traditions who drop out as adults and those raised outside of organized religions who remain secular as adults. We then generate balanced estimates for levels of secularity using multiple data sources, showing how measurement can influence results.

Chapter 2 outlines the theoretical and conceptual framework we use throughout the book. The personal and professional narrative of Lester F. Ward, a pioneering American sociologist, provides a window into the long-standing assumptions of scholarly investigations of religion and secularism. Ward's thought and narrative point to ideas that became taken for granted among academics regarding religion, science, and secularity. In contrast, we approach meaning-making both inside and outside of organized religion with tools provided by studies of culture, interaction, and cognition, conceptualizing secularities as both social statuses and cosmic belief systems.

Chapter 3 traces the historical development of secularism in the United States. By tracking the role of "freethought" in American public discourse from the late eighteenth century to the 1950s, the historical roots of contemporary secularity become more apparent. We focus on the impact of the early separation of church and state at the federal level, followed thereafter at state levels, detailing how the political and ideological context in which secularity exists shapes its concerns and organizational forms. To trace these histories we examine organizations and texts that were explicitly freethought in orientation. We carry these analyses to the Cold War era, during which the contrast between "religious America" and "godless communism" became the dominant cultural template for framing secularism in public discourse.

Chapter 4 places secularity in more recent historical context by expanding the view of secularism from that of "the platform" to that of "the parlor." Beginning in the 1970s, advances in population surveys allow us to outline patterns of secularity among the general public rather than being confined to formal, publically organized forms of secularism. We show how absolute numbers and relative proportions of secular Americans have changed over the past forty years. Generational changes to the social organization of family and sexuality have pushed against the familial traditionalism of organized religion, while divides over cultural issues and the overt use of religion as a political strategy have fueled increasing political polarization among Americans. This polarization parallels and has contributed to increasing levels of secularity. Overall, secularism has beaten demographic disadvantages in fertility to grow rapidly, thanks to a sharp rise in the apostasy rate among those raised religious coinciding with an increase in secular retention among those raised outside religion. All of these patterns are evident in trend data collected over time.

Chapter 5 outlines some specific ideological patterns among different categories of secularists, with attention to four areas: attitudes about organized religion and private spirituality, supernaturalism, life satisfaction and happiness, and views of science. Here we begin to add color and detail to the different categories of secularity. Levels of private spirituality, religious and paranormal supernaturalism, and scientism show distinct patterns between atheists, agnostics, nonaffiliated believers, and the culturally religious. We also use this chapter to address the question of whether and to what extent secularity correlates with self-rated levels of happiness and personal satisfaction. Overall, there is enough overlap *and* divergence to establish the utility of the typology for better understanding secularities.

Chapter 6 explores connections between secularity and some of the fundamental dimensions of power in American society, namely race and ethnicity, social class, and immigrant status. The dynamic life and thought of scholar and activist W. E. B. Du Bois helps illuminate some of the deeper connections between ethnicity, religion, and conventionality in American culture. In general, individuals occupying status positions with less power are less likely to be secular. There are subtleties to this tendency, such as the differential influence of increased educational attainment on supernatural belief (negative) and religious affiliation and practice (positive), but the tendency for those in less powerful positions to be religious points toward an important cultural dimension of religiosity and secularity in the United States. To the extent that religion is linked to a person's normative status as a moral, civically engaged citizen, secularity becomes deviant, and therefore subject to accompanying social penalties. This dynamic shapes the patterns and expressions of secularity in crucial ways, and we use racial, ethnic, immigrant, and socioeconomic statuses as prisms through which to understand this aspect of American culture. We close the chapter by profiling the identity, experiences, and work of David Tamayo, a contemporary leader of a nonprofit group for Hispanic American freethinkers.

Chapter 7 examines how gender and sexuality relate to secularity. We critically assess the "gender gaps" in religiosity and secularity typically found in empirical studies of religion in Western countries. These gender gaps vary depending on the type of secularity in question. To dissect the reason for these gaps, we detail the interactive relationship between gender, educational attainment, and political views. This chapter also examines patterns of sexual orientation among the varying categories of secularists. These patterns reflect organized religion's role as the guardian of traditional morality—and therefore pathway to legitimacy (or perceived deviance)—in matters of gender and sexuality. We illustrate these themes through in-depth consideration of the life and thought of Frances Wright, a nineteenth-century philosopher, orator, and feminist.

Chapter 8 focuses on family structure, outlining patterns of family formation among American secularists, including rates of marriage, cohabitation, and parenting. We then examine the influences of childhood socialization and social networks—particularly parents, peers, and spouses—on expressions of secularity. As with patterns of religiosity, familial connections, socialization experiences, and social networks strongly influence secularity. In order to understand secularities as social statuses and identities, considerations of relational networks and the interactions that occur within those networks are central.

Chapter 9 focuses on the explicitly political dimensions of contemporary American secularisms. The narrative of Cecil Bothwell, an openly atheist member of the city council in Asheville, North Carolina, provides insight into narratives of secularity as well as some of the political dimensions of secularism. Tellingly, the growth in secularity in the population has not led to a parallel increase in secular political representatives. Underrepresentation in the halls of power speaks to the continued ambivalence many Americans feel toward secularism due to its deviant designation, even as secularity has increased. In terms of political views and engagement among secularists, issues of gender and sexuality again come to the fore. This chapter closes by detailing the contemporary political landscape concerning secular Americans and examining the increasing presence of organized secular groups in the United States. The experiences of the first executive director of the Secular Coalition for America, Lori Lipman Brown, and the activities of three of the most prominent secular organizations—the American Humanist Association, American Atheists, and the Secular Student Alliance—show how changes to the political meaning of secularism and the growth of secularity are reflected in changes to organized secular groups.

In the conclusion, we provide an overview of our most important findings and discuss their implications for organized religious and secular groups. We also briefly consider the question of the U.S. case in comparative context by examining how national levels of secularity relate to societal levels of human development. We close by returning to issues of identity and morality, discussing how cultural perspectives of secularities challenge widely held assumptions and conceptualizations in both the popular and academic understandings of religion.

1

Classifying Secularities

"Secular" as a social category has religious roots and can be understood only in intimate juxtaposition to "the religious." For there to be a classificatory option of religion, its "other" (the *not it*) must exist, at least rhetorically.[1] Complicating the use of the concept is its application to phenomena of varying scope and abstraction. Most commonly, the secular and its kindred secularism are employed to reference the political dimensions of that which is explicitly *not* religious. For instance, "secular" is often used to categorize the official policies of nation-states with disestablished or nonestablished relationships to religious traditions and organizations, while "secularism" is understood as an ideological framing of political projects aimed at achieving or maintaining secular cultural space.[2]

Here we are primarily concerned with secular individuals rather than institutions. The two interpenetrate, but not necessarily in expected ways, as evinced by the history of American freethought. We use the term "secularity" to refer to the meaning-making strategies people employ who have an explicitly anti- or nonreligious referent. All people utilize an understanding of meaning that is not explicitly religious in some, indeed many, circumstances; but we are interested in individuals for whom ultimate questions of reality, meaning, and identity are not religious—at least along some basic, traditional dimensions. Our interest is in individuals whose primary identities, experiential perceptions, and routinely utilized cultural frameworks are nonreligious in nature.[3]

But what makes a person "secular"? This is a straightforward yet deceptively difficult question. In asking what counts as an instance of secularity, we are confronted with theoretical baggage freighted by the term. Two issues are of particular concern in this regard. First, the wide-ranging impact and historical importance of secularization theories have produced substantial confusion along with polemical connotations—

both political and intellectual.[4] In short, protracted conceptual and polemic debates have hindered the development of an *empirical* account of secularity. In analyzing patterns and trends in American secularity, we do not endorse secularism as right, true, or inevitable with the advance of time and culture. Conversely, we also do not endorse the conflation between the "religious" and the "good" that occurs within ethical frameworks laid out in religious and popular (and also sometimes academic) discourse. The notion that the nonreligious are immoral, depraved, or evil is clearly polemical rather than empirical.[5] Rather, we see the moral value of religion in individuals' lives as highly variable and view questions about the social impact of secularity and religiosity as empirical rather than normative issues. We confer neither denigration nor veneration, blessing nor curse. These are judgments for others to make, and they will undoubtedly continue to do so with the passionate energy that accompanies perceived righteousness. Such proclamations are not of interest to us, except as data.

Beyond the moral and polemical connotations entwined with the use of religious and secular categories, their binary classification imposes an unnecessarily strict delineation. Imposing bifurcation onto complex social realities forces a loss of accuracy, especially concerning cases that fall near the borderline. Of course, there will always be conceptual ambiguity bordering the edges of any classification scheme used to simplify a diverse reality, but a binary understanding of secular/religious is too simple and is misleading for the development of a fuller understanding of secularities as cultural phenomena.[6] To move beyond a binary classification requires the consideration of multiple dimensions of secularity and religiosity.

Basic Classifications

We use the inverse of the following dimensions of religiosity as keys to classifying secularity: affiliation, belief, and practice.[7] For affiliation, we examine whether someone claims any religious affiliation when the option of "no religion" or "none" is specifically given—in other words, whether a person claims no affiliation with an established religion. Claiming no religion does not necessarily mean that people consider themselves anti- or nonreligious in their private lives, merely that they do not identify with any organized, public religion. Religious "nones" may well be nonreligious privately too, but this is an open question. We define the category as:

Religiously Nonaffiliated—Individuals who claim no affiliation with an organized religion.

The second dimension we use is theistic belief. Here we are primarily interested in two broad categories of nontheism, atheism and agnosticism. We define atheism in a manner consistent with its popular use, meaning people who do not believe in god.[8] Further distinctions can be drawn within this category, such as between "hard" atheists (who claim definitive proof for the lack of god's existence) and "soft" atheists (who do not believe, but also do not claim definitive proof). Although these distinctions are meaningful for the way people rationalize atheism, we focus on the more general category. We consider agnostics to be those who believe knowledge of god's existence or nonexistence is beyond human capacity. For example, an agnostic might answer a survey question about the existence of god by selecting an option such as "I don't know and there is no way to find out." For our purposes, we define those with theistic dis- and nonbelief as:

(1) Atheists—Individuals who do not believe theistic claims.
(2) Agnostics—Individuals who assert that theistic claims are unverifiable in principle.

We refer to atheists and agnostics as "disbelievers" and "nonbelievers," respectively.[9] These categories are defined in reference to questions of theism, understood in the predominantly monotheistic manner of the Abrahamic traditions. To be clear, atheism and agnosticism do not always mean complete dis- or nonbelief in all supernatural entities, as someone may be agnostic about the existence of god but certain about the existence of ghosts.[10] Although clearly not true of the majority of atheists or agnostics, this possibility allows us to define the categories in reference to the most culturally central question of supernaturalism in the U.S., then employ the categories to examine the relative absence or presence of other supernatural beliefs.

We also use a category produced by considering those persons who have no religious affiliation and theistic belief in conjunction. We consider theistic dis- or nonbelief to be the most salient marker of one's secular identity. That is, self-identifying as someone who does not believe in god is a more prominent marker of identity than saying one is not affiliated with an organized religion.[11] If individuals respond to a query about theism by identifying with atheism or agnosticism, we use those designations as the starting point for further examining other social dimensions of their lives; however, theistic dis- or nonbelief and claiming no religion need not necessarily occur in conjunction. A person may quite reasonably be a theistic doubter but value other aspects of participating in a religious community such as camaraderie, social support, ethnic identification, or familial obligations. Such "belonging without believing" is relatively common in Scandinavian countries with established national religious traditions. In the U.S., only 1% of the overall pooled 1972–2010 waves of the General Social Surveys (GSS) fit the designation of belonging without believing. Compared to atheists and agnostics who also claim no religious affiliation, those who are affiliated nonbelievers tend to be older, make more money, have more children, and are slightly more likely to be politically conservative. Not surprisingly, affiliated nonbelievers also attend religious services and pray more than nonaffiliated nonbelievers. People fitting this classification according to GSS data were also disproportionately Jewish. Although theistic dis- and nonbelievers who maintain at least symbolic affiliation with a religious tradition certainly warrant inquiry, for the sake of parsimony we focus on nonaffiliated believers and theistic dis- and nonbelief as three mutually exclusive categories of secularity.

Conversely, individuals may not be affiliated with an organized religion but maintain some form of theistic belief. This trend is so prevalent in Western Europe that it has inspired a debate about the meaning and significance of "believing without belonging."[12] As we will see, the privatization of religious belief has also become increasingly common in the United States. Accordingly, we distinguish nonaffiliated believers as a useful category in an American context:

(3) Nonaffiliated Believers—Individuals who claim no religious affiliation but maintain some form of theistic belief.

A final category of secularity we distinguish is people who claim both religious affiliation and theistic belief, but do not engage in religious practice with any relative frequency. Individuals in this category can be considered as having primarily symbolic religious identities; that is, they maintain a self-understanding that includes religious elements, but they do not engage the ritual dimensions of religion in either public or private. Sociologist N. J. Demerath has termed this phenomenon "cultural religion," meaning that religious symbols retain some emotive and cultural power for individuals even as they disengage from actively practicing religious communities.[13] Cultural religion is a more ambiguous delineation than those of self-identification. Unlike religious "nones" or theistic nonbelievers, the culturally religious self-identify as religious and we as researchers determine where to draw the line separating the nonpracticing from the practicing.

To capture whether individuals are disengaged from religious practice, we primarily use two measures of religiosity, one public and one private. To assess public expression of religious commitment, we use attendance at religious services. For private religious practice, we use questions that ask about prayer outside of religious services. For each dimension, we allow individuals to engage in religious practice minimally and still be classified as culturally religious. We consider attendance at religious services twice a year or less to be evidence of a lack of public practice. That is, we consider "Christmas and Easter" Christians or Jews who attend temple annually on a high holiday but do not pray to be culturally religious rather than actively religious. Thus, our final category is:

(4) Culturally Religious—Individuals who claim religious affiliation and theistic belief, but rarely (if ever) attend religious services or pray privately.

The categorization of individuals as culturally religious is dependent upon the response options available in a given survey. Our pragmatic rule of thumb for classification is to consider the lowest options on a practice question to be nonpracticing; however, response options vary by survey, making the delineation more practical than ideal. For example, there are different response options on religiosity questions in our two primary data sources. For the Pew Religious Landscape Survey, applicable respondents who selected "rarely" or "never" for *both* public (religious service attendance) and private religious expression (prayer outside religious services) are classified as culturally religious. For the General Social Surveys, we classify applicable respondents as culturally religious if they answer that they pray outside of religious services less than once a week and attend religious services once a year or less. Such categorization is clearly debatable. Some might well argue for either more stringent or looser conceptualization, but overall it reasonably outlines the category of interest without being so rigid as to leave only a tiny grouping.[14] For the most part, we use the four mutually exclusive categories of atheist, agnostic, nonaffiliated believer, and culturally religious as a typology for understanding both the diversity and unity of American secularism. Those who do not fit one of these four categories are classified as "actively religious."

At times, we also distinguish between individuals raised within a religion who dropped out and those who were raised and stayed outside of religion.

Apostates—Individuals who consider themselves to have been religiously affiliated as children, but who are religiously unaffiliated as adults.

Socialized Seculars—Individuals who consider themselves to have been secular as children, and who remain religiously nonaffiliated as adults.

We use this distinction primarily to track changes and trends in overall religious/secular composition, and also to examine how socialization affects the resulting expressions of secularity.

These categories highlight the variety of secular expressions, while also not slicing the proverbial pie so thin as to lose utility. At the highest level of specificity, there are as many distinct forms of secularity as there are secularists. All people, religious or otherwise, represent idiosyncratic mixtures of socialization, experiences, and self-understanding. At the opposite end of this continuum, religionists often stereotype secularists as "all the same." Many staunch secularists paint religious people with similarly broad strokes. Such characterizations are generally negative in intent and effect. By outlining general but distinguishable differences in secular expressions, we attempt to strike a balance between the general and the specific, and in doing so highlight the diversity of secularism(s).[15]

Our overarching analytic strategy is to compare these groups to one another, as well as to religiously affiliated, theistic-believing, ritually practicing Americans. On occasion, such as when estimating long-term trends or examining groups that are relatively small proportions of our primary samples, we encounter data limitations that force us to use the rougher classification of religiously affiliated versus nonaffiliated. We do so only when there is no recourse. A more thorough and accurate understanding of secularism requires greater conceptual and methodological refinement than is typically employed, either in popular or academic discourse.

"Fuzzy" Edges of Secularity

As with all concepts, the borders of the categories we have outlined are "fuzzy." There are undoubtedly some people who will be placed into a category they would feel is inappropriate for them. Atheism provides a ready example. Someone may not believe in god, but also not identify with the label of atheist and all its accompanying political and social baggage. Given the considerable stigma associated with the term, avoidance is understandable. Similarly, there may be those who are agnostic with regard to theism, but quite pious in their pursuit of religion nonetheless; adherents of some versions of Buddhism or Unitarianism are notable examples. At the same time, there will be people who affiliate and believe while attending religious services regularly, but who do so for social or familial reasons and feel that religion has negligible impact on their lives. Yet ambiguity in categorization goes beyond these standard forms of mismatch between researchers' classifications and subjects' identifications.

In addition to the standard concerns with misclassification, secular statuses are also relatively unstable over time. Many people cycle through periods of secularity throughout the course of their lives. Over a period of just one year, an estimated 30% of American adults who say they have no religion will cycle back into self-identifying with some form of organized religion. Over the same time span, roughly 5% of those who identify with a religion will drop out. These fluctuations mean that in

2007 (the year the survey in question was conducted), approximately 11 million nones cycled back into religion while approximately 9.1 million former religious affiliates entered apostasy. In the U.S., individuals classified as secular based on claiming no religious preference are particularly likely to move in and out of nonexclusivist religious identities, and are more likely to be religious "seekers." There are also notable life-cycle effects that produce higher or lower probabilities of religiosity. Parents in their thirties with small children are more likely to be religiously active, while those who never marry are more likely to be secular. Similarly, divorced men are less likely to be religiously active.[16] So in addition to being categories at the edges of organized religion, secular statuses are also often temporary.

To pluck but one compelling historical narrative from a plethora of examples, William Miller

> [d]rifted away from Baptist concerns about sin and damnation . . . and made a decisive break [from religion] when he married in 1803 and moved to his wife's hometown Putney, Vermont. There he found a public library where he read Voltaire, David Hume, Thomas Paine, Ethan Allen; he found fellowship in a Masonic temple, where he rose to the highest rank; and he found that the leading citizens, men who would become valuable friends and patrons, were deists. Miller continued to believe in God, but considered the Bible to be a work of priestcraft. He amused his deist friends by mimicking and mocking the pulpit mannerisms of his grandfather and uncle.[17]

Over a decade later, after fighting in the War of 1812 and relocating to Low Hampton, New York—in an area that would come to be known as the "burned-over district" for its varied and fervent religious innovation—Miller returned to religion with a flourish. He rigorously studied the Bible, determined to answer his (and others') skepticism. He developed an interpretive method he believed unlocked predictions of future events and the true meaning of the sacred text. Between 1832 and 1844, Miller gathered an immense flock of followers, becoming the architect of the "Great Disappointment" after he prophesied a specific timeline to events of the end times. Although deflating in the short term, his prophecy ultimately produced a successful new religious movement:

Adventism. Conversely, the history of American secularism shows many examples of former ministers becoming prominent evangelists of freethought.

The high level of "churn" in the U.S. religious market is driven by the freedom to have, and corresponding narratives of, "religious choice." Combined with the inherently liminal nature of categories of secularism, it is clear that secularity may only be temporary for many; but the same is also true for religious statuses.[18] As we pursue an empirical description of American secularities, it is critical to keep in mind this pattern of switching and oscillation between categories through time. Although we analyze snapshots of these dynamics, they are but moments in the ongoing fluctuations of a religious field replete with options and mobility. Still, over time, substantial shifts toward or away from particular religious or secular statuses should be evident from accumulated still frames of the flux.

Estimating Levels of Secularity in the United States

How secularism is assessed methodologically has practical implications for the proportion and composition of Americans estimated to be secular or religious. The two primary data sources we analyze here provide a case in point. The Pew Religious Landscape Survey was collected in 2007. It is particularly useful because of its large sample size (over 35,000 respondents), which provides enough cases for more reliable analyses among groupings that are relatively small proportions of the population. This survey classified respondents' religious identities based on the following question: "What is your present religion, if any? Are you Protestant, Roman Catholic, Mormon, Orthodox such as Greek or Russian Orthodox, Jewish, Muslim, Buddhist, Hindu, atheist, agnostic, something else, or nothing in particular?" If a respondent volunteered "no religion" before the full list was read, then a follow-up question was asked: "And would you say that's atheist, agnostic, or just nothing in particular?"

On the whole, this is a reasonable methodological strategy; however, the culturally pejorative connotation of terms such as "atheist" combined with a forced choice option that does not allow people to be religiously affiliated *and* theistically dis- or nonbelieving is restrictive. For the sake of consistency, we classified respondents as nonaffiliated believers using the Pew RLS only if they said their religion was "nothing in particular," then answered a yes/no question about whether they believed in "God or a universal spirit" with yes. Those who said "nothing" to the religious identity question, then "no" to the God question we classified as atheists.[19] Although we generally prefer to let respondents' self-designations stand, multiple rounds of analyses on metrics about religion showed that the "nothing" respondents who did not believe in god were much more similar to self-identified atheists than to respondents who said "nothing" while also believing in God. Additionally, part of our primary claim here is that nonaffiliated theistic belief is a distinct expression of secularity, so we wanted this category in the Pew RLS to be similar to that in other datasets we analyze.

In comparison, the General Social Surveys provide a more inclusive estimate of the proportions of the population that would be classified as identifying with the various forms of secularity by using people's views of theism rather than self-identification. Instead of relying on a forced choice between religious affiliation and theistic nonbelief, the GSS asks, "What is your religious preference? Is it Protestant, Catholic, Jewish, some other religion, or no religion?" A second question asks about belief in God and provides "I don't believe in God" and "I don't know whether there is a God and I don't believe there is any way to find out" as response options. The two questions on the GSS allow for the classification of respondents based on theistic dis- and nonbelief while avoiding the perceived baggage of "atheist" and "agnostic" as labels. Due to these differences in the questions used for classification, atheists and agnostics identified with the Pew data are, on average, slightly more "hardline" secular than those identified with the GSS. The relationship between religious nonaffiliation and theistic nonbelief, as well as the estimated prevalence of each of the categories, is portrayed visually in Figure 1.1. The size of categories and their degree of overlap with other categories was determined using the 2010 GSS.

According to the 2010 GSS, roughly 18% of American adults said they had "no religion." Approximately 3% of Americans were atheists, 6% agnostics, 11% nonaffiliated believers, and 8% were nonpracticing

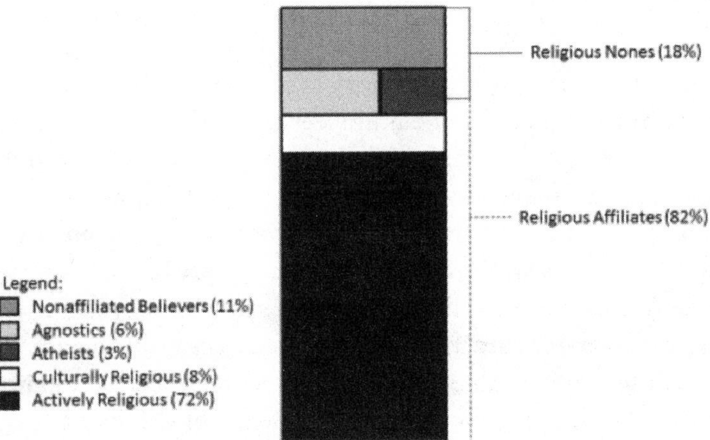

Figure 1.1. Typology of American Secularism, 2010

(culturally) religious. The combined level of secularity accounting for atheism, agnosticism, nonaffiliated belief, and cultural religion places the estimated proportion of the American population that is secular at approximately 28%, meaning there were about 65.7 million secular American adults in 2010. The forced-choice, single-question method of the Pew survey puts the estimated proportion secular at approximately 21%, about 49.3 million adults. The two-question strategy, combined with more generous measures for religious service attendance and private prayer, casts a wider net and incorporates some respondents who are, for the most part, disengaged from organized religion but would be missed with a forced-choice single question. In contrast, the single-question strategy results in smaller categories of secularists, but also classifies people into categories the respondents themselves would assent to.[20] The resulting differences in population estimates demonstrate the potentially consequential differences between varying methodological strategies for estimating and assessing secular individuals, even when applying the same conceptual criteria. Combining the two approaches, a balanced estimate of the number of secular American adults in 2010 would be 57.5 million people—about one quarter of the adult population.[21] The Data Analyses Appendix online provides further information on our classification scheme using five national datasets, along with the proportion of Americans who would be classified as secular using each.

Summary

We created a basic four-category typology of secularity: atheism, agnosticism, nonaffiliated belief, and cultural religion. Although there are other ways to categorize secularity that warrant attention, such as affiliated nonbelief, "hard" and "soft" atheism, etc., the current categories establish an initial basis for mapping the diversity of contemporary secularities. These classifications necessarily have fuzzy borders and are often temporary, but as we will show, there is enough congruence *and* divergence to warrant classifying each category as secular but distinct.[22] Measurement techniques can substantially affect the categorization of seculars, as well as the estimated population levels of secularity. Having established some basic parameters for determining and categorizing secular Americans, we now turn to outlining our assumptions about *how* secularity should be conceptualized.

2

A Cultural View of Secularities

In studying secularism, there are the usual challenges of studying the social world: neutrality, accuracy, and the availability and adequacy of information; but there are also challenges unique to the subject matter, especially for social scientists. Like all people, we are influenced by the ideas and practices of those around us, especially in our peer group and daily work. Trained by and working as sociologists, we are steeped in the conventions, history, and myths of our livelihood. For better or worse—the latter in this case—sociologists' understanding of both religion and secularity long rested on armchair speculation rooted in Enlightenment and positivist idealism that dismissed religion as an irrational holdover from primitive humanity. There were notable exceptions of course, but they were still exceptions.[1]

As a distinct intellectual pursuit, sociology is relatively young, coming of age during a Victorian era of scientism. The passionate belief that science was the key to human progress was prominent inside, but also outside of what would now be considered the "natural" sciences. Newly minted and anxious for legitimation, social scientists were some of the most outspoken advocates of scientism. In an effort to push toward professionalization and legitimacy, early sociologists relied on a utopian vision of scientific progress and a distorted perception of the field's eventual knowledge and powers. Such is often the fate of intellectuals on the make. For the most part, these missteps are behind us, but the specters of scientism still haunt the social sciences. A biographical sketch of an influential American sociologist illustrates the tenor of theistic nonbelief at the turn of the twentieth century, as well as how experiential background shapes personal philosophy. It also exemplifies why early social scientists, as well as their intellectual heirs, dealt so poorly with secularism.

An "American Aristotle"

Lester Frank Ward's life and work provides a model—both negative and positive. Upon Ward's death, prominent American sociologist E. A. Ross remarked:

> When one considers the vast range of his intellectual interests, the number and variety of his original contributions to science, and his great power of generalization, one feels that if Aristotle had chanced to be born in Illinois about the middle of the nineteenth century, his career would have resembled that of Lester F. Ward more than that of any other American in our time.[2]

Ward was born in 1841 in Joliet, Illinois, to Justus and Silence Ward, the youngest of ten children. His father was a farmer, mechanic, construction and canal worker, and itinerant millwright; "a rolling stone of the pioneer type."[3] His mother, Silence, daughter of a minister, was "scholarly, refined, and fond of literary pursuits."[4] She, like so many caught in the cresting swell of the Second Great Awakening and anti-Catholic evangelicalism in the 1840s and 1850s, was also deeply religious. As a youth Lester was outwardly shy and passive, recording in his diary that he found it "a difficult thing to conquer an inborn feeling of self-depreciation."[5] After his father died in 1857, Ward supported himself. He worked in a wagon wheel shop, on farms, and taught at a country school in the winter. His hardscrabble upbringing left an indelible mark on his personality and ideas about the world. He was a self-taught polyglot, studying feverishly in the evenings to learn multiple languages including Greek, Latin, French, and German (adding Spanish, Italian, and Russian later in life). He saved money from doing farm work to attend Susquehanna Collegiate Institute in Pennsylvania.

At the institute, Ward began to find his voice, using his rapidly expanding knowledge to engage in public debates about morality and policy. In a foretelling debate at the institute, he forced his opponents to divorce humanitarian morals from orthodox Christian dogma. His move away from orthodox religion was spurred by his views of women, sexuality, and the Enlightenment, as well as his hard-nosed pragmatism. By the end of his brief initial foray in college, he was a Thomas Paine–

inspired deist. After just three semesters, the Civil War interrupted his life and education. An abolitionist, Ward responded to Lincoln's call for additional troops in 1862. At the hellish battle of Chancellorsville in 1863, he was severely wounded—shot three times in the thighs and knee when Pennsylvania's Third Corps met Stonewall Jackson's regiment head on. He was a Confederate prisoner of war for two weeks before his inclusion in an exchange for rebel POWs. He recovered in army hospitals and was honorably discharged in late 1864 because of his injuries.

After the trauma of war, injury, and imprisonment, followed by the death of his only child during infancy, Ward busied himself by working. He soon hustled his way into the federal bureaucracy in Washington, D.C. Over the next five years, he served as a clerk in the Treasury, a "chief" in the Division of Navigation and Immigration, and a librarian for the Bureau of Statistics. Again he saved money to attend college, viewing education as his path to a better life. He took night classes to complete his degree at Columbian (later to become George Washington) University in 1869. That year marked a critical juncture in Ward's intellectual life. He began law school, started writings that would briefly sustain a freethought newsletter, and initiated work on his magnum opus, which would take nearly fifteen years to complete, the immense two-volume tome *Dynamic Sociology*. He became the primary editor and contributor (with over sixty-five editorials) to *The Iconoclast*, the media organ of the National Liberal Reform League.[6] Although Ward retained deep religious sentiments and preoccupations, he became further divorced from orthodox religion.

In 1871, he earned a law degree. A medical degree followed the next year. Soon after, Ward's wife died tragically from appendicitis and he entered a period of deep depression. He dealt with his hardship the way he always had, by working constantly. He now pursued botany full time, studying and publishing in the field throughout the remainder of the 1870s. In 1881, he began work for the United States Geological Survey. During the 1880s and 1890s, he became a taxonomist in the emerging field of paleobotany. He continued working at the USGS in various positions until 1906.

His official career as a social scientist would never have materialized if not for Albion W. Small, whose own career in sociology might not have begun without Ward's writings. Small was a Baptist minister drawn to the fledgling field in part by *Dynamic Sociology*, saying that reading it was like discovering a "philosopher's stone." Small, a teacher and for a time president at Colby College, championed and helped popularize *Dynamic Sociology*, which was largely ignored upon publication. When Ward heard that Small was using his book to teach courses at Colby, they began a correspondence and became friends. Reflecting the similarities (and differences) between freethought and liberal Protestantism at the turn of the twentieth century, they shared common ground on basic philosophical values, but differed over the assumptions upon which those values rested. When Small was asked to found the first department of sociology in the U.S. at the University of Chicago in 1892, his promotion of Ward's work gained a powerful new platform. Small established the *American Journal of Sociology* in 1895, and "anxious to add scientific respectability and the weight of a dignified author already in the general field," he asked Ward to be an advisory editor.[7] He also solicited a series of essays from Ward about what, exactly, sociology was (supposed to be).

Ward's work was initially more popular in Europe than in the U.S., where *Dynamic Sociology* sold less than five hundred copies in ten years. In 1900, Ward spent the summer in London and Paris, attending a conference organized by the newly minted organization of European sociologists, the Institut International de Sociologie. Much "to his genuine surprise," his work was in vogue in continental circles, and the members elected Ward as president of the organization for its next meeting in 1903, despite his never holding an academic appointment.[8] Two years later, in the last week of 1905, Ward and other prominent Americans pushing the new discipline broke away from the American Economic Association to form the American Sociological Society (renamed Association in 1959, removing the unfortunate acronym [after a half century!]). The cadre of aspiring discipline founders knew they needed *scientific* credibility.

Even though he had never held a permanent position at a university, Ward had the most scientific credibility of anyone in the group. International acclaim and scientific bona fides led to Ward's selection as the new organization's choice for inaugural president. As the story goes:

> Professor [Franklin H.] Giddings moved the acceptance of that part of this report which concerned the office of president. He took occasion to

> remark that nothing which he had ever done gave him so keen a sense of justice and fitness as he enjoyed in moving that Dr. Ward be made the first president of the American Sociological Society. Many years ago, when even among educated people the name of sociology was not merely discredited, but almost entirely unknown, Dr. Ward was already actively engaged in giving the word an important meaning and insisting on the great role played by reason in the evolution of human society. . . . Professor Giddings' motion was carried unanimously, and Dr. Ward was at once conducted to the chair by Professors [D. C.] Wells and Giddings. In taking charge of the meeting, Dr. Ward expressed briefly his appreciation of the totally unexpected honor thus thrust upon him, and declared himself proud of the distinction.[9]

By 1906, recognition of the social theory and philosophy laid out in *Dynamic Sociology* (and numerous other writings) had grown, and Ward finally accepted a professorship at Brown University. In many ways, his story is an American archetype: from frontier poverty to professor at an elite university through discipline, self-teaching, and seemingly tireless effort.

Ward's thought and work is by turns sprawling, overgeneral, and meticulous, an amalgamation of then state-of-the-art science, linguistics tracing etymologies and coining terminology, and most prominently, liberal social philosophy. At times, it is remarkably dense; at others, plainspoken. Although his overarching perspective is noteworthy, we are concerned primarily with his treatment of religion and science.[10]

Ward was committed to science and positivism. Hanging in his office at Brown were pictures of famous biologists such as Charles Darwin, Thomas Huxley, and zoologist/philosopher Ernst Haeckel, alongside proto-sociologists Auguste Comte and Herbert Spencer, who applied evolutionary models to "society." He frequently cited Spencer and Huxley in his work, but self-consciously set himself against "Social Darwinist" ethics, seeing social science ultimately as an interventionist effort to ease human suffering. He was, after all, a social climber of the highest order. He saw science as the beacon of—and organized religion as a barrier to—human progress. He outlined a view against, but also between, social Darwinism and the Social Gospel. In effect, he attempted a synthesis between scientific materialism and the ethics of concerted social betterment. This synthesis played an integral role in the emergence of a philosophically and, more importantly, socially viable secularism. Beginning with his work in *The Iconoclast*, Ward outlined these views in detail.

The first issue of the publication appeared in 1870, and in typical style, Ward stated his thesis clearly: "Science is the acknowledged enemy of Theology. Why? Because it teaches the truth. Theology is error. Everything that teaches truth militates against theology."[11] In an issue of *The Iconoclast* four months later, he argued:

> All will admit that charity is the highest moral virtue. Science is the only foundation for that broad and unlimited charity, which, if ever attained, will prove itself a redemption of the world. Religion, philosophy, law, government, all have failed utterly to accomplish this result. Science so far has proved a grand success. To it, and to it alone, can we attribute that great change in the treatment which man received at the hands of his fellow-man, which has taken place within the last two centuries. . . . That these are the results of science is clear, for it lifts us out of the narrow grooves of bigotry and fanaticism, and enables us to comprehend the human race as part of the vast universe of which all men are but the children, and therefore brothers.[12]

After fifteen years of tedious labor, Ward was ready to bring *Dynamic Sociology* (1883) to public light, but he could not find publishers willing to take on the intimidating treatise. He managed to get the book published only by providing $2,300 up front to cover publication costs. To raise the capital, he sold his home to his sister-in-law and became a renter. In Volume I, Ward offered an extensive treatment of religion, with reluctant nods to its benefits for humans in the past. Overall, however, he viewed it as a transitory stage of history to be swept away with the advance of science. In Volume II, he summarizes a section on these matters by saying:

> The "conflict" [between religion and science], however, arose from the simple and necessary circumstance that, with the advancement of intelligence brought about through the operation of the [scientific] method, the deeper and more obscure phenomena already claimed by religion were one after another recognized as coming within the dominion of fixed

> laws and claimed also by science. Religion had nothing to gain and every thing to lose; and it has, in fact, been constantly losing from the first, and must continue to lose to the last.[13]

Refining his position on the sequential progression of history further, Ward's series of essays in the *American Journal of Sociology* outlined his vision for the new science of society, including the place of religion and science in human evolution and progress. The following excerpt appeared in an 1896 article, the sixth in the series:

> In the primordial blank condition of the mind the anthropomorphic mode of interpretation is the only one; inanimate objects are animated and animals are endowed with intelligence. Fetishism prevails. In the next stage intelligence and will are disembodied and ascribed to immaterial or spiritual beings. Polytheism reigns. At length the number of these beings suffers a reduction and ultimately they are limited to one. Monotheism holds sway. Under monotheism the spirit of speculation finds encouragement, and with it the forces of nature and the properties of matter are erected into so many separate and independent existences or entities. Ontology or metaphysics dominates human thought. The faith in such entities is not reverential, and the bolder spirits soon question them and dare to institute investigation. The result is always the same, and the true order of nature is brought to light. How profoundly the whole social structure is influenced by the domination of one after another of these great fundamental classes of ideas, can only be understood by a careful study of human history from this point of view.[14]

Extending his own (quasi-religious) vision to its culmination in *Applied Sociology* (1906), Ward prescribed how the knowledge produced by the social sciences could be applied to human betterment. Clearing the way for his ethical system by reiterating the views that appeared in *The Iconoclast* decades earlier, he stated, "The important point is to show that the greater part of the evils from which the human race has suffered, evils unknown to animal races, are really due to error," and that "religious ideas . . . consist entirely of error."[15]

Ward's grand theory of history closely followed Enlightenment thinking about the progression of humanity through the pursuit of science.

Subscribing to the historically idealized "conflict between religion and science" popularized by scientistic philosophers John W. Draper and Cornell founder and president A. D. White (among others), Ward contended, "All this truth that science revealed had to struggle against the dense mass of primitive error it was destined to overthrow, and the resistance was enormous."[16] He cited influential deists such as Voltaire and Thomas Paine (although he once professed in a speech in Paine's honor to be "far beyond" the revolutionary's thinking), and began a section on "Truth" with a quote from the "Great Agnostic," Robert Ingersoll.[17] In Ward's view, "all heresies have been attempts to get rid of some small part of the error of the orthodox type belief."[18] Ultimately he grounded his ethics in utilitarianism, stating that "the purpose of sociology is: to *accelerate social evolution*" by facilitating "the passage out of a pain economy and into a pleasure economy."[19]

In the end, Ward thought that "church buildings would become halls of science, sermons would be scientific lectures, and the revered scriptures would be the more profound generalizations . . . discovered through the various scientific disciplines."[20] Such views of the conflict between religion and science and the inevitable progress of human history were far from anomalous in early American sociology. In fact, these views became (and often remain) part of the dominant, taken-for-granted perspective of the discipline. Although many early sociologists were, like Albion Small, reformers enacting versions of the Social Gospel, such views were marginalized from the discipline as it professionalized and secularized.[21] In effect, like secularism itself, American sociology grew out of Protestant humanitarianism, then confronted and expelled its creator. As a personification of this process, "Ward replaced God with science."[22]

Still, as with the social world more generally, and Lester Ward especially, there is more than meets the eye. Although he thought traditional religion impeded progress, his work nevertheless maintained a sacralized, naturalistic version of monism bordering on deism, and he thought that some form of religion would always be necessary as an expression of "man's inner feelings and thoughts."[23] Unlike his tone in the early pages of *The Iconoclast*, a more mature Ward tried not to alienate religious believers, but rather attempted to communicate a passion for education and science. While at Brown, Ward faithfully attended chapel, to the delight of the then quite pious administrators. Reflecting on his own experiences, he advocated for universal access to education as the great equalizer of the world, championing learning and knowledge as the key to individual and social transformation. In a speech given toward the end of his life in 1909, he argued, as he had done consistently throughout his career, against both eugenics and social Darwinism, which enjoyed popularity, especially among intellectual elites of more privileged backgrounds. He asserted:

> We are laboring under the idea that there are great natural differences among men, that the lower classes are naturally inferior. . . . [However, we] are obliged to recognize the natural equality of all men, for which I have coined a word, namely, egalitarianism. It means simply that no class has or ever did have a monopoly of brains; that there are just as good brains among the "mudsills" and the laboring men with their picks and shovels as there are in the higher walks of life. . . . All classes are equal when all are equally equipped.[24]

Ward's personal attributes of tireless scholarship, unabashedly (and unpopular) progressive views of gender, class, and race, meticulous pursuit of research, and straightforward style of communication remain laudable.[25] As with many prominent theorists, his verbiage could be impenetrable, but he also strove to clarify his position for the audience. And unlike most who sound prophetic calls—especially positivists—he was acutely aware of the constructed nature of his own perspective: "That my own contribution was simply a product of the Zeitgeist I have never pretended to question."[26] There is a recurring theme in the recollections of those who knew him personally. In spite of his knowledge in a vast range of subjects, he was humble in discussion and constantly in pursuit of new knowledge. As one of his departmental colleagues at Brown recalled upon his death, "He was as far from sham or pretence as any one with whom I have been familiar."[27]

Ironically, Ward's scientistic theoretical system was empirically unverifiable, and subsequently fell into disfavor, yet "the ideas and assumptions initially enunciated by Ward became the unconscious starting point for subsequent American sociology," particularly his ideas about religion and science. The lasting impact of Ward's thought was to set the epistemic and cultural bounds for the new discipline by "divorc[ing] American democratic faith from its orthodox religious base to a new foundation of naturalistic science."[28] Such is the (often implicit) heart of classical perspectives on secularization bequeathed to social scientists, a lineage in which we now find ourselves. This legacy has stunted a more thorough empirical and theoretical treatment of secularism. Like all interpretive communities, scholars are reluctant to question critically their founding myths and shared paradigms, lest the seemingly obvious and clear become tenuous and ambiguous. Let us be clear, we view Ward's theorizing on religion and secularism as an example of what *not to do*.[29] By treating secularism culturally, we aim to move away from the models embedded in Enlightenment and classical sociological thought and toward a view of secularizations as historical and social processes, and secularities as social statuses.

A Cultural View of Secularity

To move beyond the impasses in thinking about religion and secularism in classical as well as contemporary thought, we reframe secularism. The most common frames applied to understanding secularism have been aptly named secularization theories. As exemplified by the thought of Lester Ward, such theories are intimately tied to the formative development of the social sciences. An apparent advantage of such theories is that they deal explicitly with secularism; however, this narrow focus ultimately becomes a critical weakness. By setting out master narratives regarding the processes of religious decline, secularization theories are typically unidirectional and inflexible to the dynamics of religious fields.[30] In addition, these theories retell Enlightenment narratives, resulting in frameworks closer to ivory tower mythology than explanatory or interpretive social science.

Disciplinary iconoclasts (or imperialists, depending on your perspective) have since broken this spell by reclaiming religious behavior as decidedly "rational," but their creative destruction failed to rebuild an understanding of secularity to replace the taken-for-granted notions that were overturned. The study of religion often remains mired in the impasse between secularization and rational choice theories, with both frames flawed in mirroring, inverted ways.[31] Rather than pledge allegiance to one of these factions at the expense of empirical accuracy, we draw primarily on an understanding of social phenomena taken from studies of interaction and culture.[32] Our foremost commitment is to a view of secularisms that is both empirical and interpretive.

"Culture" is an ambiguous yet powerful concept. It has been used to refer to social practices and conventions, to learned behavior generally, and perhaps most importantly for our purposes, to interactive processes woven into symbol systems that convey collective meanings.[33] More directly, culture is the practices, beliefs, and shared understandings that make lived, collective experience both possible and meaningful. These idealistic qualities are necessarily embedded in the material, spatial, and hierarchical relations structuring a given social order. From this perspective, the division between religion and secularity ceases to impose itself as binary and instead appears as a continuum—individuals' lives may be more or less connected to organized religion, and worldviews may be more or less influenced by religious supernatural concepts.[34]

A commonsense assumption is that the lived experience of secular individuals must be categorically different from that of religious individuals. Although true in some regards (as we will see), this is highly misleading as a general principle. Regardless of overarching approaches to the world, no one is exempt from the need to render experiences meaningful through explanation or address existential dilemmas imposed by suffering and death. Cognizant agents understand their place in the world through their perceptions of social order, interactions with others, and personal sensations, all of which are channeled through interpretive frames consisting of intersubjective (shared) cultural schema.[35] That is, the stories we tell about ourselves to make sense of existence are built on more general understandings about "the way the world works," which are derived from interaction in communities, both physical and those that exist primarily or wholly through mediated communications.

Views about the basic features of the cosmos and society form the usually tacit backgrounds upon which narratives of identity are perpetually (re)told. Such backgrounds arise out of the interplay between thinking, feeling agents and the situated experiences they encounter and then remember—memory being more important to narratives of identity than historical detail.[36] This approach to meaning-making—as internalized perceptions of "the way the world works" shaped by interpretive communities—stands in contrast to hardline delineations between subjective and objective realities that permeate classic philosophical and social scientific theories.[37] Instead, we advance a synthetic approach to meaning that views the objective social and physical world and subjective, cognitive internalizations as inextricably linked. To be clear, we are not proposing that the material world is dependent upon the subjective states of humans, but rather the inverse—that subjective states are inextricably linked to the biological functioning that underpins cognition, the physical realities individuals encounter, and the webs of meaning spun by social groups. After internalizing ideas, people can put them into action, reshaping their physical and social worlds.

The subjective valuations individuals make of their experiences of physical and social worlds are central to sense of identity. Such identity work involves primarily retrospective accounting of experiences and the repeated consumption of written materials, auditory inputs including conversation and music, and visual information. Most importantly, identity definition involves the perceived views of other people a person respects. Individuals filter this stream of sensory input, selecting what to internalize by sifting information through preexisting beliefs and perceived knowledge. In the processing of experience, emotion is integral, both immediately and ultimately. All sentient individuals engage in this process at some level, whether or not in relation to organized religious groups.

This approach to the study of meaning-making pushes beyond the dead ends created by assuming that religion is either wholly rational or irrational. It is clearly both. So too is secularism. Any definitive declaration of either as ir/rational is a moral valuation. What is clear, regardless of one's personal views, is that religion or opposition to religion often plays a critical role in communities' and individuals' basic understandings of the world. The interpretive communities in which one participates, both in person and through mediated communication, create ways of seeing, filtering, and internalizing reality and experience. People do not necessarily internalize the world as it objectively exists, but rather *as it is perceived to be*. The worldview "options" available depend on one's cultural context, place in a social order, and the relative freedom within and stability of that order.

Secularity as Social Status

We examine secularity primarily at the level of aggregated individuals, so it is worthwhile to outline our foundational assumptions about the nature of "selves" and "identities." The questions of what a "self" is, and its relative permanence, have deep philosophical implications, and we cannot settle such long-standing matters here.[38] Instead, we offer a brief sketch of the assumptions that underlie the questions we ask and the analytical paths we travel.

A foundational assumption regarding one's sense of self and identity is commonly called the Thomas Theorem, although it is not a theorem in the formal sense. The name references interaction sociologist W. I. Thomas, credited as its originator: "If [people] define their situations as real, they are real in their consequences."[39] This aphorism is pregnant with implications and assumptions of its own, which helps account for its rhetorical power and longevity. It is a pithy, direct statement of the assumption underlying the concept of "definition of the situation," arguably the central idea of interactionist sociology. Definition of the situation refers to the (usually implicit) expectations people in a setting have about how they should think, feel, and act. These expectations necessarily shape courses of action. But we are not interested in definition of the situation per se. We are interested in the questions it begs.

If the position stated in the theorem is assumed to be true, it immediately implies a further question: How do people define what is real? To understand how people construct reality requires consideration of cognition and perception. There are three primary, interrelated sources furnishing the background for how people perceive and process experience, and therefore ascribe meaning to reality. The first is "structural": the social networks and routine activities in which people are embedded and the interactions carried out within those networks. An understanding of what a person fulfilling particular roles should do will be strongly influenced by how those roles have been interpreted and modeled by valued others in one's life. It is little surprise that parents, siblings, spouses, and peers strongly influence attitudes and behaviors ranging from views on politics and religion to the maintenance of mental and physical health to criminality and substance abuse.[40]

Second, one's status set, the sum total of social statuses occupied, determines the power dynamics involved with the different members of one's network. Status set can be thought of as a person's relative social location. The status of child is most activated and relevant when in the presence of one's parents, although the power dynamic of such relations can vary across time, even among the same individuals. It is situations, through the enactment of social roles, that call forth or suppress one's statuses. Situations are the embodiments through which social positions are established and reaffirmed. Medical doctors *are doctors* in specific settings, such as examination rooms and hospitals where specific interactions occur that call forth and (re)affirm the status of doctor. When the same doctor pays a convenience store attendant on the way home from the hospital, her occupational status is unlikely to be called forth, although attire may well "give it off" anyway.[41] Even so, she receives no special benefits or deference in that specific situation due to occupational position. This potential to be called forth or suppressed is characteristic of all statuses, although some are emphasized or ignored with greater frequency and veracity, depending on the degree to which the status is overtly visible through markers, is considered personally or socially salient, and is directly related to the situation in question.

Statuses influence worldviews, with the magnitude of impact from a particular status dependent upon its social and personal salience. If an individual considers a particular status salient, and especially if *others* consider a status paramount, then one's view of the world emerges from the relations continually reinforcing that status.[42] In many ways, status set determines how the world approaches you, thereby extensively coloring personal experience; but we must be careful not to essentialize or assume the relationship between status and identity. For some individuals, a particular status, say of gender, race, or social class, may be salient and prominent, while for others it may recede into the background as other statuses are socially and cognitively foregrounded. Further, statuses are not isolated, but rather exist in an interactive relationship analogous to a multidimensional matrix. The extent to which a particular status is salient (or not) in self-conception is a product of the intersection of biography and social context. For some, a secular status may be perceived as socially and personally important. For others, it may be merely a residual consideration. Sociologist Phil Zuckerman's research on secular individuals in Scandinavia showed that in an area where being a nonbeliever is common, many people rarely think about whether, why, or how they are not religious. In contrast, his interviews with people in the U.S. who were raised religious but dropped out as adults found that, in many ways, they *had to* think about their secularity because it made them different from many of their friends and relatives.[43]

Third, general views of cosmology and metaphysics, although people may not call them such, influence more specific, applied views. These background assumptions about the nature of the universe may come largely from religion, but they may also depend heavily on other institutions such as science or economics. Regardless, people must adjudicate between claims to epistemic authority—the sources of information a person trusts about the nature of reality and "the way things work."[44] Which sources of information about the world are trusted flows out of social networks and statuses. For instance, most academics place a high level of authority in scholarship and science because they have vested interests in the continuance and power of academic institutions, as that is the source of their relatively privileged positions. Such tendencies, however, may be counteracted in specific situations, such as with those teaching at private religious schools, where greater authority is given to a particular religious community than to academe. Institutional commitments are prominent in both examples, but the institutions given assent vary.

It is in cosmology and views of epistemic authority that secularisms influence the lives of those who hold them to be true—in other words, where general ideological assumptions affect positions on specific topics as well as courses of action. If, for example, secularists view the positions of organized religion as invalid on matters such as family formation and child rearing while others view them as salient, there should be noticeable differences in familial ideology and formation at the aggregate level—and indeed there are.[45] The relationship between epistemic authority and worldview produces considerable inertia toward stability in adults, as people may begin to seek out knowledge and social networks supporting their preexisting views once they have a more "settled" perspective of the world.

Once an identity is in the process of consolidation, mediated communication begins to play a more integral role. Consumption of various forms of media serves to reinforce perceived identity, as well as the statuses affecting one's view of the world.[46] While it is hypothetically possible for media consumption alone to lead to identity change, it is highly unlikely to do so absent interpersonal interaction. Social networks remain the key determinant of "conversion" and role exit. People are inspired to change their identities based on interactions with others whose views they value rather than by encountering another position in mediated form. Disembodied appeals made through media alone are not effective tools for identity change, but mediated communication plays a critical, supplemental role in identity maintenance and change.[47] Once a self-identity is in place, people consume mediated communication that reinforces, supports, or extends their views of the world. Consumption is identity maintenance in practice.

A final noteworthy aspect of identity is its rhetorical form. Identity, both collective and individual, is expressed through narrative. Narratives make sense of identity causally through time, helping individuals and groups articulate (and affirm) the *perception* of an essentialized identity. Although the essential self or group is illusory from the view of philosophers and social theorists, experiences of its permanence infer on it a circumscribed reality based on the Thomas Theorem. Rather than being fixed, identities articulated through narrative are always in the process of becoming. Viewed this way, secularity is not an absence, but rather an achieved status. It is (re)made by individuals in interaction with others—in the flesh, reflectively imagined, and through mediated communication. This process helps hide identity's constructed nature from those actively creating it.[48]

The framework we have outlined is applicable to both religiosity and secularity. By rendering both as cultural, we can avoid many of the underlying assumptions that make classical theories of secularization more prescriptive than descriptive, and also improve the purportedly acultural view of religion advocated by rational choice theorists. The distinction between religious and secular can be recalled where needed, but there is no danger of its disappearing. The rhetorical identities and public discourse of both religionists and secularists ensure that it will necessarily continue. Indeed, both can be better understood as being defined *in relation to the other*. There can be no secular without the religious, and, at least in the contemporary, pluralistic world, the inverse is also true.

Cosmic Belief Systems

In addition to being social statuses and potentially integral components of identities, we conceptualize religions and secularisms as *cosmic belief systems*.[49] In a classic treatment of the concept, political scientist Philip Converse defined a belief system as a "configuration of ideas and attitudes in which the elements are bound together by some form of constraint or functional interdependence." More informally, a belief system can be thought of as a profile or constellation of beliefs.[50] We have added the modifier "cosmic" to the concept in order to designate it as a set of foundational beliefs an individual holds about reality. That is, if someone believes in no supernatural entities, only the working of physical and natural forces, these are still assertive beliefs about the nature of reality. Likewise an agnostic assertively believes that supernatural questions are unanswerable.[51] Similarly, if a person believes that God and His angels regularly intervene in the material world to assist the faithful, this too is a belief about the basic features of reality. Thus the cosmic modifier is one that should be acceptable to both the late Carl Sagan and Jerry Falwell, housing each of their disparate views of the world, universe, and reality. Cosmic belief systems also include the most fundamental ethical values one tries to act in accordance with. They are systematized narratives making sense of internalized social experiences and perceptions.

At the individual level, cosmic belief systems may be more or less logically or socially coherent, reflecting differential levels of information and salience surrounding the beliefs in question. Indeed, Converse's lasting contribution to thinking about the concept is his observation that a substantial proportion of the public holds beliefs that seem inconsistent, or may be otherwise apathetic or uninformed about the specifics of their own belief systems compared to those articulated by ideological elites; however, we would add that ideological elites are also often not so principled as they present themselves to be. In the same way, we conceptualize secular philosophical positions as having the potential to be highly consistent and meticulously worked through, or blithely hypocritical and inarticulate. What matters is that secular belief systems have the same formal properties as religious belief systems, and both are necessarily related to political contexts, at least at the level where people attempt to translate abstract beliefs into ethical, this-worldly principles and action.

Central to understanding all belief systems is examining how they are used to generate collective and individual meaning from experiences. When individuals reflect, they make sense of their experiences by filtering them through their existing belief systems. Mismatches between previous beliefs and experiences may result in alteration of beliefs; however, changes to beliefs are highly unlikely to be wholesale, but rather piecemeal in the service of maintaining the greatest share of the belief system at the lowest cost (change). Once experiences have been processed, they become retrospective narratives, which individuals externalize through testimonials, anecdotes, and stories. Such narratives are a key source of individual identity and open (or close) particular avenues of action based on notions of maintaining consistency and authenticity for particular audiences (listeners to the narrative), including one's own self.[52] At the same time, creativity and fluidity remain important, as the same basic plot points may be embellished or downplayed for different audiences or contexts.

A constant feedback loop is thus created between cosmic belief systems, purposive action, and experiences. An individual whose belief system is taken for granted may progress through this loop with little change or difficulty. External factors, however, establish the parameters under which this process occurs, and can impose dramatic experiences that force changes to belief systems or narratives. Today's certainty is but a catastrophe away from a dramatically reorganized narrative, or even an entirely new belief system. Change to belief systems can also occur through longer processes of questioning and doubt, which may incrementally alter or dismantle previously held beliefs. Creative agency allows individuals to resist, alter, or even directly rebel against the views that they have been taught, a pathway of belief that is often applicable in the experiences of apostates. Of course, change is a rarity relative to stasis. The high cognitive and social costs of altering one's foundational beliefs about the world ensure that a tendency toward stability is the norm.

Cosmic belief systems typically have social and political ramifications. That is, constellations of belief about the fundamentals of the universe, existence, and society address issues of what lines of action are appropriate, how categories of people should be treated, and how and to what extent individuals should be involved in broader collective actions or movements.[53] In emphasizing the ideological aspects of collective and individual identity, we are not denying the importance or role of materials and resources. In fact, the relative distribution of resources shapes the belief systems available or acceptable to a social group. At the same time, we do not place priority on the ideological or the material in social processes, but rather see the two as dialectically intertwined. Resources shape ideas just as ideas shape the distribution and use of resources.[54]

Cosmic belief systems help explain and make past experiences meaningful, and thereby shape future paths of action. To be clear, not all action is based on a direct application of belief systems to concrete situations, as some forms of action are reactive or impulsive rather than deliberative, bypassing the conscious reflection and application that accompanies the practical implementation of belief systems. While this is clearly the case with some forms of "hot," reactive cognition, it is also quite clear that a large portion of the routine actions people undertake reflect the values and perceived knowledge held within a person's belief system (and vice versa).[55] From going to work to caring for one's family, and even to voluntarily assuming personal risk, actions often reflect a person's understanding of what line of behavior is proper and expected, as well as what is deemed consistent with one's identity. This is particularly the case with extraordinary, ethical, or altruistic behaviors.

Now, people may say (or even believe) one way, and act in an entirely different or contradictory manner, ranging between ideal types of authenticity and hypocrisy based on the relative correspondence of their actions, internal beliefs, and expressed beliefs. A mismatch between actions and internal beliefs may produce high levels of cognitive dissonance, while a mismatch between actions and expressed beliefs may produce social conflict. Incongruity will assuredly produce conflict between an individual and those who hold the expressed beliefs in common, but conflict can also occur with those who do not hold such beliefs, as hypocrisy is construed as a general negative mark upon character, accompanied by sanctions administered by a range of others not limited to one's in-group. Although the relationship between beliefs and actions is clearly complex, one thing should be clear: one can be highly religious in traditional ways and still act in a manner that is unethical, unjust, or hypocritical, just as a person can be highly secular and act in ways that are highly ethical, just, or authentic. The converse obviously can and does occur as well.

Summary

Many of the problems in previous social scientific theorizing about secularism spring from variations of idealized Enlightenment visions embedded in the founding myths and formative development of the social sciences. This tendency to evaluate inherited theories of secularization uncritically has impeded a more thorough understanding of secularism. At the same time, the leading contemporary alternative to secularization theories, "rational choice" theory, has little to say in the way of describing secularism. In contrast, we propose framing secularity as a cultural phenomenon analogous to religion, at least regarding certain formal and consequential dimensions of cosmic belief systems. Doing so allows secularism to be conceptualized neutrally—as a sign of neither utopia nor apocalypse—opening the door to a much wider domain of inquiry for fields engaged in the study "of religion."

3

Historical Foundations

Deism then teaches us, without the possibility of being deceived, all that is necessary or proper to be known. The creation is the Bible of the Deist. He there reads, in the handwriting of the Creator himself, the certainty of his existence; and the immutability of his power, and all other Bibles and Testaments are to him forgeries. The probability that we may be called to account hereafter, will, to reflecting minds, have the influence of belief; for it is not our belief or disbelief, that can make or unmake the fact. As this is the state we are in, and which it is proper we should be in, as free agents, it is the fool only, and not the philosopher, or even the prudent man, that will live as if there were no God.
—Thomas Paine[1]

How did secularity became a socially viable religious "preference"? The catalyst for the formal articulation and diffusion of nontheistic cosmic belief systems was, ironically enough, religious thought. Intersecting discourses of modernity, expressive individualism, and philosophical secularism coalesced into modern nonreligion in the late nineteenth century only after progressive humanism in liberal religious traditions outlined a positive system of ethical values *not* grounded on rhetorics of a transcendent God. By linking the rationale for religious faith to evidences derived from rationality, empiricism, and science, theologians and ministers unwittingly set the stage for the appearance of disbelief in the supernatural. As the cultural domain of science spread further outward, the equivalence of religion with rationality (contra emotion) left little space for a God who existed beyond this world. Simultaneously, the humanitarian impulses of progressive Victorian religion were grounded in an understanding of God's "natural" law. When natural explanations crowded out the space for God, ideological dissenters were presented an avenue to public morality without religion, an option unavailable in the past. Humanitarianism and scientism combined to produce the initial appearance of a more fully developed ethical system not grounded in supernatural theism.[2] Although these developments did not lead to an extensive or sustained popular movement of agnosticism, contemporary expressions of secularity still bear the traces and preoccupations of these origins.

The availability of a socially and philosophically viable cosmic worldview devoid of religion (other than as negative point of reference) only became possible during and after a process of institutional differentiation, where religious organizations were separated from other social institutions, particularly the state and its subsidiaries of law, and eventually education. The "immanent" focus of public discourse in Western societies is the result of assertive and successive changes in social institutions, rather than a simple receding of religion with the advance of modernity.[3] Crucial to these developments is a discourse and social order that places restrictions on absolute allegiance to spreading, but not to holding, the Truth. These are the wellsprings of the "buffered and autonomous" self, which allowed secularism to become a viable philosophical option beyond intellectual circles.[4]

To place secularism in the U.S. in historical context, we survey "freethought" movements and ideas. By freethought we mean perspectives and movements critical of and independent from organized religion; a penumbra under which the various perspectives critical of organized religion such as deism, pantheism, and rationalism have been housed throughout American history. Deism—the view that human reason and nature alone sufficiently point toward God, a perspective often combined with critiques of the orthodoxies, dogmatisms, and power of organized religious traditions—played a particularly important role in eighteenth- and nineteenth-century expressions of secularism.

Two interrelated factors consistently shaped the cultural expressions and meaning of secularity. The first is the political context of the relationship between institutions of church and state. If there were any defining issue of the various movements housed under the umbrella of freethought, it would be the separation of church and state. At times, movements for disestablishment led to alliances with religious minorities who shared this concern and fierce opposition to majority religions.

At other times, in different political contexts, freethinkers have opposed the very same religious groups they once allied with. This is particularly the case with evangelical Protestantism.

Indeed, the second primary factor shaping American freethought has been the interplay between politically conservative Protestantism and secularism. Although there have certainly been important intersections with other religious traditions such as Catholicism, American secularism is intimately tethered to opposition to and discourse about politically conservative Protestantism. Conversely, conservative Protestantism cannot be fully understood without accounting for its oppositional relationship to secularisms.[5] As we briskly cover some vast terrain in American religious history, these two factors continually recur as central to shaping the expression, vitality, and fortunes of organized American secularisms.

Aristocratic Deism

Contrary to the notion held by many in the general public who protest that the U.S. was founded as an inherently and explicitly Christian nation, furthering a particularistic version of civil religion that views American statehood as a divinely anointed project, the residents (and especially intellectual elites) of the colonies were hardly paragons of orthodox piety. For the public, lack of participation in organized religion was largely a reflection of frontier living, with limited access to clergy, transience, and de facto "unsettled" communities.[6] Organized religion was certainly prevalent in some areas such as New England, but the necessities of frontier living made organized religion scarce in many places. Meanwhile, there was deistic "infidelity" among many individuals of prominent status during the revolutionary period, who drew on movements in German, French, and British philosophy. These thinkers merged critiques of institutional religion with opposition to colonialism and monarchy, but this remained "an aristocratic cult."[7]

Deism played a limited role in public discourse and was generally cast negatively, often used by ministers as a maligned philosophical perspective to "other." In a particularly sensational example, public figures pointed to the quadruple ax murder/suicide of William Beadle, a self-professed deist; however, this horrific tale was offset by the deism of individuals such as Revolutionary War hero Ethan Allen, who published *Reason, the Only Oracle of Man* in 1784. Because of Allen's war hero status, he provided a public example contradicting the claim that deism necessarily meant depravity. Allen's treatise was the first open, public polemic of American deism.[8]

In spite of high levels of public apathy toward religion, the influence of Puritanism and biblical consciousness in early American intellectual discourse was strong. Between 1760 and 1805, texts authored by Americans referred more frequently to the Bible than to the Enlightenment. Particularly salient were ideas about a divine covenant between God and people, which was reflected by a this-worldly covenant between government and citizens. Interestingly, in formalized Federalist ideas about governance, biblical citations vanish, while they figure prominently in Anti-Federalist writings, in spite of the fact that anti-federalism was home to the prominent deists of the day.[9] Religious freedom and church/state separation were primary concerns of Anti-Federalists, who cloaked their anti-clericalism in the garb of God talk. Meanwhile, Federalists sought to downplay the institutional links between established religion and governance in order to distance themselves from monarchy in the wake of the Revolution, while still advocating for stronger central government. During the transition from the Articles of Confederation to the Constitution, Federalists sought to appease Anti-Federalist opposition to the Constitution by making provisions for individual rights. The first freedom granted in the Bill of Rights simultaneously permitted the free exercise of individual religion and prevented federal favoritism of specific religions.

When the Constitution was ratified by the states in 1789, the establishment and free exercise clauses effectively erected the first officially secular nation-state. The separation of church and state was particularly radical, but ultimately became a hallmark of American republican politics.[10] Still, the Constitution disestablished religion only at the federal level. Many states such as Connecticut, Georgia, Massachusetts, New Hampshire, and South Carolina continued to have established religions, and many more used governmental and legal means to make Protestantism the unofficial official religion. States such as Delaware, Maryland, Pennsylvania, Vermont, and North Carolina included provisions in their state constitutions that restricted holding public office to God-believing

Christians.[11] During the period directly following the Constitutional Convention, a small but visible American "freethought" movement mobilized as an antagonist to Christianization.

Revolutionary Thomas Paine authored the "Bible" of deism, *The Age of Reason*, published during and immediately following his imprisonment in France by the Jacobins during the Reign of Terror. In spite of *Age of Reason*'s reputation as a primer of irreligion, Paine states clearly up front that "I believe in one God and no more." Further, he noted that "the people of France were running headlong into atheism, and I had the work translated and published in their own language to stop them in that career, and fix them to the first article (as I have before said) of every man's creed who has any creed at all, *I believe in God*."[12] Because of the accessibility of *Age of Reason*, its argument helped diffuse deistic and rationalist ideas into public discourse beyond the educated elite. Reaction to the tract, especially Paine's direct criticism of Christianity and revealed religion, was swift, voluminous, diverse (ranging from high to low minded), and hostile. In both Britain and the U.S., a range of commentators used pulpit and pen to discredit Paine's arguments by disqualifying his legitimacy to speak about religion in public. This was done not just by taking on Paine's arguments, but primarily by attacking his character, tone, and especially his intended (or potential) audiences. In spite of these efforts, Paine would ultimately become the preeminent prophet of freethought, but not before living out his days in infamy.

Along with accessible texts espousing rationalist critiques of organized religion, the moderate growth of deism after the American and French revolutions was due in large part to the founding of fledgling "infidel" organizations sustained by the work of self-understood prophetic advocates, such as the blind, eloquent ex-Presbyterian minister and lawyer Elihu Palmer. Palmer ran the deistic newspapers *The Temple of Reason* (1800–1803) and the *Prospect* (1803–1805), and wrote *Principles of Nature* (1801), a treatise critical of Christianity, yet philosophically constructive. Palmer toured the states extensively, delivering lectures on philosophical topics. He was effectively a missionary of the Enlightenment. The prophetic and critical cast of the deist movement during this period has been characterized as "militant."[13] It is more helpful to think of freethought as akin to a new religious movement, proselytizing for converts. These efforts, however, were ineffectual in the end, as ponderous discourse and negative polemics against religion combined with minimal elaboration of the positive attributes of deism produced few converts outside of the ardently anti-religious.[14]

Although many Anti-Federalists held sympathies with freethought critiques of organized religion, public suspicion toward such views began to coalesce in the rhetorical attacks on Thomas Jefferson's purported deism/atheism during the bitterly contested presidential campaign in 1800. Meanwhile, Paine's severance of deism from liberal Christianity discouraged all but the most radical of Christians from holding deism in public esteem. The rhetoric against "infidelity" and skepticism came to play a central role in the identity of populist Protestant movements during the Second Great Awakening. Banishing doubt emerged as a central focus of both popular religious revival and political nationalism in the early years of the American republic, often in mutually reinforcing ways. Upstart Protestant groups used the veneration of doubt championed by freethought as a foil against which they could advocate the certainties and benefits of faith.[15]

In the first decade of the nineteenth century, strong antipathy toward Paine following his participation in the French Revolution and authoring of *Age of Reason* fueled a vociferous reaction from the faithful against freethought. Media of the day, both polemical and literary, portrayed "infidelity" as a contagion leading directly to sexual immorality, anarchy, and the bloodlust represented by the worst aspects of the French Revolution.[16] Paine became both scapegoat and scarecrow, losing his support even among Jeffersonian Democratic-Republicans, which consisted of a diverse alliance of religious (mostly Christian) minorities. After returning to the U.S. in 1802, Paine died in 1809 despised and alone, buried in a pauper's grave in the country where his pamphlet *Common Sense* catalyzed a revolution and his *Crisis* essays bolstered morale throughout the conflict. Only deists and secularists continued to hold Paine in high esteem, as they became the inheritors and caretakers of his legacy.

Evangelical Freethought

Like all new religious movements, the ideas Elihu Palmer championed faced a treacherous road to prosperity and public adoption, and after his death in 1806, followed closely by the then-disgraced Paine's, the movement quickly faded. The seeds of cultural diffusion had been planted though, and a second wave of freethought crested in the late 1820s and 1830s, when groups, newsletters, propaganda, and lectures proliferated.[17] This time, advocates of freethought pushed further into the public realm, responding to and adopting the tenor of their evangelical rivals—in the sense of one's perceived duty to spread the truth. This strategy was necessary to attract adherents in the hothouse of religious innovation and competition that characterized America in the early nineteenth century. Often, participants in such communities had little in common philosophically beyond their antipathy toward institutionalized Christianity, but a common enemy is enough to sustain solidarity, at least in the short term.

This manifestation of the movement spread in urban areas primarily among working-class, middle-aged men, although there were also a few women involved. Of course, there were many upper-class individuals whose views would have been considered heretical, but they had too much to lose from an open confrontation with organized religion, and in the context of history, we are confined to examining *recorded* secularisms. During the same period, state governments gradually moved toward disestablishment. Massachusetts became the last state to disestablish officially in 1833, with over 90% of voters affirming the decision, reflecting increasing pluralistic pressure from Baptists coupled with a fractious split between Trinitarians and Unitarians.[18]

Between 1825 and 1850, there were at least twenty freethought newsletters or periodicals being printed in English in the U.S., with another ten published in German, as well as some in Czech.[19] Notable outlets included the *Free Enquirer* and the *Beacon* in New York City, and the *Boston Investigator*, run by notorious Baptist-turned-Universalist-turned-visionary religious skeptic Abner Kneeland. By the time Kneeland left the paper, it had 2,500 subscribers in twenty-seven states.[20] Due to difficulties with financial solvency (especially during the extended depression of 1837–1843) and increasing antipathy toward the perceived political agitation of freethought communities, only the *Investigator* would be active by 1850. In addition to questioning the tenets of mainstream Christianity, Kneeland's publication also championed abolition, women's rights, and the causes of organized labor. Freethought organizations tended to be politically progressive, and most socialist movements were secular in orientation. During this time, charismatic and prophetic individuals such as Kneeland, socialist Robert Owen, philosopher and activist Frances Wright, and Paine disciple Gilbert Vale served as the new prophets of freethought, publically fighting against the perceived ills of "superstitious" Christianity. Many were European immigrants who sought a more hospitable environment for their heretical views.

Although explicitly opposed to traditional versions of Christianity, some expressions of freethought resembled congregational models of organization and "preaching" modes of discourse. The organization of Kneeland's "Free Enquirers" in Boston provides an instructive example. As a former minister, Kneeland was well aware of the value of a congregational structure and a vibrant community for winning and maintaining followers. In 1831, the group initiated "Sunday lectures," which covered a variety of topics on science, religion, and philosophy. When the group was forced to change venues three years later, Kneeland followed the example of Scottish secular utopian Frances Wright and leased a theater to create a "Hall of Science":

> At a considerable expense the pit was floored over on a level with the stage and a pulpit, draped in black and inscribed in Greek: "Know Thyself," erected in the center; in the rear, on both sides, were the seats for singers. On Sunday the congregation gathered, regular members taking their places in boxes marked like private pews. Then the theatre being full, the services commenced. Kneeland rose and led the assembly in the singing of a rational hymn, which was followed by selections from *The Bible of Reason*, and then another hymn. After this the lecturer delivered a sermon, which, according to a shocked observer, tended to "ridicule the Christian religion, to persuade the congregation that there is no God, no future state, and no soul." A concluding hymn and the audience was dismissed with the announcement that "the weekly ball will be held in *this place* on Wednesday evening!" On the way out, one could purchase infidel books which were spread out on a table in view of all who may pass.[21]

Between 1834 and 1838, Kneeland endured four criminal trials and seemingly endless judicial proceedings in which he stood accused of blasphemy. In the December 20, 1833, edition of the *Investigator,* three articles appeared that, respectively, questioned the virgin birth, irreverently ridiculed the idea of petitionary prayer while likening God to Andrew Jackson, and differentiated the freethought ideas of Kneeland from those of the Universalists. The state focused most of its attention on the last of these, as it was the only one clearly authored by Kneeland. After the initial trial ended in a perfunctory conviction, he appealed to the Massachusetts Supreme Court. There, consecutive retrials ended in hung juries. The arguments lodged against Kneeland contained all the primary themes of antagonism leveled by the religious establishment at freethought movements: atheism, sexual licentiousness, advocacy of birth control, amorality, anarchy, and revolution. The third time was the charm for the state, and Kneeland's conviction was upheld by the state supreme court in 1838. Convicted of blasphemy for his exploits, he became the last American imprisoned for the offense, serving two months in jail.[22] The following year, he led his congregation to the Iowa frontier to establish Salubria, a utopian community founded explicitly on his freethinking vision. It failed to thrive.

Although these proselytizers for "reason and experience" achieved some moderate successes in converting the working class to their views, their influence waned severely by the 1850s, due in part to vehement responses from religious leaders. The decades before the Civil War were a time of rapid social change and extensive immigration. For instance, in Kneeland's city of Boston, the foreign-born population increased sevenfold between 1830 and 1845.[23] Foreshadowing Red Scares of the next century, the 1850s was a time of intense public fear that religious infidelity threatened the moral order of America.[24] Notably, "Few freethinkers were atheists"; however, their deistic and scientistic arguments laid the groundwork for a more complete rejection of God that came to fruition in the years after the Civil War.[25]

For those interested in proselytizing and spreading their understanding of the Christian Gospel, there were simultaneously seas of "unchurched" citizens and governmental protections for the freedom of religion, and therefore also for religious innovation. In the period between the Revolutionary War and the 1830s, groups with a decentralized power structure, unlearned preachers, and fervor for evangelism grew rapidly. Two groups, Baptists and Methodists, were the primary winners in the battle for souls and allegiance. The latter were a particularly striking example of growth. Constituting less than 3% of all religious adherents in 1776, over one third of religious Americans were Methodists in 1850.[26] Itinerant ministers, camp meetings, and a message of personal piety and relationship to God proved highly effective recruiting and mobilization techniques.

As salt-of-the-earth sects won the hearts of ever larger shares of the public, important changes were taking place in academe, where old-line Protestant thinkers held court. The established religions of the Northeast had begun a process of intellectualization, which would eventually lead certain branches of Protestantism toward ideological secularization. In fact, prominent freethinkers in the late nineteenth century, such as Robert Ingersoll and Samuel Putnam, "felt that the secularization of liberal Protestantism was one of the most important achievements of the American freethought movement."[27] Although freethinkers' critiques of traditional religion played a role, this assessment exaggerates the influence of freethought critiques on Protestantism. Even among otherwise conservative religious groups, belief in God's working through natural law emphasized science, and Protestant theologians of all stripes had long claimed that science shone a guiding light into the designs of God. In this sense, Protestantism shared freethought's reverence for natural science; however, the evolutionary revolution in science provided new ground from which rationalists could assail not just organized religion, but God himself.[28] The groundwork had been laid for a break from theism.

Evolutionary Agnosticism

By the latter half of the nineteenth century, unchallenged belief in God's working through natural law was disrupted by the Darwinian revolution in science, expanding biblical criticism, advancing industrial capitalism, and religious pluralism; but these commonly cited sources of secularization are only part of the story. As an open market for religion led to competition and increased levels of religious organization, the seeds of theistic unbelief were ironically being sewn in religious discourse and innovation.[29] Simultaneous currents of thought in the academy began to clear the way for perpetual agnosticism with regard to God, a position that would have seemed incomprehensible only decades earlier. The dual emphasis on natural law and science in Protestant thinking provided the impetus for revisions of deism and pantheism that saw God as an expression of nature, rather than the inverse.

Importantly, American Protestant leaders espoused an "intense moralism" in the nineteenth century in conjunction with ideas of human progress and natural theology.[30] The idea that religion was "nothing but" humanitarian, this-worldly moral concerns combined with a prioritizing of natural processes opened an intellectual passageway into theistic nonbelief. If religion was about being good to one's fellow humans and God simply the sum total of the natural world, why was God necessary? Here the increasing scope and professionalization of science played a critical role. Rather than the oversimplified "conflict between religion and science" frequently portrayed in popular culture, scientific naturalism played a supplemental role by removing the necessity of God in accounting for cosmology and the origin of human morality. At the same time, the increasing power of technological applications of science pushed the understanding of everyday life toward an immanent frame—a this-worldly, practical approach to the understanding of problems, life, and nature.[31]

Further, if Darwin was right, as most institutional scientists eventually came to believe, then the "natural law" of selection was not necessarily divine and hardly benevolent. Rather, it was a slow, cruel process of death, adaptation, and survival. With this sea change in scientific thinking about human origins, Protestant theodicy was placed on precarious ground. The ideological shift in the scientific community provided a foundation on which nontheists could cast doubt about God as being *more moral than theistic belief.* This "more moral than" rhetoric was a critical turning point in the public viability of secularism, providing the foundation for the removal of the divine. The fact that theistic disbelief failed to spread prior to this is telling, as it demonstrates that regardless of one's philosophical position, religious or irreligious, both "hungered and thirsted after righteousness."[32]

In the 1860s, the thought of Herbert Spencer and Thomas Huxley won many intellectual admirers.[33] Huxley's work to officially establish, define, and defend agnosticism as a viable position on religion marked an important development in secularist ideology and the culmination of decades of work by social philosophers and scientists, most directly Spencer and Auguste Comte. Notably, both thinkers were eventually claimed by the burgeoning discipline of sociology. Regarding the origin and diffusion of agnosticism, there were three necessarily interrelated wellsprings that sustained it: (1) intellectual uncertainties surrounding traditional beliefs about God; (2) qualms with the morality connected to traditional belief in God; and (3) the transition of a reverential attitude from God to other topics such as science, humanity, nature, and art.[34] These cultural tributaries combined to produce a subcultural and public secularism that was farther from the supernatural than previous forms. The inversion of the other/this-worldly connection represented a crucial step in the development of theistic nonbelief as a self-sustaining perspective.

With the push toward theistic nonbelief, new media outlets sprang up to promote and sustain nonbelieving interpretive communities. In 1870, the Free Religion Association started *The Index*, a weekly devoted to freethought. In 1873, *The Truth Seeker* was founded as a radical freethought periodical by outspoken disbelievers D. M. and Mary Bennett. The publication remains in operation today, a miraculous feat considering the litany of freethought outlets that have appeared and disappeared over its lifespan. The most powerful force in the popularization of agnosticism was sliver-tongued gadfly Robert Ingersoll, whose lecture tours, writings, and public speeches exposed the general public to eloquent versions of freethought arguments. In the period following the Civil War, the freethought movement attained a level of intellectual respectability, even as defenders of traditional religious authority fiercely fought it. Public intellectuals such as Ingersoll, Harvard professor Charles Eliot Norton, and suffragist Elizabeth Cady Stanton were passionate and articulate advocates for religious skepticism. The popularizing of secularism during this period has led some modern secularists to reflect nostalgically on this era as the "golden age of freethought."[35] Yet, in spite of the successful diffusion of freethought ideas in certain areas of popular and intellectual culture, the movement sputtered on other fronts.

The immense diversity of perspectives contained under the broad tent of freethought contributed vibrancy, but also undermined political impact by factionalizing the movement. The story of the American Secular Union epitomizes the political fortunes of organized secularism. On the centennial of the signing of the Declaration of Independence, freethinkers gathered to form the National Liberal League. By 1879, organization members attempted to transform it into a political party uniting the diverse array of perspectives associated with the movement, mobilizing them toward common goals. Infighting instantaneously stymied the effort: "The party was probably one of the most short-lived in American history, for its birth, rise and death scarcely went beyond the imagination of those who founded it."[36]

Four years later, vigilant League members tried again, drafting nine resolutions designed to be the platform of the party. These included abolishing the U.S. presidency and replacing it with a three man-council; opposition to prohibition and temperance; designating Sunday as election day; equality of citizens without regard to sex or creed; the uniformity of the criminal and civil court system; and compulsory public schooling. At the following year's convention, impassioned debate took place over whether the organization should go beyond these general positions and advocate specific policy reforms. The League decided to restrict its activities to the resolutions laid out the previous year, to limit its overt political activity, and to change its name to the American Secular Union. The thoughts of prominent secularist Samuel Putnam on this turn of events well express the philosophical and idealistic bent of the movement, as well as the continuing influence of Paine:

> The late action of the Liberal League lifts it at once out of the details of party politics and into the realm of universal principles. . . . From this time forward, this is the one mission of the Liberal League and the American Secular Union, to set free the minds of men, to insist upon fair play in political government, to maintain equal rights for all.[37]

The American Secular Union committed itself to the separation of church and state, but in a largely apolitical, abstract, and philosophical manner. Examining the Union as a new religious movement or political party, it exhibited weak organizational structure and an inability to generate volunteerism and resource sacrifice from members. More than anything, the Union became a media hub for secularist ideas and a staging area for defensive countermovement tactics to prevent sectarian encroachments onto the separation of church and state. In 1891, under a heavily Unitarian (and therefore religiously ecumenical) influence, the annual convention split over just how anti-religious the group should be. Should only specific dogmas be assailed, or religion wholesale? The following year the annual convention managed to attract only twenty-five people. The Union, like any organization on the make, inflated its size estimates to increase member confidence. Although it claimed to have 40,000–50,000 members in 1900, only twenty-nine delegates showed up to the 1899 convention. Reality imposed itself soon enough, and by 1910 the Union "lapsed into a state of impotence from which it never emerged."[38]

The many failures of the diffuse population of freethinkers to organize effectively toward political ends stemmed from an inability to adjust the movement's focus to align with political realities. By the late nineteenth century, much of the unofficial (although often legal) establishment of Protestantism had been retracted, even though Protestants still enjoyed a majoritarian position in most areas. The visionary quality and skepticism of all forms of authority espoused by the freethinkers of this era was crippling for political mobilization, but ultimately led to the endurance of their ideas about supernatural skepticism, views on the relationship between science and knowledge, and critiques of revealed religion.[39]

Cultural Diffusion and Movement Disintegration

In the short term, however, the disconnect between the movement's tenor and the realities of modernizing America only widened. The death of the "Great Agnostic," Robert Ingersoll, in 1899 marked the loss of public secularism's most eloquent and influential advocate. Ingersoll's intellect and mastery of oration at a time when that mode of communication was prominent, coupled with the colonel's socially respectable political views—after serving in the Union Army, he became a lifelong Republican—made him uniquely qualified as a public representative for secularity. Although Ingersoll was a popular target of religious attacks, his personal attributes, like those of Ethan Allen before him, shielded him from some of the more serious charges often leveled against secularists, such as claims that they were "revolutionaries" and "anarchists." By the beginning of the twentieth century, after Ingersoll's passing, extensive immigration from Europe brought concerns about Catholicism to the fore, which resulted in a "nativist" Protestant response.

The so-called golden age quickly faded. The late-nineteenth-century generation of secularists gave way to myriad more specialized social movements (women's suffrage, protection of civil liberties, prohibition reform) and increasing virulence against leftist political movements made the costs of overt secularism extremely high. The link between socialist philosophies and secularism, both real and publically perceived, has played an important historical role in shaping secularism in the United States. It is simplest to say that, historically, most radical-left Americans were secular, but most secular Americans have not been radical leftists. The organized movements of each philosophy have tended not to officially align themselves with one another. Indeed, deism in the early republic was tied more to libertarianism than to socialism. These facts have not deterred claims about "atheistic communism" and other such epithets. The Bolshevik Revolution and the entry of the U.S. into World War I prompted the first Red Scare, and this political atmosphere not surprisingly coincided with the decline of freethought social movements, even as the ideas of such movements took greater hold in American culture and discourse.[40]

The grand public theater of the Scopes trial in 1925 pitted modern science against the movement recently christened as "fundamentalism," a dispute fundamentalism won in the short run but lost culturally.[41] The stinging and derisive words of H. L. Mencken and Clarence Darrow combined with the death of William Jennings Bryan only days after the trial seemed to signal the triumph of modernism and the impending decline of traditionalist religion. In spite of the claimed "victory" in Dayton and the widespread decrease in religious participation during the 1920s, organized freethought disintegrated as a social movement alongside the apparent retreat of evangelicalism, as the antagonisms between Catholicism and Protestantism over religious pluralism replaced earlier dialectic exchanges between the unofficially established Protestant majority and freethinkers. The increasing prominence of Catholicism and to a lesser extent Judaism signaled the diminishment of Protestantism as a national faith.[42] Secularists now found themselves in the awkward position of having to, at times, side against a rising Catholic constituency's influence on public policy while simultaneously avoiding alignment with the anti-Catholic nativism of conservative Protestants.[43] In effect, waves of immigrants led to the Catholic Church inadvertently stealing secularism's antagonistic thunder. The Great Depression further shifted public discourse away from the civil libertarian concerns that had long been the hallmark of the freethought movement. This sequence and confluence of developments effectively displaced secularists as a prominent and distinctive voice in political discourse, even as many of their ideas became more widely diffused, accompanied by institutional secularization in areas such as public education, law, and especially academe.[44]

In the end, despite its temporary withdrawal from the public stage, claims for the decline of conservative Protestantism were greatly exaggerated. The public humiliation of the anti-evolution movement among intellectual elites and the failure of Prohibition in 1933 did lead to a relative lull in partisan social movements based on religion. Concerns about economic depression and war pushed domestic "moral" politics to the periphery. Conservative Protestantism did not disappear, however, but rather began the process of building a vast subcultural infrastructure. Its political ambitions centered around codifying morality were tabled until nearly a half century later, when changing sexual mores pushed forward by the "counterculture" fueled a resurgence in conservative Christianity's political aspirations.

Following World War II, the emergent Cold War between the United States and the Soviet Union was framed as an ideological battle between communism and capitalism. Central to this prolonged international conflict was the juxtaposition of an explicitly theistic, religious vision of American national identity against "godless" communism—hence, the Congressional resolution that established "In God We Trust" as the national motto in 1956. The ideological climate in which communism was depicted as the primary out-group and enemy of the American way of life helped create a high tide of religiosity, peaking in the 1950s. The perceived link between communism and secularism, against which American culture was articulated as religious, democratic, and capitalist, was strengthened as well. Although public participation by Americans in organized religion would begin to wane again in the 1960s, the stigma of irreligion remained.

Recurring Historical Themes

Our treatment of American nonreligious history is by necessity brief, but it renders contemporary trends more intelligible by drawing out the notable themes of church/state dynamics and the cultural interplay with politically conservative Protestantism in the ideological development of secularisms in the United States. Figure 3.1 graphically presents the historical timeline we have sketched. The left-hand column provides general estimates for the periods during which these developments occurred. The right-hand column shows important parallel cultural movements (the Second Great Awakening and the Cold War) that occurred during the same periods. Drawing definitive start and end dates to these developments oversimplifies complex historical realities, but provides a useful heuristic that orients our understanding of recent developments in American secularisms. The empty ovals represent the most important historical moments in the development of American secularism. The final oval, representing the Great Abdicating, interpenetrates the resurgence of the Religious Right and is open-ended and ongoing.

Ideologies of secularity have historically been, and remain, transnational in the West, as is evident from the example of influential secular thinkers such as Paine. At the same time, the historical specifics of the U.S. have shaped both past and present permutations of secularism. This is true in numerous ways, but four are particularly relevant. First, there was no ancien régime in the U.S., and no established national church to disestablish (beyond British Anglicanism), at least at the federal level.[45] This absence is critical in the sense that social movements were less needed to fight for the extension of religious freedoms, although they were necessary to *keep them protected.* The combination of national nonestablishment and freedom of (ir)religious expression was unique, allowing for extensive religious innovation and proselytizing as well as greater protections for overt expressions of secularism. The influence of disestablishment helps explain the many incarnations of the freethought movement, as well as its inability to gain extensive ground against religious foes. Often, secularist advocates failed to take adequate account of the import of the legal victories achieved by the "godless" Constitution and the First Amendment because they were still actively battling a seemingly, and in many cases practically, established Protestant culture.

Because of the legal contexts surrounding church and state in the U.S., secularist social movements were largely *defensive* in orientation—aimed at protection rather than enactment. Some attempted the occa-

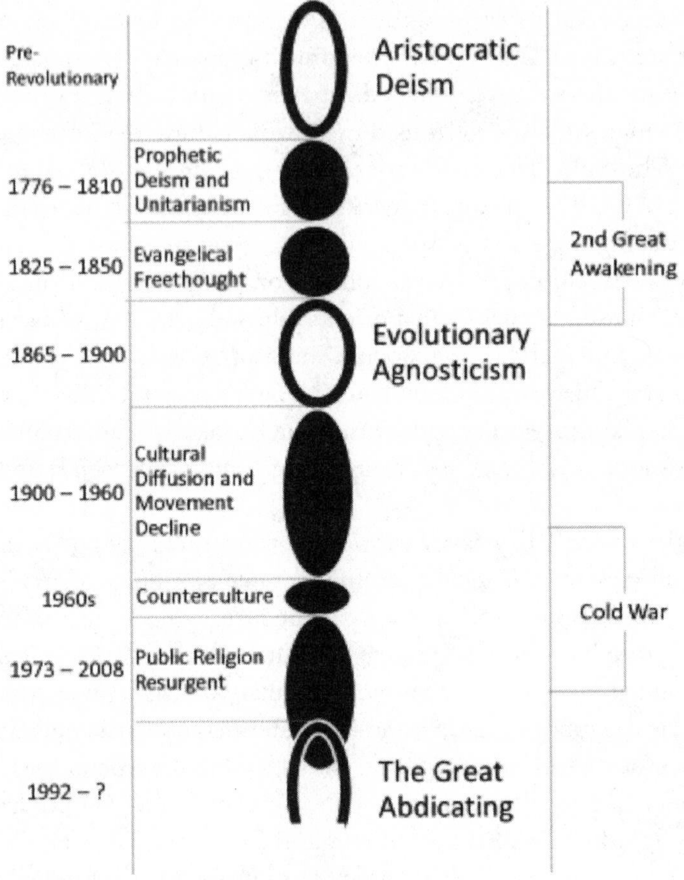

Figure 3.1. Historical Timeline of American Secularism

sional offensive action, but typically to no avail. For example, in 1894, after the American Secular Union had become a predominantly apolitical entity, Samuel Putnam, in spite of his lofty idealistic goals, again attempted to gather steam toward a politically assertive secularist organization based on the "Nine Demands of Liberalism." He initiated the Freethought Federation, merging it with the Secular Union and serving as its president, but the group mustered little traction with candidates or legislation.[46] Although it once successfully lobbied for the introduction of a constitutional amendment clarifying and furthering official state secularism, this was primarily a symbolic countermove against religious advocates pressing for "God in the Constitution." Freethinkers continually referred to Paine as their most revered prophet, a man whose views were embedded in a variety of offensive revolutionary moments and movements; yet once legal secularism was officially established, freethinkers understandably (but often unknowingly) switched largely to a defense of the ground gained. The dialectical irony deserves emphasis: public secularist movements were ultimately weakened by institutional secularization.[47]

A second historical thread is that modern American secularism grew out of traditions of freethought *and* movements in Protestantism toward humanitarianism, natural theology, and the theological split between an immanent pantheism (Unitarianism) and a highly anthropomorphized, omniscient God (Calvinism). The currents in humanism and natural theology coupled with an immanent view of the divine allowed eventual nonbelievers an avenue to public morality, meaning, and righteousness that could be divorced from theism and focused solely on humanity.[48] Ironically, but perhaps not surprisingly, the religious roots of secularism run deep. These origins, combined with the open market for religion in the U.S., forced secularisms to compete on equal footing with religious organizations, and freethought movements often adopted and adapted the organizational forms and tactics of religious groups such as weekly services and Sunday schools of secularism (the latter was advocated by atheist D. M. Bennett via *The Truth Seeker*).[49] The inextricable connection between religious and secular thought combined with the distinct legal context of the U.S. produced varied efforts at founding and sustaining communities based on secularism. These efforts were mostly organizationally ineffective, but the zeal with which the projects were undertaken helped diffuse secularist ideas from the intellectual classes to the masses.

Third, the absence of unifying goals or a unanimous perspective on issues of religion further burdened any movement's ability to compete against the proselytizing and organizing efforts of religious groups. The diversity of perspectives contained under the umbrella of "freethought" is vividly apparent upon inspection of secularity in the U.S., past or present. In many ways, the values common to the broader movement, such as independence of thought and disdain for knowledge justified by authority, served to hinder stronger organizational efforts, while at the same time fostering internal ideological vitality via pluralism. Historically, secularists were often more engrossed in disputes among themselves than between a broader movement and organized religions. Although religionists, again both historical and contemporary, typically characterize secular movements, organizations, and individuals as uniformly "godless" and anti-religious, such caricatures grossly underestimate the diversity of secular viewpoints.[50]

Finally, the nature of civic inclusion in the U.S. is such that religious organizations act as primary conduits to participation in the public sphere and recognized citizenship, ensuring a strong incentive to be religious—with the relative social penalty for secularity varying depending on the political atmosphere of a given context. A historical view shows the waxing and waning of both the antagonism directed at freethought and that directed from secularists toward religionists. High points in the vilification of secularists in the antebellum, post–World War I, and post–World War II eras corresponded with ebbs in the prominence of public secularisms. Notably during each of these periods, efforts to reintegrate and unify American society cast secularists as folk devils.[51] High watermarks in the public prominence of the various instantiations of the freethought movement occurred in the mid-nineteenth century and turn of the twentieth century, epochs when foment in secularist thought produced considerable intellectual and especially polemical output. Contemporary secularist movements advocate positions largely derived from intellectual threads traceable to these periods. To reiterate, it is this dynamic—a domestically politicized dispute over the role of religion in public life—that has produced the American religious (and secular) landscape we find historically, as well as today.

Summary

The development of secularisms through freethought movements includes characteristics unique to the American context beyond religious freedom. Although Protestantism was the normative religious tradition of the U.S., social elites were less merged with a particular religious organization than in European contexts. So while advocates of freethought could and did publically rail against the perceived and actual hypocrisies of organized religion, their efforts at secularization were *populist*, *morally libertarian*, and *politically progressive* in nature, focusing on freeing individuals from "mental slavery" rather than disestablishing religious political institutions. The contradictions and divisions between libertarianism and political progressivism served to clip the wings of efforts at movement mobilization, often before external forces might have sought to do so.

Secularists were relatively free to express their unpopular views, and did not have the unifying movement goal of disestablishing an official state religion. This freedom ironically muted the eventual impact of secularist movements on the American public, lessening their reformist political potential. Freedom of consciousness also resulted in a multitude of freethought perspectives, forcing secularisms to compete openly in the marketplace of ideas and organizations. Sectarian Protestantism and immigrant Catholicism ultimately fared much better in this environment. The freethought movement was not completely ineffectual, as it produced some fierce advocates who exercised a modicum of influence on public discourse, but overall it failed to gain sustained traction as a popular movement. Time and time again, American secularisms have been profoundly shaped by the dynamics of church/state separation and the nature of antagonisms with politically conservative Protestantism, themes that echo through history and into the present.

4

The Great Abdicating

In 1957, President Dwight Eisenhower ordered federal troops to desegregate schools in Little Rock, Arkansas, in compliance with the *Brown v. Board of Education* Supreme Court decision rendered three years earlier. The Soviet Union launched the satellite Sputnik, putting the space race, and scientific and technological competition more generally, to the fore of the Cold War. Birth control pills entered the public domain, accompanied by heated debates among religious leaders.[1] In the same year, the Current Population Survey collected by the Census Bureau sampled over 35,000 households and asked respondents about their religious preferences. The resulting data are rare and valuable because the sample size was so large, but also because the Census generally does not collect information about religion. Notably, less than 3% of those sampled said they were atheist, agnostic, or had no religion.[2]

The high tide of American religion began to wane in the 1960s, as countercultural movements emphasized highly individualistic narratives of religious seeking, personal authenticity, and self-fulfillment, broadening the diversity of religious choices available by importing commoditized versions of Eastern philosophies and giving new life to esoteric traditions. The 1960s represent a principal transformation in the religious landscape of the U.S., with more switching between faiths and the increased domestic politicization of religion. Previously salient denominational differences gradually gave way to broader coalitions between religious "conservatives" and "liberals," coalescing into and merging with the single-continuum ideological dynamic that continues to dominate American political discourse today. These shifts were particularly noticeable in matters of gender and family structure, which began to change as a result of women's increasing levels of education and labor market participation.[3]

Figure 4.1 shows the proportion of women who listed "keeping house" as their primary work status along with the estimated proportion of all

Americans who were married, ever divorced or separated, and never married in each wave of the General Social Survey. From 1972 to 2010, the percentage of women keeping house fell from 53% to 18%. Over the same span, the percentage of all Americans currently married fell from over 70% to 44%. In correspondence, the percentage of people who were ever married that had ever been divorced or separated more than doubled (from 17% to 41%). The percentage of adults who had never been married also more than doubled (from 13% to 28%). Over the same time frame, the percentage of all births that were to unmarried mothers increased from 11% to 37%. These trends show a realignment and diversification of family structures in the U.S., accompanied by changes to the social organization of gender, especially concerning the intersection of work and family.[4]

The "God Strategy"

These sociodemographic and economic processes destabilized mainline forms of religion, clearing the way for an ethic of personal authenticity and changes to the social organization of gender and sexuality. Countercultural and feminist movements in the 1960s challenged the social organization of sexuality, gender, and by implication, religion. As would become apparent in the religious reaction to the counterculture, gender and sexual order were at the very heart of traditional religious authority and power. The cohort of Americans who came of age during the 1960s would ultimately be less involved in traditional religions than those before them, initiating greater religious experimentation and individualism that continued in succeeding generations.[5] When the GSS was first fielded in 1972, just over 5% of respondents claimed no religion. By the mid-1970s, the percentage of Americans who claimed no religion was about 8%, where it would remain until the 1990s.

The counterculture of the 1960s was followed by a backlash that increased the internal politicization of American religion. When countercultural movements challenged prevailing ideas about the links between morality and traditional religion with ethics of individualism and self-expression, the continuance of the Cold War provided sustenance for a backlash of cultural conservatism that included a heavy emphasis on political religion. Conservative religious believers responded to cultural changes by forming political coalitions and mobilizing around resis-

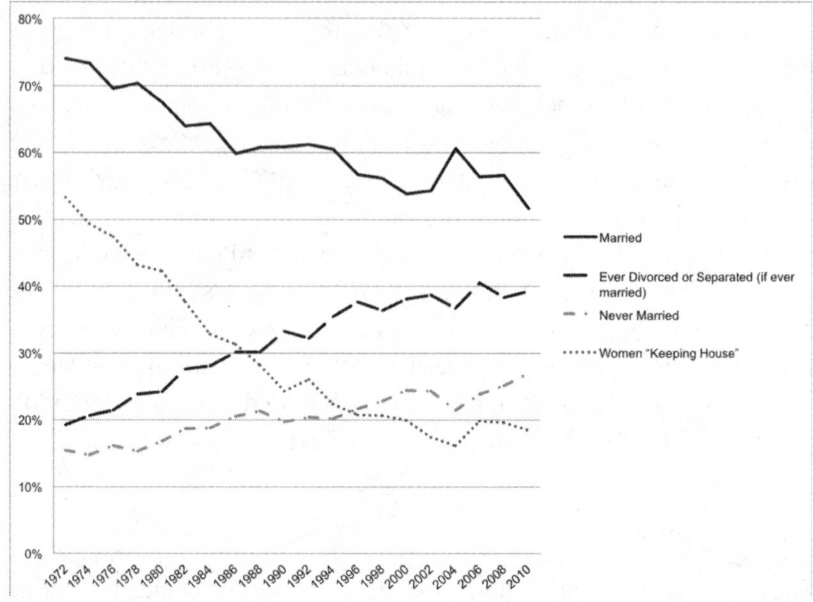

Figure 4.1. Changes to American Family Structure, 1972–2010

tance to issues perceived as threatening traditional morality, often focusing on gender and sexuality. In the 1970s and 80s, the religious Right (re) emerged as a political vehicle for rejuvenated forms of morally conservative, public religion. The movement formed and rallied around perceived instances of encroaching liberalism such as the Supreme Court's decision in *Roe v. Wade* (1972) to legalize abortion, opposition to states ratifying the progressive stance on gender embodied in the Equal Rights Amendment, and other divisive cultural issues such as homosexuality and prayer in public schools.

This mobilization gained power and status by aligning with the Republican Party in electoral politics during the 1980s. The end of the Cold War was accompanied by a lessening of the more aggressive forms of stigmatization tying secularism to communism and anti-Americanism, but also provided political conservatives the opportunity to put more energy toward domestic issues, often focusing on matters of sexuality. A decade of strong rhetoric by the Moral Majority and similar advocates about the fall of American culture and the seductions of secularism culminated in the midterm elections of 1994, in which Republican candidates rode the wave of "values voters" to majorities in the House and Senate.[6] These developments led to yet another countermovement in the long-running interplay between secularism and conservative Protestantism, as the rise of the religious Right coincided with the coming of age of the children of the baby boomers. Following these political developments, there began a dramatic decline in the proportion of Americans claiming religious affiliation. By 2012, surveys of American adults consistently reported that over 20% claimed no religion.[7] The sharp rise in secularity is demographically astounding considering the birth advantage held by religious affiliates over seculars. The reasons for these changes lie in the relationship between religion and politics, changing patterns of demography, and changing rates of religious (and secular) transmission from parents to children.

Political Polarization and Secularity

Communications scholars David Domke and Kevin Coe conducted an authoritative study of the use of religion in presidential rhetoric from the Great Depression (1932) until the Great Recession (2008).[8] From the 1930s until 1980, they found relative stasis in the political uses of religious rhetoric. Further, when presidents and political platforms invoked religion, they tended to espouse a generic, inclusive vision of civil religion built around nondenominational theism. During this period, religious issues—other than those relating to communism—were in the relative background of domestic politics.

The coalescence of conservative religion and politics in the 1980s altered the relative calm surrounding religion and domestic politics. The post–World War II era saw America with a booming economy and an external threat portrayed as godless. Religious affiliation was often a taken-for-granted signifier of ethnic identity, but it was not a primary marker of domestic political positioning. Beginning in the late 1970s and early 1980s, the use of religious rhetoric changed, and an increased connection between personal religiosity and voting patterns soon followed. During the 1950s, knowing Americans' religious affiliations or levels of practice was little help in predicting their voting patterns. By the 1990s, religiosity rivaled the ever-salient categories of "race" in its ability to predict political views and voting behavior.[9]

In the 1980s, conservative believers from multiple traditions of Protestantism, as well as Catholicism, began forming political coalitions around social issues such as abortion, feminism, gay rights, and prayer in schools. The rhetoric of the movement targeted secularism, but also liberal religion. Influential religious-political organizations such as Jerry Falwell's Moral Majority and the Religious Roundtable were founded in 1979 and expanded throughout the 1980s. Unifying over conservative theological and social doctrines while casting those with liberal (or often moderate) religious views out of the camp of "true believers," the movement defined right religion as that which was politically Right.[10] Beyond grassroots activism, opportunism and electioneering drove political elites to enact a strategy to woo morally conservative religious voters concerned about the changing mores of sexuality and gender.

Domke and Coe identified four primary themes in political rhetoric using religion since the presidential administration of Ronald Reagan. First, politicians, especially Republicans, began communicating prophetic rather than priestly messages about religion. Rather than, for instance, asking for God's favor and guidance, politicians *assumed* God's favor and guidance of their agenda. This type of speech sent signals to the faithful that these politicians were not hoping for divine blessing over their "mission," but rather enacting God's will via political crusade. Indeed, the use of these prophetic religious metaphors increased fourfold in presidential addresses from 1981 to 2009 compared to the era from 1933 to 1980.[11] The president who employed this rhetorical strategy the most was George W. Bush, followed by Reagan in a distant second.

The prophetic theme fusing God, America, and divine will cast the United States as set apart, a chosen nation. To be sure, the idea of exceptionalism has been present in political rhetoric throughout American history, but the degree of emphasis and repetition of this theme intensified in the past three decades. For example, presidential inaugural addresses employed the trope of America as "set apart" twice as often during this period compared to the previous half century. Another example is how national addresses were closed: from Franklin Roosevelt to Gerald Ford, individual presidents ended between 15% and 46% of their addresses with requests for divine blessing, with Harry Truman and Gerald Ford on the high end and Dwight Eisenhower and Richard Nixon on the low end. The most common phrases used were "May

God give us wisdom" and "With God's help." Ironically, the nadir of this trend came with openly evangelical Jimmy Carter, who ended fewer than 10% of his speeches with a call for divine favor. Ronald Reagan forever changed this, closing over 90% of his national addresses with such a petition. In his first term, he started by using the phrase "God bless you," which transitioned into "God bless America," a phrase that had been used to conclude just a single address from Franklin Roosevelt to Jimmy Carter. Since Reagan, every president has used the phrase to close at least 87% of his national addresses. Although the phrase itself is not new, its use signals the broader shift toward using religion in overtly political ways. The genie is out, and there seems to be no looking back.[12]

The third theme of religious communications in politics in recent years is a rise in public displays of faith by politicians. These take the form of visits to religious sites, schools, and organizations to give addresses, as well as the promotion of ceremonial religious behavior and discourse. Concerning visits to religious locations, between Franklin Roosevelt's and Richard Nixon's administrations, presidents made an average of fifteen trips to religious locations per four-year term. During the period from Ronald Reagan to George W. Bush, this number more than doubled, with presidents making an average of thirty-two visits per term. In addition to these pilgrimages, proclamations of national days of prayer for various concerns increased dramatically, with much of the focus on conservative religious issues. Similarly, explicit references to Christ and Christianity increased rapidly in Christmas communiqués, while generalized references to God declined. In multiple ways, politicians, especially Republicans, increased the volume and specificity of their public religious messages, signaling communion with conservative religious believers.[13]

The final theme Domke and Coe identified, the one most apparent to even the casual observer, was an increasing discursive emphasis on and intensity around issues of moral—particularly sexual and gender—politics. Since the 1980s, abortion has often served as a prominent target. The vehemence of the rhetoric concerning abortion in the Republican Party platform has steadily increased since 1980. In 1992, opposition to same-sex marriage was introduced into the platform; and the issue became an increasing point of emphasis in conservative discourse, especially in 2004, when ballot initiatives were used to motivate "values voters" to the polls. Accompanying this emphasis on homosexuality, there has been a dramatic increase in the use of "family values" and "faith" in politically conservative discourse.

The 1990s proved to be the most important period in the solidification of the religious Right's influence within the Republican Party. In 1988, charismatic evangelist Pat Robertson contended for the party's presidential nomination. Although he lost, his campaign mobilized conservative Protestants, and perhaps more importantly, led to an increasing presence of religious conservatives among the party's active members, such as delegates to national conventions. In the 1990s, the influx of religious conservatives became apparent in the party's official discourse. The 1992 Republican National Convention provides two important texts in the burgeoning "culture wars" that signaled the influence of the religious Right.

The opening night of the convention, the keynote speaker was Pat Buchanan, who had contended for the GOP nomination, but not surprisingly lost to incumbent George H. W. Bush. Buchanan had initially championed isolationism and laissez-faire economics, but turned to moral conservatism as the primaries progressed. He used the RNC pulpit to deliver "one of the most scathing speeches in party convention history," with ample references to metaphors of war and sexuality.[14] He began by calling the Democratic National Convention, which had occurred the previous month, "the greatest single exhibition of cross-dressing in American political history" because "radicals and liberals came dressed up as moderates and centrists." He emphasized that George Bush was a "lifelong champion of Judeo-Christian values," while Democratic nominee Bill Clinton had a "different agenda. At its top is unrestricted abortion on demand." A "militant leader of the homosexual rights movement," he declared, had been a featured participant at the DNC. Discussing Hillary Clinton, Buchanan said she had "compared marriage and family as institutions to slavery and life on an Indian reservation." Over chants of "Go Pat, Go, Go Pat, Go!" he continued:

> This my friends, this is radical feminism. The agenda that Clinton and Clinton would impose on America—abortion on demand, a litmus test for the Supreme Court, homosexual rights, discrimination against religious schools, women in combat units—that's change all right. But that's

> not the kind of change America needs. It's not the kind of change America wants. And it's not the kind of change we can abide in a nation that we still call God's country.

In the most famous segment of the speech, Buchanan emblazoned the language of culture "war" into political discourse and signaled the transition in focus from the external communist threat to the new internal target, saying, "There is a culture war, as critical to the kind of nation we will one day be as the Cold War itself, but this war is for the soul of America."[15]

Buchanan's speech was not the only expression of the culture war at the 1992 RNC. The influx of delegates affiliated with or sympathetic to the Christian Coalition, a vestige of Robertson's presidential campaign, helped push through a substantial overhaul of the party platform. In the 1988 platform, economics and jobs dominated. Although the platform opposed pornography, abortion, and sexual education including instruction in birth control, these issues were subsumed within broad sections concerning education and individual rights—with the exception of pornography, which had its own short section. In 1992, Bush campaign officials estimated that more than 40% of delegates were evangelicals. Of the platform committee members, 20% were officially aligned with the Christian Coalition, whose spokesperson, Ralph Reed, advocated for a strong emphasis on "family values." In an act of limited governance, President Bush decided not to exercise much influence over the content of the platform, letting the committee members and delegates create it.[16]

Reed was successful. The committee moved "family values" to the forefront, making it the organizing principle for the platform. The first sections after the preamble were titled "Uniting Our Family" and "Family: The Home of Freedom." Metaphors of conflict in the context of the family permeated the platform, which stated, among other things: "Today, more than ever, the traditional family is under assault," "For more than three decades, the liberal philosophy has assaulted the family on every side," "This is the ultimate agenda of contemporary socialism under all its masks: to liberate youth from traditional family values," and "Republicans oppose and resist the efforts of the Democrat [*sic*] Party to redefine the traditional American family."

While the platform is suffused with religious language about families, one section in particular warrants reprinting in its entirety. Under the heading "Family: the Home of Freedom," a subsection on "Promoting Cultural Values" read:

> The culture of our Nation has traditionally supported those pillars on which civilized society is built: personal responsibility, morality, and the family. Today, however, these pillars are under assault. Elements within the media, the entertainment industry, academia, and the Democrat Party are waging a guerrilla war against American values. They deny personal responsibility, disparage traditional morality, denigrate religion, and promote hostility toward the family's way of life. Children, the members of our society most vulnerable to cultural influences, are barraged with violence and promiscuity, encouraging reckless and irresponsible behavior. This undermines the authority of parents, the ones most responsible for passing on to their offspring a sense of right and wrong. The lesson our Party draws is important—that all of us, individuals and corporations alike, have a responsibility to reflect the values we expect our fellow citizens to exhibit. And if children grow to adulthood reflecting not the values of their parents but the amorality with which they are bombarded, those who send such messages cannot duck culpability.[17]

Although the convention included the final public address given by Ronald Reagan and the nomination acceptance speech of President Bush, the story of the event became culture war. For instance, a column in *Newsweek* about the convention was entitled "A Feast of Hate and Fear."[18] Foretelling the election outcome, Bush received minimal to no "bounce" in post-convention polling numbers, but Republican electoral success would come in the midterms.

The discourse promoted by the religious Right through interest groups like the Christian Coalition spread outward to the general public. In perfect synchronization with the rising influence of the religious Right was a growing antipathy toward "fundamentalists." Data from the National Election Surveys demonstrate that overall dislike of fundamentalists increased substantially in 1992 and 1996, and that anti-fundamentalism became a significant predictor of vote choice where previously it had been irrelevant. At the same time, antipathy lessened toward fundamentalists among Catholics and political conservatives, thanks to the work of organizations such as Reed's. Dislike increased among political progressives, Jews, and seculars. Anti-fundamentalist sentiment grew most among the highly educated and those who watched more television coverage of presidential campaigns. Further, where previous waves of National Election Survey data indicated that culture war issues operated in a sphere distinct from political identity questions such as party affiliation and liberal/conservative orientation, these issues began to align strongly in data from 1992 and after. Positions on issues such as abortion and homosexuality had become strong predictors of vote choice.[19]

Direct evidence of polarization over time is also present in data on U.S. political elites. Political scientist Geoffrey Layman places the beginnings of political and religious polarization in the early 1970s, when Democratic delegates to national conventions became increasingly secular. A countermovement of religious traditionalists entered the elite ranks of the Republican Party beginning in the late 1970s, displacing nominally religious mainline Protestants. For example, the percentage of evangelical delegates to the Republican National Convention increased from under 4% in 1976 to nearly 40% in 1996. Although the shift was less dramatic than that in the GOP, the delegates to Democratic Party conventions continually became more secular over the same time. This polarizing shift of delegates to the national conventions was most pronounced in 1992 and 1996.[20]

The Great Abdicating

Organized Religion and Political Polarization

Overall, the "God strategy" has been an effective electoral play for political conservatives. While the upside of the overt politicization of religion is high for politicians, it is also accompanied by the potential for backlash—one felt by religious organizations. Over time, the so-called culture wars led many Americans who were nominally religious to reject formal ties to organized religion. The sentiment of many former nominally and liberally religious individuals was effectively: "If that's what it means to be religious, then I'm not religious." As religious rhetoric became more prominent in political discourse during the same period that saw increasing political polarization, religious affiliation and confidence in organized religion decreased. As shown in Figure 4.2, which uses GSS data, while distrust of organized religion briefly had risen higher than confidence in 1988–1990 and 2002, 2008–2012 represents the most sustained period in which more Americans said they had "hardly any" confidence in organized religion compared to those who said they had "a great deal."[21]

The GSS only began asking about belief in God in 1988, so we can track the composition of different types of secularity only from that time. As Figure 4.3 shows, although there has been modest growth in atheism and agnosticism, the greatest amount of growth has been among nonaffiliated believers, suggesting a crisis of public confidence in organized religion rather than declining supernaturalism per se.

The two-question classification method using the GSS also allows us to examine the coupling between theistic nonbelief and claiming no religious affiliation. An estimated 60% of agnostics claimed religious affiliation in the late 1980s, while only 23% did by 2012. Similarly, the proportion of atheists claiming affiliation dropped from an estimated 71% in 1991 to 20% in 2012. Not only were more formerly religious people moving into apostasy, more nonbelievers were also dropping their affiliations with organized religion. This trend illuminates a shift in the conventionality of religious membership, and provides evidence that the resonant normative power of organized religion has waned in the last two decades.

Changes are also apparent in patterns of political identity. Political liberals have become increasingly likely to be religiously nonaffiliated. Where there may have been little cognitive or cultural dissonance involved in being strongly religious and politically liberal in the 1950s, this was no longer the case for many Americans by the 2000s. Where 12% of political liberals were religiously nonaffiliated in 1990, 29% were in 2010. There were also substantial increases in the percentages of political moderates and conservatives who were religious nones, from 7% to 16% and 5% to 11% respectively, but the largest increase occurred among liberals.

We can assess the political polarization thesis empirically by looking at the standard deviation of a consistent measure of political identity queried over time. Standard deviation provides a measure of how closely

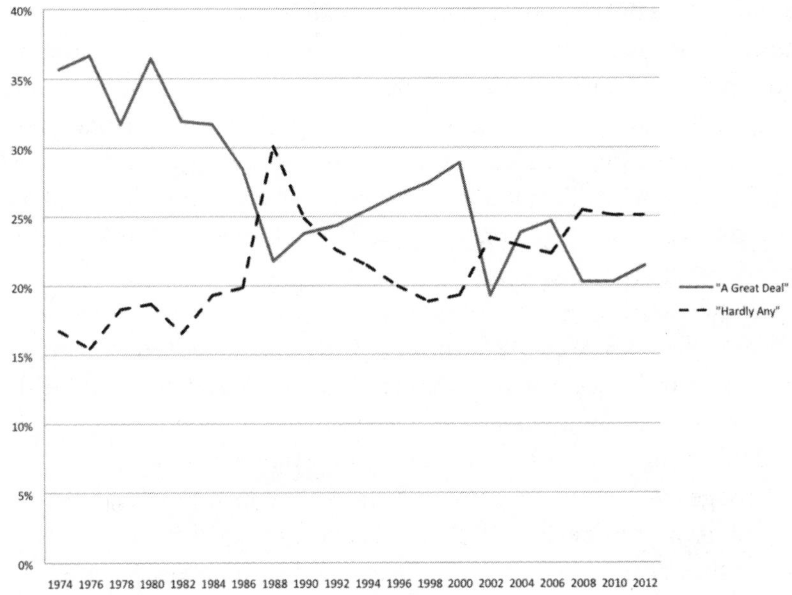

Figure 4.2. Confidence in Organized Religion, 1974–2012

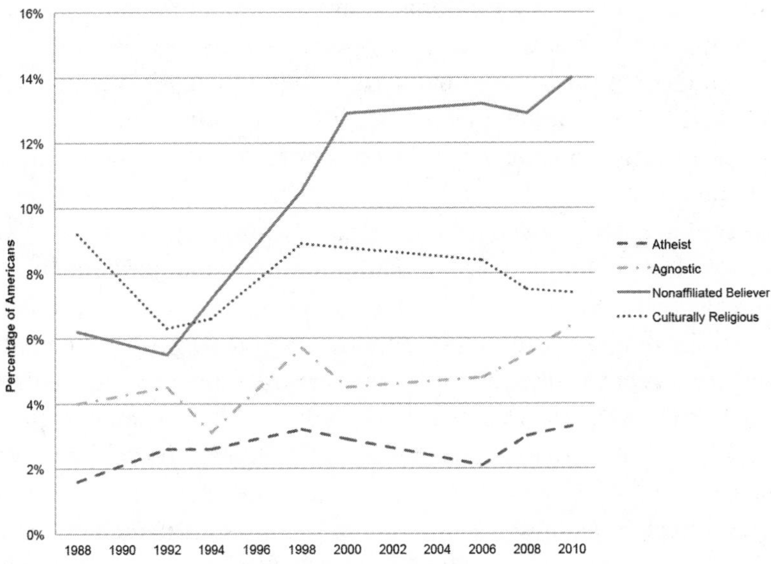

Figure 4.3. Percentage of Americans by Secularity Type, 1988–2012

the points in a distribution cluster around the average, with higher scores indicating greater dispersion—in this case meaning greater polarization. From 1974 to the present, the GSS has asked respondents whether they "think of [themselves] as liberal or conservative" and provided a seven-point scale ranging from "extremely liberal" to "extremely conservative," with "moderate" as the middle category. Since the 1990s, the trend has moved toward increasing political polarization in GSS samples, corresponding tightly to the increase in religious nones.

We can see this by turning each year of the GSS into a "case" with specific attributes. We gave each year of the survey an overall standard deviation for the political identity measure and also an attribute for the proportion of respondents reporting no religion. Values for the standard deviation of the political identity question across all years of the GSS range from a low of 1.27 in 1978 and 1980, to a high of 1.47 in 2010. Although these values are relatively small and close together in absolute terms, they represent a considerable range of dispersion because they are standardized estimates for a variable that is limited to values from 1 to 7.[22] Plotting political polarization and secularity together in Figure 4.4, the standard deviation of political identity for a sample correlates strongly with the proportion of the sample claiming no religion (Pearson's r = .86; correlations can range from -1 to +1, with 0 being no relationship). Looking at the samples by decade cluster, the data from the 1970s and 1980s show less than 8% claiming no religion and relatively low levels of polarization. In the 1990s, there is a noticeable increase in both polarization and secularity. In the 2000s, we find the highest levels of each.

A sophisticated study of religious group voting patterns between 1960 and 1992 found little evidence of changing rates of mobilization among conservative Protestant and religious nones as voters, but both conservatively religious and secular Americans have become more politically homogenous—identifying and voting the same way—since then, at least for presidential elections.[23] As Figure 4.5 shows, Ronald Reagan in 1980 was the only Republican able to win a majority of the nonaffiliated vote.[24] Similarly, Jimmy Carter in 1976 was the only Democrat in recent elections to win a majority of white fundamentalists' votes. Since the 1990s, the gap between the religiously nonaffiliated and white fundamentalist vote has widened, with the greatest difference between

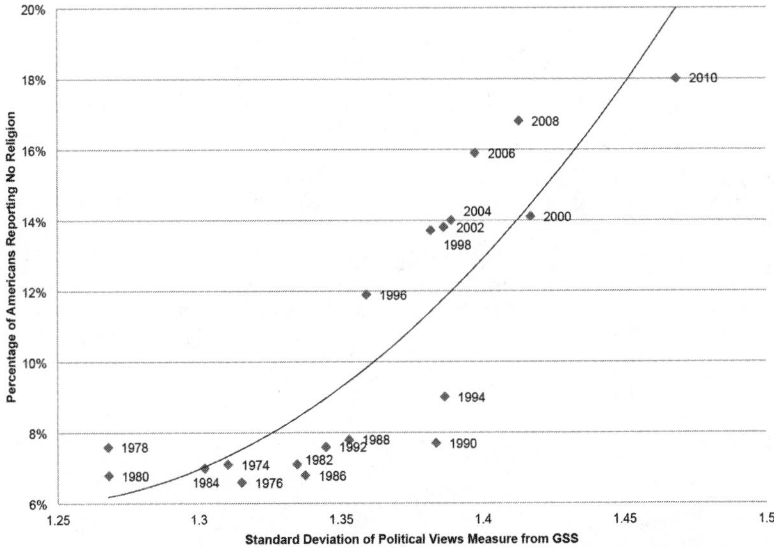

Figure 4.4. Political Polarization and Percentage of Americans Reporting No Religion

the two occurring in the 2008 election, when approximately 76% of the religiously nonaffiliated voted for Barack Obama, compared to 29% of white fundamentalists. It seems he had just cause for mentioning nonbelievers in his first inaugural address.

At the 2012 Democratic National Convention, the secularity of the delegates and the resistance of the American electorate to a noticeable absence of God met head on. Before the convention began, delegates rewrote the platform so that a phrase about government giving "everyone willing to work hard the chance to make the most of their God-given potential" was removed—the last remaining reference to God. When the convention opened, the delegates adopted the platform. The media quickly made the change a twenty-four-hour-news talking point. While Obama may have been the first president to mention secularists in his inaugural address, he was hardly secular himself, and perhaps more importantly, knew a political liability when he saw it. Obama personally had the platform amended to put the reference to God back in, along with another excised reference—to Jerusalem as the capital of Israel. At the beginning of the convention's second day, Los Angeles mayor and

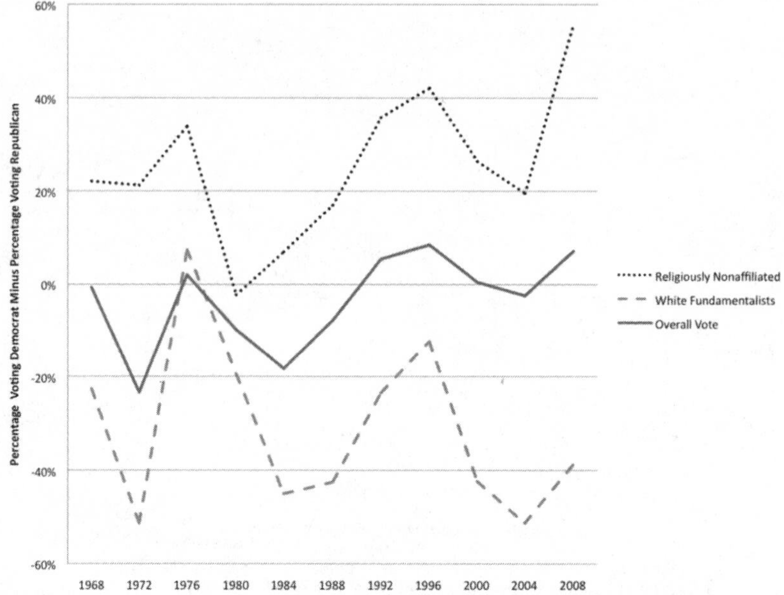

Figure 4.5. Presidential Voting of Americans Overall, Religiously Nonaffiliated, and White Fundamentalists, 1968–2008

DNC chair Antonio Villaraigosa brought the changes to a vote on the floor. Needing two thirds of those present to vote affirmatively to reinstate the removed phrases, Villaraigosa conducted the vote three times. Each time there was roughly equal support and opposition. After the third vote, he passed the motion by fiat, which was booed loudly. Although the external political liability was neutralized, the internal dissent was palpable.[25]

Apostasy and Secular Retention: The Lifeblood of Secularity

As important a role as political polarization has played in the shift toward increasing secularity among Americans, an explanation of that shift must also take into account apostasy and retention in religious groups, as well as conversion and retention among those raised outside of religion. Seculars can come from only one of two sources: apostasy or socialized secularity. Tracing these trends shows how a social category with a severe demographic disadvantage was able to gain substantial ground as a proportion of the population.

The overall level of secularity (or religiosity) in a society has four potential sources of change: demography, immigration, apostasy (or conversion), and retention. The birthrate of a group clearly has a direct impact on its staying power, as the celibate Shakers discovered when their numbers dwindled precipitously over time, while the pronatalist Latter-day Saints have become the newest world religion. Groups with high average levels of childbearing hold an innate advantage in keeping or gaining position relative to other religious groups. Often changes to religious markets, such as ground gained by conservative groups, have predominantly demographic explanations.[26] But secularists are at a severe birthrate disadvantage, so demographics are clearly not the cause of rising secularity. Immigration is not the source of increasing secularism either. Pooling all years of the GSS since 2000, 15.4% of native-born respondents claimed no religion, very similar to the 15% of first-generation immigrants. Estimates from the Pew Religious Landscape Survey are similar, with 79% of those born in the U.S. actively religious compared to 78% of foreign-born respondents. Although studies indicate that religiosity is higher among immigrants who are less integrated into their new environments through work and those who have language barriers, these differences disappear as integration occurs.[27]

The third potential source of change, apostasy, is where the action is. Figure 4.6 shows the number of individuals raised in a religious tradition who stay religious as adults for every one person who becomes a religious apostate for specific birth cohorts, using pooled GSS data from 1973 to 2010. We make no distinction between switching to another religion and staying in the same religious tradition. That is, if a person raised Catholic marries a Protestant and converts, s/he is still considered "religious" by our classification. For those born before 1911, there were over forty people raised Protestant who remained religious for every one person who became a religious none. For the same cohort there were over thirty-five people who stayed religious that were raised Catholic, and over twenty-five who stayed religious after being raised Jewish for every one that became a none. The ratios drop over time and cohorts, with all three religious traditions having retention-to-apostate ratios of about five to one in the most recent birth cohort (those currently under age forty). The ratios are even lower for those under thirty, but the sample size remains small and we can expect a slight increase in this rate as these individuals age. Based on these ratios, the proportion of the population that is religiously unaffiliated would be approximately 17% in the most recent cohort, *even if every American were raised in a religious tradition.*

The increase in Americans claiming no religion also reflects the growing presence of individuals who were raised outside of organized religions. Figure 4.7 shows that, according to pooled GSS data, following the increase in religious nones that occurred among those who came of age during the 1960s, there has been an increase in the rate of those raised outside of religion among the cohort born between 1961 and 1980. Among those born between 1941 and 1950, fewer than 10% reported attending religious services twice a year or less as children. Among those born after 1970, that percentage more than doubled to 23%. Similarly, where only 2% of those born before 1911 never attended religious services as children, over 12% of those born since 1970 report never attending.

But the increase in individuals raised outside of religion tells only part of the story of secular socialization. The final source of potential religious change, retention—in this case meaning individuals who continue to claim no religion as adults—is the other piece of the puzzle. Unlike religious groups who have seen their retention rates fall over time, the retention rates of religious nones started quite low and have now risen to match those of established religious traditions. Figure 4.8 shows the adult religious affiliations of individuals raised outside of religion by birth cohort. Until the baby boomers, over half of those raised outside religion became Protestants as adults. Since that generation, secular retention has risen rapidly. While religious retention has fallen, secularity has nearly caught up with organized religion in terms of keeping people in the belief system in which they were raised. Among those born after 1970, over 70% of socialized seculars still claimed no religion as adults. Only since the increase in religious nones that started in the 1990s have more than 2% of all American adults claimed no religion after having been socialized seculars—in the 2010 GSS, it was up to 5%. This proportion should increase as more secular adults in the current generation translate into more socialized seculars, and higher secular retention keeps a greater share of those raised secular out of religious

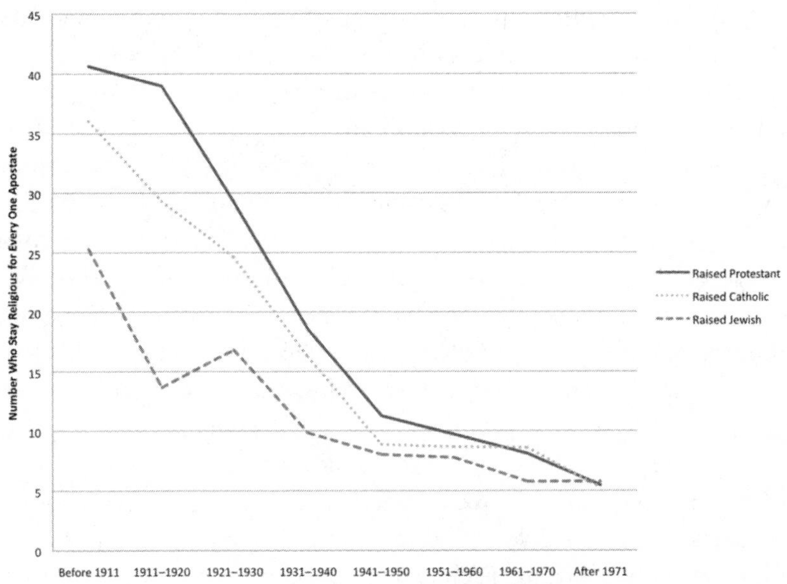

Figure 4.6. Retention-to-Apostate Ratios for Those Raised Protestant, Catholic, and Jewish by Birth Cohort

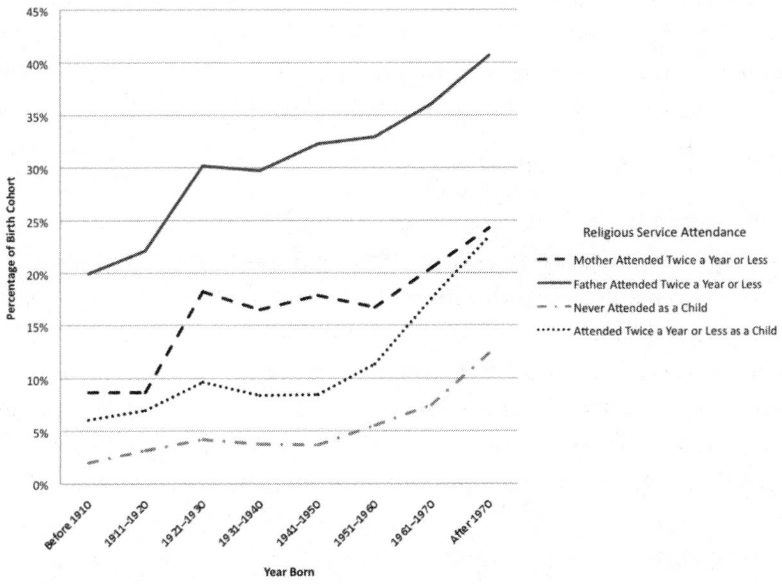

Figure 4.7. Secular Socialization by Birth Cohort

groups. Taken together, apostasy from religion coinciding with greater retention of socialized seculars accounts for the rising tide of secularity.

So what makes an individual more or less likely to drop out of religion if they were socialized into it? Conversely, what makes those raised outside of religion more likely to convert? The strongest associations between social characteristics and apostasy occur among the never married, political liberals, people living in the West, and the childless. Men, college graduates, and the divorced are also more likely to drop out. African Americans, Southerners, political conservatives, women, those with less than a high school degree, and parents are all more likely to remain religious. These factors mirror those that predict secularism in general because apostates comprise a substantial majority of secularists.

The strongest factor leading to conversion after being raised secular is political conservatism, followed by marriage and having children. Women, Southerners, and the divorced were also more likely to convert, but the effects were not as strong. Factors making people more likely to remain religiously nonaffiliated were, in order of strength, never marrying, being childless, living in the Northeast, being African American, being politically liberal, being male, and having a college degree. The fact that African Americans are less likely to switch, both into or out of religion, is particularly interesting. Socialization and familial influences are stronger for African Americans, regardless of whether they are raised religious or secular.

The Future of American Secularity

Although longitudinal patterns in family structure and politics are trending toward apostasy and greater retention for socialized seculars, how long can secularity grow in defiance of demography? Under a basic formula for the level of secularity among a given population, the proportion secular will be equal to (proportion raised religious * proportion apostates) + (proportion raised secular * secular retention). At present, all of these variables are *trending toward increased secularity*, which is how the proportion of Americans who claim no religion tripled in a relatively short time, in spite of the demographic disadvantages of secularity relative to active religiosity.

To give a better idea of how fertility constrains the growth of secularity, consider the current situation, with 20% of American adults claiming

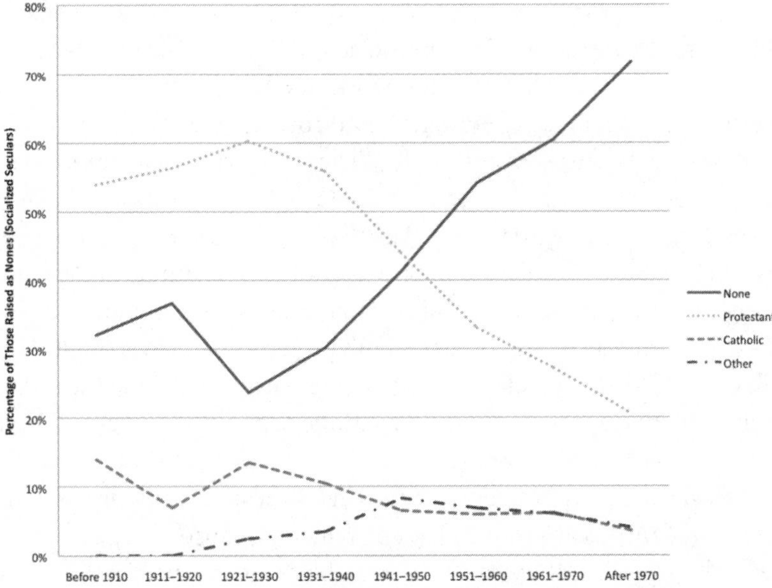

Figure 4.8. Adult Religious Preferences of Socialized Seculars by Birth Cohort

no religion and an average birthrate for nones of 1.17 and religious affiliates of 2.04.[28] The birthrate differential imposes severe growth penalties every generation. Even assuming increased retention, we can expect the proportion of those raised outside of religion to be a relatively small share of adults claiming no religion. For example, among respondents to the GSS born in the 1980s, only 24% of the nonaffiliated were socialized seculars. In short, the birthrate differential limits how much market share seculars can attain before plateauing if apostasy rates do not continue to increase at a rapid pace. Secularity in the U.S. has already beaten a thorough, long-term projection of its future published recently in the leading academic journal for empirical studies of religion, which estimated 17% to be the ceiling on American secularity.[29] Recent changes defy demography because they are cultural.

Leaving aside the complications of multivariable demographic projections in favor of a stripped-down, basic model of apostasy/retention and birthrate ratios, we can make some rudimentary projections about the immediate future of secularity in the United States. The following is an outline of what the proportion of American adults with "no religion" would be under different scenarios. We make projections for 2025 and 2050 based on varying assumptions. One projection assumes that the apostasy rate of all those raised in a religious tradition rises to 20% and the other assumes the apostasy rate plateaus at its current 15%. The low projection assumes retention rates of 65% for those raised outside of religion, while the high projection assumes 80% retention rates. We calculated the estimated proportion raised religious and secular for 2025 by applying the birthrate information above to current estimates of secularity, and project these numbers to 2050 by applying the birthrate to our respective projections for 2025. At the high end, we have loaded the deck in favor of secularity by making the (risky) assumption that apostasy rates will continue to rise at their current pace, while secular retention rates remain at 80% rather than dropping as the most recent cohort of Americans ages. Under these assumptions, roughly one third of Americans would claim no religion by 2050.

On the low end, if apostasy rates stabilize at 15% rather than continuing to rise, and socialized secular retention rates settle at 65%, then nones will plateau at just over 20% of the adult population. Given current trends, these are indeed conservative assumptions, but it is also possible that the high tide of apostasy has already occurred. Occupying the middle ground between the high and low projections, we predict that the proportion of people claiming no religion will be around 25% by 2025 and stabilize thereafter, rising slowly to 27% by 2050. To reiterate, unless the apostasy rate continues to rise, the proportion of the population with no religion is constrained by its demographic characteristics and will necessarily stabilize. Social scientists are notoriously bad at prognostication, and we may well be off by a wide margin if cultural dynamics shift in unforeseen ways. At the same time, current indicators point toward the growth of secularity. Not only are the numbers of American secularists rising, the social sources of secularity are also trending upward. Only time can judge whether the exodus from organized religion is beginning to ebb or has yet to crest.

Summary

Since the 1970s, and especially since the 1990s, the proportion of Americans who identify as secular has increased rapidly. This change

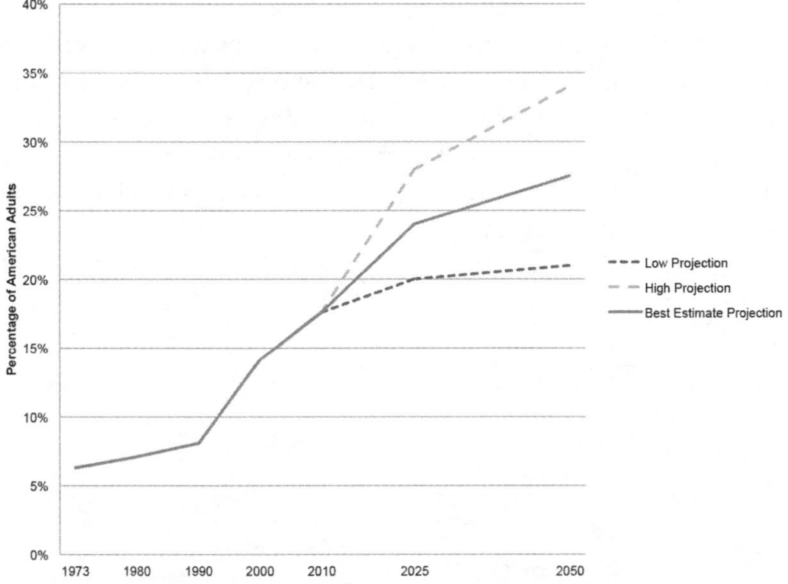

Figure 4.9. Projections for Percentage of American Adults Claiming No Religion to 2050

has occurred despite seculars' considerable demographic disadvantage in terms of having children. The forces driving this change are both cultural and political. The decline of marriage rates and female domesticity combined with increasing levels of divorce has facilitated a rise in secularity. At the same time, the political meaning of "religion" in the United States has changed dramatically since the 1960s, particularly in the late 1980s and 1990s. Countercultural movements promoting individual expression in the realms of religion, sexuality, and politics fueled a conservative backlash that wielded religion as a political weapon, catalyzing yet another backlash from the political Left. In an ironic self-fulfilling prophecy, the religious Right decried America's purported secularity, ultimately leading to an increase in the number of Americans who were secular, and diminishing organized religion's social standing among large segments of the public. Over time, data show that confidence in organized religion has fallen, that political polarization correlates closely with the rate of secularity, and that the religious Right and secular Left have become relatively homogenous, consistent voting blocs. The confluence of these factors led to a rapid increase in apostasy rates among those raised in organized religious traditions, as well as increasing retention rates among those socialized secular. Together, changes to family structure and the politics of religion have driven Americans out of organized religion in droves—the Great Abdicating.

5

Nonreligious Belief Systems

To understand secularisms as cosmic belief systems, we begin by examining the ideological patterns of different expressions of secularity. First, we analyze each category in light of how secularity is often understood—in relation to religion. We also look at patterns of private spiritual expression and supernatural belief. Next, we examine the relationship between secularity, life satisfaction, and subjective well-being. We then examine views of science. We also outline the degree to which individuals perceive or experience social conflict as a result of their secular status. Finally, we outline some themes of secular identity and the sociocognitive patterns of atheism, as outlined in the ethnographic and psychological literatures.

Secularity in Relation to Religion

We used the General Social Survey (GSS) to examine the proportion of atheists, agnostics, and nonaffiliated believers who never attend religious services or pray privately. The culturally and actively religious are excluded from this analysis because attendance and prayer are the dimensions of (non)religiosity used to create the categories. Among the three secular categories, the rates of those who never attend religious services are similar, with atheists most likely to never attend (67%), followed by nonaffiliated believers (59%) and agnostics (58%). Notably, two out of five agnostics and nonaffiliated believers and one third of atheists still attend religious services, at least occasionally. Substantial differences, however, are apparent between different types of secularity regarding levels of private prayer. Nearly four out of five atheists say they never pray (79%), compared to two out of three agnostics (66%), and only one out of four nonaffiliated believers (26%). These patterns show that nonaffiliated believers are more likely to draw a line between public and private religion, rejecting the former, but not necessarily the latter.

The same pattern was evident in the 2008 GSS regarding whether people think of themselves as religious and/or spiritual, as presented in Figure 5.1. Over 60% of atheists and agnostics did not consider themselves to be either spiritual or religious, compared to 22% of nonaffiliated believers and 27% of the culturally religious. The "spiritual but not religious" identity is highly prevalent among nonaffiliated believers, 63% of whom reported it, further evidence that this category often represents those alienated from organized religion *and* interested in privatized spirituality. One third of the culturally religious also selected the "spiritual but not religious" option, while just under 20% of atheists and agnostics did. The culturally religious, meanwhile, have the highest rate of those who consider themselves "religious but not spiritual"—28%—compared to 15% or less for each of the other types of secularity. Exemplifying the inevitable blurriness of the boundaries, 11% of atheists and the culturally religious, along with 9% of nonaffiliated believers and 6% of agnostics, consider themselves both religious and spiritual. On the other side of misclassification, 3% of those who fall into the actively religious category consider themselves neither religious nor spiritual.[1]

Regarding views of organized religion, a slight majority of atheists, agnostics, and nonaffiliated believers express "hardly any" confidence in religious institutions. In contrast, only about one quarter of the culturally religious express similar sentiments. Over 65% of those in each of the secularist categories agree that "religion causes more conflict than peace," with atheists and agnostics the highest at around 80%. Regarding whether there are any truths found in organized religions, roughly 30% of atheists believe there is "little truth in any," compared to 19% of agnostics and 8% of nonaffiliated believers and the culturally religious. Interestingly, 62% of atheists, 76% of agnostics, and 86% of nonaffiliated believers report believing that there is "basic truth in many" religions. In spite of the apparent acknowledgment of religion's potential benefits, a 2008 Pew survey designed to examine fluctuations in Americans' religious identities found that only 34% of those reporting their religious preference as "nothing in particular," 25% of agnostics, and 9% of atheists said they simply had not found the right religion yet. So while most secularists acknowledge the potential value or functionality of at least some aspects of religion, they also generally remain skeptical of the overall and personal worth of organized religion.[2]

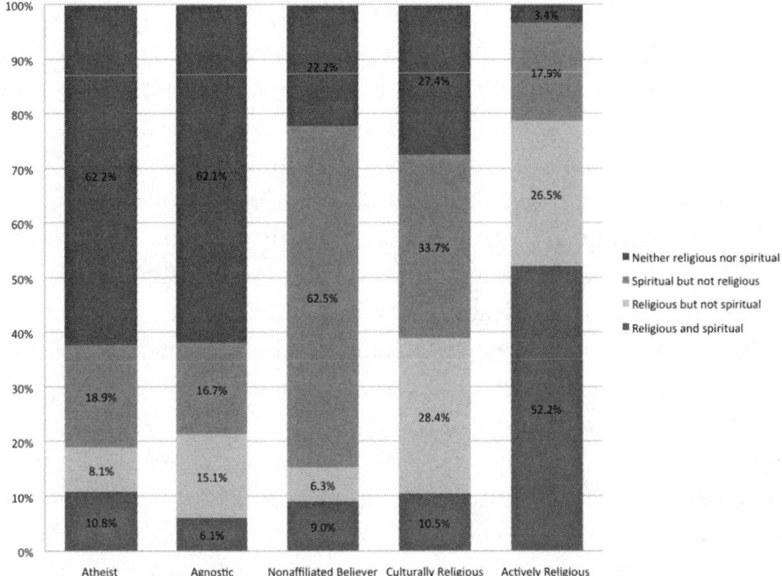

Figure 5.1. Identification as Religious and/or Spiritual by Secular or Religious Category, 2008

We also examined patterns in the Pew Religious Landscape Survey (RLS). Mirroring their low levels of religious service attendance, secularists of each type are not members of a local congregation at similar rates (all over 75%); however, the categories diverge regarding whether individuals believe that religion is "not at all important" in their lives. Atheists (74%) are much more likely to report that religion is not important compared to agnostics (41%), nonaffiliated believers (27%), and the culturally religious (18%). Again, the difference reflects distinctions between public and private religion. Each type of secularist was equally disengaged from local congregations, but there is considerable variation in the self-evaluated importance of religion to one's life.

Next we looked more closely at private spiritual practices and experiences. Over one third of agnostics and nonaffiliated believers reported meditating at least once a month, compared to 23% of atheists and 18% of the culturally religious. A similar pattern is evident regarding whether people report feeling a "deep sense of spiritual peace" at least once a month. Over half of nonaffiliated believers (51%) and 48% of agnostics say they regularly feel spiritual peace, compared to 39% of atheists and 31% of the culturally religious. Finally, 65% of agnostics say they "feel a deep sense of wonder" at least once a month (presumably often at human limitations), compared to 53% of atheists and nonaffiliated believers, and 38% of the culturally religious. On each of these dimensions of private spiritual practice, the culturally religious are distinctly the lowest category, while nonaffiliated believers and agnostics report slightly higher levels of private spiritual practices and experiences.

Finally, we considered whether secularists have different belief profiles with regard to supernatural concepts—both religious and "paranormal." Using data from the 2007 Baylor Religion Survey (BRS), we looked at whether respondents "probably" or "absolutely" believed in five religious supernatural concepts: heaven, hell, Satan, demons, and angels. For each concept believed in, respondents were assigned a one, a zero if they did not believe (five as maximum). Atheists essentially believe in no religious supernatural entities. Agnostics also exhibit little religious supernatural beliefs, averaging belief in less than one item, while nonaffiliated believers (2.5) and the culturally religious (3.2) hold higher average numbers of beliefs. Similar patterns occur regarding paranormal supernaturalism. The same battery on the BRS also asked about the existence of extraterrestrials, ghosts, Bigfoot, and extrasensory perception (ESP). Again we assigned respondents a one if they believed and a zero if they did not for each item (four as maximum). Atheists (1.1) and agnostics (1.3) had the lowest levels of belief, but still believed in at least one paranormal item on average, as did the actively religious (1.7). The culturally religious (2.1) and nonaffiliated believers (2.2) had higher levels of belief in the paranormal, averaging more than two beliefs held.[3]

The portrait these data draw of the different types of secularity in relation to religion and supernaturalism is one of some similarity, but mostly of gradation. Atheists, agnostics, and nonaffiliated believers are equally disenchanted with organized religion, although atheists are the most likely to say that there is little good in any form of religion. While there is relatively uniform disengagement from public religion, there are varying levels of engagement with private spiritual pursuits and practices. The primary matters distinguishing different expressions of secularity are distinctions drawn between public, organized religion and privatized, spiritual pursuits. The combination of similarities and distinctions lends credence to the treatment of these categories as possessing some commonalities, but also enough differences to warrant a classification scheme with greater refinement than a single, generalized category of secularity. We now proceed to address a matter of longstanding debate in both popular and academic discourse: the relationship between secularity and personal happiness and well-being.

Happiness and Life Satisfaction

One widespread notion about the nonreligious is that they are more negative than the religious in overall outlook, either as an antecedent to secularity or because their rejection of religion leads to more pessimism.[4] This narrative is sometimes presented as one in which those who accept religion into their lives become more optimistic and thankful. Alternatively, it can be a story in which a previously religious person experiences great loss or tragedy and forsakes religion.[5] In line with this idea, there is evidence that secularists are more likely to think of themselves as "critical." In a battery of questions about self-described personality traits on the BRS, 68% of agnostics, 63% of atheists, 60% of nonaffiliated believers, and 57% of the culturally religious described themselves as "critical," compared to 47% of the actively religious. Of course, whether being critical is a negative attribute depends on one's valuation of "critical," but we can directly test the assumption that seculars experience less subjective satisfaction by looking more broadly at how Americans view their own lives in terms of optimism or pessimism.

Looking at the Pew RLS, among all secular respondents, atheists have the highest average level of satisfaction with their personal lives, while agnostics are the least likely to be "very dissatisfied." Overall, there is little variation between types of secularity. Fifty-nine percent of atheists were "very satisfied," similar to 57% of nonaffiliated believers, 56% of the culturally religious, and 55% of agnostics. All these categories are slightly less satisfied than actively religious respondents, of whom 63% were "very satisfied," but these apparent differences reflect *degree* of satisfaction. Combining "somewhat satisfied" and "very satisfied," about 88% of actively religious Americans were satisfied, mirrored by 88% of atheists, 89% of agnostics, 87% of the culturally religious, and 86% of nonaffiliated believers. All types of Americans are quite similar in whether they are satisfied with their lives overall, but religious Americans are more likely to describe themselves as "very" satisfied, while secular respondents have a higher propensity to choose "somewhat" satisfied.

These differences in outlook are a matter of nuance, rather than overall more positive or negative perspectives. The choice to be moderately rather than strongly secular suggests a less absolutist and more relativistic outlook on life, which may well be reflected in a decision to select the weaker "somewhat" rather than "very" to qualify "satisfied." For all types of secularity, individuals are choosing to not accept at least some elements of the normative assumptions about what it takes to be a "religious" American. The culturally religious and nonaffiliated believers are in liminal positions however, accepting some elements of religiosity while denying or avoiding others. In turn, this ambivalence translates to their higher likelihood of being "somewhat" rather than "very" satisfied or dissatisfied compared to their religious counterparts. Similarly, agnostics, who are by definition ambivalent on a central worldview element, are the most likely to choose a "somewhat" response at 41%.[6]

There is not a statistically significant difference between atheists and the actively religious for predicting personal satisfaction when controlling for sociodemographic characteristics like age, gender, income, education, and marital status, a remarkable result considering the large sample size (n = 26,495).[7] The difference between agnostics and the actively religious was the second *weakest* predictor in the model, and the difference between the actively religious and atheists was the weakest. The predicted probabilities of being "very satisfied" show that while there is a small advantage to being actively religious (.38), it is very similar to the probabilities for atheists (.37), agnostics (.35), nonaffiliated believers (.35), and the culturally religious (.33).

Among theistic believers in the Pew RLS, it is those who are "not too certain" about theism who have the lowest levels of self-rated satisfaction with their personal lives, while those with high levels of certainty and those who say "not at all certain" each exhibit the same, higher levels of satisfaction. Similarly, respondents to the survey who disagreed that there "are clear standards of right and wrong" have the highest levels of dissatisfaction with their personal lives. These results indicate that it is *degree of certainty* about cosmological views that correlates with personal satisfaction and happiness rather than religious belief per se.[8] These results are replicated in a question about satisfaction with one's current standard of living. The highest satisfaction with standard of living occurs among both those who embrace and reject religion, regardless of whether they are impoverished or affluent.

Similar patterns are evident in the GSS. Using pooled data from 2006 to 2010, we examined the frequency with which different types of secularists reported considering themselves "very happy," "pretty happy," or "not too happy." Actively religious Americans are more likely to report being "very happy," although the differences are again a matter of degree. In further support of the hypothesis that certainty/ambiguity of belief and identity (either religious or secular) is driving the correlation with self-rated happiness, a regression model controlling for basic sociodemographic factors showed no significant difference between the actively religious and atheists, agnostics, or nonaffiliated believers. The actively religious, however, were significantly more happy than the culturally religious. The predicted probabilities for each category show little difference, with the actively religious the most likely to report being "very happy" (.29), and the secular categories slightly lower (all around .25). For predicting the likelihood that someone will report being "pretty" or "very happy" compared to "not too happy," there are effectively no differences between the categories, with actively religious Americans and each of the secular categories having a probability of .88 or .89 of selecting one of these response options. Results of the full models are available in the Data Analyses Appendix.

In sum, actively religious Americans are slightly more likely to report being "very happy" or "very satisfied" with their lives compared to those in the liminal positions of nonaffiliated belief and cultural religion, but differences between the religious and theistic non- and disbelievers are negligible after controlling for social and demographic characteristics. The popular stereotype about unhappy atheists is not supported empirically; if anything, the notable pattern is the unhappy culturally religious, but even this would be an exaggeration. At the same time, religious participation does relate to self-rated happiness and satisfaction, albeit in a much smaller magnitude than is often portrayed. The weakness of the association partly derives from the bidirectionality of influence. People experiencing major life stressors may turn to religion for support, but these individuals tend to have lower levels of happiness and satisfaction than those experiencing less severe life stressors. Further, the types of stress in question influence whether negative emotions push an individual toward or away from religion. A panel study found that people who experienced financial strain were more likely to be uncertain of their religious faith, and that such strain tended to push people out of, rather than back into, religion. Conversely, stress from the death of a loved one pushed individuals on the margins back into organized religion.[9] Overall, the relationship between religiousness and personal happiness is complicated, and does not lend itself easily to the conclusion that religious people are happier, while secular people are more dour. We now turn to an assessment of the more constructive dimensions of the worldviews of American secularists by examining views of a primary institution in which they place epistemic authority: science.

Views of Science

> In surveying the history of man, it is clearly discovered, that the miseries and misfortunes of his existence are, in a high degree, the result of his ignorance and his vices. Ignorance renders him savage and ferocious; while science pours into his mind the benign sentiments of humanity, and gives a new colouring to his moral existence. Reason, which every kind of supernatural theology abhors; reason, which is the glory of our nature, is destined eventually, in the progress of future ages, to overturn the empire of superstition, and erect upon its ruins a fabric, against which the storms of despotism may beat in vain; against which superstition may wreak her vengeance without effect, from which she will be obliged to retire in agonizing tortures. (Elihu Palmer, deist speaker, author, and organizer, 1801)[10]

In 2006, "New Atheist" Sam Harris wrote, "The conflict between religion and science is inherent and (very nearly) zero-sum. The success of science often comes at the expense of religious dogma; the maintenance of religious dogma always comes at the expense of science."[11]

As the writing of Elihu Palmer (and others such as Lester Ward) makes clear, the supposed conflict between religion and science has long been a central argument of secular advocates, and is hardly a new or unusual expression of secularity. Accordingly, secularists often rely on science and reason as pivotal rhetorical elements in the construction of narrative identity; however, the degree to which different types of secularists place emphases on, and faith in, science varies.[12]

Using the 2007 BRS, we looked at whether members of each category thought "science and religion are incompatible," supported teaching creationism in public schools, accepted evolutionary accounts of human origins, or thought "science will eventually provide solutions to most of our problems." Atheists are most likely to believe that science and religion are incompatible (50%), followed by agnostics (26%), and the culturally religious (18%). Consistent with high-profile atheists who use the rhetoric of science to advance their political and moral positions, atheists are more likely to espouse a form of "scientism" as rhetorical grounding for identity and political positioning. Fourteen percent of actively religious Americans affirm the view that science and religion conflict, but most of these individuals are biblical literalists who believe religion is the "winner" of the conflict.[13] Notably, nonaffiliated believers (9%) are the least likely to perceive science and religion as incompatible.

Concerning the evolutionary, biological origins of humanity, over 90% of both atheists and agnostics accept this account of human history. Meanwhile, 72% of nonaffiliated believers and 58% of the culturally religious accept evolutionary accounts of human origins. Only 30% of actively religious Americans accept human evolution. Regarding support for creationism, there is a steady gradation by type of secularity, with the culturally religious (25%) most likely to support teaching creationism in public schools and atheists (6%) the least likely. Over half of actively religious Americans support such policies. The last question, concerning whether respondents think science "will eventually provide the solutions to most of our problems," serves as a proxy for the amount of "faith" individuals put in science to deal with social issues. Atheists place the most faith in science (79%), followed by nonaffiliated believers (73%), agnostics (64%), and the culturally religious (58%). Actively religious Americans put far less faith in science to solve human problems, with only one third agreeing with the statement.

The 2008 GSS contained multiple batteries of items about science, including questions about interest in science and basic factual knowledge. Agnostics averaged the highest scores for the number of factual questions answered correctly, followed by atheists, the culturally religious, nonaffiliated believers, and the actively religious. Agnostics were the most likely to say they were "very interested" in scientific discoveries (56%), followed by nonaffiliated believers (47%), atheists (46%), the actively religious (38%), and the culturally religious (34%). Agnostics also reported higher levels of comfort concerning whether they have a "clear understanding" of what constitutes a "scientific study." Taken together, these data show that agnostics have more interest in and knowledge about science even though atheists place more faith in it.

The Pew RLS also asked the question, "When it comes to right and wrong, which of the following do you look to most for guidance?" Overall, "practical experience" was the most frequent response for all secular categories, followed by "philosophy and reason," then "science." Individuals in each of the secular categories chose these options at higher rates than actively religious individuals, but the distribution of responses varied by secular type. Atheists were the most likely to choose science, agnostics were the most likely to choose philosophy and reason, and nonaffiliated believers and the culturally religious were the most likely to choose practical experience. Here we can see some of the subtle differences in the moral orders of different types of secularities. So while scientistic rhetoric is often used in high-profile secularists' public discourse, most secular Americans say they look to more pragmatic sources for guides to ethical action.

Secularity in a Religious Society

The Pew RLS also asked questions about whether respondents perceived conflict between their religiosity or secularity and the broader culture. Responses to these questions reveal an interesting dynamic. Among seculars, atheists (46%) and agnostics (43%) perceived such conflict due to being nonreligious at a higher rate than nonaffiliated believers (33%). On the other side of the coin, the actively religious felt there was a conflict between being a religious person and living in contemporary American culture at a rate (43%) mirroring nonbelievers' perceived otherness. The culturally religious, however, mirrored the nonaffiliated believers on perception of conflict (34%). These findings show that identification with both nonaffiliated belief and cultural religion often represents an effort to be nonreligious while reducing the level of conflict that typically accompanies secularity. Meanwhile, both solidly religious and secular Americans perceive relatively equal levels of conflict as a result of living out their belief systems. From this perspective, it is not surprising that more people have moved toward the middle ground of being neither thoroughly religious nor strongly secular.

Over half of nonaffiliated believers (56%) say they disagree with their families about religious matters, as do 48% of atheists and 44% of agnostics. Given that atheism is the most pejoratively perceived of the categories—a fact acknowledged by atheists themselves, as they are more likely to report feeling their views are ridiculed in the media—these results provide a clue to how secular identity is constructed through social interaction. Even though "atheist" is a more publicly disliked label, nonaffiliated believers perceive more familial conflict as a result of their religious views, which likely plays a major part in why they are not more definitively secular. Indeed, nonaffiliated believers are more likely to report keeping their religious views private to avoid conflict (27%) compared to atheists (19%) and agnostics (15%). Atheists, agnostics, and nonaffiliated believers are all more likely to hide their views of religion from others for fear of reprisal compared to Protestants (11%) and Catholics (8%), who are more likely to enjoy the privileges of conventionality.

The relations between secularity and other social institutions necessarily vary according to the degree that religion is used to demarcate and differentiate normative cultural membership, as well as subcultural group membership. In the American context, secularists are publicly disliked, but their civil rights are also shielded by law, and public institutions are prohibited from favoring or persecuting specific religions (or lack thereof). These political protections create an environment where secularism is legally protected but remains informally costly, a context conducive to "passing" (hiding one's discreditable quality) in potentially antagonistic public settings.[14]

Themes of Secular Identity

We created questions for an online survey that asked respondents who said they had "no religion" how important a series of potential reasons for not affiliating with a religion were.[15] We asked about lack of interest in religion, negative encounters with religious people, distrust of clergy and religious organizations, science undermining religion, pluralism of religions (ergo "all refute all"), concerns about the influence of religion on government, religions having too many rules or being too dogmatic, personal suffering, injustices in the world, and finally a lack of knowledge about religion.

The most commonly selected reasons for being secular were science undermining religion, concerns about the influence of religion on government, distrust of clergy and religious organizations, and uninterest in religion. Atheists were the most likely to be both personally uninterested in religion (63%) and concerned about the influence of organized religion on politics (67%). Reiterating our findings about attitudes toward science, atheists were the most likely to select the science versus religion narrative (86%), with fewer agnostics (66%) and nonaffiliated believers (42%) selecting this reason. Interestingly, nonaffiliated believers were the most likely to select negative encounters with religious people (41%), pluralism of religions being a case of "all refute all" (50%), and thinking that religions have "too many rules" (32%). Agnostics were not the highest category for any of the reasons offered, although they still had relatively high levels of concern about the influence of religion on politics (54%), as well as uninterest in religion (52%). A clear majority (59%) of atheists, agnostics, and nonaffiliated believers all listed distrust of clergy and organized religion as an important reason for being religiously nonaffiliated. The least selected reasons for all types of secularity were ignorance about religion and personal suffering.[16]

While much remains to be done to better explain the identities of different types of secular Americans, there are a number of informative qualitative examinations of American atheists. Some consistent themes have emerged. First, atheists' self-conceptions typically construe atheism as *more moral* than religion. As we noted, a "more moral" identity played a critical role in facilitating the initial historical development of atheism and agnosticism as viable religious preferences, and contemporary work points toward the continued importance of this dimension of identity. This "more moral" position is structured around narratives that highlight the irrationality and oppression of organized religion and religious dogma, both contemporary and historical. Naturally, a hardline "more moral than" stance requires selective observation that ignores the positive social roles religion can and does play, again in both contemporary and historical contexts. Lest we be misunderstood, secularists are hardly alone in stereotyping, and discrimination against secularists by religionists has been the historical norm. Still, overgeneralizations flow both ways.

The "othering" that some religious individuals and organizations direct toward secularists plays a prominent role in both sides' self-understandings. Stereotyping forces those who choose to be secular to opt into a deviant social status. Even when chosen, social stigma (hidden or revealed) must always be socially managed. Stigma can be managed through various strategies, for example restructuring one's social network to consist of more friendly or accepting contacts. Of course, rarely are people able to select everyone in their network, so other strategies such as passing, rhetorical efforts to neutralize the deviant label, and open confrontation are also options. The strategy of the vast majority of secularists is a combination of selective passing and norm neutralization, with confrontation engaged in sparingly (unless one's mission is to be *always* overtly political and confrontational). Still, open confrontation gets the most attention, both from the press and academics. For the popular media, this is because secularists who have joined "open" movements are more vocal. For academics, it is because they are easier to find and more politically engaged.

On the whole, seculars tend to be politically "progressive," by whatever standards such a relative distinction may mean in a given context. In the nineteenth century, progressivism involved stances such as opposing slavery, promoting women's suffrage, and advocating birth control. Today, it often means supporting reproductive rights and same sex marriage, environmentalism, and (still) advocating for access to birth control. There have certainly been and currently are politically conservative secularists, but progressivism is far more common. Much of this tendency stems from humanist ethics of equality that are central to most seculars' framing of questions of morality.

In addition to humanism, scientism is a recurring theme in the discourse of many American seculars, particularly atheists. This rhetorical focus on science represents an alignment between the this-worldly focus of secularity and the materiality of science. Put another way, because science is the institution with the most cultural power to study, describe, and define material reality, there is an understandable tendency for atheists to employ the rhetoric of science to justify their moral and political positions. Although science cannot actually tell right from wrong (although some secularists certainly believe this), atheists' frequent use of science is, well, natural.

Studies of atheists also highlight that the development of secular identity is often a long process, especially for apostates, with three distinct phases of identity development: (1) questioning theism; (2) rejecting theism; (3) "coming out" atheist.[17] Many atheists report long periods of questioning and uncertainty before considering themselves nontheists. Once acceptance was reached, however, atheists described their new identities as "liberating," and more consistent with their perception of their authentic selves. Part of this sense of authenticity stems from open acknowledgement of their critical stances toward conventional religion.

An important dimension of contemporary secular identities is media and communication technologies that facilitate interpretive community, such as books, newsletters, and especially the internet. Just as Thomas Paine attempted to diffuse deism to sections of the public who had previously lacked access to such arguments, the internet and other communication technologies have democratized the possibilities of imagined and mediated communities. Access to secular communities through mediated communication remains a relatively new phenomenon, but the possibilities are intriguing.[18]

The Psychology of Atheism

Recent research in social psychology points toward multiple pathways into supernatural disbelief. Psychological studies have found higher average levels of intelligence and a tendency toward critical thinking among theistic dis- and nonbelievers, suggesting that a particular cognitive style is one pathway to secularity. These studies indicate that a high proportion of nontheists employ material rationalism as an overarching cognitive style that is applied to most areas of social life, including religion.[19] An emphasis on rationalist cognition leads to a greater likelihood of skepticism regarding supernatural or otherwise empirically unverifiable claims. Perhaps not surprisingly then, academics are among the most secular populations.[20] This highly analytical expression of secularity is also given public voice by atheist apologists such as Richard Dawkins. Here we find heavy rhetorical reliance on science as a dominant and superior way of knowing. A potential explanation for this expression of secularity draws on a dual processing model of cognition that distinguishes between intuitive and analytical thinking. Intuitive thinking is quick and reflexive, whereas analytical thinking is slower, deliberative, and cognitively taxing. Individuals who employ analytic thinking in a greater range of circumstances, for longer periods of time, and to greater problem-solving effectiveness are less likely to accept supernatural accounts of events, be they religious or "paranormal." In general, nontheists are more likely to employ a cognitive processing style emphasizing logic and rationality at the expense of intuition.

Another potential pathway to secularity is an inability to mentally project the "minds" of supernatural agents. That is, individuals who have difficulty empathetically imagining the mental states of other individuals, and therefore also supernatural agents with humanlike qualities—which is how the vast majority of religious supernatural agents are conceptualized—are less likely to be religious believers. In support of this pathway's existence, an innovative study has shown that individuals with autism spectrum disorders are more likely to be atheists.[21]

Another pathway to atheism is especially prevalent in cultural contexts where religious institutions are weakened and social welfare programs create high levels of existential security. In such contexts, the lack of social pressure to be religious and corresponding reduction in the penalty for being irreligious create situations in which individuals may be indifferent to questions of religion and theism, or at the very least uninterested in pursuing serious religious beliefs and practice in their lives. This pattern is typified by Western European and Scandinavian countries where rates of disbelief are high and levels of religious practice are low. Conversely, cultural contexts with high levels of death, suffering, and uncertainty are typically characterized by higher average levels of religious belief and practice.[22] Beyond the general connection between existential insecurity and religiosity, in moral communities where a particular expression of religious faith is associated with communal belonging, the penalties for secularity increase substantially.

This line of research remains in the developmental stages, but points to some noteworthy themes in the personality traits of atheists. At the same time, there is essentially no research on other expressions of secularity, such as agnosticism or nonaffiliated belief. Unfortunately, "atheism" often remains shorthand for all expressions of secularity in both academic and popular discourse. Although some of the findings for atheism likely apply, the extent to which there are differences between atheists and other secularists with regard to psychological traits and dispositions is an area particularly in need of development.

Summary

There is a considerable amount of overlap in some areas of social life between the different categories of secularity we outline. At the same time, there are substantial differences between the secular types concerning private spiritual beliefs and practices. A primary difference between atheists, agnostics, nonaffiliated believers, and the culturally religious is the totality of their disengagement with religion—both public and private. Atheists tend to be the most secular overall, rejecting religion and supernaturalism more completely. Agnostics are less opposed to religion in toto than atheists, with greater openness to privatized spirituality. Agnostics are also less opposed to organized religion than both atheists and nonaffiliated believers. Nonaffiliated believers are more likely to be "spiritual but not religious," drawing firmer distinctions between organized religion and privatized spirituality. Culturally religious individuals are not interested in private spirituality, scoring lower on the related measures than all other categories examined, and were the most likely to think of themselves as "religious but not spiritual." Nonaffiliated believers are less likely to perceive general social conflict due to their nonreligious views, but more likely to perceive conflict with family members and hide their views to avoid confrontations. This is because nonaffiliated belief is often a form of conventional passing, taking what are seen as the positive aspects of religion, such as private spirituality and theism, while leaving behind organized religion as a negatively valuated aspect of conventional religiosity.

Yet the divergences are not limited to approaches toward religion. Nonaffiliated believers and the culturally religious reported slightly lower levels of self-rated happiness, but it is primarily the level of *certainty* in one's cosmic belief system that relates to higher levels of self-rated happiness and satisfaction, as atheists and actively religious Americans score essentially the same on these outcomes. In terms of ideology, atheists tend to place an emphasis on analytic thinking and more "faith" in science than other secularists. Agnostics tend to be interested in and knowledgeable about science, but they are also less scientistic in their overall outlook than atheists. While strongly opposed to organized religion, nonaffiliated believers were less scientistic than both atheists and agnostics, and were more open to deinstitutionalized forms of both religious and paranormal supernaturalism. Overall, the categories of secularity we have outlined share enough commonalities to be considered under the broad umbrella of nonreligion, but are also distinct enough to warrant separation in future studies of secularity.

6

Ethnicity, Assimilation, and Secularity

"To-day," he said, with a smile, "the world cares little whether a man be Baptist or Methodist, or indeed a churchman at all, so long as he is good and true. What difference does it make whether a man be baptized in a river or wash-bowl, or not at all? Let's leave all that littleness and look higher." Then, thinking of nothing else, he slowly sat down. A painful hush seized that crowded mass. Little had they understood of what he said, for he spoke an unknown tongue . . .
—W. E. B. Du Bois[1]

The Other(ed) American Aristotle

William Edward Burghardt Du Bois was a revolutionary intellect. A modern prophet, Du Bois relentlessly critiqued racialized social order.[2] Born in Massachusetts in 1868 in the immediate aftermath of black emancipation in the U.S., he died August 27, 1963, in Ghana, the day before the March on Washington that culminated in Martin Luther King Jr.'s "I Have a Dream" speech. Even though Du Bois was a founder of the National Association for the Advancement of Colored People, the executive secretary of the NAACP in 1963, Roy Wilkins, only ambivalently acknowledged his influence during the march. Du Bois had joined the Communist Party in the last years of his life as a final protest against the economic exploitation he saw as intimately connected to racial domination throughout the world. Wilkins's words at the March on Washington speak simultaneously to the power and controversial nature of Du Bois's thoughts, words, and deeds, emphasizing their prophetic qualities: "Now, regardless of the fact that in his later years Dr. Du Bois chose another path, it is incontrovertible that at the dawn of the twentieth century his was the voice that was calling you to gather here today in this cause."[3]

Du Bois possessed a prodigious intellect and work ethic throughout his life. When old enough to attend college, he longed to go to Harvard, but was told that his high school education was not sufficient for the university's entrance requirements, even though he was valedictorian. He attended Fisk University in Nashville, where he sang in the choir, wrote for the school paper, and studied German, Greek, physics, chemistry, and philosophy. After graduation, he applied to Harvard again, and this time was admitted—as a junior, in spite of having already earned a bachelor's degree at Fisk. While enrolled at Harvard, he studied for two years at the University of Berlin, where he learned from innovative intellectuals such as philosopher Wilhelm Dilthey, economist Gustav von Schmoller, and sociologist Max Weber. He became the first African American to graduate with a doctorate from Harvard, after studying with, among others, pragmatist philosophers William James and George Santayana. Du Bois would put the ideas of his teachers to use in innovative, emancipatory ways.

Du Bois was to become an accomplished researcher, historian, novelist, community organizer, and sociologist; yet, contra Lester Ward, he was largely ignored by scholars in the mainstream of sociology, in spite of the fact that it was his disciplinary home for most of his career. His efforts to raise the personal and collective conscience of African Americans, combined with his broad academic interests, led to his ostracism from a discipline eager to establish itself as "scientific" by downplaying the role of "activists" and enforcing rigid rules about what counted as legitimate research. Concerning the perpetual matters of morality facing all students of society, Du Bois found that, much to his chagrin, dispassionate facts about inequality moved people little toward justice. Reluctantly, he began to assume a prophetic rather than scientific stance. While still grounding his activism in the facts of the social world, he was unafraid to levy unpopular, acrid criticism against power and injustice, using a variety of communicatory forms including social science, fiction, and poetry to get his message across to diverse audiences. As he noted, "My career as a scientist was to be swallowed up in my role as master of propaganda. This was not wholly to my liking."[4]

Du Bois was (and often still is) excluded from his rightful place as a founder of sociology, in spite of groundbreaking empirical studies such as *The Philadelphia Negro* and *The Negro Church*, trenchant theorizing on problems of race, class, and power, and consistent articulation of ideas that would eventually form core principles of the discipline. Du Bois's central analytical concepts of the divided "self" (double consciousness) and the racial "veil" that necessarily colored American society (and the Western world more generally) threatened early sociology's insistence that knowledge be fully "objective."[5]

Consider, for instance, what happened after Du Bois outlined a systematic research plan to study African Americans and their place in American society in 1941. Many influential academics and the presidents of black colleges pledged support for the program. He proposed to use traditionally black land-grant colleges as centers of study on African Americans using disciplines ranging from history to economics to psychology. The information produced would then be systematized.[6] By 1943, plans to put the program into action were moving forward. The following year, a conference was planned to begin implementation. Then Du Bois was suddenly and forcibly "retired" by Atlanta University:

> At any rate, without a word of warning I found myself at the age of 76 without employment and with less than $5,000 of savings. Not only was a great plan of scientific work killed at birth, but my own life was thrown into confusion. I felt the world tottering beneath my feet and I fought back in . . . despair. [But t]he whole scheme died within a year or two. It has never been revived.[7]

Where Lester Ward's armchair philosophizing about the social world and interdisciplinarity (in the natural sciences)—along with his scientific credentials—took him from the periphery to the center of sociological thought, only to be forgotten as the discipline became more grounded in empirical research, Du Bois used grounded empiricism, critical theorizing, and interdisciplinarity (in the humanities)—all hallmarks of the discipline today—but was nevertheless perpetually marginalized. Only recently have social scientists rediscovered his visionary work. Yet even today, his voluminous writings are typically pigeonholed as studies of race rather than acknowledged for their general excellence.

Here we examine specific aspects of Du Bois's life and work for two reasons. First, his theorizing about power provides insights that are not limited to the analysis of race, but are widely applicable. Second, the role of secularity and religion in his life provides insight into the connections between race, religion, public conceptions of morality, and politics in the United States. Religion functions as a key to understanding pivotal themes in his work, an interpretive angle scholars have only recently realized.

Du Bois's most influential work, *The Souls of Black Folk*, centers around a question pertinent to all who inhabit a disempowered and socially degraded status: "How does it feel to be a problem?" A primary answer to this question became one of his most influential ideas: the experience of double consciousness, which refers to the state of being inside yet also outside of societal (cultural) boundaries. In *Souls*, Du Bois said of double consciousness:

> It is a peculiar sensation, this double-consciousness, this sense of always looking at one's self through the eyes of others, of measuring one's soul by the tape of a world that looks on in amused contempt and pity. One ever feels his two-ness,—an American, a Negro; two souls, two thoughts, two unreconciled strivings; two warring ideals in one dark body, whose dogged strength alone keeps it from being torn asunder.[8]

In essence, anyone occupying a position not given normative status is forced to reconcile the devalued meaning imposed by others with her own self-concept—at least for those able to fight the degrading view the "generalized other" holds of them. To the extent that the marginalized can overcome and not internalize the pejorative evaluations attached by others, they gain the ability to see the world from the perspective of conventional culture as well as from the viewpoint of the "othered." This multioptic positioning provides unique perspectives and vantage points, but also places the marginalized at risk of becoming doubly ostracized—caught in between communities with no true home.

The concept of double consciousness is applicable to those of any status who must interact with others in contexts that devalue aspects of their identities. Further, devalued status positions often act as "master status" markers. That is, devalued statuses color a person's entire identity as perceived by others.[9] Others emphasize minority statuses via interaction, necessarily differentiating or "marking" an individual as set apart from conventional expectations. In this way, those with a culturally devalued, deviant status are forced to operate in, but not be part of, the normative social order.[10] The taken-for-grantedness that accompanies privileged positions validated (often implicitly) by conventional social mores is simply not feasible.

Extending the generality of the concept, double consciousness leads to a better understanding of Du Bois's own relationship to religion, which itself reveals deeper insights about his ambivalent and conflictual relationship to conventional (white) American society, and sometimes also to black communities. Raised in the Congregationalist Church, Du Bois left formal religion during his schooling in the U.S. and Germany. His philosophical position was a thoroughgoing sociological perspective applied to the empirical world and, following his pragmatist intellectual mentors, knowledge itself. In other words, he saw knowledge and ideology as the products of social relations and interactions, no more, but also *no less*. The understanding of religions (and all ideologies) as social constructs often leads to the corollary view that the ultimate-truth claims of religious dogma are suspect, as was also evident in the thought of Lester Ward.[11] Consistent with his pragmatist philosophical stance, Du Bois wrote the following in correspondence with his friend and collaborator, the historian Herbert Apatheker in 1956:

> I gave up the search for "Absolute" Truth; not from doubt of the existence of reality, but because I believe that our limited knowledge and clumsy methods of research made it impossible now completely to comprehend Truth. I nevertheless firmly believed that gradually the human mind and absolute and provable truth would approach each other nearer and nearer . . . and yet never in all eternity meet. . . . I assume the existence of Truth, since to assume anything else or not to assume was unthinkable. . . . I did not rule out the possibility of some God also influencing and directing human action and natural law. However I saw no evidence of such divine guidance. I did see evidence of the decisive action of human beings.[12]

The scholarly consensus about Du Bois that has formed over the last thirty years is that he was decidedly irreligious, so much so that when sociologist Phil Zuckerman was compiling an edited volume of Du Bois's work on religion, "a highly respected professor['s] . . . immediate reaction was 'Du Bois on religion? Why that's like doing Hitler on democracy.'"[13] But this mischaracterization is only part of the picture, and obscures much that is profound in Du Bois's work. Although his personal reflections and other writings indicate that he was a freethinker in the sense of personal identity, he used religious language, metaphors, idioms, and narratives to convey deep moral truths in ways intended to reach beyond the mind and into the souls of his readers. He wrote stories that identified Jesus with victims of lynching and much of his profound work, such as *The Souls of Black Folk*, included arguments that presaged those of black liberation theology.[14] He even began his own "credo" with "I believe in God, who made of one blood all nations that on earth do dwell."[15]

Du Bois employed religious imagery often, as it was the only way to convey the depths of his criticisms of injustice in the world, and also his hopes for human betterment. For someone who is supposed to be definitively irreligious, he wrote an inordinate number of texts in the form of sermons, prayers, jeremiads, parables, hymns, and creeds. Further, he likened himself to a prophet, and saw it as his job to speak truth to power on matters including but not limited to racism, materialism, colonialism, exploitation, and violence.[16] Du Bois can be best understood in the prophetic tradition, albeit one in which "pragmatic religious naturalism"—that is, religious idioms shorn of their supernaturalism—is the overarching perspective rather than the supernatural legitimations that have historically justified prophetic visions. For Du Bois, religion is always a *this-worldly* affair.[17]

The parable "Of the Coming of John," which serves as the climax (or nadir) of *The Souls of Black Folk* and from which the epigraph to this chapter is taken, is a case in point.[18] The story tells of two Johns, one white and the other black, who were playmates as children. John Jones, the young black man, leaves his home amid the rice plantations of coastal Georgia for college at an all-black school, while John Henderson, the white son of a local judge, leaves home for Princeton. While away, black John learns of the sublime truths found in the sciences, arts, and humanities. During a trip to New York City with the school's singing quartet, he learns that, although sublime, the ideals of high culture cannot overcome the ever-present color line in American society. While attending a performance of Wagner's opera *Lohengrin*, black John encounters white John. White John, refusing to sit near him, has black John removed by ushers after the prelude. As black John is escorted out, white John recognizes him as his childhood playmate, but pretends not to know him. As he rides a train back to the south, black John quotes Queen Esther, saying, "I will go in to the King, which is not according to the law; and if I perish, I perish."[19]

After his education, both formal and informal, John returns home, initially to the cheers, but then the bewilderment and dismay of his community. The epigraph is the moment when, from the pulpit of the local Baptist church, John delivers the conclusive message of the lessons he has learned to the overflowing and anxious congregants, who refute his blatant impiety, because he is promoting new "ideas at the expense of the slave religion the community embraces."[20] John now faces double estrangement, from both white and black communities. As he leaves the church, his younger sister, follows him:

> "John," she said, "does it make every one—unhappy when they study and learn lots of things?" He paused and smiled. "I am afraid it does," he said. "And, John, are you glad you studied?" "Yes," came the answer, slowly but positively.[21]

Turned out by his community of inheritance, John nevertheless takes a job as a local schoolteacher to instruct black youth. Upon learning that he is teaching equality and uplift to his pupils, Judge Henderson, father of white John, shuts down the school. On his way home, black John happens upon white John attempting to rape his sister. Rushing to her defense, black John strikes and kills white John, sealing his fate as a sacrifice to the racialized social order of Jim Crow. Rather than flee, John returns to the scene of the "crime" and placidly accepts his fate, temporarily elevating himself above the pettiness and violence of the unjust world by imaginatively returning to the sublime realm he encountered in the New York opera house. A mob lead by Judge Henderson lynches John, while "the world whistled in his ears."[22]

In this pithy narrative, John Jones plays the role of a John the Baptist character, or as political theorist Robert Gooding-Williams suggested, given his speech at the church, "John the anti-Baptist."[23] Although John succumbs to the pitfalls of double consciousness, he prepares the way for a new voice of black leadership—one that remembers, mourns, and celebrates the past and traditions of black America, relentlessly decries contemporary injustice, and strives toward a future where African Americans take their rightful places as "co-worker[s] in the kingdom of culture."[24] It deserves emphasis that the kingdom of culture *is* the kingdom of God for Du Bois, an epitome of his use of religious idiom to drive home a this-worldly point. The narrative of John and *Souls* more generally cleared the way for Du Bois's own prophetic voice, and he spent the rest of his life tirelessly sounding its call.

"Of the Coming of John" operates on multiple levels: philosophical, literary, moral, and polemical. It is a work of existential tragedy with intertextual links to the Bible, Continental and American philosophy, Greek mythology, and Wagner's opera. It also plays a distinctive intratextual role within the arc of *Souls*, casting the dehumanization and accompanying violence of America's racial caste into stark relief. It exposes whitewashed expressions of "justice" as hypocritical in the deepest sense, while it exhorts African Americans, especially black churches, to pursue consciousness raising through remembrance of the past, but also through knowledge acquisition and activism, in spite of the perils they entail—sadness, pain, and death itself. At the same time, it warns black leaders that allowing the white visionary aspect of double consciousness to prevent them "from avowing and embodying in their actions black Americans' slavery-based spiritual (and racial) identity will fail to mobilize the black masses."[25] The only piece of fiction in a masterwork of nonfiction, Du Bois uses the story to illustrate his broader arguments and criticisms through metaphor.

In "Of the Coming of John" and numerous other works of social science, literature, and activism, Du Bois's double consciousness with regard to religion and race served as the vantage point from which he launched jeremiads against injustice and inhumanity. This inside-yet-outside stance on all matters, including religion, allowed him the flexibility to speak to multiple audiences, outlining the empirical and historical dimensions of race while also denouncing the immorality of racial subjugation. In spite of his heterodox religious views, he foresaw the potential for political organizing and community building in the black church, while excoriating the blatant racial hypocrisy of white "Christians."[26]

By standing outside of organized religion, which some scholars have termed a "semi-involuntary" institution for African Americans due to its historical centrality to community integration, Du Bois forged a critical perspective not beholden to religious expectations. His simultaneous use of religious language and expression of skepticism reflect the cultural contexts in which he lived and thought. Trained in the Victorian era of scientism, but speaking to minority communities where religion functioned as the primary conduit of remembrance and the central social institution, Du Bois leveraged double consciousness to uplift the disempowered as forcefully as he could:

> I have been in the world, but not of it. I have seen the human drama from a veiled corner, where all the outer tragedy and comedy have reproduced themselves in microcosm within. From the inner torment of souls the human scene without has interpreted itself to me in unusual and even illuminating ways. For this reason, and this alone, I venture to write again on themes on which great souls have already said greater words, in the hope that I may strike here and there a half-tone, newer even if slighter, up from the heart of my problem and the problems of my people.[27]

Du Bois understood that religion could be destructive but also transformative, especially in ostracized communities where employing its potential for political mobilization was imperative. Similarly, his understanding that religious rhetoric and rationale could be useful in combatting racialized social institutions foresaw the integral role of black churches in the civil rights movement. At the same time, his thoroughgoing pragmatism and skepticism about the supernatural and organized religion provided grounds from which he could detail the uses and abuses of religion in the oppression of people of color. As Cornel West noted about the paradoxical nature of Du Bois's religious views:

> He also didn't fall into the kind of narrow reductionist traps of scientistic, positivistic, ties to science, the kind of narrow Darwinism that you get today among the number of more sophomoric atheists like our dear brothers Christopher Hitchens, [Richard] Dawkins, and others. . . . But you can be religiously sensitive without being religious, and Du Bois cer-

> tainly was one of the most religiously sensitive of the secular thinkers. . . . He is a thorough-going radically democratic humanist . . .[28]

In a speech in honor of Du Bois given just weeks before his assassination, Martin Luther King Jr. declared that "Dr. Du Bois' greatest strength was his committed empathy with all the oppressed and his *divine dissatisfaction* with all forms of injustice."[29] With an ethnographer's eye and a prophet's pen, W. E. B. Du Bois changed the world through his thought and scholarship, even as his own discipline largely ignored his luminous and voluminous contributions.

Du Bois's emphasis on the connections between race and social class pointed toward what has more recently been termed the intersectionality of social statuses.[30] Intersectionality refers to how multiple statuses combine to create emergent contexts of oppression beyond those of single status positions. For example, the experiences of being a young person of color without a high school degree are not simply a matter of "adding together" the influence of race and social class on life chances. Rather, the combination of statuses produces an emergent form of overlapping disempowerment that cannot be reduced to the effects of individual statuses. That is, the inequality and domination faced by individuals with multiple minority statuses is beyond the additive effects of isolated statuses. The policing and imprisonment of poor racial minorities in the United States perniciously demonstrates this principle.[31] Power reflects the interactive rather than additive effects of social statuses, especially regarding race and ethnicity, social class, gender, and sexuality.[32]

Ethnicity, Social Class, Immigration, and Secularity

Secularity remains deviant in the U.S. and is accompanied by the penalty of being perceived as "immoral." This penalty is even more costly for those who already occupy other minority statuses. For instance, religion offers women and ethnic minorities a claim to worth and citizenship even amid cultural contexts that devalue their positions relative to men and whites. Conversely, the absence of religious identity and especially the presence of an assertive secular identity is more costly to minorities. Due to cumulative stigmatization, if one's status position is already devalued, a further devaluing is more costly than an initial devaluing for someone who otherwise occupies full majority status.

This interactive character of minority statuses is at the core of the relationship between social status and secularity in the United States. Because religious, theistic believing identity is normative and tied to claims about full citizenship and public morality, secular identity is less prevalent among members of minority positions, especially those relating to the primary axes of power: social class, race and ethnicity, and gender. Further, religious or secular identity is typically an achieved status, where many other minority statuses are not. If a person already occupies a position with relatively less social power, the *choice* to compound stigmatization with an additional degraded status becomes extremely difficult.

But there are nuances to this pattern. As we have noted, it is "atheism" that is especially "othered" in American culture, and thus the relationship between having higher status and a higher likelihood of secularity applies more strongly to theistic disbelief and nonbelief. In contrast, nonaffiliated believers are more likely to be individuals who are disconnected from religious institutions, but do not take the additional step of becoming nonbelievers. At the same time, higher social status is linked to higher rates of civic participation, and this relationship holds for public (but not private) religiosity.[33] As a result, "nones" who retain theistic belief may do so because they are disconnected from organized religion but wish to avoid the substantial social penalty applied to open nonbelievers. The relationship between minority status and lower likelihood of secularity is evinced by the general relationships between socioeconomic status and secularity. Higher levels of education are present among atheists and especially agnostics relative to other categories. In the 2006 to 2010 waves of the GSS, 44% of agnostics and 37% of atheists had a bachelor's degree or higher, compared to 25% of the actively and culturally religious and 24% of nonaffiliated believers. Results from the Pew RLS are nearly identical, with the exception that slightly more self-identified atheists had a college degree (42%).

Similar patterns are evident for income level. Forty-three percent of atheists and 41% of agnostics make over $75,000 per year in the Pew RLS, compared to 34% of the culturally religious, 30% of the actively religious, and 28% of nonaffiliated believers. In GSS data, agnostics (44%) are substantially more likely than the other categories to make over $75,000 per year, including atheists (34%). High-income levels are least prevalent among nonaffiliated believers (27%). In short, higher social class is associated with Americans who are more likely to be atheists or agnostics, while nonaffiliated believers are similar to the actively religious in terms of their tendency to be of comparatively lower social class. To examine the influence of social class more generally, we standardized and combined measures of annual income and level of education in order to create quartiles of low, mid-low, mid-high, and high categories for social class, which we use to examine if and how class affects secularity among different racial and ethnic groups. We also outline how generational immigrant status affects the probability of secularity.

White (Americans)[34]

Among white Americans, higher levels of income and education correlate to a higher likelihood of atheism or agnosticism. Among the lowest class level, .5% of whites are agnostic and 2.1% are atheist. Among the highest social class category, 4.2% are agnostic and 6% are atheist. For nonaffiliated believers, social class has a slight negative relationship, moving from 12% of the lowest class category to 8% of the highest class. Cultural religion is stable across levels at roughly 5%. Immigration status has little relationship to the secularity of whites, with the exception that people become slightly less likely to be culturally religious as generations progress (from 7% of first-generation immigrants to 5% of those who are third generation or later). Political views are a central aspect of white Americans' religiosity or secularity, and the association with political identity is stronger for firmer expressions of secularity such as atheism. Because the mobilization of the religious Right and its merger of conservative political and theological positions has occurred primarily among white Americans, political positioning has become tightly coupled with whether whites identify as secular or religious.[35]

African Americans

> Bitter was the day, I say,
> When the lyncher's rope

Hung about my neck,
And the fire scorched my feet,
And the oppressors had no pity,
And only in the sorrow songs
Relief was found—
Yet no relief,
But merely humble life and silent death
Eased by a Name
That hypnotized the pain away—
O, precious Name of Jesus in that day!

That day is past.

I know full well now
Jesus could not die for me—
That only my own hands,
Dark as the earth,
Can make my earth-dark body free.[36]

Like his Harlem Renaissance mentor Du Bois, Langston Hughes struggled to find a way to use, but also criticize, religion in his work while maintaining a persona that did not alienate his audiences. His poem "A New Song," partially reproduced above, provides an example of this dynamic although one that is far less dramatic than his infamously radical poem "Goodbye Christ." In the latter, he excoriates the hypocrisy of religion in America and upholds a communist, proletarian ethic. Written in his twenties, the poem would cause Hughes problems for years afterward, as he incessantly fought off the label of "atheist."[37]

So vociferous were the denunciations by everyone from black clergy to conservative politicians that Hughes publicly renounced the poem in an effort to distance himself from communism as the Second Red Scare spread. He argued that "Goodbye Christ" was intended to satirize hypocritical religion. Nonetheless, right-wing critics used the antireligious sentiments it conveyed as a rhetorical bludgeon against him. For example, charismatic evangelist Aimee Semple McPherson, called out by name in the poem, mobilized her enthusiastic followers to protest Hughes's public appearances. He later recalled a scene where he was forced to withdraw from a "literary luncheon" because McPherson's followers were protesting outside the hotel where it was being held:

> There Aimee's sound truck had been backed across the roadway blocking all passage so that limousines, trucks, and taxis were tangled up in all directions. The sound truck was playing "God Bless America" while hundreds of pickets milled about with signs denouncing Langston Hughes—atheistic Red.[38]

Meanwhile, a 1945 speech written by J. Edgar Hoover, which later became a favorite pamphlet of his entitled "Secularism—Breeder of Crime," quoted "Goodbye Christ" in its entirety.[39] The following year, U.S. Senator Albert Hawkes denounced Hughes on the chamber floor and had the poem entered into the *Congressional Record*, as would Senator Joseph McCarthy during the legendary hearings of the Permanent Subcommittee on Investigations in 1953. Called before the subcommittee, Hughes read a prepared statement in which he declared, among other expressions of innocence relating to charges of communism, "I am not now an atheist, and have never been an atheist."[40]

Like Du Bois, the example of Hughes shows the peril African Americans face in criticizing religion (and liberal economics), with its potential for alienating multiple communities and audiences, and leaving public figures susceptible to attacks on their character and morality. Nonetheless, a rich history of black thought encompasses a this-worldly humanism with sufficient depth to establish personally and communally meaningful cosmic belief systems absent supernaturalism.[41] Still, the social penalty imposed on minorities for secular identity remains readily apparent in aggregate data, especially for expressions of theistic dis- and nonbelief, as well as for being culturally religious. In the Pew RLS, less than 1% of African American respondents were atheist or agnostic, while less than 2% were culturally religious.

Among African Americans, socioeconomic status (SES) is a predictor of secularity, but the patterns depend on the type of secularity in question and black Americans are more likely to be actively religious as social class increases. At the same time, black atheists and agnostics also tend to have higher levels of social class. Regarding income level, 39% of black atheists make more than $75,000 a year, as do 34% of black agnostics. In contrast, 18% of actively religious African Americans have incomes above $75,000, as do 17% of the culturally religious and 14% of nonaffiliated believers. Similarly, 32% of black agnostics and 30% of black atheists have a bachelor's degree or higher. By comparison, 19% of the actively religious have a four-year college degree, while only 13% of nonaffiliated believers and 12% of culturally religious African Americans do.

Examining our general measure of SES shows that higher levels of social class are associated with African Americans who are in the active religiosity or theistic nonbelief categories, rather than the nonaffiliated believer category. Fourteen percent of African Americans in the lowest social class category were nonaffiliated believers, while 7% in the highest social class quartile fit this category. The proportions of agnostics (.2% to .8%) and atheists (.5% to 1.8%) increase slightly between the lowest and highest class categories, as does that of the actively religious (84% to 89%). In effect, higher social class holds a polarizing potential for African Americans with regard to religiosity. Although African Americans who adopt a secular identity, especially atheists or agnostics, tend to have higher levels of SES, the vast majority still choose to engage with organized religion. Where whites can give up religion and still receive the benefits of conventional citizenship because conventional American society *is* "white," ethnic minorities must connect to their communities subculturally, making it more likely that religion plays an integral role in their lives.

Asian Americans

Upon first glance, the case of Asian Americans contradicts the trend of minorities having lower rates of secularity, as a higher percentage of Asian Americans are atheists, agnostics, nonaffiliated believers, or culturally religious compared to whites in the Pew RLS. Rates of secularity are highest among Japanese and especially Chinese Americans, who make up a large share of the pan-ethnic population of "Asian Americans." However, closer analyses reveal a fascinating dynamic at play across generations. Dividing respondents into those who were born outside the U.S., those born in the U.S. who have at least one parent born abroad, and those whose parents were born in the U.S., it is second-generation Asian Americans who are most responsible for the higher levels of secularity within the category overall. Seventy-five percent of first-generation immigrants are actively religious, similar to 77% of the third (or later) generation respondents; however, among second-generation respondents, only 60% are actively religious.[42]

The religious preferences of individuals in these three categories help explain the differences. Among the first and second generations, only 15% and 8% respectively are evangelical Protestants, but 43% of third or later generation Asian Americans are evangelical. Meanwhile, the percentage who are Muslim, Buddhist, and especially Hindu (from 20% to 0%) declines across generations. In effect, first-generation immigrants are more likely to maintain a religious tradition that is "Eastern," while the second generation faces the dual pressure of being raised by parents likely maintaining the religion of their ethnic origin and also being raised in the U.S., where Eastern religions remain nonnormative. These cross-pressures result in a high proportion of second-generation Asian Americans dropping out of the religions of their parents while also not adopting new religious traditions. Third and later generations, less constrained by familial expectations about maintaining non-Christian religious traditions, adopt Protestantism at relatively high rates. Socialization across generations also plays an important role, as the percentage of those reporting that they were raised in Protestantism increases from 14% among the first generation to 60% of those in third or later generations. Among the latter, nearly 80% are Christian, with the remaining split primarily between secularity and Buddhism.

Thus over time there is an assimilative process whereby Asian Americans become more likely to adopt Christianity, especially Protestantism, and less likely to adhere to non-Western religious traditions. In the third or later generation category, Asians are actually more likely to be evangelical, or Protestant in general, than whites. On the other side of the coin, rates of secularity are basically equivalent between whites and third- or later-generation Asians. Notably, Asian Americans' similarity to whites in rates of secularity reflects relatively higher levels of social class compared to other racial and ethnic minorities. According to the 2010 Census, Asian Americans had higher average levels of education and income than all other ethnic groups, including whites.[43]

Among Asian Americans, higher levels of social class are associated with lower rates of active religiosity. The largest increase in secularity as social class rises occurs for nonaffiliated believers, which increases from 0% among the lowest class category to 14% among the highest. The culturally religious category increases substantially as well, going from 0% of the lowest class to 8% of the highest class. Atheism increases from 5% among the lowest class to 9% among the highest. These findings highlight that overall level of achievement in class status among ethnic groups relates to rates of secularity that mirror those of whites. Further, the rise, then fall, of secularity across generations of Asian Americans occurs as individuals leave non-Western traditions and enter Protestantism at high rates, underscoring the linkages between Christianity and full "American" citizenship.

Hispanic Americans

The case of Hispanic Americans combines themes present among both African and Asian Americans. Similar to African Americans, Latinos are less likely to be secular compared to whites. Like Asian Americans, there are fluctuations in religious affiliation and identity based on immigrant and socioeconomic statuses. For Latino Americans, there is a higher likelihood of secularity among the upper class. For example, a study of Latinos living in and around Richmond, Virginia, found that while Catholicism was, not surprisingly, the dominant religious preference of respondents, a substantial proportion chose "no religion," and this pattern was concentrated among respondents who were the most thoroughly assimilated to American culture. Indeed, Latinos in the sample who spoke English at home, consumed media in English, held more prestigious jobs, were native born, and were more politically and civically engaged were more likely to claim no religion.[44]

We tested this relationship using data with a wider geographic range, intended to be a nationally representative sample of Latino adults living in the United States. The 2011 National Survey of Latino/as collected by Pew includes small but adequate samples size for native- (n = 492) and foreign-born Latinos (n = 728) to assess the relationships between socioeconomic status, immigration status, assimilation, and secularity. A limitation of this dataset is that it does not include a question about prayer, so we were forced to use low religious service attendance and personal religious salience to create the culturally religious category.

Regarding class status, we again used educational attainment and annual income to create four quartiles of low, mid-low, mid-high, and high. Those in the lowest SES grouping had a low likelihood of being secular in any form, especially atheists (0%) and agnostics (.4%), but also nonaffiliated believers (7%) or culturally religious (1.4%). In the highest SES classification, the percentages were higher for all four secular categories. Atheism (1.8%) and agnosticism (.6%) remained relatively rare, but there were substantially more nonaffiliated believers (13%) and culturally religious (6%). Results by immigrant status show a rise-and-fall dynamic for secularity across generations similar to Asians, with 9% of foreign-born Latinos responding that they have no religion, compared to 17% in the second generation, and 13% in the third or later generations. Also similar to Asian Americans, Protestantism increases significantly in the third and later generations (from 16% of foreign born to 32% in third or later generations). For each of the nonwhite categories, secularity was the highest among second-generation Americans. In contrast, second-generation whites were slightly more likely to be actively religious than those in the first or third-plus generations.

Along with immigrant status, language also proves to be an important factor. Among respondents who were Spanish dominant, only 5% claimed no religion. Among those who are bilingual, the percentage claiming no religion was 10%. Among those who were English dominant, 22% claimed no religion. In general, we see very low rates of theistic disbelief, but rapidly increasing rates of religious nonaffiliation with increasing assimilation, reflecting the high cost of atheism for minorities and the tendency toward secularity among those with greater levels of cultural assimilation.

"Question Anything and Everything"[45]

To delve further into some of the cultural issues involved in the connections between ethnicity and religion, I (Joseph) interviewed David Tamayo, founder of the nonprofit organization Hispanic American Freethinkers (HAFree). Tamayo's personal narrative and that of his organization help flesh out some of the general patterns we have observed between ethnicity and secularity by providing illustrations from the experiences of Hispanic Americans.

The idea for starting a group specifically for Hispanic Americans grew out of Tamayo's personal experiences as an atheist and the absence of Hispanics in organized secularist groups.

DT: So I became an atheist about eight years ago. My wife was already an atheist and we had been married for almost twenty years, and we just . . . y'know, looking and thinking about science and so on . . . I tell people, "You can't choose to believe or not believe. It just happens." So you either believe or you don't, but it's nothing you can control. You can't *make* yourself believe or not believe something. So I started going to some of the local skeptics groups, and atheist groups, humanist groups and so on, and I noticed how very few Hispanics were in these groups. Now in looking at the statistics, I knew that they composed about 16% of the U.S. population, and certainly that was not reflected in the number that I was seeing there. So I decided to, just for fun, create a meet-up group and see if there were any Hispanics that would show up to the meeting. And the first three meetings no one showed up. It was just my wife and I having a nice dinner.

JB: (laughter)

DT: Which is not bad at all, y'know? But then after the fifth meeting or so, all of the sudden there were a dozen people sitting around the table. And I thought, "Oh, well this is nice." So we all went around the table telling our stories and how did we become atheists, or nonbelievers, or agnostics, or whatever, whatever anyone was calling themselves. And we got to the last person and it was this day laborer. And you could tell that he had been working hard. His clothes were dirty and smelled of work and so forth. But then we get to him and he started talking, and he said, "Well, I've never believed. I always thought there was something wrong with me because I didn't believe. I didn't think there was a god and I didn't see any evidence for god." He could barely talk because he was so emotional about it. So at that moment I decided, if I could make a group so that if anyone feels like him—that there's something wrong, they're out of place, that they have no one to talk to—that at least there would be a group they can talk to that would understand things, you know, from a cultural point of view. From a language barrier, or whatever, and that way

> they would feel more at home and see that there are other people like him or her, that can serve as a sounding board for ideas and so forth. And so I did that. And we started the group about three years ago I guess—since then we've had that same scene, or a similar scene has repeated half a dozen times.

A secularist organization specifically for Hispanic Americans begs the question of why such a group is necessary given the numerous existing secularist groups in the United States. Tamayo explained that the combination of family, culture, and interpersonal relationships places Hispanic seculars in different situations than many other American secularists.

> JB: Is there something that you felt like was a unique challenge that was faced by Hispanic Americans? That there was a need there to be served from a particular point of view?
>
> DT: Yes. And in fact, so let me give you some differences. The Hispanic family unit seems to be, um, more respectful of the elders than the typical American family. And I'll tell you how. A lot of the people that are coming out as atheists in the mainstream community, they're usually afraid that they're going to be ostracized, that they're going to be kicked out of their house. People worry they may be out in the streets. With Hispanics, that's not the concern. It typically doesn't happen. The norm is that they don't want to hurt Grandma's feelings, that they don't want to hurt their parents' feelings. And in my own case I didn't tell my family that I was an atheist for a while because I was afraid that my parents—you know, they're older now—they were gonna go to their grave feeling that they had been failures as parents. So they're much more concerned about not hurting parents' and grandparents' feelings about religion, and themselves as being failures in raising you. That, I think that was an example of one unique thing. I think *a lot* of cultural things with Latinos are interweaved with religion. And so, when you think back, most of the major events in a Latino family are baptisms, are marriages, and first communions, or other religious events. And so that's part of the problem.[46]

To Tamayo, the connections between family and secularity are not abstract, but personal.

DT: I think what you find with Hispanics is that a lot of them will hide [secularity] much more. Again, because of that cohesive family, y'know, they don't want to create waves in the family. I'm the black sheep in my family. Now they're still nice to me. Some of them look at me with pity. Every Christmas for the last eight years I've received a lot of religious books.

JB: (laughter)

DT: You know, believe it or not I'm very—I tried to be nice about it and so forth because I want them to engage [with] me. And you know a lot of them, the older ones look at with me pity. Like "Aw, poor bastard he's going to go to hell." And it's fine. I know they still care.

Tamayo sees the mission of the group as helping to dispel not only reliance on religion, but also supernaturalism more generally, an issue that influenced the selection of the name "freethinkers."

DT: We debated that a lot when we were trying to pick a name for the group.

JB: OK, what was that debate like? What were some of the options?

DT: Well, so we initially, when we got together we had said, "Let's meet for atheism." It started with the atheism part. But very shortly I realized that it's not just the god question, but that Hispanics in general believe a lot of bullshit when it comes to superstition.

He noted the number of paranormal or superstitious beliefs and behaviors he sees as prevalent in some Hispanic communities, including items sold at botánicas, the practice of Santería and the use of palm readers and astrologers.

So we decided that "freethinking"—initially we did it in Spanish, but then we figured a lot of the Hispanics, people who consider themselves Hispanic in the United States, do not speak Spanish, and even a lot of the people who do speak Spanish don't know what that word means, and so we said, "You know what? The language of this country—and we're trying to assimilate and be part of the American culture, and we are Americans—so let's put the name in English." So we actually started with the name in Spanish and changed it to English officially, the IRS and all of that. And we

> use the word "freethinkers" because that encompasses everything, so the religion part, the atheist thing is just a subset of freethought, and then it's about the superstition, the Friday the Thirteenth, the ghosts, the chupacabra, whatever. So all that to show—to question all of that—because it's the same question. It's critical thinking and asking, "How do you know this?" and "How do you know that?" and "Show me the evidence."

Tamayo sees assimilation and education as necessary for improving the lives of Hispanic Americans, and also as laying the groundwork for more seculars.

> In general, I would say there is a lack of critical thinking. That it's not taught in our culture that much. There is far more authority. You know someone with authority says X, Y, or Z, so they believe what this person says. I think part of it is the culture we inherited from the Spaniards. You know, we're still "conquered" in a lot of ways. And when people come here they feel they are second-class citizens because of their language, their lack of cultural understanding. The jokes—you know they don't get the jokes, even when they speak some of the language—they don't feel part of the culture. And that means that religion traps them a little bit more because, "Here's some sort of faith that is going to accept me as I am, period." So there's a lot of questioning that needs to take place for someone to become more secular.

While Tamayo sees successful assimilation as a potential route to secularity, he also believes the desire to assimilate and the need for social services often drive the high rates of religiosity among new immigrant populations:

> A lot of them are trying to melt into the pot, you know what I'm saying? They're trying to become part of America. And a lot of them are just being grateful. In other words . . . like near my office here there are at least ten churches. I believe every single one of them probably has "clases de Ingles." English classes, or citizenship classes, or you know, free babysitting. That kind of stuff. It's a way of attracting folks who are needy. They need to learn English, they need to assimilate. So they go in, and they have nothing to pay with, and so they feel they owe something to their

> benefactors. And their benefactors say, "You don't owe me anything. Just come in and stay for services, and we'll have dinner afterwards." And before you know it, now they're there and they are going to Sunday School and they're part of that community, and now: Bingo! You've converted.

HAFree sees matters of assimilation as a central aspect of its mission and service to the Hispanic community. At the same time, they encourage a skeptical view of culture:

> And to the Hispanics [we're] saying, "Hey, you need to assimilate. You need to become part of the American fabric. You need to become an American. Do not just follow old beliefs and old ways without question. Culture needs to be questioned. And this is a good time to question your own culture, and all cultures. Because you only get better from there."

As another part of the group's mission, Tamayo visits schools to talk with "at risk" youth, encouraging them to pursue higher education in the sciences.

> What we do is encourage them to go into the hard sciences. There's a shortage, a very bad lack of representation of Hispanics in the hard sciences. In engineering, physics, chemistry, you know that kind of stuff, mathematics. And so the idea is to encourage them to be into those sciences. . . 'Cause you know what? That creates secularism, in my opinion. I know that correlation is not causation, but once you start thinking logically, you start taking steps. And you can question everything. And you understand that there's only very few ways that we can know things. And one is the scientific method. Well, the only one in my opinion. Feeling is not a way of knowing. Imagining is not a way of knowing, and so forth. Then people become more secular.

Overall, HAFree has been relatively successful, receiving little public pushback on its efforts and inspiring other Hispanic Americans to start organized secular groups:

> But this year, Hispanic American Freethinkers, one thing that we can claim as a positive is that we've gotten about, I'd say we have maybe seven

or eight groups, Hispanic secular groups that were started this year in different parts of the country. Now, they're local groups. They're not 501(c)(3)s yet or anything like that. We're the only national group, but all of these groups started because they heard me talk or saw what we did and so forth. And we encouraged them to get started locally.

In addition to Tamayo's organizational efforts, aspects of his personal narrative of secularity also speak to other interesting themes, such as deconversion:

When someone converts from, say, Catholic to Pentecostal, or Mormon or whatever, they just have to shift their beliefs a little bit. So they're not really, they're still believing in the same God, or they're still believing in a God. It's a lot of the same. If you look at the differences, the differences are minor compared to what's the same. So I think it's much easier to convert from one religion to another than it is to convert, um, y'know to just leave it all together. And a lot of people feel scared. And it's scary. Now for me it was a great relief. When I became an atheist, it was like a weight had been lifted off my shoulder. I felt, all the sudden I felt like, "Oh, I don't have to second guess that judge. That person that was gonna be judging me, you know afterward for my entire life. I can now be sorry for things I did wrong and be done with it, and not worry that someday I'm gonna be judged for those things." And what amazed me the most about my self is that six months after, I realized I was the same person. I was still compassionate, I was still giving money to the poor, and doing the charities that I like. And I was pretty much the same person except without any guilt—I mean I was Catholic, so that guilt plays pretty good in the Catholic religion. (laughter) But it's not easy for a lot of people and I think it's impossible for many others.

While his organization has received little negative publicity for its efforts, Tamayo's own apostasy inevitably led to disappointment among his family. *How* he received negative feedback from his family illustrates a fascinating and increasingly important issue: the projection and fragmentation of the self through communication technology.

JB: So how's the reception been? Have you had any negative responses from different groups or people?

DT: No, actually. If there have been negatives, I have not come across them, or they haven't been directed towards us. The only negatives that I've seen are people defriending me on Facebook.

JB: OK. (laughter)

DT: What I ended up doing was I created a second Facebook page for my parents and some of my family that didn't like the things that I posted. And so I told them, I said, "Look, if you don't like the real me, I have this other me over here that is gonna be quiet and not say anything." Because I still want to see pictures that they post and I wanna see events that happen in the family. All my parents and my siblings and my nieces and nephews they all live up in New England together, in Rhode Island. I live in the Washington, D.C., area, so I'm the only one in the family who lives far away. Everybody lives together there. They're always seeing each other and they're always talking to each other and always having parties and things. So I wanna know what's going on there. And Facebook is a good way of seeing pictures and seeing things that are going on. And so when they were defriending me because of things I was saying online—you know, I was not pulling any punches, about religion or superstition or anything, questioning everything, and having debates online—then they didn't wanna see that. They felt uncomfortable, so once I opened the second page, where I'm just like a dead David Tamayo, then they friended me there and that way I can have both.

JB: (laughter)

DT: And it was good. I'd say only about 20% of my relatives went to the new me. And the others stayed with my old me. So it worked out well.

In the end, Tamayo felt that most people accepted his authentic, secular self. His experience with social networking sites demonstrates how greater connectivity and the diversity of available forums on electronic communication allow people to, if they so choose, divide and segregate their presentations of self for different contexts and audiences. Here, the language of "a dead David Tamayo" makes it clear where our informant's authentic sense of self lies, but the principle that the fragmentation of self is facilitated by new forms of communication technology should be evident. Cyber forums have become, and will become even more so, central venues for the presentation of self and corresponding positive and negative sanctions thereof. Advancements in communication technology also create new contexts for deception, as well as surveillance—anonymity as well as authenticity.[47] In short, the frontier of identity work is cyberspace. Inevitably, this alters face-to-face interaction as well.

Summary

> Reveal, Ancient of Days, the Present in the Past and prophesy the End in the Beginning. For this is a beautiful world; this is a wonderful America, which the founding fathers dreamed until their sons drowned it in the blood of slavery and devoured it in greed. Our children must rebuild it. Let then the Dreams of the dead rebuke the Blind who think that what is will be forever and teach them that what was worth living for must live again and that which merited death must stay dead. Teach us, Forever Dead, there is no Dream but Deed, there is no Deed but Memory. (W. E. B. Du Bois)[48]

Culture outlives individuals. Cultural remembrance or amnesia determines whether and how ideas live on. *What* is remembered, however, is a collective question. If remembrance is central, perception is preeminent. Ever the prophet, Du Bois reminds us of both the promise of high ideals and the vast injustices littering our past, present, and future. At the very least, his words remind us that formal religion does not have a monopoly on languages of transcendence, morality, or prophetic critique.

Social power and secularity are positively related in the U.S. population, in spite of, indeed, because of the cultural connections between normative civic status and religion. Those with an ample supply of social status can better afford the penalties applied for the ideological and cultural deviance of secularity. This pattern is evident in the relationships between secularity and ethnicity, social class, and immigration. Because social penalties are more severe for atheism and agnosticism, the connections between majority status and secularity are more pronounced for theistic dis- and nonbelief. In many ways, the prevalence of nonaffiliated belief among Americans appears to result from the cross-pressures of religious politics and the penalties applied to those perceived as irreligious; it is a way to express distance from organized religion without incurring the penalties that accompany being labeled an "atheist." Further, the extensive links between the civic sphere and religion in the U.S. mean that connections to community are often predicated on religious organizations, especially for minorities. To the extent that conventional society and culture is "white" in the U.S., minority groups must create and sustain subcultures to generate cultural worldviews, products, and understandings that are not "whitewashed." There is perhaps no social institution better equipped for subculture formation and maintenance than religion. Religion, and its cultural Other of secularity, necessarily bear the imprint of societal distributions of racialized power.

7

Gender and Secularity

What is the purpose of our souls? When we speak of reform, what hope we to produce? *The universal improvement of our human condition.*
—Frances Wright[1]

The High Priestess of Infidelity

One of the most prominent voices in the freethought movement during the Second Great Awakening was notable not only for the content of her message, but also because of her personal characteristics. Frances "Fanny" Wright was a radical visionary—morally, socially, intellectually, and politically. Born in Scotland in 1795 and raised in England after the death of her parents, she was a formidable intellect and a cultural revolutionary.[2] Born to a family of prominent status, she and her sister moved when Frances was eighteen to live with her uncle, James Mylne, chair and professor of moral philosophy at the University of Glasgow, a position previously held by famed economist Adam Smith. While there, Wright had access to the university's library and her caretakers' considerable social circle, which was ensconced in the Scottish Enlightenment. She applied her talents to learning the art of philosophy. Still eighteen, she wrote *A Few Days in Athens*, a parable of and meditation on Epicurean philosophy that, in keeping with the heretical nature of Epicurus, identified organized religion as the primary source of social problems and ignorance. As articulated through the character of the sage, Theon:

> What master error, for some there must be, leads to results so fatal—so opposed to the apparent nature and promise of things? Long have I sought this error—this main-spring of human folly and human crime. . . . I have found it,—Fellow-men, I have found it in—Religion![3]

During this time, she became fascinated by the American Revolution, and envisioned America as a land of unparalleled freedom.[4]

In the summer of 1818, Wright sailed to America. During her tour of the fledgling republic, she authored a series of letters that would become *Views of Society and Manners in America*, a sprawling work extolling the virtues and promises of the United States. Although panned by critics of conservative political ilk, influential utilitarian philosopher Jeremy Bentham adored the book, and Wright quickly became his pupil. After sending a copy to American Revolutionary War hero Marquis de Lafayette, she made another influential ally. The nature of her relationship with the much older Lafayette remains mysterious, but it became the subject of intense speculation by critics throughout her life.

Wright returned to America in 1824 in the company of Lafayette on his celebratory farewell tour of the states, meeting with some of the most important public figures of the day. Thomas Jefferson thoroughly enjoyed *A Few Days in Athens*, as well as *Views of Society and Manners in America*, and happily received Lafayette and Wright at his Monticello plantation.[5] As Lafayette ventured further south on his tour, Wright went west to New Harmony, Indiana, Robert Owen's utopian socialist commune. Inspired by Owen's efforts, Wright embarked on her own communal experiment of Nashoba in 1825, situated on a plot of land outside of Memphis, Tennessee. She purchased thirty slaves, proposing that they work their way out of bondage and compensate their former owners, thus providing a precedent for America to make its way out of dependence on a slave-based economy. Nashoba never actualized Wright's vision, and the venture languished for a few years before dissipating in utter failure.[6]

In June 1828, Wright became co-editor of the *New Harmony Gazette* (later the *Free Enquirer*); she was the first woman to hold such an editorial position in America. The next month, she embarked on perhaps her most notable accomplishment in the New World. On July 4, she addressed the public at New Harmony Hall. At the time, women were forbidden by cultural mores from addressing "promiscuous audiences"—public gatherings of men and women together.[7] In daring to address such audiences, Wright shattered a critical barrier to women's participation in the public sphere. But she was not content to achieve this only with an address to a favorable audience on the margins of the Western frontier.

Envisioning a role as a secular, political prophetess, Wright embarked on a speaking tour of major U.S. cities, addressing, in a series of lectures, matters no less than the foundations of inquiry, knowledge, morals, religion, and politics. Her withering critiques of conventional social institutions skewered many sacred cows, repudiating sexist marriage laws, exploitative systems of labor, and the hypocrisy and superstitions of organized religion. Over the next eighteen months, she traveled and lectured extensively, imploring audiences to establish "halls of science" where citizens could listen, learn, and discuss how to realize the ideals of equal rights and democracy. She donated the proceeds accrued from her appearances toward this end, in efforts to catalyze organized freethought groups.

Her acts of defiance caused a sensation wherever she ventured. At first, audiences were taken with her eloquence, vast intellect, and command of argument. Among her admirers was a young Walt Whitman, whose father took him to hear Wright speak. Whitman would become an avid reader of both her articles and books, cherishing her work throughout his life. Recalling her in the highest esteem, he said she "had a halo: is almost sacerdotal." Further, he reminisced, "She was one of the few characters to excite in me a wholesale respect and love. . . . It was not feature simply but soul—soul. There was a majesty about her. . . . I never felt so glowingly towards any other woman. . . . She possessed of her-self my body and soul."[8] Unlike Whitman, the forces of conventional social order were horrified, and a din of misogynistic voices soon made themselves heard. Ministers began publically referring to Wright as the "High Priestess of Infidelity," while papers labeled her "a bold blasphemer, and a voluptuous preacher of licentiousness." Indeed, "not one editor encouraged or supported her."[9] In a variety of expressions, "the press called her a whore who threatened the very foundations of society."[10]

Undeterred by such negativity, in 1829 she spent $7,000 of her own capital to convert an old Baptist church into a hall of science in New York. Across the street from a Bible repository, "boldly in the window they showed the heroes of heterodoxy—among them Paine, [Percy Bysshe] Shelley, [William] Godwin, and Richard Carlile—and the pamphlets and books Fanny and Robert [Dale Owen] printed themselves."[11] Wright marked its consecration with a public address. The speech she delivered at the opening of the hall of science warrants in-depth attention for at least two reasons. First, the location, occasion, and unique qualities of the narrator in the context of 1829 offer insights into the historical connections between gender, religiosity, and conventionality. Second, by coming at the end of her most important speaking tour of the United States, it provides a window into Wright's philosophy at the most critical time in her public life.

The importance of Wright's defiance of the restriction on speaking to promiscuous audiences, especially about matters such as politics, religion, and sexuality, should not be underestimated. By restricting speech to nonpublic or female-only forums, women's potential political power was effectively neutralized. So pervasive was the view that a woman could not be a public rhetor while maintaining feminized morality that the early female political reformers, typically abolitionists, worked through rather than around the charge of women's delicate moral sensibilities. To do so they framed claims about political matters as stemming from women's unique moral insights, rather than "ground their defenses in appeals to justice, law, equity or constitutionalism."[12] Wright, however, did appeal to these broader ideals. Further, she fearlessly criticized organized religion in her public addresses:

> To awaken the people's attention, therefore, to the affairs of earth, it was necessary first to draw their thoughts from the clouds. . . . Now, during this process of preliminary enquiry, I meddled neither with the faiths nor the forms of the popular superstition. . . . I criticised neither bible nor catechism, objected to no translation, quarrelled with no readings, challenged no discussion, but ventured the remarks—that theology was very expensive, its disputes very injurious, and its teachers very intermeddling, and encouraged the public to examine, whether its utility was equal to the cost. . . . These questions were plain and simple, and the clergy, apprehensive apparently that the answer would be unfavourable to their calling, declared, that to have them heard was immorality, but that to answer them would be atheism, which last term they explained to signify the infraction of all the laws of the decalogue, and of the states and the United States into the bargain.[13]

Unlike women reformers in the 1830s and 1840s such as Lucretia Mott and Sarah and Angelina Grimké, Wright argued for equal rights for slaves *and women* by leveraging the discourse of equality found in the Declaration of Independence and the Constitution, a strategy that would not gain prominence until long after her brief career as a public speaker. Further, rather than appealing to (supposedly irrational) emotion and moral suasion, which was regarded as the domain of women, Wright argued overtly from reason and philosophy. Given that such gendered strictures were upheld most vociferously by clergy, Wright's identity as a freethinker provided a grounding from which to ignore the conventional restrictions on female orators. At the same time, her secularity limited the pragmatic impact of her speech, because she was operating in a different cultural and cognitive frame than most of her listeners, even among the radical and liberal circles in which she traveled.

These attributes of thought and speech make Frances Wright a woman out of time, not only because she was advocating reforms that would only come to fruition long after her life, but also because she paid no heed to the strictures placed on her by virtue of gendered behavioral expectations. As such, her arguments were advanced far beyond what public audiences could understand or be open to. Yet her life and ideas warrant our attention precisely because of what they tell us about both her time and our own.

Wright opened her speech at the hall of science by saying, "The object that assembles us here this day is the same for which, through all past ages, the wise have labored, and the good have suffered," which was "universal knowledge." The collective pursuit of knowledge, she argued, required people to

> [t]hrow aside the distinctions of class; the names and feelings of sect or party; to recognise, in ourselves and each other, the single character of human beings and fellow creatures, and thus to sit down, as children of one family, in patience to inquire—in humility to learn.[14]

Attempting to persuade her American audiences, Wright grounded this view of human rights in a version of American civil religion cast in secular terms: "And what must supply our discipline? Self-government. . . . The efforts of a hierarchy, the denunciations of orthodoxy, or the jealousy of wealth and pretension, can do nought against free thoughts and free speech in a country *politically free*."[15] Later in the speech, she continued this line of thought with critiques that remain valid today:

> Surely it befits a people acknowledging political liberty, to investigate the meaning of the word, and the power involved in the principle. Surely it concerns a people claiming equal rights to examine how they may exert those rights with a view of equal benefit. What has been done towards this, let the state of society attest. How far we have studied human life as a science, let our human condition bear witness. How far the people of this land have improved their republican institutions, or reduced to practice the declaration of '76, let the state of society declare. We speak of equality, and we are divided into classes; of self-government, and we fit not ourselves to govern. We hear of law and legislation, and the mass of people understand not the one, and take no interest in the other. We complain of existing evils, and seek neither their source nor their remedy; we see pauperism on the increase, and vice travelling in her footsteps, and we ask only for more jails and larger poorhouses.[16]

Rather than emphasizing emotion or feminine moral benevolence, Wright stressed that her arguments were based on reason and intellect, which could lift people above the shame imposed by conventional rules of thought, feeling, and behavior:

> The object we have in view, namely the acquisition and diffusion of knowledge, is so noble, so rational, and so pure, that, in pledging ourselves to its pursuit, we may feel elevated above all unworthy feelings, and not merely willing, but eager to exchange passion for reason, and to immolate selfishness at the shrine of the public good.[17]

In the speech, Wright also addressed religion in a variety of ways, criticizing arguments for theism from first cause, the existence of the soul, the afterlife, and supernaturalism generally, calling clerics "advocates of mental darkness" and imploring listeners (and readers) to think for themselves while using science as the collective method for verifying knowledge, in contrast to subjective belief or opinion. The rhetorical reliance on science as the method for framing new cosmic belief systems—although Wright would surely find our phrase problematic—again shows the historical tethers that connect "new" atheists to secularists past.

A particularly interesting aspect of Wright's thought that has thus far gone unnoticed by historians and scholars is her advocacy for *social* science. Like her contemporary Auguste Comte, Wright advocated a positivist application of science to matters of human institutions and societies. And, like Comte, she saw science as providing the pathway toward a new "religion" of humanity.

> We cannot enter the hall of science to learn nor to teach Christianity, nor Judaism, nor Islamism, nor paganism, nor deism, nor materialism; we can enter it only to study the world we live in, to study ourselves as inhabitants of that world, and to form our opinions in conformity with the results of our studies. I have said—*to study ourselves* . . . . The master science—the centre path and fairest avenue in the field of knowledge, and from which and into which all others, if rightly followed, would be found to branch and converge—*the science of human life* remains to this hour in its infancy.[18]

To the extent that social scientists claim Comte's thought as a foundational attempt to establish a philosophical grounding for contemporary social science, which is considerable, Frances Wright's ideas warrant similar recognition. Ultimately, her secular utopian vision projects "full republican instruction" as the salvific path to enlightenment, and public schools available to all citizens as the means through which it could be achieved. Throughout her public life, Wright championed many progressive causes, but she consistently argued that open public education was the lynchpin of equal rights: "Your institutions may declare equality of rights, but we shall never possess those rights until you have *national* schools."[19]

Also noteworthy in Wright's speech at the hall of science was her recognition of the potential for dogmatism also present *in secularism*. She instructed the members assembled in the hall, "Let us preserve our popular meetings in this place uncontaminated and undistracted by religious discussions or opinionative dissensions." Again voicing criticisms that have weathered the test of time, she implored fellow freethinkers:

> Or, on the other hand, have we learned to doubt the lessons of books, and the laws of men, let us beware in what spirit we set forth our scepticism, lest, haply, while discarding the dogmas, we retain the dogmatism, and lend, even to truth, the tone of presumption and the spirit of error.[20]

Closing her remarks, Wright returned to the theme of American civil religion for a final call to action:

> Yet great is the victory [the American republic] hath yet to achieve. It is over the tyranny of ignorance, and the slavery of the mind. Noble be her weapons and spotless is her cause! let her seek them at the hand of knowledge, and wield them in the spirit of justice, of charity, and of love to man.[21]

Her groundbreaking speaking tour concluded, Wright left New York City, traveling to Memphis to gather the slaves from Nashoba, then to New Orleans and, ultimately, Haiti in October 1829, where they were freed, officially ending her failed experiment in emancipation.

Gender, Education, and Politics

The relationship between gender and religion is knotty, existing at the intersection of sexuality, domesticity, and public views of morality. The case of Frances Wright speaks to these relations in two important ways. First, religion and sexuality were used as rhetorical weapons to publicly attack her, showing how these matters often intertwine in the heart of gendered expectations for thought and behavior. As a case of public deviance, punishment, and the maintenance of conventional boundaries, reactions to Wright's ideas and actions show how religious piety is often tied to conventional, public moral standing, especially for women. Since religiosity is typically seen as a prerequisite for feminine moral status, the lack thereof is necessarily viewed as an aberrant, deviant social position.

Second, and directly relevant to the matters we examine here, Wright's philosophical and political work provides insight into the gendered "nature" of religiosity, and by inverse implication, secularity in American culture. Her philosophy drew from and expanded upon the Scottish Enlightenment, (especially Jeremy Bentham's) utilitarianism, utopian socialism, and French and American revolutionary conceptions of liberty and freedom grounded in "moral sense" philosophy. Wright's thought and reform efforts revolved around two consistent themes: political progressivism and free, open, and public education for all children as a panacea for numerous problems of inequality.[22] These foci—political progressivism and educational advancement—offer clues not just to the thought of a nineteenth-century radical egalitarian, but also to the puzzle of contemporary gendered patterns of religiosity and secularity.

The relationship between gender and religiosity (and secularity) is one that has proven difficult for social scientists to understand. Among Western populations, women are disproportionately prone to religiosity, in spite of the patriarchal power structures of most organized religions. This paradox has perplexed many theorists, and confused researchers still more due to the lack of empirical findings that adequately account for these gendered patterns of religious expression.[23] When potential explanations such as differential labor force participation and child care responsibilities failed to account for differences in religiosity, some sociologists even suggested in high-profile journal articles that physiological differences created varying "risk preferences" between men and women, which could be responsible for gender gaps in religious expression.[24]

The gaps in religiosity are inverted for secularity, such that men are more likely to be secular than women. Using GSS data from 1988 to 2010 and data from the Pew RLS, we calculated gender ratios based on the proportions of men and women claiming each of the various expressions of secularity. To generate a balanced assessment, we averaged the gender ratios across the two datasets. Atheism is the most strongly gendered form of secularity, with 2.6 male atheists for every female atheist, followed by agnosticism and cultural religion (2.1 men per woman), then nonaffiliated belief (1.4 men per woman). For active religiosity, there are 1.2 women for every man.[25]

The literature that has followed in the wake of claims that there were "universal" gender differences in religiosity due to biological causes resoundingly criticizes arguments from innate difference, but at the same time has generally failed to offer an alternative theory supported by empirical tests.[26] One exception is a study showing that women raised by mothers with a high level of personal (rather than familial) occupational prestige tended to have lower levels of religiosity as adults. These findings are framed in light of power-control theory, a body of ideas in criminology about how boys and girls are socialized differently with regard to "risky" behavior.[27] This study makes substantial advances in the understanding of how and why risk preference may relate to religiosity without recourse to innate sex differences, but continues to work within the bounds of the risk preference model.

In contrast, we employ a perspective that draws on cultural sociology (and the thought of Frances Wright) by examining two dimensions in relation to gender and secularity: education level and political views. Specifically, we tested whether gender differences in secularity were altered for political liberals with high levels of education. In order to test our hypothesis in an empirically rigorous manner, we controlled for a number of other variables known to be significantly related to levels of religious expression, such as age, income, race and ethnicity, marital status, and region of the country. We also controlled for mother's and father's levels of educational attainment as a proxy for the socioeconomic status of one's parents.

In order to access an adequate number of cases on which to test this idea, we used the general category of all those claiming no religion as compared to respondents who reported a religious affiliation so that all years of the GSS could be used rather than just the waves since 1988. As we have noted, it is certainly more preferable to examine varying expressions of secularity separately, but to assess highly specific subsets of Americans (such as politically liberal, highly educated women claiming no religious affiliation), we used the more ambiguous (and therefore more numerous) designation of religious nones versus religious affiliates. In addition, we compared those who attended religious services twice a year or less to those who attend services more than that, giving us rudimentary assessments of both religious affiliation and public religious behavior. Here we graphically present the results based on gender, education, and political views; the results from the full models are available in the Data Analyses Appendix.

Figure 7.1 shows the probability that an American claims no religion for men and women by education level and political views for those who identify as "extremely conservative," "moderate," or "extremely liberal."[28] Among liberal Americans, the gender gap in secularity closes as education rises. For those with less than a high school degree, men have a much higher probability (.17) of being religious nones compared to women (.08). In contrast, among liberals with a graduate degree, the probabilities of men (.31) and women (.30) being religious nones are almost identical. Among moderates, higher levels of education have a slightly positive association with the probability of men claiming no religion, and a slightly negative association with women doing so, such that the gender gap increases as education rises. Among conservatives, there is a general tendency to be religiously affiliated, and the gap between men and women again increases slightly as levels of education increase.

Figure 7.2 shows the same pattern at play concerning infrequent attendance at religious services. Among respondents self-identifying as "extremely conservative" and "moderate," the gender gap in infrequent attendance is relatively consistent across education levels. In general, higher education is associated with a lower likelihood of nonattendance. Stated positively, increased education is associated with more religious service attendance for political conservatives and moderates. Meanwhile, for those self-identifying as "extremely liberal," the differences between men and women decrease as education increases. For extremely liberal women, increased education is positively related to the likelihood of infrequent attendance, the only social category for which education is *negatively* related to religious service attendance. For extremely liberal men, increased education slightly decreases the likelihood of infrequent attendance. These countervailing influences converge among highly educated liberals such that there is no gender gap in infrequent attendance, with men and women having an equal probability of nonattendance (.52).

We replicated these findings with data from the Pew RLS. In a multivariate model controlling for nearly the same variables as we did with GSS data, politically liberal women with postgrad degrees had a higher probability of being atheists, agnostics, or religious nones (.43) compared to men with those characteristics (.32). Overall, these findings suggest that gender gaps in religion and secularity are more about the *politics* of the body than the body per se. Specifically, political progressives are more likely to question convention and tradition with regard to gender and sexuality. To the extent that organized religion is perceived as aligned with conservative views of sexuality and gender,

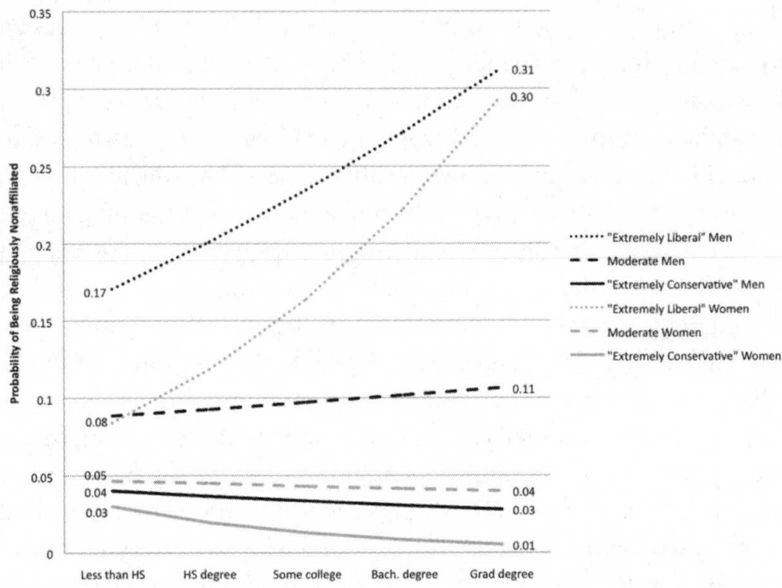

Figure 7.1. Probability of Religious Nonaffiliation by Gender, Education, and Political Position

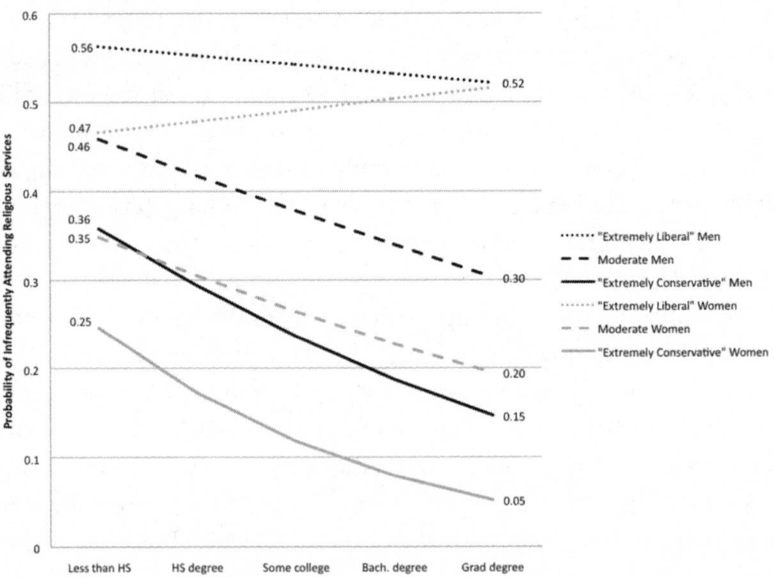

Figure 7.2. Probability of Infrequent Attendance at Religious Services by Gender, Education, and Political Position

which, as we have shown, is substantial, those willing to identify as politically liberal are also more likely to reject organized religion. These analyses demonstrate that under certain combinations of social characteristics the gender gap in religiosity and secularity disappears, casting doubt on the claims that biological differences are driving the relationship between gender and religiosity. Rather, as we have shown, individuals occupying minority statuses are more likely to be actively religious, which is the case for women—under most circumstances. This suggests, as some scholars have recently argued, that gender gaps in religiosity and secularity should decline to the extent that a society experiences a broader trend of secularization that is accompanied by greater gender equality.[29]

Sexual Orientation

A notable exception to the general relationship between disempowerment and religious identity is sexual minorities. Direct prejudice by religious organizations against gay, lesbian, bisexual, transgendered, and queer individuals leads to lower levels of religious engagement. But even here the dynamics between gender stratification and religion remain influential, as gay men attend religious services more and have rates of apostasy similar to heterosexual men after accounting for social and demographic characteristics. Indeed, it is women who reject traditional gender and sexuality roles who are more likely to be outside organized religion because they see it as patriarchal.[30] Further, studies have shown that gender orientation (e.g., masculine/feminine characteristics) is more important than sex characteristics (male/female) for predicting religiosity. Specifically, levels of "femininity" predicted variation in religiosity, especially for men.[31]

GSS data suggest that people who identify as gay, lesbian, or bisexual are not drastically different from heterosexuals with regard to secularity. Among individuals with same-sex orientation, there are slightly more atheists compared to heterosexuals (6% to 3.3%), but very similar levels of agnostics, nonaffiliated believers, and the culturally religious. Among bisexuals, there are more agnostics (12% to 6%) and nonaffiliated believers (14% to 12%) compared to heterosexuals, but fewer atheists (2.3% to 3.3%) and culturally religious (5% to 8%). Tests for differences in secularity or religiosity at the population level based on sexual orientation were statistically nonsignificant.

We must exercise caution with these data due to a small number of cases, as the GSS has asked about sexual orientation only since 2008. At the same time, a study that classified people as gay, lesbian, bisexual, or heterosexual on the basis of respondents' reports of the gender of the people they had sexual relations with in the past five years found that gay men have rates of religious participation similar to heterosexuals, while lesbians and bisexuals had lower rates of participation. While non-heterosexual Americans were more likely to drop out of religion than heterosexual women, they had rates of apostasy similar to heterosexual men. Reiterating our findings concerning gender, the general pattern is that "female alternative sexuality cannot be easily wedded to extant religious traditions."[32] Taken together these findings suggest that it is alternative conceptions of gender roles rather than alternative sexuality that leads to higher levels of secularity.

The Fall of Fanny Wright

> Yes! my democracy has no reservations; my yearnings for the liberty of man acknowledge no exceptions, no prejudices, no predilections. Equal rights, equal privileges, equal enjoyments—I would see them shared by every man, by every woman, by every nation, by every race on the face of the globe. (Frances Wright)[33]

Upon return to the states after visiting Haiti, an extramarital pregnancy forced Frances Wright into hiding in France. Before leaving the U.S., she played an active role in organizing the first labor-based political party in America, and delivered a series of public lectures. In June 1830, she delivered her "Parting Address" at the Bowery Theatre in New York.

As in all her public addresses, she appealed to American civil religion, arguing that the Constitution was "the only inspired scripture, written for human kind, and destined to be acknowledged by all nations."[34] Summarizing her arguments, she intoned:

> This only will I say, that I have assailed what I believe abuses; that I have advocated equal rights in place of unequal privileges, appealed to fact from faith, to reason from credulity, to justice from law, to virtue from prejudice, to the ever-during principles of the inner mind from the changing and fleeting forms of ceremony and superstition, and, bear witness, fellow citizens! from the unconstitutional and antirepublican divisions of sect, class, and party, as existing around us, to this sacred charter of the common rights of equal free-men and American citizens.[35]

She concluded by telling listeners that her respite from public life would be brief, but necessary for the furtherance of the progressive movements she championed:

> So long as I alone was concerned, the noise of priest and politician was alike indifferent to me, but I wish not my name to be made a scarecrow to the timid, or a stumbling-block to the innocently prejudiced, at a season when all should unite round the altar of their country, with its name only in their mouths, and its love in their hearts.[36]

In the short term, this anticipation was perhaps her most prescient prophecy. The birth of a daughter in secret, followed by a subsequent marriage to legitimize the child led Wright to avoid the public eye for over five years. In the meantime, in spite (or because) of her litany of accomplishments and undeniable intellectual prowess, she was transformed into a pariah so reviled that "Fanny Wrightism" became a political epithet to be avoided at all costs.

Although her transgression of gender norms was used against her at all phases of her public life, it was Wright's criticism of religion and then-conventional forms of marriage and sexuality that were exploited as the primary rhetorical cudgels used to silence and marginalize her critiques of systemic injustices in American society.[37] Further, when a caretaker engaged in scandalous sexual relationships at the Nashoba commune in Wright's absence, she publicly and explicitly criticized Victorian sexual mores, defended sexual pleasure as central to human happiness, and endorsed miscegenation as a method of hastening emancipation.[38] Her criticism of religion and Victorian strictures on marriage and sexuality led to her being publically branded as, among other slanders, "the great Red Harlot of Infidelity," "the whore of Babylon," "Priestess of Beelzebub," "a bird of ill omen," "a crazy atheistical woman," and more generally as a "female monster."[39] One of the most frequent charges made against Wright was that she advocated "free love," a denunciation that dogged her from Nashoba onward.[40]

In a particularly damning assessment, when Wright briefly returned to public speaking in 1836, Catharine Beecher, influential education reformer and abolitionist, daughter of famed evangelist Lyman Beecher, and sibling to abolitionists Henry Ward Beecher and Harriet Beecher Stowe, histrionically said of Wright:

> The apropriate [sic] character of a woman demands . . . a shrinking from notoriety and public gaze, a love of dependence, and protection . . . and an instructive abhorrence of all that tends to indelicacy and unpurity. . . . Fanny Wright, with her great masculine person, her loud voice, her untasteful attire, going about unprotected, and feeling no need of protection, mingling with men in stormy debate, and standing up with bare-faced impudence, to lecture to a public assembly. And what are the topics of her discourse . . . ? Nothing better than broad attacks on all those principles that protect the purity, the dignity, and the safety of her sex. There she stands . . . attacking all the safeguards of all that is venerable and sacred in religion, all that is safe and wise in law, all that is pure and lovely in domestic virtue. . . . I cannot conceive any thing in the shape of a woman, more intolerably offensive and disgusting.[41]

Wright's career as a public speaker declined as her audiences became both smaller and more hostile, public meeting houses denied her requests to speak, and her thought became increasingly abstract. When she left America for France in 1839, former mayor of New York Philip Hone wrote, "Let her go home or go to the Devil, so that she never visits us again."[42] Although she continued to write, she was effectively banished from the public sphere and increasingly isolated, ultimately dying amid a toxic combination of infamy, obscurity, and loneliness in Cincinnati in 1852. Adding posthumous insult to injury, Wright's daughter Sylva testified before Congress in 1874 *against* women's suffrage.[43]

Walt Whitman spoke longingly of writing corrective histories of the lights of radical freethought, especially Paine, Wright, and abolitionist Quaker Elias Hicks, "superb characters . . . who were much maligned or much misunderstood." Whitman noted that Wright was ultimately more vilified than Paine, as the latter at least maintained cadres of defenders. Recalling her thought and oratory, he said.

> In those days I frequented the anti-slavery halls in New York. . . . It was there that I heard Frances Wright . . . a woman of the noblest make-up whose orbit was a great deal larger than [the audiences']—too large to be tolerated for long by them: a most maligned, lied-about character—one of the best in history though also one of the least understood. . . . Yes, they may object to her—object as the priestly class would object to Jesus, Socrates . . . [but s]he was sweeter, nobler, grander—multiplied by twenty—than all who traduced her.[44]

Although she espoused a uniformly egalitarian philosophy focused on providing public education to all people regardless of race or gender, reform of marriage and divorce laws, and the use of birth control, the burgeoning movement for women's rights distanced itself from Wright, with the exception of Ernestine Rose, her successor as a public orator.[45] In direct contrast to Wright, who argued for gender equality and women's direct participation in politics, early women's movements sought to capitalize on women's purported differences from men and their transcendence of petty partisan politics, appealing to women's supposedly unique virtue of benevolence to stake claim to moral high ground. As such, Wright's contributions were largely recognized only after her lifetime, when later generations of leaders in the suffrage movement, especially Elizabeth Cady Stanton and Susan B. Anthony, celebrated her as an inspirational pioneer. Except among historians of feminism and oratory, Wright remains largely obscure today, outside passing references to her utopian efforts to end slavery at the Nashoba commune.[46] Although she would ultimately lose the fight, Frances Wright well understood that "her battle with the evangelicals was fundamentally political."[47] Her insight is as true now as then.

Summary

The oft-noted gender gap in religiosity and secularity is intimately connected to progressive political views and education levels. Although we have admittedly engaged in the armchair historian's sin of "presentism" by telling the historical story of Frances Wright to make a contemporary point, the connections between politics, education, gender, and religiosity nonetheless echo through the ages. Taking these connections as the starting point, we outlined how the confluence of political identity and educational attainment can serve to exacerbate or diminish the gender gap in secularity. What role women play in public life has historically been and remains a central matter of conservative/progressive political divisions, and therefore relates directly to differential rates of religiosity and secularity.

8

Marriage, Family, and Social Networks

Family is a foundational unit in every community, acting as the central source of socialization into cosmic belief systems and behavioral expectations. Children are typically guided to the cultural perspective of their caregivers and family, and in turn attempt to pass their own views on to the next generation. Religious leaders recognize this, and accordingly place importance on programs for socializing children within their organizations. These may take the form of daycare, after-school activities, Sabbath schools, youth groups, camps, and numerous other types of programs. Providing socialization courses is integral to the success or failure of religious groups, especially in the U.S., where congregations are voluntary associations. Many immigrant religions adopt congregational forms in the United States that facilitate the maintenance of such programs, even when the tradition itself has not been historically oriented to a congregational model.[1] So what happens when a family is *not* religious? What leads some who are raised religious to become secular as adults? And how do familial connections shape these processes?

Life course changes, especially those associated with marriage and family, are some of the most important factors influencing religiosity or secularity among individuals. These processes exert influence both "up" and "down" generationally. Downward generational impact is well understood in a general sense. Children learn from their parents and elders. Few young children would spontaneously envision the religious myths of the great traditions or seek out a specific religion. Instead, parents or caregivers introduce children to their religion or secularism, both formally and through modeling—messages that carry stories and lessons about who "we" are. At least initially, the vast majority of people are introduced to a particular religion without having any sense that there are innumerable other traditions. This socialization is integral to understanding both the religious and secular views of adults.

While most people understand the connection between socialization and intergenerational religious transmission, fewer are apt to notice how connections to religion are also driven by *upward* generational forces. For example, many twenty-somethings experience a drift or shift away from organized religion, at least in its institutional forms. While religious beliefs and often even private practices may persist during this period, organizational affiliation and salience of faith may wane. What often reverses apostasy are marriage and having children. These life course events with the potential for or involving new generations are important stimuli for prospective or new parents.[2] Feeling the need to raise children in a moral environment is a strong motivation for many people to return to religious organizations. In the absence of marriage or children, the relative freedom from familial ties may help crystalize secular identities.

The bidirectional influence of family ties brings us back to the dialectical cultural influences of secularism. As with many of the relationships we have examined, culture and social structure influence the presence or form of secularism, but also vice versa. In the case of family, not having children can make individuals more likely to stay outside of organized religion, while being less religiously attached in the first place influences decisions about ideal family structure and size.[3] As we draw out these patterns, it is vital to realize that both are reciprocally intertwined in the lives of individuals and groups through time.

Interfaith Marriage

Understanding interfaith marriage is important to understanding the role religion and secularism play in relationships, especially considering the increasing occurrence of interfaith marriage in the United States, comprising almost half of all marital unions.[4] Similarly, evidence suggests that young Americans continue to become more accepting of the idea of marrying someone with a different religious tradition.[5] There is a substantial body of research on interfaith or interreligious marriages, but little work has been done on couples in which one member is religious while the other is not, in part due to the rarity of such occurrences, although such unions are increasing. Examining marriages between two secular individuals and between religious and secular individuals is one of the most critical areas for future research development in the study of secularism.

In the meantime, the research on interfaith marriages provides a solid starting point, as preliminary research on marriages between two seculars indicates patterns of marital stability similar to those for interreligious unions.[6] At a basic level, research suggests that couples who share the same religious identification will experience lower rates of divorce and higher marital satisfaction than those who do not.[7] The potential challenges of interfaith relationships are evident in applied research, where family therapists discuss how to treat couples who have different religious beliefs, as well as how to interact with their children.[8] These effects are by no means uniform, though. Among interreligious couples, the difference between religious traditions may be an issue at the forefront of the relationship, but it is more likely that couples who choose to have interfaith marriages will be those who can "bracket off their religious practices from their partners' and the rest of the marriage."[9]

A particularly relevant finding from studies of interreligious marriage is that the "distance" between worldviews matters more than simple binary distinctions of different affiliations. Intuitively, we can recognize that spouses' respect for one another's belief systems is critical to the amount of conflict generated by interfaith unions. For example, immigrants are more likely to marry natives of their new country if their religious traditions are similar.[10] These tendencies can be applied to the choices of secular and religious individuals to marry each other. It is one thing for a religiously affiliated person to marry someone who is religiously nonaffiliated or apathetic, but quite another to marry someone who is actively opposed to one's faith system. Thus, we should expect that religious partners in secular/religious unions will tend to be nominally religious. Indeed, while research shows that the overall "link between religion and marital quality is both reciprocal and weak," empirical evidence suggests that the "distances" between couples on matters of theology and religious practice are more powerful as predictors of marital satisfaction or strife than individuals' levels of general religiosity or denominational heterogamy.[11]

Recent research has outlined two important patterns in the connections between religiosity and marital quality. First, it is not religion per se that makes marriages better or less likely to dissolve, but rather specific attitudes *about one's marital relationship* that religion tends to instill in individuals. Four factors have been identified as being of primary importance in this process: the extent to which an individual sees the union as sacred or sanctified, level of commitment to the union, willingness to make sacrifices for one's partner, and willingness to forgive one's partner.[12] In combination, these relational traits account for the positive relationship between religiosity and marital quality. A second finding of note is that the negative effects of religious heterogamy on marital quality are declining across recent generations of Americans. Sociologist Scott Myers analyzed longitudinal data from three generations and found that dissimilarity between couples regarding the importance of religion in their lives declined in predictive power for both marital happiness and stability across generations. This decline was precipitous enough that religious heterogamy ceased to be a significant predictor of marital happiness or stability among the most recent generation. Further, the positive effect of religious affiliation relative to nonaffiliation in the first generation also declined to insignificance by the third generation.[13] Taken together, this body of research informs secular or interfaith couples about *how* religion operates positively for religiously homogamous marriages, and also suggests that the deleterious effects of religious heterogamy are declining over time. In effect, these studies provide a roadmap to successful partnerships, as well as good news for seculars about the improving state of their marital unions.

There is good reason to predict that in addition to increasing rates of interreligious marriage there will also be higher rates of secular Americans marrying other seculars as they compose larger proportions of the population. As studies of Catholics have shown, the frequency of interreligious marriage can be explained in large part by the rarity or commonness of similar others in the local population. Simply stated, if there are a lot of religiously similar potential partners available, people are less likely to consider or find a spouse with different religious views.[14] The same should hold true for seculars. If seculars are sufficiently rare, then finding a partner may almost require marriage to a spouse who is religious, but if secularism is more common, it will lessen this occurrence by providing a stronger mate market for homogamy.

Children and Marriage in the Life Cycle

The primary way we can see the relationship between family and secularity moving "upward" generationally is by looking at having children.

In the Pew RLS, there are 5,540 respondents who reported that they were between thirty and thirty-nine years old. Fifty-nine percent of the secular respondents have kids compared to 74% of actively religious respondents. Put another way, for a thirty-something without kids, there is a 34% chance s/he will be secular. For a thirty-something with kids, the likelihood decreases to 20%. This general pattern is repeated with specific categories of secularity. From this snapshot, we can see much of the trend in the relationship between having children and secularity. While it is certainly not the norm to be secular as a thirty-year-old, it is much less likely for people with children.

There are similar differences between respondents who are married and unmarried. Again, for respondents between the ages of thirty and thirty-nine, only 17% of those who are married are secular, compared to 29% of the people who have never been married. The percentage is even higher for those who report "living with a partner" (32%). It is not only intimate relationships, but also type of relationship that influences secularity. Similar to the low rates of secularity among married Americans, the divorced (20%) and separated (19%) have relatively low rates of secularity, suggesting that those who enter into marriage are more likely to be religious than those who avoid the institution, or at least have not been part of it yet. The widowed are the least likely to be secular, with only 10% who are not actively religious. Due to these life-cycle patterns, marital status accounts for some of the standard "aging" effects found for both religiosity and secularity.[15]

Differences by Gender

While we previously looked at gender differences in general, it is worth noting how specific life course events influence men and women differently in regard to secularity.[16] One of the biggest distinctions lies in the association with having children. Men who have kids are more likely to be actively religious, at a rate of 77% compared to 72% for childless men. For men, the presence of kids is a potential encouragement to be more religious. In addition, being secular leads men to avoid having children. This difference does not exist for women. Instead, about 85% of women with no children are actively religious, compared to 84% of women with kids. For men there is a drop off across all types of secularity if they have any children. Among women, there are slight decreases for dis- and nonbelief, while nonaffiliated belief actually increases for women having children (from 8% to 11%). In contrast to men, having children does not affect women's rates of religiosity versus secularity, although the distribution for types of secularity is slightly altered. Even here, there is less change for women concerning expressions of secularity and religiosity. Men have distinct pre- and post-children distributions, but women look basically the same at both points.

We see a similarly gendered effect for marriage. Married men are more likely to affiliate and declare a belief in God (79%) than unmarried men (68%). For women, there is less of an association between marriage and secularity or religiosity, with 83% of unmarried women and 86% of married women being actively religious. Compared to women, men are more likely to be pushed by divorce or separation away from religion and toward secularity. Seventy-one percent of divorced or separated men are actively religious, while 85% of divorced or separated women are. Divorced or separated women look essentially the same as married women regarding secularity, while divorced or separated men are more secular than married men. In other words, there is a drop-off in rates of religiosity for men after the dissolution of a marriage, but not for women. The largest differences in expressions of secularity occur among nonaffiliated believers and the culturally religious. This pattern is also evident among widowers, where 82% of men are actively religious compared to 92% of women. Overall, living outside of marriage, as a result of having never been married or being divorced or widowed, more strongly influences men than women toward secularity.

Looking instead at people who are "living with a partner," cohabitation has more influence on women than men. Three fourths of men who are *not* living with a partner are actively religious, as compared to 85% of women. As we would expect, this number drops for both men and women if they are cohabitating. Living together outside of marriage is a practice that many religious traditions oppose as a matter of private, but also public and political morality. People who are willing to engage in such unions tend to be less religious, and it may even push people away from organized religion. It is easy to understand that someone living with a partner would be uncomfortable participating in a congregation where cohabitation is frowned upon. Many men and women in these types of relationships maintain religious beliefs, but forego specific religious identities. As rates of secularity rise, we see that nonmarital cohabitation has a gendered influence opposite to that of marriage. For cohabitating men, the drop is to 64% actively religious, or about 10% fewer, while for women it is a 13% drop, to 72%. Each of the various secular categories increases with cohabitation. The most pronounced increases for women come in the form of nonaffiliated belief (8% to 18%) and atheism (1.7% to 3.3%). Thus, women are roughly twice as likely to be nonaffiliated believers or atheists if they are living with a partner. In fact, slightly more cohabitating women are nonaffiliated believers than cohabitating men (17%). Further, of the different marital statuses examined, cohabitating women are the most likely to be in each of the secular categories, with the exception that never-married women are the most likely to be agnostic.

Socialization

In combination, marriage and children produce one of the most important processes for understanding belief systems of all types: socialization (the transmission of culture across generations). Building on a previous theme, we observe that having parents with different religious views is a crucial factor in socialization. The kind of split socialization that results, with one set of cosmic beliefs from one parent and a different set from the other, makes children more likely to be secular as adults, especially when a parent claims no religion, and most especially if that parent is the mother.[17]

The Pew RLS allows us to look at some specific ways people socialize children. Seventy-two percent of actively religious respondents, for instance, report reading sacred texts or praying with their children. At least for these behaviors, religious practice is by no means universally transmitted, even within religious families. Interestingly, the socialization of religious practices is taking place in many secular families as well. Thirty-eight percent of nonaffiliated believers read sacred texts or pray with their children. Even though they self-identify as being part of no specific religion, some nonaffiliated parents apparently make a conscious effort to pass along private religious practices to their children. Even among atheists, who are the least likely to engage in private religious practices, 9% read scripture or pray with their children. Agnostics are higher at 19%, with the culturally religious in between at 11%. If we made a ranking of secular socialization, on this measure the culturally religious would be more secular than agnostics. Of course, part of our criteria of who is culturally religious relies on lack of private religiosity. The culturally religious are not enacting religious practices themselves and most also choose not to pass them along to their children.

There is also information about enrolling children in religious education programs such as Sabbath schools, which yields some quite different results. While praying and reading scripture with a child can be thought of as private religious devotions, sending a child to a religious education program is a more public activity. For respondents who are actively religious, it is a less common behavior, with 67% sending their children to such programs. This parallels the behavior of adults themselves, among whom prayer is more common than service attendance.[18] In contrast, secularists are actually *more likely* to enroll their children in religious education programs than they are to read scripture or pray with them. The rate of public socialization is about the same as that of private devotion for nonaffiliated believers rearing children (39%), but program participation is significantly higher than private religiosity for agnostics (31%) and the culturally religious (22%). Perhaps the most striking finding in this regard is that almost one in four atheists (24%) are having their children attend some type of religious education program, in contrast to the less than one in ten who pray or read religious texts with their children. It appears that many atheists (or their spouses) want their children to learn about a religious tradition (or at least like the childcare or education offered), but they do not want to engage in religious teaching or practice themselves. This one-in-four figure also reflects the relatively high levels of intermarriage between atheists and more religious spouses. The culturally religious are the least likely to engage in religious education for their children, reinforcing that nonparticipation is the defining characteristic of this category. Although they express some religious beliefs, the culturally religious are unlikely to act on them or expose their children to religious socialization—public or private. While atheists and agnostics are personally opposed to key religious beliefs, many still expose their children to at least some religious education.[19]

Reversing perspective, we can look at how the belief system in which one is raised influences adult religious outlook. While about 20% of Americans are in one of the secular categories according to the Pew RLS, this is true of 47% who were raised as atheists, with 32% staying atheists as adults. Even among those raised atheist however, over half end up as actively religious adults. So while there is some continuity to secular transmission, there is also a lot of religious "mobility" in this category. Interestingly, people who were raised agnostic (which is even less common than being raised atheist) are actually much less likely to become actively religious later in life (23%). One possibility is that being asked questions about childhood religiosity prompts retrospective narrativizing. For example, part of the reason more people who report being raised as atheists may now be more actively religious than those who were raised agnostic is that respondents *retrospectively* understand their childhood in this way. Put in different terms, a very religious adult may look back on a nominally religious upbringing by saying, in effect, "My parents were such atheists. They only took me to services a couple of times a year and barely ever talked about faith." While nominal religious socialization is in fact a standard level of religious activity for many Americans, it could be seen as "atheistic" in contrast to a person's current, active religiosity. This is not to claim that people are intentionally lying about their past religious experiences, but as we have noted, "atheist" serves as a primary out-group against which religious Americans define themselves. Retrospective narrativizing of events is more important than empirical history in terms of meaningfulness to identity, but it must still be understood as narrative recounting.

About 7% of respondents to the RLS report that they were raised as "nothing in particular," and their cosmic belief systems later in life look different than any other upbringing. About half of these respondents become actively religious, but their next most common choice is nonaffiliated belief (31%). These are presumably people raised without a specific religious identity, but with some sort of religious beliefs at least in the background. As adults, most have become attached to specific traditions, but many, a much higher proportion than among the general population or those raised atheist or agnostic, have maintained religious beliefs without any particular affiliation. Ten percent become atheists, while only 4% each become agnostic and culturally religious. For this category, adopting a religious identification typically comes with engaged practice too.

In general, people raised in religious households tend to stay religious later in life, although as we have shown, this is much less the case now than in even the recent past. Rates of active religiosity in adulthood are similar for those raised Protestant (83%) and Roman Catholic (81%). For both of these traditions, 2–3% of children socialized end up being atheist adults, and about 2% become agnostic. Those raised as Roman Catholics become culturally religious as adults at a slightly higher rate than those raised as Protestants (5.2% vs. 3.8%). Overall, about four out of five of those who are raised in Christian households maintain Christian beliefs, identities, and practices, but approximately 8–9% become unaffiliated, 4–5% become nonbelievers, and 4–5% stop participating. Parents are thus able to strongly influence, but not determine, whether their children grow up to be religious or secular.

We can distinguish this process further between different Protestant denominations. Evangelical forms of Protestantism have relatively high rates of retention, in the sense that a higher percentage of members stay affiliated with a religious tradition (although perhaps not the same one), maintain theistic beliefs, and continue practicing. Of the groups that are large enough to examine on the basis of national data, Baptists, Pentecostals, the Church of Christ, and Methodists have above average numbers of adults who are still actively religious. Lutherans and Presbyterians maintain their religiosity in adulthood at the same rate as the general population.[20] Liberal Protestant denominations such as the Episcopalian, Congregational, and United Church of Christ traditions have the highest rates of secularity once members grow up. Interestingly, only 77% of adults raised in nondenominational congregations are actively religious, a relatively low rate. Although we would expect nondenominational members to be actively religious based on the common understanding of nondenominational churches as likely to be evangelical and Pentecostal, these numbers may also be a matter of retrospective accounting. That is, individuals raised in nominally or culturally religious households may report nondenominational Christianity simply because their childhoods did not involve strong socialization into any particular religious tradition, but rather a vague sense of cultural Christianity.

Another group worth examining are those raised in the Church of Jesus Christ of Latter-day Saints. Adults raised Mormon have rates of secularity almost identical to Protestants and Catholics: 83% are actively religious, 10% are unaffiliated believers, 1.9% are agnostics, 1.6% are atheists, and 3.2% are culturally religious. These patterns support the idea that Mormons are becoming similar to other Christian groups in the United States, at least in their ability to keep members affiliated and engaged into adulthood. A group that has lower rates of active religiosity in adulthood is Jews (68%). A relatively high rate of people who were raised Jewish become culturally religious as adults (17%). A smaller proportion of those raised Jewish become unaffiliated believers (6%). Overall, while most American Jews retain some religious affiliation and beliefs, many are not engaging in religious life through a synagogue or personal practice.

Based on sophisticated analyses of multiple generations of Californians, sociologist Vern Bengtson found that a central component of successful religious (or secular) socialization—that is, the transmission of cosmic belief systems from parents to children—is the degree of perceived closeness and warmth between children and their parents.[21] Of particular importance is the relationship between fathers and their children. When relationships are close and warm, fathers tend to have levels of religiosity similar to their children, while there is a significant mismatch between religious beliefs and practice for "distant" fathers and their children. Bengtson's data also replicate our findings that the successful transmission of secularity across generations has become far more likely in recent generations of Americans—seculars are now nearly as effective at transmitting their specific belief systems to their children as religious Americans.

In the 2007 Baylor Religion Survey (BRS), less than 7% of those who were actively or culturally religious reported having fathers who claimed no religion, compared to 25% of agnostics, 22% of atheists, and 25% of nonaffiliated believers. Tellingly, nonaffiliated believers were by far the most likely to report that they did not know the religious affiliation of their fathers (21%). The second highest category for not knowing the religious view of their fathers was for the culturally religious (11%). None of the other categories reported not knowing the affiliation of their fathers at a rate higher than 7%. The same pattern, in lower proportions, is found regarding the religious affiliation of respondents' mothers. Only 2% of actively and culturally religious adults had secular mothers, compared to 16% of atheists, 13% of agnostics, and 14% of nonaffiliated believers. Again, nonaffiliated believers (15%) and the culturally religious (9%) were most likely to report not knowing the religious affiliation of their mothers. None of the other categories responded that they did not know at rates higher than 2.5%.[22]

The 2006 Faith Matters survey provides further insight into the influence of parents' religious views by asking about the religious views of respondents' children. Among those with children, 32% of agnostics, 55% of atheists, and 81% of nonaffiliated believers said their children had "no religion." It seems that absence of religious affiliation has a higher rate of intergenerational transmission than does theistic dis- or nonbelief.

Beyond general secular identity, the frequency with which children are socialized into religious practices strongly influences the probability of their identifying as secular in adulthood. Although a lower frequency of religious service attendance in childhood generally correlates with greater likelihood of secularity in adulthood, there are interesting differences regarding the type of secular expression. In 2008, the GSS asked a question about how often respondents attended religious services at age twelve. A larger share of atheists reported going at least once a week (43%) compared to nonaffiliated believers (32%) and the culturally religious (34%). Agnostics reported the lowest levels of childhood attendance, with 24% reporting that they attended at least once a week.[23] It seems that intensive religious socialization may lead apostates to assume a more hardline secular position as adults. Bengtson uncovered a similar pattern in his data gathered across generations of Californians. He found that religious "rebels came from strongly religious families . . . where parents' religious socialization efforts were experienced as excessive or intrusive." Summarizing his research team's findings in this regard, Bengtson said, "We were struck by how often we found parental religious fervor associated with the child's religious rebellion."[24]

Concerning the influence of another aspect of parental style on adult secularity, a fascinating difference in the childhood experiences of secular and religious individuals appears regarding the use of corporal punishment. The 2007 BRS asked respondents to what degree the following statement accurately described their childhood: "My parents often used corporal punishment (such as spanking) as a form of discipline." Three fourths of actively religious adults said their socialization experience included corporal punishment, as did 69% of the culturally religious, 66% of atheists, and 65% of agnostics. A large gap separates these categories from the nonaffiliated believer group, of which only 43% said their parents used corporal punishment. It seems a "softer" parental style of correction strongly correlates with less rigid religious/secular boundaries and firmer public religious/private religiosity boundaries in adulthood. Concerning their own children, agnostics and especially atheists were the most likely to disagree with the use of corporal punishment to discipline their children, and also to feel that "praise" is more important than "discipline." Taken together, the increasing number of secular Americans and the declining rates of the use of corporal punishment by parents in the United States suggest the potential for a continued increase in religious nonaffiliation across future generations.[25]

Spouse's Religion

The most important relationship for many people is to their spouse or partner. The Pew RLS asks about the religious affiliation of respondents' spouses, and some interesting patterns emerge. First, people who have spouses who are either Protestant or Mormon are very likely to be actively religious themselves (89%). The flipside is that they are very unlikely to be atheists (0.5% and 0.6%, respectively) or agnostics (1.0% and 1.9%, respectively). Similarly, both nonaffiliated believers and the culturally religious are underrepresented. Roman Catholics' partners are actively religious at a lower rate of 83%, with almost all of the difference accounted for by an uptick in marriage to nonaffiliated believers (9%) and the culturally religious (6%). So while the partners of Catholics do not necessarily tend to have opposing belief systems, they are more likely not to self-identify as religious and less likely to engage in religious behaviors.

Looking at religious adults by specific denomination, there is little difference regarding the likelihood of marrying a secular spouse. The patterns are quite similar to the responses for what religious denomination a person was raised in, as detailed in the previous section. One exception is nondenominational Christians, who have the lowest rates of secular partners at 6%. This finding provides further evidence that the apparent weak socialization found among those raised nondenominational is the result of retrospective accounting for cultural Christianity rather than engaged nondenominational Christianity. Church of Christ and Pentecostal Christians also have low rates of secular partners at 8%. These relatively intense types of Christianity lead adherents to choose partners who tend to be relatively devout themselves. Only 0.1% of the partners of Church of Christ members are atheists and 1.2% are agnostics. Similarly, only 0.5% of the partners of nondenominational Christians are atheists or agnostics. Among Pentecostals' partners, 0.6% are atheists or agnostics. Baptists (90%), Methodists (89%), Lutherans (87%), and Presbyterians (87%) also tend to have actively religious partners. The spouses of Congregationalists, United Church of Christ members, and Episcopalians are less likely to be actively religious—about 83%—matching the patterns for these denominations' less effective religious socialization.[26]

As we would expect, those who are in significant relationships with atheists and agnostics are much less likely to be religious, but they are still actively religious at fairly high rates. Twenty-six percent of people who have atheist partners are atheists themselves, while 39% of people who have agnostic partners are agnostics. People with atheist partners are slightly more likely to be actively religious (41%) than those with agnostic partners (35%). Apparently, agnostics have a stronger tendency to group together, while atheists are more likely to interact intimately with religious partners. Atheists, almost by definition, have more at stake in religion, albeit in an antagonistic manner, and it seems that atheism may be at least partially sustained through regular interactions with those who are actively religious. In this way, the cognitive styles of atheism and active religion are more proximate than those of agnosticism and religion, even though socially and philosophically there would appear to be a larger divide between them. For those who have partners they describe religiously as "nothing in particular," there are two distinct categories. Forty-three percent of these respondents are actively religious themselves (similar to those with atheist partners) and 48% are nonaffiliated believers. So, in order, the secular categories whose members are most likely to marry spouses with the same secular outlook are nonaffiliated believers, agnostics, and atheists. This ranking also reflects the relative prevalence of each status among the general population.

Secular Peers

A final network influence on secular identity is the religious or secular composition of one's friends. In models analyzing data from the 2005 BRS, including a measure of how many of a respondent's friends were "not at all religious" substantially improved prediction of nonaffiliation, even when accounting for parents' affiliations and a person's frequency of attendance at religious services as a child. Further, the inclusion of a measure for the secularity of peer networks explained more of the variance in whether someone claimed no religion than parental nonaffiliation or childhood service attendance.[27] Peer networks also accounted for the vast majority of variance previously explained by having a father who was nonaffilitated. In other words, children of secular fathers are more likely to select secular friends, so much of the transmission between secular fathers and children occurs *indirectly through selection of secular friends.*[28]

The Faith Matters Survey we used to assess parental secular transmission also asked a question about close friendships. Of their closest friends, 80% of atheists, 75% of agnostics, and 50% of nonaffiliated believers reported having at least one close friend who is "not religious." By comparison, 44% of the culturally religious and 40% of the actively religious had at least one close friend who is not religious. Concerning familial connections, 41% of atheists, 26% of agnostics and nonaffiliated believers, and 19% of the culturally religious reported that no one in their extended family shares their religious views. This finding is corroborated by data from the 2007 BRS, which asked respondents to indicate which among a list of statuses was "most important in describing who you are." Atheists were the least likely to select "family," while the culturally religious were the most likely.[29] Taken together, the absence of agreement between individuals and their families combined with a higher probability of having secular friends indicates that peers' views may play a more important role for agnostics and especially atheists relative to other secularists; however, friendship networks clearly play an important role for all types of seculars. Further, contrary to the idea that nonbelievers have isolated social networks, nonaffiliated believers (8%) and the culturally religious (7%) were the most likely to report having no close friends at all, while atheists (4%) and agnostics (3%) look the same as the actively religious (4%) on this measure.[30]

Summary

Much of the variation in peoples' religiosity and secularity can be explained by the push and pull of their relationships with family members—particularly parent-child and marital relationships—and friends. There is a strong tendency for people to adopt and maintain the religious or secular views and habits of those around them, but there are also countervailing currents. A majority of Americans maintain religious stances the same or similar to the ones their parents instilled in them, but there are also a considerable number of people who shift away from their religious or secular socialization. In particular, there is a strong current toward religion, as exhibited by the relatively low rates of nonbelievers even among those who were brought up as atheists or agnostics.

These patterns of religious mobility demonstrate the influence of cultural forces, as many religious concepts, especially Christian and theistic, are normative in American culture. Even in a devoutly atheistic household, the pervasive presence of statements like "In God We Trust" on currency, the Pledge of Allegiance, and many other expressions of American civil religion explicitly link theism to citizenship. The normative cast of religiosity and the continuing high levels of distrust of seculars provide strong disincentives against open secularity. Conversely, religious socialization perceived as too intensive or invasive carries with it the potential to push people away from religion altogether as a reactive stance.

A less obvious force influencing secularity is the effect children have on parents. For many people, religion is not an especially salient part of their lives until they need to provide moral order for their children. This upward generational influence creates a mutually reinforcing pattern wherein children adopt the religion of their parents even as parents encounter or reencounter religion by virtue of having children. Further, the upward trends in secularity can be partly explained by shifting rates of marriage and childbearing. In a cultural context where more people wait longer to get married, have fewer children, or forsake these life events entirely, religion will be less likely to enter people's lives. In this sense, falling rates of marriage and childbirth bode well for the future of secularity. In short, familial and peer relations matter, and their influence on the transmission (or not) of religiosity or secularity is strong.

9

The (Explicit) Politics of Secularity

When a national sample of Americans was asked whether certain attributes would make them more or less likely to vote for a candidate for political office, "atheist" was the attribute that the largest percentage of respondents said would make them less likely to vote for someone (53%), more than having an extramarital affair (35%), marijuana use (22%), or never previously holding political office (52%). Even 24% of nonaffiliated respondents reported they would be less likely to vote for an atheist compared to a theist.[1] In the 112th U.S. Congress (2011–13), 57% of senators and representatives self-identified as Protestant, 29% as Catholic, and 7% as Jewish, all higher than the national averages for American adults, among whom 51% are Protestant, 24% are Catholic, and 2% are Jewish. The most pronounced difference from the American populace is the fact that there was but a single senator or representative who self-identified as secular. Pete Stark, a representative from California with four decades of service in the House, came out publicly as an atheist in 2007 at the urging of the Secular Coalition for America, but qualified that he is an active Unitarian. He lost his bid for reelection in 2012. The 113th Congress included Krysten Sinema, a new member who openly identified as having "no religion," making her the first member of Congress to do so. Sinema was raised Mormon, but left the faith.[2] She swore the oath of office using the Constitution instead of a Bible.

The sparse presence of declared seculars in government is clearly below the level of secularity among Americans in general. It follows that some senators and representatives are likely only nominally religious, culturally religious, nonaffiliated believers, or belong without believing, but because of their public position, astutely claim a religious affiliation. Some members of Congress are likely choosing the path of least political resistance so as not to alienate potential voters.[3] Openly secular politicians remain quite rare, and those who succeed in winning elections may still face strident opposition to their public service. The experiences of a city council member who considers himself "post-theist" help illustrate these trends, as well as some prominent themes in personalized narratives of secularity.

Who Shall Deny the Being of Almighty God?

Cecil Bothwell is nothing if not active. His business card lists him as a publisher, author, artist, and handyman/builder, while the biography he made public during a run for the Democratic nomination in a U.S. congressional primary stated that he also had experience in "private land-use planning and forestry, computer and large appliance repair, automotive and tractor repair, agronomy, the arts (wood, clay and paint) and alternative energy systems." On his regularly updated blog, he describes himself this way: "Born in 1950. Write for a living. Three cats. Other car a canoe. Live in Asheville, North Carolina in a fixer-upper. Very much in love. Garden. Fix up. Read. Fix up. Blog. Fix up. Rinse. Repeat." He adds that his "career includes . . . intermittent stints as a singer/songwriter and slam poet."[4] When I (Joseph) spoke to him, he was busy writing his first novel.

I met Bothwell in a hip coffee shop just outside of downtown Asheville, a bustling city with over 400,000 residents nestled in the Swannanoa River valley at the western foot of the Blue Ridge Mountains. A stroll around the city quickly reveals it as a haven of progressivism, liberalism, and alternative culture. Bookstores, coffee shops, other locally owned businesses, and the arts are plentiful. Bothwell knows the city well. He has lived in Buncombe County, of which Asheville is the county seat, for three decades, written a popular guidebook for visitors to the city, and worked as managing editor and lead correspondent for the *Mountain Xpress*, a local paper. He now sits on the city council. Interesting as these skills and accomplishments are in themselves, I wanted to talk to him about how his nonreligious views connect to his now very public life as a politician.

Bothwell publicized information during his political campaigns that presented him as raised Presbyterian and an active member of a Unitarian Universalist congregation, even though he thinks of himself as "post-theist," an interesting example of "belonging without believing."[5]

JB: I read in a newspaper story you were raised Presbyterian. Is that right?

CB: Well, sort of. I mean . . .

JB: How would you classify it?

CB: Well, Mom would have called herself a Presbyterian. Pretty much the family went to church on holidays. Dad was apparently raised Methodist, but he was openly agnostic. So I went to Presbyterian Sunday school occasionally. I think there was one year where Mom thought it was a good idea and maybe I went multiple Sundays in a row, in third grade or something, but it was pretty nominal. I mean if anybody had asked me I would have said I believed in God as a child. By the time I was in my teens I really fell out.

JB: Was your father a strong influence on your position?

CB: What he did was he made it permissible. For example, the Methodist church says the Lord's Prayer "forgive us our trespasses" and the Presbyterian church says "forgive us our debts." And so when we did go to church and we did the Lord's Prayer, Dad would very loudly say, "Forgive us our TRESPASSES." He was kind of ornery. And so one time I asked him about it. I said, "Why do you . . . ," and he said, "Well, because that was the church I grew up in, they said 'trespasses.'" And I said, "What's the difference?" And he made some kind of explanation and I said, "Well, what do you believe?" And he said, "I'd call myself an agnostic." And I said, "Whoa, that's a big word, what is that?" I don't remember the exact conversation, but he said, "I don't believe there's a God" or "I don't know." But he still went to church and he was a Scout leader and he led us in the Scout oath and stuff like that. To God and my country, etc. And so he didn't really make waves about it, but it gave me permission to think that maybe the church wasn't necessarily right about everything. At least.[6]

Bothwell's secularity, like every individual's, involves unique biographical experiences and remembrances. For instance, a clear turning point in the narrative of his nontheistic identity occurred during his Eagle Scout board of review process:

And then it really fell apart for me. . . . I think I was fourteen, I'm pretty sure I was fourteen, when I got my Eagle Scout badge. When you go, at

> least in those days, there's an Eagle board of review, and it was three adult leaders not from your troop, so they were strangers. They kind of give you a cross-examination. Dot all the I's, cross all the T's. And this one guy said, "I notice you don't have the God and Country award." And I said, "No, sir." And he said, "Well, I like to see a boy get his God and Country award before he gets his Eagle badge." And I said, "Okay." And he said, "Now, if we approve you, will you promise to get that God and Country award?" And I thought, "This asshole. It's not a requirement. I have more than enough merit badges." I had three extra already over what I needed. I had done all the requirements and he's holding this over my head. And I thought real quick, "Well, I'm not gonna *not* get this." My dad was big into Scouts. He'd been an Eagle. He wanted me to be an Eagle. So I said, "Yes sir," knowing that I was lying to him, that there wasn't a chance in the world I would go after [that badge]. And that was my break. I walked out of there an atheist. At one point I realized that I had lied to get an award that is basically supposed to be awarded to you for being totally upright and not lying—among other things. But I felt like this religionist was trying to shove it down my throat. And it really kind of popped for me that I don't believe in god. I'm not gonna pretend.

Although Bothwell flirted briefly with religion again after his senior year of high school via Campus Crusade for Christ (now Cru) because "there was a very charismatic young leader" and "it was a lot of fun and there were pretty girls there," he soon returned to atheism. He said bemusedly, "I don't know if I was saved. I was tempted to be saved." By the end of his first year of college, his disbelieving stance on theism was relatively firm. He says his ethical perspective is based on the Golden Rule, which he roots in an evolutionary, biosocial understanding of cooperation, combined with philosophical pragmatism:

> I think the Golden Rule is derived biologically. Most animals are cooperative. Even fairly aggressive carnivores are cooperative and take care of each other's young and that kind of thing. As you go up the chain the hominid apes are extremely social and inclined to take care of others in their group. I think it's because it works. And so moving from that, I think most other ways of treating the world seem to emanate from that.

He believes that secularists' commitment to science is what makes their voice needed in public discourse. Further, he says that "better educated people tend to be more skeptical, and I think science is moving god further and further off the map. What's left to explain?" In spite of grounding his nontheism in scientism, he is ambivalent about the aggressive tactics of some of the figureheads of the "New Atheist" movement. Asked if there are specific thinkers or movements he has looked to for inspiration regarding ethics and worldview, he said:

CB: I read widely, but I don't necessarily credit any one authority. I mean I've read all the New Atheists. Dawkins and Hitchens and . . .

JB: What are your thoughts on that? Do you think it's a good thing for secularism or not?

CB: I think it's interesting, but especially Hitchens is so caustic at times. You know, I don't know if it's good or bad. He was so . . . sort of evangelical about it. . . . I mean it's fun to read. *God Is Not Great* was a really good look at some of the damage that Christian religion has done, or religions more broadly. Dawkins of course comes at it from a more scientific angle having been a scientist first. He's a debunker. Vonnegut was a big influence in my teens and of course he's decidedly humanist. His message over and over again was to be kind to each other. Chomsky appeals to me, but that's more political than spiritual.

Although skeptical about theism, Bothwell is an active member of his congregation.

JB: I've seen some things where you say that congregational involvement is important. Given your stance on theism, why?

CB: It's often good and I think it is one of the only institutions in most communities that provides solace when people die. It provides ceremony for when people wanna get married, or rites of passage. You know for Jewish people Bat Mitzvah or Bar Mitzvah are important for coming of age. At the UU church we have a coming of age program the year when they're sixteen. It's more like learning to be involved, that kind of stuff. All those things are good effects. The

> homelessness work we do, other kinds of charity. Working in the jails. All of it is organized often under the auspices of church.

Later on, he told an insightful story about a prison "ministry" he initiated and continues to maintain. In one of his many books, Bothwell detailed abuses of power perpetrated by Bobby Lee Medford, a corrupt sheriff in Buncombe County who was ultimately convicted of extortion, bribery, and money laundering for coordinating an illegal gambling ring.[7] As part of his investigative reporting, Bothwell tried to gain access to the local jail.

> We had unexplained deaths occurring in the jail and there were allegations leaking out that there was abuse going on. I tried to get in there as a reporter and they said, "No, you can't come in here." But I set up a church ministry with my UU church, and they let jail ministries in. Churches are allowed. So I've been going into the jail for about six years now.

In spite of his congregational involvement and extensive charity and social justice work, Bothwell's personal views on theism became a political issue when he published *Prince of War: Billy Graham's Crusade for a Wholly Christian Empire*, a critical biography of the Christian folk hero. The book portrays Graham as a shrewd, political man who acted as a war hawk in his long-running role as presidential counsel. The book was indeed a bold statement, especially considering Graham is from and resides in North Carolina and has made Gallup's top ten list of most admired men an astounding fifty-five times since 1955.[8] In the postscript of the book, Bothwell stated, "I suppose I should acknowledge my understanding that I will find myself labeled as Satan's helper, instrument, vehicle and whole lot more upon publication of this work. So, for the record, I don't believe in supernatural beings of any stripe and I happily acknowledge that I could be wrong."[9] His premonition that he would be publicly attacked was unsurprisingly accurate, especially once he entered politics.

In the end, Bothwell's risky critique of Graham inadvertently led to his first political foray. Asked if he experienced any negative reaction to the book, he replied:

CB: Very little. Here and there. Although I did get fired from the *Mountain Xpress.*

JB: Really?

CB: Yeah. I was fired two weeks before the book was released. And I have to think that it was advertiser pressure. . . . It was weird. I was furious for a week or so. And I calculated my output and I had published more than twice as many words as any other writer at the paper in the last year. I'd won awards for the paper. When there was an event, I would be sent to represent the paper. For two years running I won a reader poll for best reporter. The second year I got it, I won it on a Wednesday. Friday I was called into the publisher's office and told to pack up my stuff, I was out of there.

JB: That's a pretty serious negative consequence.

CB: I was never told that that was it. I don't know. It changed my life, among other things. A few months later . . . I'd always thought, when I covered meetings for local government, I thought, "Damn, I could do better." A few months later, I ran for county commission and lost by .8% to a twenty-year incumbent. After that, I was fed up with fundraising and campaigning. I didn't enjoy it. But later that summer a friend, who's a number cruncher, said, "Man you killed 'em in the city. You lost outside." That kind of worked on my head, so a year later I ran and won for city council.

During the campaign for council, Bothwell's theistic disbelief and claims about Graham were used to question his morality, as well as that of anyone who would vote for him.

CB: During the election campaign a direct mail piece went to, we think possibly 30,000 people. We've tried to guess from what we can figure about the spread. And it accused me of being an atheist. And said Asheville was going to hell if it elected me.

JB: OK. Was that how it was characterized?

CB: Yeah, it was that kind of thing. And then a second piece came out from the same people. The second direct mail said that I had said that Billy Graham was a follower of Adolf Hitler. Or that he was influenced by Adolf Hitler. And those letters probably made a differ-

> ence because I finished first in the primary out of ten, and we have an open primary; but I finished third in the general. And I don't doubt that those letters had an effect in cutting down my vote total. But there were three seats so I still got a seat.

Bothwell did not let the accusations later stand in the way of working with the source of the negative ads. He says, "We know who funded it and everything. He's actually an ally of mine on a different issue, now three years later. Politics—strange bedfellows . . ."

After he was elected to the city council in 2009, Bothwell made national news after he declined to take the standard oath of office that involves swearing on a Bible and concludes with the words "So help me God." Instead, he gave his "solemn affirmation." Some political muckrakers soon threatened to sue for his removal because, they argued, as an open atheist, Bothwell was not allowed to hold public office under the North Carolina constitution. The precise wording of the constitution states that those "who shall deny the being of Almighty God" are disqualified from serving public office. Of course, Article VI of the U.S. Constitution declares, "no religious test shall ever be required as a qualification to any office or public trust under the United States." Jurisprudence based on interpretations of the First and Fourteenth amendments has ruled similar laws in other states unconstitutional, making the North Carolina requirement effectively unenforceable.[10] The Associated Press ran a story on the dispute that was picked up by outlets such as the *New York Times* and *USA Today*. MSNBC's *Rachel Maddow Show* aired a segment on the story, while Fox News conducted a poll that asked viewers whether Bothwell should have to give up his seat—75% of those who responded to the conservative network's poll said "no." In the wake of all this attention, Bothwell was transformed into a secularist hero.

When asked how he felt about this transition, he said:

> It was awkward. Because the truth of the matter is that I didn't think religion had any bearing on my running for office. I don't think it has any bearing on life, frankly. For people who find comfort in it, that's great and I'm happy for them. I don't dispute that they shouldn't feel comfort. And for all I know they may be right. When the press came to me during this flap and they said, "Are you an atheist?" And I said, "Really I think of myself as post-

> theist." That was the term I came up with, because in my life I've really not felt much need for a god explanation. I was born in 1950 and by that point we had sorted out the theory of evolution, Darwin and so forth. We sorted out the atomic level pretty thoroughly—although there was the [Higgs] boson they just finally found—but we had a pretty good sense of how things started, that the Big Bang occurred. It didn't seem to me there was any room left. So I didn't think of it. To me the question of god is not a relevant question. And when they made a big deal about it, it was like, "Oh . . ." And then when the atheists made me the "most courageous elected official in 2010," I was like, I haven't done anything courageous. I got elected. And I affirmed. They said, "Do you promise?" and I affirmed.

The effect on Bothwell of the heightened attention has been generally positive. Since he primarily makes his living by writing and publishing, the higher book sales that resulted from the publicity in 2009 were certainly welcome. He has also become a sought-after speaker for various secular groups and functions, allowing him to disseminate his political ideas to a wider audience, and increasing book sales even more.

Meanwhile, on the council, his election along with other non-Christians resulted in a perceptible change of organizational culture, exemplified by the reading of an invocation that begins each meeting. Asked whether his nontheism was an issue once he was on the council, he said:

> Well it has definitely changed at least one major aspect of the council. A couple years before I got on council there came the issue of ministers doing an invocation before each council meeting. Other municipalities had gotten in trouble for that. So they switched to where each of the council members in turn does the invocation. So when I got elected, at the same time a Jewish woman got elected. This was a big shift because it had pretty well been a Christian organization. Since then, she tends to do invocations written by her father, who is an educator and kind of a poet, so she leans on him. I give decidedly nontheist exhortations. And then a guy who just left council last fall who's married to a Presbyterian minister, although I don't know what he professes, he would almost always quote Jewish rabbis in his invocations. Another guy elected when I was elected is quietly atheist and refuses to give invocations. And then this

> last election two more UUs were elected. So there's now three UUs on city council. We're the majority religion! Anyway, they both tend to give fairly secular talks. The mayor and another long-time council member are straightforward Christians. They, and they never used to say this, they now say, "If you'd like to bow your head . . . ," instead of "let us bow." *So there's not the assumption anymore.*[11]

Cecil Bothwell's experiences highlight a number of cultural themes in American secularism. His nominal religious socialization and the influence of his theistically doubting father are apparent. His articulation of a metanarrative relying heavily on rhetorical references to science and pointing to the influence of higher education on his thinking are also reflective of broader trends. His experiences in politics provide situational examples of the public's distrust of atheists and the potential personal liabilities of being critical of mainstream religion. At the same time, his story shows that public acceptance of secularity is growing to the extent that a theistic disbeliever can win a general election, at least in certain areas. His experiences also contain the unique biographical moments that personalize broader narratives of secularity. Other secularists cannot cite an Eagle Scout board of review as a critical turning point, or recount the experience of being fired from a job where they thrived because of publishing a negative book about a beloved religious icon, but all will have their own personally notable experiences recognized as turning points in their identity narratives.

One of the most important themes that emerged in our discussion with Bothwell is how secularist positions represent assertive belief systems that influence one's perception of "the way the world works," and therefore how it should be approached through practical action. When asked whether his nontheism affected his political views or the subjects he addressed in his public role, Bothwell said succinctly:

> Yes, it does. I think this is it. I think that the only time we ever have to do good is now. I don't think I'm coming around again to have another shot at it or anything. I think that we need to take care of the people we love and the people in our community, and that we have to do it now. There's no putting it off or praying for a better outcome. There's doing it or not doing it. It has made me feel committed to action.

He further discussed positions on specific issues he sees as growing out of his secular understanding of the world and society. For instance, his identity as a humanist leads him to work for affordable housing and wider access to health care, while his view that climate change will have catastrophic consequences in the future, which he bases on scientific projections, leads him to push for public transit, energy conservation, and local food sourcing. One thing is clear after talking with this affable jack-of-all-trades: in spite of the problems he sees, his view of the world is hardly despairing, but rather one that emphasizes persistent activity and service, regardless of whether you agree with his political and philosophical positions or think he is a "radical" whose "extremism doesn't just stop with bashing religion and the Reverend Graham."[12]

Political Views of American Seculars

We now turn to how political perspectives vary among secular Americans, which affords a richer understanding of what it means to be nonreligious in particular ways, and also how one's cosmic belief system shapes views of government and society. In the contemporary U.S., religious and political views are often conflated, with the assumption that a religious affiliation or tradition relates directly to particular political views and party affiliations, but there is great variation among different types of religious individuals and nuanced relationships between religious and political views. In the same way that all Protestants are not the same when it comes to politics, so too we should not be too quick to assume that all secular Americans will share a particular view or political identity.[13] Regarding political outlook, we are interested not just in political party identification, but also how people understand the role of government, decide which candidate to vote for, and generally think about the governing institutions of society.

View of Government

In the Pew RLS, atheists and agnostics tended to be especially dissatisfied with the perceived direction of the United States, with only 25% and 23% respectively saying they were satisfied with "the way things are going." In contrast, the culturally religious and nonaffiliated believers were very similar to actively religious Americans. Majorities in all categories were dissatisfied, ranging from around 70% for actively religious Americans to 77% for agnostics. The degree of satisfaction or dissatisfaction further elaborates these patterns. Forty-nine percent of atheists and over half of agnostics were "very dissatisfied" with the country's direction, while actively religious Americans, the culturally religious, and nonaffiliated believers had similar, lower levels of dissatisfaction, with values ranging from 40–43% "very dissatisfied" and 29–30% "somewhat dissatisfied."[14] The sources of these dissatisfactions, however, vary substantially depending on the category in question. When asked whether the political system was working, all secular respondents were more likely to be "very dissatisfied" than actively religious Americans were. It is worth remembering that this sample was collected in 2007, a time of unpopular foreign wars, a president who regularly used religious rhetoric for their justification, and a population of seculars who were more likely to be opposed to those wars than actively religious Americans.[15]

A commonly held assumption about the religiously nonaffiliated is that they are anti-institutional, and that the choice to avoid religious organizations signals a lack of support for other public organizations. However, there is little evidence that secularists are opposed to institutions in principle. When forced to choose between a preference for a larger government with more services and a smaller government with fewer services, Americans overall were almost evenly split, with 46% selecting smaller government. Agnostics were slightly above the national average in preferring a smaller government (50%), but the same percentage of atheists and the actively and culturally religious reported wanting a smaller government (46%). Nonaffiliated believers were the least likely to support having a smaller government (41%). In contrast to the historically perceived link between secularism and socialism, there is no clear "secularist" stance on bigger or smaller government distinguishable from that of the actively religious.

Regarding government involvement in domestic issues, all types of Americans thought there should be more of a welfare safety net. Nearly uniform percentages of Americans across all categories thought the government can and should do more to help the needy. Sixty-nine percent of nonaffiliated believers thought the government should help more, similar to the 67% of atheists and 66% of the culturally religious. The actively religious (64%) and agnostics (63%) supported government assistance for the needy at similar, slightly lower rates. But differences are evident on other issues that members of each category thought the government should be involved in. One example is environmental policy. Actively religious people (63%) were the least likely to agree that stricter environmental laws are worth the loss of (hypothetical) jobs, and the culturally religious (64%) were not much different. Nonaffiliated believers (68%) occupied a middle ground, while atheists (77%) and agnostics (79%) were the most likely to favor environmentalist social policies.[16]

The ordering of the categories was almost identical concerning whether people favored diplomacy over military strength as a means of ensuring peace, with secularists more likely to favor diplomacy. Actively religious respondents (59%) and the culturally religious (63%) were the least likely to prefer diplomacy, nonaffiliated believers were in the middle (68%), and atheists (72%) and agnostics (74%) were the most likely. Only 35% of Americans thought the military is the best means to ensure peace *and* that there should be stricter environmental rules, or that diplomacy is the best choice *and* that environmental protections would "cost too many jobs," so these two policy questions clearly do not measure the same underlying issue, but they do provide insight into how secularists see the world, with distinct patterns for the type of government involvement desired in both environmental issues and foreign conflicts. When asked about an interventionist or isolationist foreign policy, atheists (43%) and agnostics (42%) were more likely than actively religious respondents (37%) to think the U.S. should pay more attention to problems overseas, while the culturally religious (35%) and especially nonaffiliated believers (30%) were less likely to favor interventionist efforts. Combining these results with the question about military action versus diplomacy, nontheists were the most likely to favor a policy of "active diplomacy" internationally.

Overall, it is opposition to specific practices of government, rather than institutions in general, that concerns American secularists, as there are ways they want to see government play a more active social role. While most secular Americans tend to oppose religious institutions, they are not opposed to the idea of government. At the same time, they are hardly the stereotypical secular socialists of yesteryear. Rather, many would like to see the government play an expanded role on issues they care about, such as the environment, while they oppose government intervention in other areas, such as foreign wars. Like most Americans, secularists resent government when it goes against their beliefs, but support it when it promotes their values. There is no overriding anti-institutional bent among secularists, only a slant toward holding progressive views and wanting a political system that supports the same. What then are the sources of secularists' dissatisfaction with the government's role in citizens' lives? Asked whether the government should be involved in "issues of morality," secularist respondents to the Pew RLS overwhelmingly thought the government should be less involved. Eighty-five percent of agnostics, 77% of atheists, 67% of the culturally religious, and 63% of nonaffiliated believers thought the government was "too involved" in issues of "morality," compared to half of actively religious respondents. Issues of "morality" are often interpreted as dealing with sexual politics, and secular Americans want less governmental involvement in such areas.[17]

Attitudes about Gender and Sexuality

Two of the most contentious issues that concern how morality and government intersect in the contemporary U.S. are homosexuality and abortion. Pooling data from the GSS from 2006 to 2010 allows us to assess how secular statuses relate to views of sexual politics. Secularists are much more likely to think homosexuality should be socially acceptable. Regarding the view that same sex relations are "not wrong at all," agnostics are the most accepting of homosexuality (69%), followed by atheists (64%), nonaffiliated believers (58%), and the culturally religious (55%). There is far less acceptance among the actively religious (35%). The same pattern exists regarding the view that same sex marriage should be legal. On an issue of sexual morality such as homosexuality, Americans likely think of government involvement in restrictive, rather than supportive ways, because in the past that has been the most common form of legal involvement in the matter.[18] Should governmental involvement in same-sex partnerships become more supportive, as is the case in an increasing number of states, a different set of assumptions about the government's role in issues of sexual politics may take hold, and most secularists would likely become more supportive of such governmental involvement.

Similarly, seculars are far more permissive in their views of abortion. Just over one third (36%) of actively religious Americans think abortion should be allowed for "any reason," compared to 53% of the culturally religious, 58% of nonaffiliated believers, and 70% of atheists and agnostics. Again, nonaffiliated believers and the culturally religious occupy a territory between actively religious respondents and atheists and agnostics. Not identifying with an organized religion or not engaging in standard religious behaviors correlates with a steady transition away from the political views of religiously engaged and affiliated people, but not to the same extent as rejecting or persistently doubting theism. There is greater uniformity of opinion among different types of secularists on allowing abortion in cases of rape. Only 6% of agnostics, 8% of atheists and the culturally religious, and 11% of nonaffiliated believers think abortion should be illegal in cases of rape, compared to 27% of those who are actively religious.

Other issues of sexual politics exhibit similar divisions between actively religious and secular Americans. For example, over 70% of atheists, agnostics, and nonaffiliated believers think birth control should be made available to teenagers, compared to 50% of those who are actively religious. Similarly, a sharp divide exists in views about the morality of premarital sex, with over 70% of the respondents in the four secular categories stating that it is "not at all wrong," in contrast to 41% of the actively religious. Regarding censorship of pornography, 42% of the actively religious say porn should be made illegal, compared to less than 22% for each of the secular categories.

Differences between religious and secular individuals are also apparent in general views of gender roles, evidenced by varying levels of agreement with statements about gender and social roles such as "women are not suited for politics," "men should work, women should stay home," and "preschool children are hurt if their mother works outside the home." Agnostics hold the most egalitarian views of gender, followed by atheists, nonaffiliated believers, and the culturally religious, while actively religious Americans show the highest levels of gender traditionalism. A consistent pattern emerges, with agnostics the most liberal on issues ranging from environmentalism and diplomacy to matters of sexual politics and women working, followed by atheists, nonaffiliated believers, and the culturally religious. It is over matters of sexuality and gender that political differences between actively religious and secular Americans are most evident.

Political Identity and Voting

Looking at political identity in the 2007 Pew RLS across the four secular categories, there was a strong tendency among seculars to self-identify as more liberal than the average American. This tendency was most pronounced among atheists, 24% of whom considered themselves "very liberal." Almost half of atheists in the United States self-identified as liberal, one in three were moderate, and only about three in twenty were conservative. Agnostics, the culturally religious, and nonaffiliated believers showed a similar trend, but with a stronger propensity to select the moderate label. Thirty-eight percent of actively religious Americans were politically moderate, similar to the 40% of agnostics, 41% of the culturally religious, and 44% of nonaffiliated believers; but only 18% of actively religious Americans self-identified as liberal, while this was true of 32% of the culturally religious, 33% of nonaffiliated believers, and 45% of agnostics.

Considering the divergence on issues of gender and sexuality previously outlined, it is clear where secular respondents hold views typically considered more "liberal" than actively religious Americans. Similar views on the role of government in the economy keep religious and secular Americans from being even more pronouncedly different. There is also a visible gradation of political views by type of secularity. The group we have characterized as the most secular on average, atheists, shows the highest rate of liberal or very liberal self-identification and the lowest rate of conservative or very conservative identity. Agnostics are the next most likely to be liberal and the next least likely to be conservative. The rates at which nonaffiliated believers and the culturally religious hold liberal views are similar to each other and also above the national average, but not as high as those of atheists and agnostics.

An alternative way to look at political identification is through party affiliation. Even more definitive distinctions are evident in Pew RLS respondents' self-descriptions as Republicans, Democrats, or independents. Just as many secularists remain independent of religious organizations, the most common choice for secular Americans is to remain

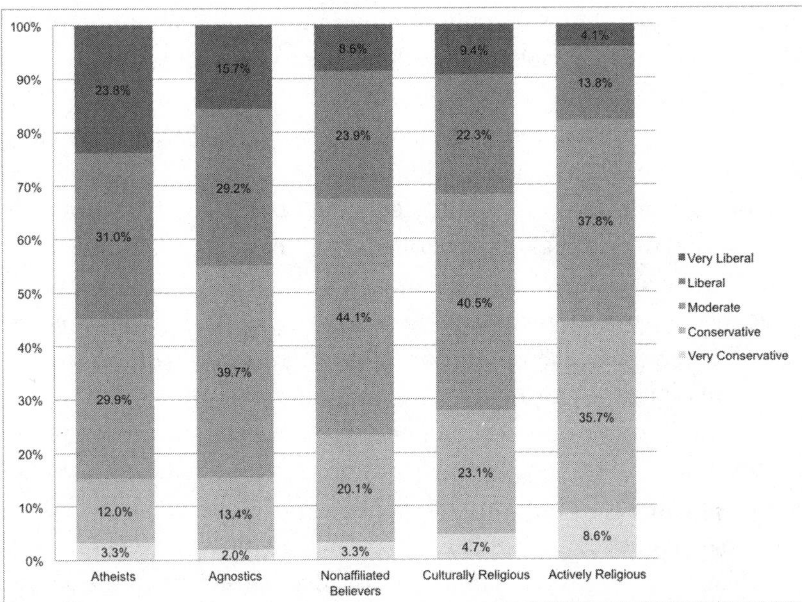

Figure 9.1. Political Identity by Secular Category, 2007

independent of political party affiliations. While 30% of actively religious Americans in the survey identified as politically independent, this was true of 37% of the culturally religious, 45% of nonaffiliated believers, 46% of atheists, and 51% of agnostics. The choice to not claim an affiliation is mirrored in politics and religion, with the nonaffiliated and nonbelievers more likely to claim independence than those who are culturally or actively religious. There is a distinct tendency for secular respondents *not* to be Republicans, if they affiliate with a party. Avoidance of the GOP was most prominent among atheists and agnostics, among whom only 11% and 12% were Republicans, respectively. Fifteen percent of nonaffiliated believers and 21% of the culturally religious were Republicans. Among actively religious Americans, 30% self-identified as Republicans. So while it is most common for all types of secular Americans to see themselves as politically independent, those who did choose a position in 2007 overwhelmingly sided against the Republican Party.

We can distinguish these patterns further by looking at which party secularists pick when forced to make a choice, as they typically are in elections since the U.S. maintains a winner-take-all system. Respondents who self-identified as politically independent were subsequently asked which party they leaned toward. Secular Americans overwhelmingly selected Democrat when forced to choose. Among atheists, this was true of 77% of independents, as it was for 74% of the culturally religious, 72% of agnostics, and 68% of nonaffiliated believers, while it was the case for 57% of actively religious Americans. For many secular Americans, identification as politically independent appears to be more about issues of identity construction and management coupled with political alienation than any particular opposition to the liberal policies of Democrats, which are more likely to align with their political views.

It is one thing to have certain political views, but another to act on them. Looking at one of the most common political behaviors, voting in a presidential election, members of each of the secular categories other than agnostics are less likely to participate than actively religious Americans are. Just as secularists are less likely to engage in the voluntary behavior of going to a church, synagogue, mosque, or temple, so too they are less likely to enter the voting booth. Not voting is especially common for the culturally religious, less than 60% of whom reported voting in the most recent presidential election in 2012. Nonaffiliated believers had relatively low levels of voting as well, with 63% reporting they voted, while 67% of atheists reported voting. Agnostics and the actively religious voted at similar reported rates of 75%. Of the different secular groups, nonaffiliated believers and the culturally religious again are the least likely to be institutionally engaged.[19]

Looking more closely at different types of secularity and voting in presidential elections in the GSS shows the same patterns that are present in the Pew RLS. Taking the general category of all those who are not religiously affiliated across all years of the GSS, we find a consistent 10% gap in voting in presidential elections between religious nones and the religiously affiliated. The smallest gap (6%) occurred in the 1978 presidential election, while the largest gap (14%) occurred in the 1988 election. Pooling data on questions about the 1984 through 2008 presidential elections for the waves of the GSS with the questions used to classify secularists into our typology, 73% of eligible, actively religious respondents voted. The percentage was the same for agnostics. Sixty-nine percent of atheists voted, as did 63% of the culturally religious and

60% of nonaffiliated believers. Combined with the data about political affiliation and views, this information on voting at least partially explains why the overwhelmingly liberal leanings of secularists do not show up in law or policy. Collectively, they do not vote with enough frequency to exert an influence on who is elected to office that reflects their share of the voting population.

The 2004 presidential election provides a useful example of recent voting patterns based on religion and secularity. Of culturally and actively religious respondents, 43% said they voted for Democratic nominee John Kerry. Among conservative Protestants, George W. Bush won nearly 80% of the vote, while he split mainline Protestants and white Catholics at around 50%. Bush lost among Hispanic Catholics, seculars, Jews, black Protestants, and non-Judeo-Christian traditions. Fifty-nine percent of atheists, 67% of agnostics, and 63% of nonaffiliated believers voted for Kerry. Secular Americans were also slightly more likely than religious Americans to vote for a third-party candidate. Atheists were the most likely to vote for Ralph Nader, which is why the proportion voting for Kerry was not higher. If it made sense, perhaps more secularists would choose a third-party candidate for president, but in a winner-take-all system, such options are not electorally viable, so many simply do not vote.

Collectively, these voting patterns provide further evidence that self-identification as politically independent is a symbolic statement of political autonomy rather than a reflection of a moderate stance on political issues. For many secularists, the choice of Kerry over Bush reflected their liberal views in spite of their pronounced political independence. Low secular turnout hurt John Kerry, especially in swing states, many of which had same-sex marriage ballot initiatives that helped mobilize the faithful. Ultimately, religion played a critical role in the 2004 election, especially the voting of religious traditionalists for George W. Bush.[20] This realignment of religion and politics to a conservative religious/liberal secular dynamic with more mainline religious individuals split between Republican and Democrat is a relatively recent and consequential development.

One way of thinking about the overlay of political and religious views is to focus not on differences in particular attitudes, liberal or conservative identities, Republican or Democrat affiliations, but on whether these matters are part of a person's everyday life. When asked whether they follow government and public affairs, a very interesting difference among secular respondents appears. Both atheists (62%) and agnostics (63%) report paying attention "most of the time," compared to 53% of actively religious respondents. Both nonaffiliated believers (46%) and the culturally religious (48%) have lower rates of cognitive engagement with political matters. A similar pattern is present for reading news about politics, and interest in international affairs. The more secular individuals are, the greater the likelihood they report being interested in politics and public affairs. Forty-six percent of atheists and 40% of agnostics say they are "very interested" in public affairs, compared to 26% of nonaffiliated believers, 22% of those who are actively religious, and 18% of the culturally religious. These differences reflect varying average levels of education among different types of secularists. Overall, nonaffiliated believers and the culturally religious are not only disengaged from religious social life, but they are also less likely to be engaged in political affairs. In contrast, atheists and agnostics tend to direct substantial energy and attention toward government and politics, in spite of the fact that they are almost completely unrepresented by openly secular politicians. This engagement can be seen by examining recent developments in nonprofit, nontheist organizations. Brief profiles of three prominent nonprofit secular organizations show the growth of organized secularism in recent years.

Growth in Organized Secular Groups

American Humanist Association

Founded in 1941, the American Humanist Association (AHA) has become a central organized secular group in the United States. Although it has been around for a (relatively) long time, the AHA has undergone considerable growth and change in recent years. We spoke with Roy Speckhardt, the current executive director, about how the organization has changed. For many decades, the focus of AHA was on publishing its magazine *The Humanist*, and also on organizing an annual conference. In recent years, however, the group has devoted more time and resources to public advocacy, legal action, and establishing a web presence. Speckhardt said that where 90% of the budget used to go toward the magazine and conference, the ratio is now flipped, so that about 10% of the budget goes toward these efforts, while 90% goes toward advocacy, which takes a variety of forms. Much of the change in strategy revolves around establishing a more media savvy operation, with a strong presence on the internet, but also in other media forums such as television and radio. Speckhardt noted that in the past, humanist groups had almost no access to mainstream media, whereas today they regularly have representatives taking part in various media forums.

In 2001, the organization counted less than 5,000 donors, while in 2013 it had 28,000. Some of this reflects more people giving small donations, but it nonetheless indicates considerable growth. AHA's budget for 2012 was $2,143,370. Going forward, Speckhardt sees the primary goal of AHA as overcoming the stigma of nontheism, then switching to more policy-oriented projects. That is, to the extent that identity politics can be successful, AHA hopes to transition to the model of European organized humanist groups by focusing on issues such as public education, charity, and nonviolence.

American Atheists

American Atheists (AA) was founded in 1963 by Madalyn Murray O'Hair, in the wake of the Supreme Court's decision against mandated Bible reading in *Abingdon School District v. Schempp* (merged with *Murray v. Curlett*). The stated goals of AA are securing the "civil rights of non-believers" and the separation of church and state. O'Hair remained the iconoclastic leader and primary spokesperson for the organization until her abduction and murder in 1995. After O'Hair's death, the group moved from a primary focus on legal challenges to a broader strategy incorporating more forms of activism and media outreach. For instance, in 2002 AA helped organize the Godless American March on Washington, and in 2005, it created the Godless Americans Political Action Committee, which endorses political candidates based on their views on issues of church/state separation.[21] Like AHA, AA has continued to expand its media outreach into new forums in recent years, particularly through the internet. In 2014 the organization launched Atheist TV, an internet television channel streaming a variety of content related to atheism. AA's budget for 2011 was $1,757,542.

Secular Student Alliance

The Secular Student Alliance (SSA) was founded in 2000 as an umbrella organization for connecting atheist, agnostic, and humanist student groups on college campuses, and has since expanded to include high school secular groups. Its stated mission is to "promote the ideals of scientific inquiry, democracy, secularism, and human-based ethics." The number of student groups affiliated with SSA has grown rapidly, expanding from 43 groups in 2004, to 195 groups in 2009, up to 325 by 2014.[22] Along with the number of affiliated groups, SSA's budget has also increased dramatically in recent years, going from $118,432 in 2009 to $968,618 in 2012. Part of this growth reflects an effort to organize students on high school campuses in addition to colleges.

Although SSA is nonpartisan on many issues—for example, it explicitly refrains from taking policy positions on economic matters—it does focus on civil rights for minorities, and, like all organized secular groups, the separation of church and state. Director August Brunsman IV noted:

> We are in favor of marriage equality and many of our groups have done activism for LGBT equality in a lot of ways. Some of our groups are known for being very trans friendly. I actually had a conversation with a young trans woman at our conference this summer who is a member of one of our groups at a large state school. She said that she actually found the members of her SSA group on her campus were more at ease with her being trans than the members of the major LGBT group.[23]

SSA is also following a program model from the LGBT community by offering SafeZone sessions on campus to train staff to be "people that young students who either identify as secular or who are questioning their faith can talk with. The mandate of the allies is not to convert or change any student's mind. They are simply there to be supportive and let the students know that there is nothing wrong with them for doubting." In addition to acting as an organizing platform for smaller groups, SSA is connected to many other secular organizations such as AA, AHA, and Hispanic American Freethinkers, all of which are voting organizations of the Secular Coalition for America.

"Ripe Time for Political Action"

Lori Lipman Brown is a lawyer, teacher, former state senator, and founding director of the Secular Coalition for America (SCA), a 501(c)(4) organization that lobbies Congress on behalf of numerous 501(c)(3) nonprofit organizations representing nontheists, secularists, and freethinkers. As the first federal lobbying organization representing secular interests, Lipman Brown's work with the SCA offers an interesting vantage point for understanding changes to American secularism in recent years, particularly regarding politics and culture. Her work for SCA from 2005 to 2009 meant being a public spokesperson for secularism, not only in the halls of power, but also in a diverse array of other forums including television, where she was interviewed on both the *O'Reilly Factor* and its satirical doppelganger *The Colbert Report.* I (Joseph) spoke with her about her personal secular/religious identity, experiences in public office and as a lobbyist, identity politics movements based on nontheism, and matters of church/state separation.

JB: How would describe yourself in terms of a religious or secular identity? What words or what label would you put on it?

LLB: Generally I would say I'm a humanistic Jew who's an atheist. And that's not necessarily the most accurate way to say it, because the "who's an atheist" part doesn't really matter in that context. But the reason I add it is because that particular label is the one that has been denigrated. And people have been harmed when they identify as atheist. So, as with any oppressed minority, I'm going to make sure that I'm using the term that needs to be regained. Atheist just means, what it really is, I'm a-god, non-god. In any event, what I really am is a humanistic Jew. The humanist part means I don't have supernatural beliefs, but I have ethical standards and life philosophy that I live by. And Jewishness is more my culture.

In addition to Jewish culture, Lipman Brown has also participated in Unitarian traditions, both as a child and for a time, as an adult.

LLB: My family has been members of Unitarian Universalist congregations for many years. Mostly because there weren't any humanistic

Judaism ones where we lived in Nevada. My spouse and I got very involved with the social justice work of homeless projects and such at the Nevada UU congregation.

JB: How would you characterize the influence of your parents on your secular or religious identity?

LLB: Most people, including religious people, turn out the way they are raised. We went to a Reform Jewish temple when I was younger. And so the children went to Sunday school, Hebrew school. So at one point I actually knew how to read and write in Hebrew, but unfortunately I don't remember much of that. But we also, every week, learned all the Bible stories and it was theistic. When I was about ten, my family got very involved in the Unitarian Church in Hollis, New York, because of all of the civil rights work they were doing. So then we went to their Sunday school. And they had more teaching about *all* the world's religions, which was rather interesting too. By the time I was a teenager, my parents, and actually the whole family, wasn't really thinking of god as a real entity or anything, just that we had these traditions, and we had this culture.

In 1992, Lipman Brown campaigned for and was elected as a state senator in Nevada. Prior to and during her reelection bid in 1994, she endured a smear campaign by Republican challenger Kathy Augustine, which focused on portraying Lipman Brown as an unpatriotic outsider by directly linking Christianity to patriotism, and by contrast portraying non-Christians as un-American:

> The assemblywoman who was already planning to run for my senate seat had set it up, because I was the only Jew in the state senate, that when the lieutenant governor was out of town, and they had their own person running the senate, that they would have someone come in and pray to Christ every day. So that it would become real obvious by my response that I was a Jew in the senate. So by doing that for two weeks, they did get me to step outside and come in after the prayer, for the Pledge of Allegiance part, from the back of the room. Y'know, don't wanna walk across the room during the pledge, right? And then when I started running for reelection they did some polling. Friends were calling me saying, "I just got a call." This is what they asked: "If someone told you that Lori

Lipman Brown refused to pray in the state senate, would you vote for her?" And then they asked, "If someone told you that Lori Lipman Brown refused to pledge allegiance to the flag, would you vote for her?" And, I said to my campaign manager, this is just a week before the election, "You know, we're fighting on the issues, and she's terrible on the issues for this particular district, do we really even have to say anything about this? I mean who cares whether I prayed. Or didn't pray. Or pledged or didn't pledge." I had a 100% voting record for veterans, and there were tons of veterans in my district. So my campaign folks said, "Let's do a tiny little poll of our own and see if it matters." And 50%, this was in 1994, 50% of the Democrats in my district—I'm a Democrat—said they would not vote for me if someone told them that I refused to pledge allegiance to the flag. The lie about the pledge of allegiance really got them. But they said, "Brown doesn't pray or take part in the traditional prayer," and they made it sound like every day I just wouldn't pray with them, even when they were nonsectarian, which wasn't true. But they followed this with, "We don't understand why she turned her back on the flag and refused to say the pledge." And they just made that whole thing up.

At times, Augustine's campaign also made (thinly) veiled references to Judaism by referring to Lipman Brown as a "New Yorker" or a "New York banker," despite her having lived in Nevada longer than Augustine:

So, by pointing out that, "Oh, she's Jewish, that must be why she's not a patriot," it had an effect. Because of the little poll we had done, I got out there, on TV, a couple of days before the election and said, "No, it's not true." And I had the Jewish war veterans behind me. And said, "I proudly say the pledge," etc., etc. And the day before the election, they sent everyone a letter—and this was before the time of early voting—signed by three state senators who said, "She's lying to you, we saw her turn her back on the pledge. Every day she refused to pledge allegiance." And, "She wouldn't take part in the traditional prayers." So when it came time to vote, 8,000 people who showed up to vote in other races in my district didn't vote for either of us, and I lost by less than 2,000 votes. And I think if I were in that district, hearing what I heard at that point, I probably would have been one of those 8,000 people, because I would not have been able to vote for my opponent because of her stance on everything

> and her record, but I also couldn't vote for someone who I thought had just lied to me.[24]

Interestingly, the negative campaign focused on Lipman Brown's Jewish identity rather than nontheism:

> Even though I was a member of some humanist groups, I don't think they even knew what a humanist was. If they knew I was an atheist that would have been the big issue, but at the time nobody asked about that part of belief systems. That was like, not even on the table. Back then it was anti-Semitism.

Afterward, Lipman had a heightened sense of her Jewish identity, both personally and communally:

> As a result of that attack—there's a couple of things you can do when someone attacks you for being a Jew. You can start trying to blend in more and pretend there's not much Jewishness to you, one response. Or you can get really, *really* heavily involved in the Jewish community and say, "I have nothing to be ashamed of. I am who I am and there's no problem with who I am." And so, after that we joined a Reconstructionist synagogue, Valley Outreach Synagogue, that was very social justice activism oriented. I did fundraising work for Hadassah and the Women's American ORT. I just got really heavily involved in the local Nevada Jewish community. Y'know, even the different kind of Jew that I am, when I was attacked, all the rabbis, including the Orthodox one, who knew I was nontheistic, said, "Doesn't matter. We're supporting her. That shouldn't be a reason to attack somebody."

Lipman Brown's reelection effort coincided with the sea change in domestic politics in the U.S. that saw Christianity become increasingly tied to both patriotism and right-wing political identity.

> [Anti-Semitic tactics] wouldn't have worked if they hadn't had the thing about the prayers to hang their hat on. Right after, in 1996, the next election cycle, when I was walking door-to-door in that district for another candidate, a regent candidate, I started hearing, quite often, when I would

> knock on a door, "Is he Christian? Because we only vote for Christians." So it was sort of like, just putting that in people's minds, that only people of a certain religion should be elected. If you go back a little further to about 1970, there was a time when it didn't seem to be quite such a big deal, what someone's religion was. I think during the eighties it started becoming a really big issue. Although I guess in different parts of the country it's always been more important. I lived in some pretty big cities, but I've heard stories from small towns in the Midwest that were kind of rough.

Lipman Brown sees the rise in secularity and organized secularism in the 1990s and 2000s as a result of the domestic politicization of religion coinciding with generational changes in American attitudes about organized religion:

> But there are really two things that were happening. One is, many people who had grown up with their social and community life revolving around a church or synagogue no longer believed the theology of it, but they still wanted that community. So there are the groups that are there for community, and also for raising your child to not be religiously ignorant. Because I would hope most people would want their children to be familiar with religion. A lot of what goes on in the United States is about religion. But then there was also the political end of it. And I think really, there may have been little things happening, but I think it got *really* to a fever pitch during the George W. Bush administration. Because so much was happening with attacks on science and education, public education—based in our president's belief system—so people started really paying attention to the fact that environmental science, or reproductive science, was being ignored. And we took on the abstinence-only sex education, because that, again, the idea that the only way that you should be is abstinent until marriage is based on someone's religion, it's not a science thing. Granted a science-based full sex ed class, government paid for in a public school, would certainly include abstinence, but that's not the only thing it would teach.

In addition to matters involving science and sexual politics, she views the Islamophobia of post–9/11 politics as sending frightening signals to religious minorities, including Jews and nontheists, or in her case, both.

Overall, the linking of Christianity to American patriotism and nationalism provided a spark to nontheist movements:

> Politically, it was a pretty ripe time for political action on the part of nontheists. The other thing is the rhetoric about people having to have a god to have morals and to have religion, I mean to have any ethics or to have any values at all. That was also pretty destructive.

Although organized secularism has grown substantially, it remains to be seen how effective organized secular groups can be in the political arena.

JB: Do you think secularism can operate effectively as a form of identity politics?

LLB: The word "secularism" I wouldn't associate with identity politics because many people who are for secular government are religious people. So when I lobbied, I often lobbied with members of the Interfaith Alliance, the Baptist Joint Committee for Religious Liberty, and the National Council of Jewish Women. So a lot of people who are secularists, meaning that they believe that our government should not endorse a specific religion, that the government should be separate from religion, are religious people. But the identity movement for nontheists, people who don't believe in any gods, that was and still is an important movement for the same reason as identity politics for other minorities have been—all the different civil rights movements, for African Americans, for women, for gays, lesbians, transgendered people. Not because we want to be separate, but because we're being treated differently, and there's power in coming together and saying, "This is who we are." I mean, take pride day. And people say, "Well why should you be proud to be gay?" Well it's not that you're prouder to be gay than to be heterosexual, it's that you're *not ashamed* of it. And it's the same thing I think for nontheists.

JB: Do you think that is a good analogy, to the LGBT movement? Or are there some differences there too? Because I've seen some resistance to that idea.[25] Do you think that analogy holds up?

LLB: Well, there's two sides of the coin. In terms of the issues, it's more like religion, because if you're being discriminated against because

> you're a Jew, you could just stop being a Jew. At least religiously, you could stop being Jewish and convert. Right? If you're being oppressed because you're a nontheist, you could believe in God, and then you don't get oppressed. So it's more like that in terms of an *issue*. But in terms of a change in societal attitude, it's much more like being gay or lesbian. Or being a transgendered person who can pass. Most of the people in these categories never have to let anyone know that they are in that oppressed category. Just like a nontheist doesn't ever have to say, "I don't believe in any gods." And so, you can hide. Or you can say, "Wait a minute. This is who I am and there's no problem with it."

As the founding director of SCA, Lipman Brown's job was to lobby congressional representatives on issues the organization viewed as involving the separation of church and state, although there was occasionally internal dissent about *which* matters were church/state issues. For instance, marriage equality for same-sex couples was initially not acknowledged by the SCA board as a church/state matter, but Lipman Brown ultimately persuaded the board members to recognize it as within the group's purview. An issue of particular concern was George W. Bush's faith-based initiatives; the SCA argued that the faith-based service organizations needed to meet two basic requirements to make the distribution of federal funds to them constitutional: (1) provision of services to all, regardless of faith, creed, or lack thereof; and (2) no discrimination in the hiring of employees based on faith, creed, or lack thereof.[26]

In general, Lipman Brown and SCA advocate a position that government should respect religious freedom by protecting the religious rights of individuals, but not allow for the imposition of others' beliefs through social policies.

> If we go with the LGBT analogy, it's like people who say that gay people getting married infringes on their rights to be heterosexual. It has nothing to do with their rights to be heterosexual. And people saying, "I don't believe in a god" has nothing to do with your belief in your God. And the thing is, your religion, your religious rights give you the right to live by your religion, as long as you're not harming someone else. Your re-

ligion doesn't say you should kill me, that kind of thing. Whatever you believe—if you believe gay marriage is wrong, don't marry anyone of the same gender. If you believe contraception is wrong, don't use contraception. But once you start telling me that I should follow *your* religion, that's going too far.

This position echoes Thomas Jefferson's argument for freedom of conscience: "The legitimate powers of government extend to such acts only as are injurious to others. But it does me no injury for my neighbor to say there are twenty gods, or no god. It neither picks my pocket nor breaks my leg."[27]

Although she sees identity politics as a potentially positive strategy for nontheists, Lipman Brown's experiences in politics have also convinced her of the vital need to form coalitions with religious people and organizations who share nontheists' values or policy positions.

> There were groups that had been working on church/state separation for many years, with religious members. So you had the Interfaith Alliance, the Baptist Joint Committee for Religious Liberty, which is one of the *best* church/state separation groups. You had Americans United for Separation of Church and State, whose leader is a minister. Things like that. But there hadn't been—the identity politics part of it, the trying to deal with the social aspects of how people treat people, or what other people think about atheists, and nontheists in general—having the Secular Coalition come into existence and actually go lobby with these groups was pretty powerful. I mean walking from lobby meeting to lobby meeting, the most fun I had was chatting with the Baptist and the Sikh—one of the key lobbyists that I worked with was Sikh—just learning about each other was so fantastic. Each one of us, when we would talk to these legislators or their staff, would have our own moment to say, "This is how this bill will affect nontheists." Or, "This is how this bill will affect the Jewish community," for the woman who worked for that group. And so it was really a huge step to be included in all of that.

Such contact fosters respect across religious lines, strengthening mutual tolerance and acceptance, exemplified by how representatives from different groups came to a better understanding of one another. Further, she sees positive contact between religious and nonreligious people as key to changing negative social views of nontheism.

> One of the meetings we went to we were speaking to a U.S. senator, we had the opportunity to meet with her directly, and the woman from the Jewish organization, when it came her turn, she said, "God willing . . ." And then she stopped herself and said, "Well, I know we don't all believe in God around the table, but you know what I mean. Hopefully it will work!" And when we got out into the hall I said, "Becky it's OK if you say that, I mean that's appropriate for you." And she said, "I know but I just wanted you to feel included, so I didn't mean to say anything that would exclude you." It was just a great feeling.

Lipman Brown's vision of the best way to change negative public views of nontheists is to, as it were, humanize the humanists:

> The other thing I think is really important is that we get the society around us to understand that we're like *everybody else*. Meaning, we're not better than other groups, we're not worse than other groups. We're not more moral, or less moral. There are so many of us who do such great charity work and helping others. And then there are some nontheists who are just horrible, very selfish people who don't care about anybody. And, although I really am one of the happiest people I know, there are some people who are just miserable.[28] *As with every, single group*. And, we have as much distinction amongst us as—I mean if you said a Christian is this kind of person, that would be crazy because there are so many people who fall into that category and they are not all the same. If you're going to look at every nontheist as a Christopher Hitchens, then you have to look at every Christian as a Pat Robertson; but that's not accurate. I think we need to keep working on the societal *recognition* of who we are. And hopefully—yes, I mean there are good and bad—but I would hope that people happen to meet more good people who are nontheist. I just, I think that if nontheists are respectful of others and explain ourselves, we could really change hearts and minds.

As a result, Lipman Brown considers negativity toward religion in toto to be counterproductive:

> There are nontheists out there who are *anti*-religion, and I think that is really destructive to the movement. I find it really annoying when people are aggressively antireligious. I'm vehemently antitheocracy. Vehemently. And so I will tell somebody, "You can have any belief you want, so long as you're not harming someone with that belief. But you can't make me abide by *your* beliefs." And so, with that in mind, I've worked with lots of religious people. And I know lots of religious people who share my ethical values and live the same values I live. Just because they happen to believe in God and I don't doesn't matter to me. It's irrelevant.

Lipman Brown's vision of how personal religiosity or secularity should interact with politics is pragmatic, and she reiterates that secularities are social statuses:

> JB: How do you think individuals' secularity or religiosity should influence politics? Because it will, so what would be the optimal way for that to happen?
>
> LLB: Well, the same way anyone's views influence them. Or their upbringing. The same way class influences you. Did you grow up in a poorer area and now recognize the problems of poverty? Did you grow up in great wealth, but with a view toward empathy toward poverty? Or did you grow up in great wealth and think, "People in poverty deserve what they get"? I don't know that *where* your belief comes from really matters. It's, what are your thoughts on the issues?

As with our other biographical profiles, Lori Lipman Brown's experiences reflect both individualized circumstances and broader cultural trends. Her experiences in public life track some of the important cultural and political changes we have highlighted. Her role as the first lobbyist for secular groups reflects the growth of the organizations SCA represents. Although not all in the organized secular movement embrace her strategy of being open to working with religious individuals and organizations, politically engaged, ecumenical secular individuals and organizations appear to represent seculars' best chance to increase their influence on public policies and cultural norms.

Summary

Secularities, like all cosmic belief systems, are necessarily social, and therefore political. The degree of explicit politicization varies by context, but secular belief systems are always situated relative to religions and public perceptions of what it means to be religious (or not). In the contemporary United States, public perception of secularists is more favorable than in the past, especially relative to the Cold War era, but it remains poor overall. The increasing presence of secular Americans may cause such antipathy to wane, but that remains to be seen. Americans remain highly suspicious of people who are not religious and tend to be unwilling to vote for them. As a result, secularists are more dissatisfied with the government as a whole than are actively religious Americans, who are overrepresented in politics. Seculars' lack of proportional representation combined with the rising numbers of secular Americans has led to substantial growth in the size and activity of organized secular groups such as AHA, AA, and SSA, as well as the formation of the Secular Coalition in an effort to influence legislators and make the voices of nontheists more audible in public discourse.

Most secularists are not opposed to government in principle. Further, theistic dis- and nonbelievers are more likely to report being actively interested in politics. Many secularists would welcome a more prominent role for government, as long as it fits with their generally progressive-leaning views. On some issues, including welfare and redistribution of wealth, there is little difference between secular and religious Americans. Where political divisions occur is over sexuality, gender, and so-called "moral" issues. The culture wars have come home to roost over matters involving (women's) bodies and "the" family, along with the government's role in regulating the social organization of sexuality and gender. Disputes over these matters have fueled rising apostasy among younger generations of Americans, whose views on such matters are substantially more liberal (or libertarian) than those of previous generations, providing an integral piece of the story about why the number of secularists in the U.S. is on the rise.

Conclusion

A Secular, Cosmical Movement?

And we all have a duty to do good. And this commandment for everyone to do good, I think, is a beautiful path towards peace. If we, each doing our own part, if we do good to others, if we meet there, doing good, and we go slowly, gently, little by little, we will make that culture of encounter: we need that so much. We must meet one another doing good. "But I don't believe, Father, I am an atheist!" But do good: we will meet one another there.
—Pope Francis[1]

Delivering these words during a morning Mass in Rome in 2013, Pope Francis signaled the increasingly prominent place of secularists in the world. From presidents to popes, there is growing awareness of secularity as a way of life for multitudes. Where secular individuals, especially atheists, have long been reviled and condemned, the figurehead of the largest religious organization in the world now counseled collaboration with secularists toward humanitarian ends. AHA director Roy Speckhardt responded, "While humanists have been saying for years that one can be good without a god, hearing this from the leader of the Catholic Church is quite heartening." Of course, not all shared or endorsed this wide ecumenical vision, since both sides still define themselves as *not the other*.[2] Still, recognition of secularists' role in civil society continues to grow.

As secular individuals become both more prevalent and open about their beliefs, increased awareness and humanizing of the "other" may begin to reduce intergroup antagonisms.[3] However, for this to occur in the U.S. requires the ascendance of a more inclusive understanding of American nationalism and citizenship—one that makes room for secular Americans to be considered full citizens with legitimate moral standing. Such civil discourse is in contrast to visions of godless villains, be they criminal or communist. To the extent that such a shift occurs, it will alter the forums in which secular voices may be heard. What secular advocates will choose to voice with such newfound recognition remains to be seen.[4]

U.S. Case in Comparative Perspective

Returning to our opening gambit, the U.S. remains a relatively religious country compared to most other Western societies. At the same time, the recent increase in secularity has made the U.S. case less distinct. Other Western countries with relatively high levels of religiosity have also seen a drop-off in levels of religiosity among recent generations. Ireland makes a particularly interesting comparison point. Religious affiliation in Ireland was extraordinarily high during the period of "the Troubles" (the late 1960s until the late 1990s) between British Unionists and Irish Republicans in and around Northern Ireland.[5] As the external political threat has lessened, so have levels of affiliation among younger generations of Irish. Reduced political conflict coincided with increasing secularization at the individual level and declining respect for the orthodoxy and moral authority of the Catholic Church.[6] Similarly, in the U.S. there was a drop-off in affiliation from its 1950s peak as the Second Red Scare subsided, and especially as the Cold War ended. This suggests that where ethnicity and/or nationalism is linked to religion, external conflict can operate to keep levels of religiosity unusually high.[7] In contrast, *domestic* politicization of religion, particularly concerning matters of sexuality and family, can drive secularity up. There is not a simple or one-way relationship between political conflict and religiosity/secularity, but rather a dynamic interaction that hinges on the source and focus of conflict and the role that organized religion plays.

There is also a clear difference between locations with "organic" secularization and those with "imposed" secularization. Communist and former communist countries tend to have high levels of secularity but also far lower health, economic, and quality-of-life indicators than postindustrial social democracies. This is in direct contrast to locations where individual level secularity increases organically, tending to accompany the highest levels of economic, social, and health development and infrastructure.[8] For example, using Waves 5 (2005–2009) and 6 (2010–2014) of the World Values Survey aggregated to the national level, we correlated levels of societal development with the percentage of those in a country who, when asked whether they consider themselves to be religious persons, select "not religious" or "atheist," and when asked about attending religious services report doing so only on high holidays or less often. After removing communist or former communist countries from the analysis, the strongest correlate (ranging from -1 to +1, with 0 as no relationship) was an index of societal gender equality (r = .80). Similarly, there was a strong correlation (r = .74) between secularity in a country and the Human Development Index (HDI) compiled by the U.N. that incorporates levels of education, life expectancy, and distributions of income and wealth.[9] There were also significant correlations between secularity and other political and societal health indicators, such as stronger rule of law (r = .78), gross national income per capita (r = .77), greater civil liberties (r = .66), adult literacy rate (r = .54), greater religious freedoms (r = .54), and lower levels of income inequality (r = -.48).[10] As we all know, correlation is not causation. At the same time, it is clear that rather than occurring in disorganized, dangerous societies, organic secularity is most likely to occur in relatively stable, healthy social contexts. In short, more secularity is not a sign of apocalypse, but rather often a sign of "existential security."[11] This, however, is not the case for areas that have undergone *forced* secularization, indicating that secularity does not cause societal health, but rather the inverse.[12]

Further, as Figure C.1, plotting HDI and secularity shows, the U.S. is well within the distribution pattern.[13] While still relatively low in secularity given its high HDI, the U.S. case is similar to others such as Switzerland, Canada, Singapore, Finland, and Argentina. So while the U.S. remains relatively religious compared to some Western European countries, it is hardly an outlier in the statistical sense, at least globally speaking. Although the particulars of the American case certainly warrant attention, the time has come to cease understanding the U.S. as "exceptionally" religious. Although it is more religious than the average postindustrial nation, it is not exceptional. Further, this analysis fails to adjust for desirability bias and the overreporting of religiosity, which occurs more often in American samples.[14] To reiterate, the cultural specifics of *any* case warrant close attention, but thinking of the U.S. as set apart from other developed counties in terms of its piety is more normative than empirical.

The comparative study of secularity remains relatively open to empirical exploration.[15] We have not undertaken it extensively here because our focus has been on the American case. Still, the possibilities and potential are evident from this brief example.[16] Moving forward, there are a number of elements important for understanding population levels of secularity in a comparative context. Foremost is the formal relationship between organized religion and politics, especially in terms of institutional arrangements, religious freedom, and (dis)establishment. Beyond institutional arrangements lie the cultural meanings of religion, which are shaped by both foreign and domestic political conflict. Understanding how religion is used to delineate in- from out-groups is a necessary component of understanding the meanings of secularity in specific contexts. At the demographic level, patterns of marriage, sexuality, fertility, and immigration are potential sources of changes in religious/secular composition, and vice versa. Levels of retention, switching, and apostasy are also potential sources of change, ones that point back to the cultural meanings of religion.

Primary Themes

Variety and Complexity of Secularities

The diversity of secularity is evident between and within the four broad categories of atheist, agnostic, nonaffiliated believer, and culturally religious. As would be expected, atheists are the most consistently nonreligious in ideation and practice; they are more likely to be strongly opposed to organized religion and also to exhibit low levels of interest in private spiritual concerns. In short, atheists tend to be neither spiritual nor religious. Ideologically, many atheists place heavy emphasis on institutional science, and often on the mythologized "war between science and religion," to frame their understanding of the world and their experiences. Nonaffiliated believers are also strongly opposed to organized religion, but are more likely to have privatized spiritual concerns and practices. This results in identities such as "spiritual but not religious," through which individuals draw firmer distinctions between

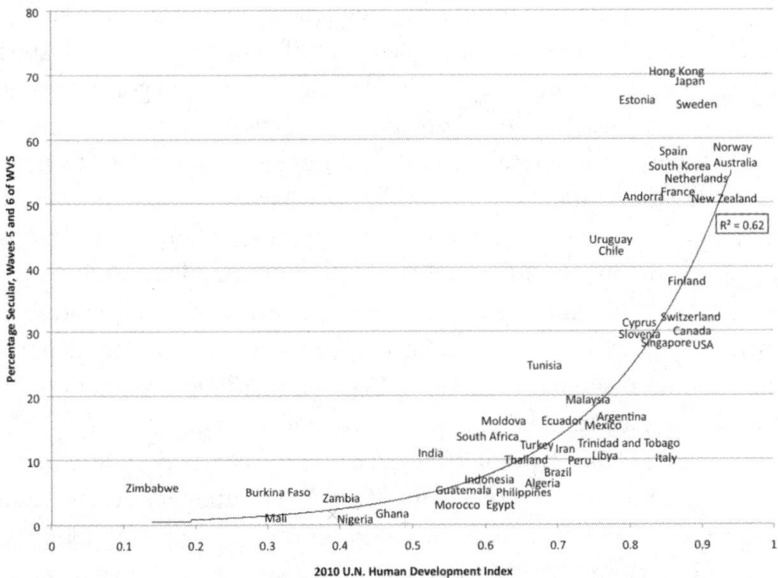

Figure C.1. Percentage Secular by Human Development Index

public and private religiosity. One of the causes and consequences of such distinctions is the ability to maintain a conventional identity by passing as, effectively, *not* irreligious, while also not adhering to a particular religious perspective. Agnostics fall somewhere between atheists and nonaffiliated believers, being generally opposed to organized religion, but also relatively open to spiritual, emotive experiences such as wonderment and awe.[17] The culturally religious, by contrast, maintain the importance of organized religion while exhibiting little to no interest in personal religious practice. Each type of secularity shares some similarities with other types, but is also distinct enough on a variety of dimensions ranging from demography to politics to warrant treating these categories as analytically separate where possible.

In addition to these categories, there are potentially relevant distinctions to be made between apostates and socialized seculars, affiliated nonbelievers, and any number of other combinations or refinements of belief, identity, and practice. Regardless of the categorizations used, public knowledge and perception of the labels themselves can guide adoption or rejection. This can be seen among and within the secular population in the United States. Self-identification as religious, spiritual, irreligious, or anything else is premised on the categories that are avoided just as much as the labels that are adopted. We find evidence of this in disconnects between responses about belief and identity, such as when atheists say they believe in God, or when people say they do not know whether there is a God but (ironically) do not know what "agnostic" means. Because of this, it is essential to understand how individuals, and also their surrounding communities, perceive and understand secularity. What it means to be secular in a given cultural context depends on what it means to be religious, and vice versa, as such distinctions are created and maintained through negative delineation.

Beyond our basic typology, the variation in secularity should be apparent from the examples of Thomas Paine's revolutionary deism, Lester Ward's secular monism, W. E. B. Du Bois's this-worldly prophetic religious idiom, Fanny Wright's secular utopianism, David Tamayo's broad understanding of freethought, Cecil Bothwell's "post-theist" Unitarianism, and Lori Lipman Brown's humanistic Judaism. The variation in secularity also raises important questions about variations in religiosity. If we think of cosmic belief systems as ranging from thoroughly secular to zealously religious, a vast middle ground opens for study. The religious/secular binary has precluded systematic study of positions that do not neatly fit ideals of conventional religious expressions. Particular areas in need of further development are forms of nominalism, noninstitutionalized supernatural beliefs and subcultures (paranormalism), and privatized expressions of religiosity and spirituality.[18] Complicating binary distinctions between religion and secularism opens a host of unexplored topics for study in fields typically focused on institutional religion.

Implications for Theories of Religion

Examining secularity from an empirical standpoint has been our primary focus, but we have also outlined a theoretical perspective for studying secularity (and religiosity) that avoids or corrects some of the shortcomings of existing paradigms. Although both secularization and rational choice theories provide insight into certain areas, they each fail to function as dynamic theoretical frameworks that allow for open study of *both* religiosity and secularity. Neither of these paradigms is particularly useful for empirically studying secularism. Debates about whether religion or secularism is rational or irrational do little to advance our knowledge of either, as such disputes hinge on the contextual meaning of "rational." If by rational we mean providing tangible benefits and instrumentality, as rational choice theories of religion use the term, then religion can clearly be rational, as can secularity. If by rational we mean subject to empirical verification or falsifiability, as typically conceived in "disenchantment" versions of secularization theory or secularist polemics, then religion and secularity are *both* nonrational, as each is premised on assumptions about ontology that are not empirically falsifiable.[19] This point seems lost on polemicists and theorists on all sides eager to prove their worldview as rationally superior. A reconceptualization that avoids the dead ends created by such disputes stands as a primary theoretical challenge facing scholars "of religion."

Many of the problems in creating a theoretical framework that includes both religiosity and secularity stem from how religion is defined. The primary approaches to definition in the study of religion remain the "substantive" and the "functional."[20] There are benefits and drawbacks to each, hence the long-running debate about which is preferable. A substantive approach uses the content of beliefs to classify religion, arguing that supernaturalism or gods are what makes a belief system religious.[21] Substantive definitions are useful for studying organized religion, but effectively exclude humanistic religions, and often diffuse or nontheistic versions of supernaturalism as well. Further, distinctions between the religious and secular are typically not as clear-cut as strict substantive definitions make it seem. More directly for our current study, such approaches draw secularisms completely outside the domain of disciplines focused on religion.

On the other hand, functional approaches define religion as any belief system that provides the grounds for "ultimate" meaning, offering a flexibility that the substantive approach precludes.[22] Still, there are problems with purely functional definitions of religion too. In particular, labeling all belief systems focused on ultimate meaning as religious obscures substantive differences between them. This also requires either subsuming belief systems, including secularities, into "religion" in order to validate their study, or conversely "flattening out" the supernatural elements of religious belief systems.[23] In short, neither definition both (1) effectively provides a broader framework under which religion, non-institutionalized spirituality or supernaturalism, and secularism can all be studied; and (2) allows for meaningful distinctions between different types of belief systems.

In place of such perspectives, we have outlined a cultural view of *cosmic belief systems* that provides conceptual tools for both examining and making distinctions between religious and secular communities and worldviews, as well as privatized versions of spirituality or noninstitutionalized supernaturalism.[24] The organization and functioning of religious, noninstitutionalized supernatural, and secular beliefs can be studied in similar ways. For while some varieties of secularity are premised on *dis*believing in supernatural precepts, they nonetheless *posit* particular beliefs about reality and the social world, and also appeal to particular traditions and epistemic authority. To be clear, we are not arguing that religion and secularity are the same, but rather that they can be studied under the same paradigm, with the same conceptual tools. The substantive distinction between natural (empirical) and supernatural remains a useful category in mapping constellations of belief, but it should be obvious that not all supernatural belief systems are examples of organized religion (e.g., paranormalism) and that not all organized religion deals extensively, or at all, in supernaturalism (e.g., this-worldly, predominantly humanistic religious traditions).

Cosmic belief system is a broader general concept than religion, which can then be subclassified into religious, noninstitutionalized supernatural or spiritual, and nonreligious belief systems.[25] This provides a functional understanding of cosmic beliefs as addressing existence, meaning, and explanation, but highlights that such experiential frames are not limited to organized religion. Distinctions between supernatural and materialist, cosmic and practical, organized and diffuse, or any number of other substantive or organizational distinctions can be incorporated into the wider study of belief systems. Such an approach is not meant to be closed and perfect, but rather useful, allowing for comparison and contrast across studies of different types of belief.[26] For studying secularities, we have argued that nonreligion refers to belief systems that *explicitly* define themselves as not religious, rather than referring to all types of belief systems other than organized religious traditions.

In essence, religiosity, noninstitutionalized supernaturalism, and secularity can all be studied under the rubric of belief.[27] The concept of belief proves useful even when other dimensions of group membership are in question, such as affiliation or ritual practices. Indeed, when individuals engage in symbolic membership absent practice (cultural religion) or affiliate and practice absent specific beliefs (affiliated nonbelievers), belief remains a central aspect of identity and self-concept. For instance, the culturally religious still believe in the meaningfulness of the group they are identifying with, while affiliated nonbelievers believe in the meaningfulness of a group's collective interaction, even if they do not believe in specific religious precepts. Similarly, atheists may believe in the authority of science and humanist ethics, or nonaffiliated believers in the meaningfulness of maintaining a relationship to the divine without engaging formal religious organizations. Agnostics believe in the value of skepticism and humility in the face of the unknown, or perhaps the futility of debating unresolvable questions. No cognizant human can escape belief, as even disbelief or assertion of absence is effectively *belief in* absence, skepticism, or any of a number of similar negating concepts. This fact should make belief a central component of social scientific study rather than a subject that is studiously avoided.[28]

In studying cosmic belief systems, some basic methodological and interpretive considerations should be kept in mind. Within the folk cosmologies articulated by interpretive communities, formal philosophical distinctions about epistemology, ontology, and ethics often blur. In other words, people generally develop their sense of "what ought" from their understanding of "what is," in spite of David Hume's famous separation of the two and continuing debates about the philosophical validity of such linkages.[29] While we advocate upholding the idealized distinction between facts and values in research, it is imperative to recognize that folk cosmologies often collapse such distinctions in practice.[30] For researchers this leads to two basic directives. First, it emphasizes the importance of understanding that public belief systems often do not conform to the formal systematization of ideologies proposed by intellectuals or elites. Second, it means conceptualizing both religiosity and secularity in a way that privileges neither, treating each with respect, but not reverence.[31]

To better understand the intersections of secularity and culture requires constructing and using theoretical frameworks that broaden the scope of what those engaged in the study "of religion" examine and do. Our proposed concept of cosmic belief systems, along with a broader view of both religiosity and secularity as culture, provides a way forward. We have shown that secularity can be empirically studied in a manner similar to religiosity, but there is obviously much more to do and say.[32]

Historical, Cultural, and Political Dimensions of Secularities

To understand each, religiosity and secularity must be examined in relation to one another rather than separately, with particular attention paid to the political and historical contexts of the indefinite cultural boundaries between religious and secular. Because secularity is linked to the cultural, particularly the political, meanings of religion, empirical studies of secularity must take care to understand historical dynamics between secularity, organized religion, and politics. In the American context, sectarian Protestantism has historically held a particularly important dialectical relationship with secularisms, and both have shaped and been shaped by the political and legal environment of the United States. The early disestablishment of religion at the federal and then at the state level ironically served to weaken the long-term viability of organized secular movements by removing the political necessity for anti-clerical movements. As a result, organized secularism engaged in largely defensive political tactics, concentrating the bulk of its energy and efforts toward ideological and proselytizing endeavors. The history of secular movements in the U.S. can thus be broadly characterized as populist, libertarian, and ideologically progressive in orientation, but also often as politically reactive.

The American public's views of secularity have remained generally negative, but also become less stigmatizing in recent years. Accompanying this lessening of the stigma against secularity, the proportion of Americans claiming no religion increased threefold between 1990 and 2010—the Great Abdicating. This change in religious/secular composition is particularly interesting considering the significant demographic disadvantage seculars have relative to religious individuals. Changes to the political meaning of religion, particularly among conservative Christians, and its corresponding politicization, have driven this transformation. Views of sexuality are a particularly salient political boundary between religious and secular Americans. Stances on issues such as premarital sex, abortion, same-sex relations and marriage, and gender roles more generally are all microcosms of larger debates about moral authority and the social organization of family and sexuality. The polarization of political discourse and identity has resulted in two large, relatively consolidated voting blocs in American politics: the conservatively religious Right and the secular Left.[33] This political organization follows shifts in the social and demographic organization of gender and family over the past forty years. The future of these trends is uncertain, but at present secularity continues to grow.

Atheists and agnostics are more interested in formal politics than the average American, while nonaffiliated believers and the culturally religious tend to have lower levels of political interest and engagement. In spite of strong political interest and engagement among atheists and agnostics, secularists remain underrepresented in the halls of government relative to their levels in the population. Open secularity in particular remains a political liability for public figures, reflecting continuing distrust of secularists among the public. While this antipathy is stronger among specific segments of the population such as evangelical Protestants, these sentiments spill over into American culture more generally.

American nationalism and civil religion continue to rely on exclusionary references to Christian theism. Patterns of secularity by immigrant status and ethnicity help demonstrate these connections. Asian Americans are much more likely to be secular in the second generation, with high rates of exiting non-Christian religions and adopting secularity. In the third and later generations, Asian Americans look similar to white Americans, adopting evangelical Protestantism at high rates. Conversely, among Latino Americans, recent immigrant status and less integration into American culture correlates with lower levels of secularity due to reliance on religious communities for social support, while assimilation leads to higher rates of secularity. In other words, once Latino Americans have achieved the normative status of assimilation through higher social class, secularity, particularly in the form of cultural religion, becomes more common. In effect, immigrants may use religion to assist with assimilation in different ways, but Christianity remains tethered to nationalism in many prominent streams of discourse.

Overall, the political meanings of secularity have shifted in response to the changing political meaning of religion over the past forty years, particularly as framed by morally conservative Christianity. With the end of the Cold War, secularity has become less taboo, and the growing size of the secular population makes it more politically important. This underscores that a key consideration in understanding the political context of secularisms is the extent to which religion is linked to political conflict, and whether such conflict is centered on external threats or internal disputes about governance.

Sociological Patterning of Secularities

Regarding the social and demographic patterns of secularity in the U.S., a number of findings stand out. Atheists and agnostics tend to be of higher social class, while nonaffiliated believers tend to have lower socioeconomic status. Among white, Latino, and Asian Americans, higher social class leads to higher levels of secularity and lower levels of active religiosity. This pattern reflects the relative deviance of secularity, such that people of higher social standing can, as it were, more "afford" to be ideologically different. For those of lower social class, the inclusionary status offered by religion is comparatively more valuable, and its abdication more costly. An exception to this pattern is African Americans, where higher levels of social class push people away from nonaffiliated belief and toward nontheism or conventional religiosity, more usually the latter. This tendency speaks to the continuing centrality of organized religion in black communities, a product of the historical importance of black Protestantism as the primary institution controlled by African Americans.

Mirroring the case with religiosity, there are gender gaps in secularity. Atheism is the most gendered, followed by agnosticism, cultural religion, and nonaffiliated belief; however, there is gender parity in rates of secularity among political liberals with high levels of education. This finding casts doubt on claims that innate differences account for such gender differences. Instead, gender gaps in religiosity and secularity reflect the cultural links between gender traditionalism and religion, particularly conventions about sexual purity and normative status for women. For women with high levels of educational attainment and a progressive view of politics, secularity is a viable option. For politically conservative and less educated women, secularity is extremely costly, and rare. We also find evidence of the gendered nature of secularity in patterns of marriage and parenthood. Those who have never married or do not have children are more likely to be secular, but the effects are stronger for men than women. The one relationship status where there is a stronger pull toward secularity for women than men is cohabitation, again reflecting the connections between cultural expectations about normative marital sexuality and religiosity for women.

Finally, as with religiosity, expressions of secularity are strongly influenced by those in one's social network, particularly parents, spouses, and peers. Children tend to adopt the cosmic belief systems of their parents, although there are also distinct patterns of rebellion, as evinced by adult atheists having higher rates of religious socialization compared to other types of secularity. Patterns of perceptions about familial conflict demonstrate that nonaffiliated belief and cultural religion are often efforts to navigate the cross-pressures of normative religiosity, familial expectations, and personal disinterest in organized religion. Meanwhile, peers play an important role in the formation and maintenance of identity for all types of secularists, especially atheists and agnostics.

Taken together, the sociodemographic patterns of secularity confirm the continuing importance of cultural linkages between religiosity and conventionality to understanding patterns of secularity in the United States. Because open secularity remains deviant, it is more costly to individuals who already occupy culturally devalued status positions. Patterns based on gender, marriage, and children also reveal the considerable extent to which religiosity remains connected to traditionalist expectations about gender, sexuality, and family, particularly for women.

Implications for Organized Religion and Secularism

For religious communities, the question of whether and how to respond to secularists is ever pertinent. For exclusivist groups, the answer presumably will be to continue othering secularists. In terms of internal social cohesion, it is quite effective to target a group that is mistrusted and disorganized. Fear of the godless is, after all, a storied tradition. Perhaps more importantly, rhetorically framing secularity as immoral facilitates the corollary claim that a particular religion or theism is the only path to morality. At the same time, overtures such as those made by Pope Francis suggest the possibility of collaboration between religious and secular communities on common goals. While such coalitions remain unlikely, they are certainly not impossible. Exclusive religion will undoubtedly continue to survive and thrive, but the humanity and dignity of secular individuals will also gain wider recognition. As a result, fear mongering may inadvertently delegitimize polemicists in the eyes of more moderate constituents. The contemporary political disputes over homosexuality involving exclusivist religious groups provide an instructive example of such dynamics.

For moderate and liberal religious groups, the question of when and how to engage seculars is more complicated, but also holds more potential for coalitions on matters of social justice and political activism. Since the 1960s, liberal religious groups in the U.S. have steadily lost ground in terms of proportion of the population, yet there is also now a vast pool of Americans outside of organized religion who are not necessarily disconnected from some of the political and service concerns advocated by liberal religious groups.[34] The upside for collaborating with secular organizations or providing ways for seculars to volunteer through ecumenical religious organizations is potentially high—at least if the goals are politically, rather than theologically, oriented.

The Unitarian Universalist Association (UUA) offers an interesting example of this potential.[35] Recall Cecil Bothwell's use of the UUA prison ministry to facilitate his social justice work with prisoners and Lori Lipman Brown's involvement with homelessness programs through a UUA congregation. Their stories are not unusual, but rather indicative of the approach the UUA takes to matters of politics and social justice. Indeed, while the membership of their denomination is relatively small, Unitarian Universalists are disproportionately active in social causes. Further, leaders of the group seek out coalitions with a wide range of other social justice organizations, both religious and secular, to the point where the UUA website includes a page titled "Atheist and Agnostic People Welcome," laying out the reasons why secularists should consider joining the group.[36] The benefits of this activity are apparent not just in terms of civic engagement, but also in the relative health of the denomination. Although the UUA's numbers fell alongside other liberal groups' in the 1970s, the denomination reversed that trend by adding members in the past three decades. Between 1980 and 2010, the UUA added ninety congregations, doubled its number of clergy, and expanded by 55,320 members. By contrast, not a single denomination classified as "mainline" (liberal) Protestant grew during the same time period. The Disciples of Christ, Episcopalians, the Presbyterian Church USA, and United Church of Christ all declined by over 30%, while the UUA grew by 35%. It seems Unitarians' efforts to engage seculars and other religions are yielding benefits, both in terms of organizational engagement and growth.[37]

One of the significant changes in American secularism over the last decade revolves around the increasing organization of secular groups.[38] Particularly with modern technological capabilities, it is possible for relatively small groups to attain high levels of social recognition.[39] For example, a group such as the Freedom from Religion Foundation (FFRF), which self-reports about 20,000 members, attempts to have a national presence through legal action and advertising.[40] One result of increasing communication technology and public relations campaigns by organized secular groups is that those interested in the topic can easily find a wealth of information, and group membership is possible in ways that did not exist a generation ago.

In spite of the growth in organized secularism that we have documented, the history of freethought in the U.S. portends continued difficulty in sustaining organized secular movements, especially those that are organized as general nonreligious groups rather than political nonprofit organizations. In order to achieve long-term organizational success, secular groups would need to—dare we say it—look to religious communities. If we conceptualize organized secular movements as akin to religious movements, we can apply established models of group growth to evaluate the relative chance of success for organized secularisms.[41] Doing so immediately reveals important shortcomings for organized secular groups. The low fertility rates of seculars we have discussed at length, and the implications for the success or failure of a social group across succeeding generations are self-evident. Given that secular retention has increased in recent years, organized secular groups can certainly persist with low fertility, but compensating for mortality and keeping pace with organized religious groups will remain difficult. Generating member commitment is another issue that organized secular groups will have to address. Since religious groups in the U.S. are voluntary associations, they rely extensively on member sacrifice in terms of time, money, and talent. Most organized secular groups tend toward a more libertarian stance on members' behavior and ideological views. While consistent with the ethos of freethought, this is a liability for long-term organizational success. One possible remedy would be to create service or other requirements for membership in organized secular groups.

The problem of establishing an organizational power structure that members see as legitimate is a related issue. Who speaks for secularism? As we have shown, secularists are more of a mixed population than a highly cohesive social group. Outside of leaders of the various humanist associations and New Atheist authors, there are few public advocates for organized secularism, and there is no organizational authority among or between such spokespeople. Organizing secularism more formally necessarily entails an internally ecumenical yet cohesive stance coupled with overcoming the anti-hierarchical leanings of many secularists. Given that skepticism toward authority and freedom of consciousness are hallmarks of freethought, the problem of establishing an effective organizational hierarchy without factionalizing or losing membership is particularly acute. In contrast to the difficulties facing long run success for organized secularism, the future for *dis*organized secularism looks relatively bright. Because noninstitutionalized secularity functions as the default position for those who are not interested in organized religion, it holds a unique advantage in generating constituents as rates of religious participation wane.[42]

Onward, Upward

Secularisms and secularities are diverse. The past and present bear witness to this fact. Secularities should be understood as social statuses that individuals can develop varying levels of commitment to, and which are subject to varying levels of stigmatization depending on cultural context. Both the likelihood and the content of secular statuses reflect the social positioning of individuals and the cultural meanings of both religiosity and secularity. Particularly relevant in this regard are primary relational statuses such as family, ethnicity, social class, gender, and sexuality. In all these ways, the conceptual tools useful for understanding secularity mirror those useful for understanding religiosity. It is in the political and cultural dimensions of secular statuses that we find the sources of the dramatic changes to the religious/secular composition of the United States. The meanings and future trajectory of these changes remain dynamic and open-ended.

Secularities are a vital part of the cultural landscape in the United States and elsewhere. Responses to secularisms are clearly driven by the perspective one begins with. Although we have avoided advocating for specific groups' interests, we do believe in the value of broader recognition of the humanity and dignity of people holding different worldviews. The increasing presence of secularisms in the postindustrial world requires tolerance and compassion from and for multiple vantage points—both secular and religious. Regardless of what one makes of the increasing presence and visibility of secularity or the persistence of traditional religious perspectives, both are here to stay. A place at the multicultural table of public discourse will assuredly be part of the future, so working together in spite of (a)theological differences presents itself as an ongoing challenge for building more inclusive communities.

DATA SOURCES APPENDIX

Our primary data sources for results presented throughout the book are the 1972–2010 General Social Surveys (GSS) and the 2007 Pew Religious Landscape Survey (RLS). At various points throughout the study, we also analyze data from supplementary data sets. The Data Sources Appendix provides information on how those samples were collected and how the measures were used to create our categories of interest.

General Social Surveys

Waves of the GSS have been collected by the National Opinion Research Center for the National Data Program for the Social Sciences at the University of Chicago since 1972. Collection and processing of the surveys has been funded by grants from the National Science Foundation. The surveys were collected nearly annually until 1994, then biannually with slightly larger samples since. The surveys contain core items focused on demography and basic attitudes that are included in each wave. Different years also contain rotating modules on varying topics. The principal investigators for the GSS are James A. Davis, Tom W. Smith, and Peter V. Marsden.[1] Overall, the GSS "is by far the best source of available information about continuity and change in Americans' religiosity over the past four decades."[2] In all, the pooled dataset across the years 1972–2010 contains 5,545 variables, 2,072 of which can be tracked over time.

Each wave of the survey represents a new cross-section intended to be a representative sample of noninstitutionalized American adults. The survey was collected only in English until 2006, and has been collected in English and Spanish since. The GSS uses multistage probability sampling based on data from the Census Bureau to ensure representativeness, and collects the surveys in face-to-face interviews. For the collection of sensitive information, such as sexual history, the GSS now uses computer-assisted personal interview techniques that allow respondents to input answers directly without having to verbalize their answers to interviewers. Due to slight changes in collection design over time, and the fact that the sample is representative of households rather than the overall population, all analyses employ the WTSSALL weight designed to correct for these features.[3]

Concerning our categories of interest, the GSS only began asking the questions necessary to classify respondents as atheists, agnostics, nonaffiliated believers, or culturally religious in 1988. The religious affiliation question, however, has been asked across the range of the survey. It is for this reason that in the analysis of trends we sometimes resort to using the "no religion" category broadly. When analyzing the GSS for contemporary data patterns and in comparison with the 2007 Pew Religious Landscape Survey, we use pooled data from the 2006–2010 waves of the GSS.

Pew Religious Landscape Survey

Our other primary data source, the Pew RLS, was commissioned by the Pew Forum on Religion and Public Life and collected by Princeton Survey Research Associates International between May and August of 2007. The focus of the survey was the religious affiliations, beliefs, and behaviors of the general American public. The sample is relatively large (n = 35,556), yielding enough cases to conduct analyses on smaller groups with a reasonable amount of statistical power. In all, there were 5,048 respondents who self-identified as secular in the survey.

The RLS sample was collected using random-digit dialing. As many as ten attempts were made to contact numbers selected, with varying call times and days of the week. Successful contact was made with 80% of the working numbers generated. The cooperation rate for those contacted was 35%, and the completion rate for those who agreed to participate was 86%. This makes the total response rate including all attempted calls, refusals, and break-offs 24%.[4] Telephone interviews were conducted in English or Spanish. We use the continental dataset, which excludes Alaska and Hawaii.

The weight created for the dataset to make it more representative of the American public was designed to correct for two features. First, the survey oversampled Muslim, Hindu, Buddhist, and Orthodox Christian traditions. Second, the weight adjusts for demographic patterns of nonresponse so that analyses more closely match the population parameters of the American public. The demographic dimensions included in the weight were "sex, age, education, race, Hispanic origin, region, country of birth (for Latinos) and population density."[5] Cases were then balanced using the Deming Algorithm to ensure that individual cases did not exert extraordinary influence on analyses. The weight was used for all analyses presented.

Pew Asian American and Latino/a Surveys

In addition to the RLS, in Chapter 6, we present data from the Pew Asian American survey (2012) and the National Survey of Latino/as (2011). The Asian American survey consisted of 3,511 completed phone interviews, primarily with Americans of Chinese, Filipino, Indian, Japanese, Korean, and Vietnamese background. Interviews were done in English, Cantonese, Hindi, Japanese, Korean, Mandarin, Tagalog, and Vietnamese. Potential respondents were contacted with stratified random-digit dialing. The goal was to obtain a sufficient number of responses to generate reasonably representative samples for the ethnic groups listed above.[6] Data for the 2011 National Survey of Latino/as were collected by Social Science Research Solutions. Interviews were conducted by phone in English and Spanish based on random-digit dialing, with 1,220 respondents completing the questionnaire and identifying as having Hispanic ethnicity. The goal of the survey was to generate reasonably representative sample sizes for both native- (n = 492) and foreign-born Hispanic Americans (n = 728).[7] The questions on theism and religious affiliation in the Asian American and Hispanic surveys are the same as those used in the Pew RLS.

Faith Matters Survey

In Chapter 8, we analyze data from the 2006 Faith Matters Survey, a sample of 3,108 American adults based on telephone interviews using random-digit dialing. The sample was collected by International Communication Research, which included a $25 incentive for participating in the survey. The response rate for the survey was 53%.[8] The Faith Matters measure for theism asked, "Are you absolutely sure, somewhat sure, not quite sure, not at all sure, or are you sure you do not believe in God?" Respondents who answered that they were sure they did not believe in God were classified as atheists, and those who responded that they were "not quite sure" or "not at all sure" were classified as agnostics. This measure of agnosticism is problematic, but the Faith Matters survey includes unique measures on social networks and civic engagement that warrant its limited use in our study.

Baylor Religion Survey, Wave II

In Chapters 5 and 8, we also use Wave II of the Baylor Religion Survey (BRS), which was fielded by Gallup in 2007. The survey was intended to provide extensive data on the religious identities, beliefs, and practices of American adults. The survey design was mixed-mode, with initial efforts to contact respondents done through random-digit dialing. Those reached by phone were told about the survey and asked if they would be willing to complete a mailed questionnaire. In all, 3,500 potential respondents were successfully contacted, and 2,460 questionnaires were mailed out. Each mailing contained a description of the survey, a number to call for questions about the procedure, and a $5 reward for agreeing to receive the survey. A total of 1,648 questionnaires were returned. Gallup created a weight based on data from the Census Bureau on region of the country, race, gender, age, and education to better match the sample's characteristics to population parameters (as measured by the Census).[9]

The measure used to classify atheists and agnostics in the BRS sample was the same as the question in the GSS. The religious affiliation question on the BRS asked, "With what religious family do you most closely identify?" Respondents were provided with a list of over forty options, with "no religion" at the end. This wording maximizes the classification of respondents into religious affiliations, creating a stricter classification of nonaffiliated believers than the measure in the GSS or the Pew RLS. As such, the nonaffiliated believer category in the BRS sample represents a slightly more secular grouping than the classifications in other data sets.

NOTES

INTRODUCTION

1 Our claim about the total number of secular individuals is based on the estimated proportion of the population that is secular using the most recent wave of the WVS multiplied by the population of the country in question. These numbers are based on the WVS question, "Independently of whether you attend religious services or not, would say you are a religious person, not a religious person, [or] an atheist?" Respondents who said they were not religious persons or were atheists, then responded to a question about frequency of attendance at religious services with "only on special holy days" or less were counted as "not religious." We use this two-question classification method with WVS data because the question wording misclassifies some people who think of themselves as "not religious," but also as nondenominational Christians, "having a relationship with Jesus," etc. (the same issue arises with a different question on religious affiliation); cf. Dougherty, Johnson, and Polson (2007); Smith and Kim (2007). Our analyses showed that this form of misclassification was more frequent in the U.S. sample than in comparison countries, so we created a more conservative classification for counting respondents as "secular" in the WVS data. Data from the World Values Survey are publically available at http://www.worldvaluessurvey.org/wvs.jsp. All links referenced in endnotes were active when last accessed on February 5, 2015.

2 E.g., Berger, Davie, and Fokas (2008); Finke (1992); Norris and Inglehart (2004).

3 Similarly, "no" responses to the question on the WVS about whether a respondent belongs "to a religion or religious denomination" increased from 6% in 1981 to 33% in 2011.

4 The full text of the speech is available at http://avalon.law.yale.edu/21st_century/obama.asp. On a personal level, Obama's upbringing by an anthropologist mother "who stressed that religion was an expression of human culture," and also by nominally religious grandparents undoubtedly informed his recognition of the humanity and dignity of nonbelievers. On Obama's personal religious views and use of biblical rhetoric, see Jeffrey S. Siker, "President Obama, the Bible, and Political Rhetoric," *Political Theology* 13:5 (2012): 586–609, 588. The line referenced from the inaugural is a slight reworking of part of a 2006 speech that Obama delivered to an annual conference for Jim Wallis's Sojourners, a progressive religious organization. That talk more directly speaks to issues of faith and democracy than the inaugural, including open discussions of secularity and the public sphere. The most direct reference to secularism is in the following excerpt:

> In fact, because I do not believe that religious people have a monopoly on morality, I would rather have someone who is grounded in morality and ethics, and who is also secular, affirm their morality and ethics and values without pretending that they're something they're not. They don't need to do that. None of us need to do that. But what I am suggesting is this—secularists are wrong when they ask believers to leave their religion at the door before entering into the public square. Frederick Douglas, Abraham Lincoln, Williams Jennings Bryan, Dorothy Day, Martin Luther King—indeed, the majority of great reformers in American history—were not only motivated by faith, but repeatedly used religious language to argue for their cause. So to say that men and women should not inject their "personal morality" into public policy debates is a practical absurdity. Our law is by definition a codification of morality, much of it grounded in the Judeo-Christian tradition. Moreover, if we progressives shed some of these biases, we might recognize some overlapping values that both religious and secular people share when it comes to the moral and material direction of our country.

The full text of the speech is available at http://obamaspeeches.com/081-Call-to-Renewal-Keynote-Address-Obama-Speech.htm.

5 David A. Frank, "Obama's Rhetorical Signature: Cosmopolitan Civil Religion in the Presidential Inaugural Address, January 20, 2009," *Rhetoric & Public Affairs* 14:4 (2011): 605–30, 621.

6 See Wade Clark Roof, "American Presidential Rhetoric from Ronald Reagan to George W. Bush: Another Look at Civil Religion," *Social Compass* 56:2 (2009): 286–301. For an analysis of Bush's extensive use of the "melodramatic narrative," which paints characters and narratives as wholly good or evil, see Herbert W. Simons, "From Post–9/11 Melodrama to Quagmire in Iraq: A Rhetorical History" *Rhetoric & Public Affairs* 10:2 (2007): 183–94. For an analysis of Bush's use of religious rhetoric in light of theories of democratic discourse, see Rogers M. Smith, "Religious Rhetoric and the Ethics of Public Discourse: The Case of George W. Bush," *Political Theory* 36:2 (2008): 272–300.

7 Even more so because in response to the advantage Bush had among religious voters in 2004, the Democratic primaries in 2008 involved an unusual degree of focus on religion. See Bruce Ledewitz, *Church, State, and the Crisis in American Secularism* (Bloomington: Indiana University Press, 2011), 175; Corwin Schmidt, Kevin den Sulk, Bryan Froehle, James Penning, Stephen Monsma, and Douglas Koopman, *The Disappearing God Gap? Religion in the 2008 Presidential Election* (New York: Oxford University Press, 2010), 74–75. Obama's connection to black liberation theologian and preacher Jeremiah Wright was a prominent topic during the 2008 presidential campaign. See Clarence E. Walker and Gregory D. Smithers, *The Preacher and the Politician: Barack Obama, Jeremiah Wright, and Race in America* (Charlottesville: University of Virginia Press, 2009).

8 The religious or secular nature of A. Philip Randolph's views is still debated, much like those of W. E. B. Du Bois, whose ideas and work profoundly influenced

Randolph. On the secularity of Randolph, see Jervis Anderson, *A. Philip Randolph: A Biographical Portrait* (New York: Harcourt Brace Jovanovich, 1972), 25–26, 49; on the influence of African American Methodism and progressive religion on Randolph's thought, see Cynthia Taylor, *A. Philip Randolph: The Religious Journey of an African American Labor Leader* (New York: NYU Press, 2005). For a balanced overview of Randolph's relationship to religion and the black church, see Cornelius L. Bynum, *A. Philip Randolph and the Struggle for Civil Rights* (Urbana, Chicago, and Springfield: University of Illinois Press, 2010). On both Du Bois's and Randolph's relationship to black churches, see Barbara Dianne Savage, "W. E. B. Du Bois and 'The Negro Church,'" *Annals of the American Academy of Political and Social Science* 568 (2000): 235–49. Similar debates also continue about Twain's religious views. See Harold K. Bush Jr., *Mark Twain and the Spiritual Crisis of His Age* (Tuscaloosa: University of Alabama Press, 2007); cf. John Bird, "The Mark Twain and Robert Ingersoll Connection: Freethought, Borrowed Thought, Stolen Thought," *Mark Twain Annual* 11 (2013): 42–61.

9 E.g., Porterfield (2012); Stewart (2014). On the global influence of Paine's ideas on democracy and civil society, see Michael Howard, *War and the Liberal Conscience* (New Brunswick, NJ: Rutgers University Press, 1978), 29–32; Thomas C. Walker, "The Forgotten Prophet: Tom Paine's Cosmopolitanism and International Relations," *International Studies Quarterly* 44:1 (2000): 51–72.

10 David Domke and Kevin Coe, *The God Strategy: How Religion Became a Political Weapon in America*, updated edition (New York: Oxford University Press, 2010), 161, 234(fn22). The full text of the speech is available at http://www.presidency.ucsb.edu/ws/index.php?pid=4694.

11 Approximately 38 million viewers watched the speech in the U.S. on television, and many more watched it on the internet. These figures were over 25% higher than those for the first inaugural speeches by George W. Bush and Bill Clinton, but lower than those for Ronald Reagan's first inauguration in the pre–cable TV, pre-internet era (Oliver Luft, "Barack Obama's Inauguration Watched by 40m Americans," *Guardian* [January 22, 2009]). On the prominence of civil religious themes in inaugural speeches, see Cynthia Toolin, "American Civil Religion from 1789 to 1981: A Content Analysis of Presidential Inaugural Addresses," *Review of Religious Research* 25:1 (1983): 39–48.

12 The data analyzed were taken from the 2003 American Mosaic Survey, publicly available from the Association of Religion Data Archives at http://www.thearda.com/Archive/Files/Descriptions/MOSAIC.asp. For each of the questions, we excluded respondents with the characteristic in question from analysis. For example, when asking about atheists, disbelievers were excluded and when asking about whites, only racial minorities' responses were analyzed. This prevents the size of the groups in the survey from influencing the resulting frequencies and provides a better assessment of tolerance across social boundaries. Homosexuality was an exception, as there was no question about sexual identity on the survey.

For the "conservative Christian" questions, we excluded biblical literalists. For an extensive report on the rhetorical and symbolic exclusion of atheists from civil society, see Edgell, Gerteis, and Hartmann's (2007) research analyzing the same data. In spite of the remaining antipathy towards atheists, public acceptance of anti-religious individuals has also been moderately increasing. For example, according to the General Social Surveys, in 1972, 67% of Americans said that individuals should be allowed to speak publicly against "churches and religion," 63% said anti-religious books should be allowed in public libraries, and 42% said that anti-religious professors should be allowed to teach at colleges and universities. In 2010, 75% of Americans said anti-religionists should be allowed to speak publically and have books in the library. The greatest increase in tolerance occurred regarding irreligious teachers, with 62% saying they should be allowed to teach. Further, the 2014 Boundaries of American Life Survey replicated the questions from the 2003 Mosaic survey and found that Muslims had become slightly more distrusted than atheists. This suggests that Islamophobia may be replacing concern for "atheistic communism" in the constructions of a primary "othered" category against which normative American identity is constructed. Preliminary results from the survey can be found at http://www.soc.umn.edu/assets/doc/BAMPreliminaryFindingsReport.pdf. Even so, atheists and the nonreligious remained highly distrusted.

13 For instance, James Dobson, founder of the powerful Christian parachurch organization Focus on the Family, used his first "Family Talk" radio program after the Sandy Hook Elementary School shootings in 2012 to make the following statements:

> Our country really does seem in complete disarray. I'm not talking politically, I'm not talking about the result of the November 6th election. I am saying that something has gone wrong in America. And we have turned our back on God. I mean, millions of people have decided that either God doesn't exist or He's irrelevant. And we've killed 54 million babies and the institution of marriage is right on the verge of a complete redefinition. Believe me, that is gonna have consequences too. And a lot of these things are happening around us. And somebody is gonna get mad at me for saying what I'm about to say right now, but I'm gonna give you my honest opinion. I think we have turned our back on the scripture and on God Almighty, and I think He has allowed judgment to fall upon us. I think that's what's going on.

Full audio of the broadcast is available at http://drjamesdobson.org/Broadcasts/Broadcast?i=32d0ea7c-eeb2-41fb-9c05-f6e0c733d58a. For a positive response to the increase in secularity, see Paul Kurtz, "Bravo! Secularism Growing in the U.S.," *Free Inquiry* 22:3 (2002).

14 For the claim that the increase in religious nones is measurement error, see Rodney Stark, "The Myth of Unreligious America," *Wall Street Journal* (July 4, 2013). A more moderate version of this argument is presented in Dougherty, Johnson, and Polson (2007).

15 Examples of high-profile headlines include Laurie Goodstein, "Study Finds One in 6 Follows No Religion," *New York Times* (December 18, 2012): A9; Michelle Boorstein, "15 Percent of Americans Have No Religion; Fewer Call Themselves Christian; Nondenominational Identification Increases," *Washington Post* (March 9, 2009): A4; Nica Lalli, "No Religion? No Problem," *USA Today* (April 6, 2009): A15.

16 Shook (2010: 13).

17 Williamson and Yancey (2013: 17) fall into this trap. They argue that "atheism seeks to negate religion." As a description of some atheists' views this would be apt, but as a general definition of atheism it is clearly problematic. Although many atheists undoubtedly seek to counter the influence of religion on culture, just as undoubtedly there are many who are indifferent to religion rather than antagonistic. Indeed, this characterization is only fair if we define religion as "that which seeks to negate atheism." While there is some truth to this statement, it is misleading as a definition, and, so far as we are aware, has never been seriously proposed as a social scientific definition of religion.

18 Our theoretical perspective is particularly applicable at a level of analytic scope more micro than the one we pursue here. Qualitative work using life histories and in-depth interviews is required to understand the personal, narrative dimensions of secularity. Ideally, such work will be done on various expressions of secularity, and with individuals holding varying levels of commitment to secularity. Work on American atheism (LeDrew 2013; Smith 2011, 2013) and apostasy (Zuckerman 2011), as well as on Scandinavian secularity (Zuckerman 2008), has laid the groundwork for a broader comparative and qualitative understanding of secularity as a social status.

19 To be fair, some versions of secularization theory—not coincidentally those that prove most insightful—examine *religious responses* to secularization (e.g., Bruce 2008; Casanova 1994; Martin 2005). We are advocating understanding the religious and secular in relation to one another as a general principle, while also attempting to avoid the overgeneralization and lack of empiricism that plagues classical theories of secularization.

20 By performing analyses primarily at the level of aggregated individuals representing generalized public opinion, we necessarily miss many of the interesting biographical experiences that color personalized narratives of secularity. Indeed, one of the most challenging aspects of studying identity of any kind is parsing shared aspects of self-understanding from the truly personalized. Although we also provide biographical examples throughout, our analyses necessarily obscure many "negative cases" to the patterns we highlight (e.g., the atheist who is very spiritual in other ways, but whose survey response is outweighed by the majority of atheists who are not religious or spiritual). Similarly, we generally do not explore more macro levels of analysis than individuals in the U.S., although we certainly think such comparative endeavors are worthwhile. Our intent is to provide a better understanding of basic patterns, establishing a baseline against which other studies can be usefully framed.

21 We are also aware of the danger of overinterpreting aggregate patterns of public opinion, as large portions of the public may be ill-informed, indifferent, or incoherent about the belief systems they adhere to or espouse. The now classic statement of this problem is Philip Converse, "The Nature of Belief Systems in Mass Publics," pp. 206–61 in *Ideology and Discontent*, edited by David Apter (New York: Free Press of Glencoe, 1964). This interpretive caveat is well taken, but most people are also able to articulate at least the basic tenets of positions they hold, such as view of God and religious affiliation. Whether secularists are ideologically more diverse or less coherent than other segments of the population is an open empirical question.

22 For a thorough account of the origins and meanings of "secular," see Asad's (2003: 21–66) genealogical anthropology of the category.

23 Lee (2012a: 131) provides a discussion of the various terms used in the study of secularism and an argument for "nonreligion" as the organizing concept under which others should be housed.

CHAPTER 1. CLASSIFYING SECULARITIES

1 Taylor (2007: 269) argues that it is debatable "whether there could be unbelief without any sense of some religious view which is being negated."

2 Calhoun, Juergensmeyer, and VanAntwerpen (2011).

3 Defining what is secular forcefully implies the corollary of defining what is religious. On this count we default to our exegetical discussion of the fundamental axiom of social construction in chapter 3; given the social constitution of religious/secular, the definitions that matter are those of the people making the distinctions. If people define themselves as "not religious" (or "religious") in some way, we treat these designations as meaningful. We do, however, complicate this principle by introducing the component of nonbehavior (religious practice) into one of our primary classifications.

4 On the tendency for debates over secularization to obscure more than they clarify, see Gorski and Altinordu (2008).

5 For rebuttals of such pejorative designations of secularism using social science, see Zuckerman (2008, 2011: 121–38).

6 Hurd (2011). We are guilty of furthering this confusion by adding to academic research using an either/or of religious/not religious (Baker and Smith 2009a). Although our analyses of a binary classification were justified in the sense of laying down a baseline empirical understanding of American secularity (or so we like to tell ourselves), we quickly saw the inadequacy of such an overgeneral delineation. On the constructed nature of conceptualization more generally, see Howard Becker's *Tricks of the Trade* (Chicago: University of Chicago Press, 1998), 109–45.

7 Our categorizations are based on the typology of religious commitment developed by Charles Y. Glock and Rodney Stark, *Religion and Society in Tension* (Chicago: Rand McNally, 1965). Glock and Stark proposed dimensions of religious

belief, practice, feeling, knowledge, and effects. Each of these dimensions can be applied negatively to appreciate an individual's distance from organized religion, and can even be applied positively to assess a person's engagement with explicitly secular communities, either "imagined" via mediated communication or face-to-face.

8 See Shook (2010) for an overview of the variety of imputations of these general categories, as well as a discussion of the historically variable meaning of terms such as "atheism."

9 It is important to clarify that nonbelievers still believe theism is real in the sense that it affects others' belief and actions. In other words, that theism has a *social* reality. Otherwise, critiquing religion would be absurd. It is also noteworthy that there may be believing agnostics, that is, people who say there is no way to know about God's existence, but who choose to believe anyway.

10 We use the lower case spelling of "god" when referring to the views of atheists or agnostics, as this more accurately represents their views—since, for most, "god" is not a proper noun, if it even represents anything that exists at all. Elsewhere, we follow the cultural convention of capitalizing "God" to signify a specific, anthropomorphic view of theism.

11 The "costs" in terms of time and investment, ranging from lowest to highest, would be religious belief, affiliation, and practice. That is, espousing belief is relatively "easy" to do, while practice takes time and commitment. Of course there are also psychic costs to expressing beliefs one does not truly hold.

12 Grace Davie (1994, 2000) and David Voas (2009; Voas and Crockett 2005; Crockett and Voas 2006) are the primary figures in the discourse over the meaning of "believing without belonging." Although they agree on the increasing prevalence of the trend, Davie sees it as evidence of privatization, primarily a shift in the manner in which religiosity is expressed. In contrast, Voas argues that widespread theistic belief is merely the cultural residue of a once preeminent Christendom in Western Europe. In essence, he argues that theistic belief is also waning, and will continue to decline in the near future. Implicitly embedded within this discourse is a debate on whether privatized belief "counts" as a meaningful form of religious expression.

13 Demerath (2000, 2001). On the closely related concept of symbolic religious identity, see Gans (1994). Notably, our definition of cultural religion is different from that of Zuckerman (2008), who defines it in relation to theistic belief rather than practice.

14 We based these classificatory decisions on the measures available in the GSS. The "less than once a week" distinction for prayer is looser than we would prefer, but was the next category used after "never" on the GSS. Ideally, the classification of "cultural religion" using private levels of practice would offer a response option such as "rarely" in addition to "never." As an ideal type, we are interested in people who retain some level of religious self-understanding, but for whom religious practice is at most a rarity.

15 The best-known statement of this understanding of sociological inquiry is C. Wright Mills, *The Sociological Imagination* (New York: Oxford University Press, [1959] 2000). More recently, the tension between general/specific modes of explanation has arisen regarding historiography.

16 Estimates for the proportion of the U.S. population exiting religious and nonreligious statuses were calculated using results from the Faith Matters Survey (for details, see Putnam and Campbell 2010: 557–61) combined with an estimated 16.8% religious nones (2008 GSS) and a Census Bureau estimate of the population of American adults as 219,259,405 in 2007. Lim, MacGregor, and Putnam (2010) use the same data to provide an in-depth analysis of the relative instability of the "no religion" category using longitudinal data. On the interactive effects of age and family status to produce life cycle effects on religiosity, see Stolzenberg, Blair-Loy, and Waite (1995).

17 Grasso (2002: 473) provides information on Miller's journey from traditionally religious to freethinker to prophet. For an excellent history of the "burned-over district," see Whitney R. Cross, *The Burned-Over District: The Social and Intellectual History of Enthusiastic Religion in Western New York, 1800–1850* (Ithaca, NY: Cornell University Press, [1950] 1982).

18 As Robert Putnam and David Campbell (2010: 136) summarized in their wide-ranging examination of American religion, "entirely apart from genuine conversion or apostasy, American religious identities are fuzzy around the edges." Also see Sherkat (1991); Sherkat and Wilson (1995); Vargas (2012).

19 Interestingly, 21% of self-identified atheists answered "yes" to the God question. It is unclear what, exactly, these respondents thought "atheism" meant. Fully two thirds of agnostics said yes to the God question. Based on a follow-up question, 39% of "God-believing atheists" then reported that they were "absolutely certain" about this belief, as were 32% of "God-believing agnostics." About 31% of "theistic atheists" said they believed in an anthropomorphic God, as did 26% of "theistic agnostics." This disjoint between self-identification with secular labels and responses to theistic belief questions reinforces the fuzzy nature of these classificatory boundaries and the possible differences depending on operationalization and measurement of secular identities.

20 We also used a sample of Americans matched to population characteristics and collected by Knowledge Networks to assess levels of self-identified salience with the labels "irreligious," "secular," and "religiously indifferent." "Irreligious" (1.1%) and "secular" (2.2%) had low levels of recognition or salience, but "religiously indifferent" was a label affirmed by a substantial proportion of respondents (11%). Analyses showed that Jews (17%), Buddhists (15%), Catholics (12%), Hindus (12%), and religious nones (28%) were more likely to think of themselves as religiously indifferent compared to Protestants (3%). It is telling that only 28% of nones thought of themselves this way, and that nonaffiliated believers were more likely than disbelievers (7%) to describe themselves as religiously indifferent. Nonaffiliated belief thus appears to be a category selected by people who have

privatized their spiritual beliefs and practices *or* those who are apathetic about religion. Those at certain levels of social class were also more likely to be apathetic. Specifically, individuals with upper-middle-class incomes ($75,000 to $125,000) and the rich (more than $175,000 per year) were the most likely to be religiously indifferent.

21 Our estimate for the number of adult Americans in 2010 is based on Census data, which put the figure at 234,564,071.

22 In addition to the GSS and Pew Religious Landscape Survey, analyses of Wave II of the Baylor Religion Survey (2007) show distinct sociodemographic and religious patterns for atheists, agnostics, and nonaffiliated believers (Baker 2012a; Baker and Smith 2009b).

CHAPTER 2. A CULTURAL VIEW OF SECULARITIES

1 W. E. B. Du Bois conducted some of the earliest empirically grounded studies of religion, but his work on religion has often been ignored or misunderstood. See Robert A. Wortham, "Du Bois and the Sociology of Religion: Rediscovering a Founding Figure," *Sociological Inquiry* 75:4 (2005): 433–52; Wortham, "W. E. B. Du Bois, the Black Church, and the Sociological Study of Religion," *Sociological Spectrum* 29 (2009): 144–72; Phil Zuckerman, "The Sociology of Religion of W. E. B. Du Bois," *Sociology of Religion* 63:2 (2002): 239–53.

2 James Q. Dealey, Edward A. Ross, Franklin H. Giddings, Ulysses G. Weatherly, Charles A. Ellwood, George E. Howard, Frank W. Blackmar and Albion W. Small, "Lester Frank Ward," *American Journal of Sociology* 19:1 (1913): 61–78, 66. Also see Samuel Chugerman, *Lester Frank Ward, the American Aristotle: A Summary and Interpretation of His Sociology* (Durham, NC: Duke University Press, 1939); Andrew A. Sorensen, "Lester Frank Ward, 'The American Aristotle,' in Illinois," *Journal of the Illinois State Historical Society* 63:2 (1970): 158–66.

3 James Q. Dealey, "Masters of Social Science: Lester Frank Ward," *Social Forces* 4:2 (1925): 257–72, 258.

4 Emily P. Cape, *Lester F. Ward; a Personal Sketch* (New York: G. P. Putnam's Sons, 1922), 21.

5 Clifford C. Scott, *Lester Frank Ward* (Boston: Twayne Publishers, 1976), 17.

6 In many ways, the thought of Ward parallels that of Frances Wright.

7 Scott, *Lester Frank Ward*, 33.

8 Ibid., 35.

9 "Organization of the American Sociological Society: Official Report," *American Journal of Sociology* 11:4 (1906): 555–69, 568–69.

10 On Ward's place as a founder of American sociology, see Samuel C. Mitchell, "Some Recollections of Lester F. Ward and James Q. Dealey," *Social Forces* 16:1 (1937): 44–47, 47. On the importance of Ward's work to contemporary sociology and an argument for his inclusion among the "classics," see James J. Chriss, "The Place of Lester Ward among the Sociological Classics," *Journal of Classical Sociology* 6:1 (2006): 5–21. Regarding the importance of Ward to liberal social

philosophy and his impact on social policy in the U.S., see Henry S. Commager (ed.), *Lester Ward and the Welfare State* (Indianapolis: Bobbs-Merrill, 1967).

11 Lester F. Ward, "The Situation," *Iconoclast* 1:1 (1870). Reprinted in *Glimpses of the Cosmos*, Vol. 1 (New York: G. P. Putnam's Sons, 1913), 46.

12 Lester F. Ward, "What Has Been Gained? No. 2," *Iconoclast* 1:5 (1870). Reprinted in *Glimpses of the Cosmos*, Vol. 1 (New York: G. P. Putnam's Sons, 1913), 79.

13 Lester F. Ward, *Dynamic Sociology: Or Applied Social Science as Based upon Statical Sociology and the Less Complex Sciences*, Volumes I and II (New York: D. Appleton and Co., 1883), 305.

14 Lester F. Ward, "The Data of Sociology: Contributions to Social Philosophy, VI," *American Journal of Sociology* 1:6 (1896): 738–52, 749–50. Purveyors of classical social theory will recognize Auguste Comte's "law of three stages" in Ward's arguments here. Although Comte is not cited in the article referenced, Ward begins *Dynamic Sociology* with an extensive treatment of Comte's work. He also makes his admiration for and knowledge of Comte's work plain in other places. For example, see his review of *The Positive Philosophy of Auguste Comte*, by Lucien Lévy-Bruhl, in *Science* 19:479 (1904): 376–80.

15 Lester F. Ward, *Applied Sociology: A Treatise on the Conscious Improvement of Society by Society* (Boston: Ginn and Company, 1906), 65, 68.

16 Ibid., 75–76. John W. Draper's *History of the Conflict between Religion and Science* (New York: D. Appleton and Co. [1874] 1897) and Andrew D. White's *A History of the Warfare of Science with Theology in Christendom* (New York: D. Appleton and Co., 1896) became seminal texts for those advancing a conflict thesis between religion and science. This position is historically inaccurate (see Evans and Evans 2008), but nonetheless maintains some rhetorical currency among agnostics, and most especially among atheists (Baker 2012a, 2012b).

17 Regarding Paine, see Lester F. Ward, "The Struggle of To-Day," *Truth Seeker* 39:7 (1912): 98–99. Reprinted in *Glimpses of the Cosmos*, Vol. 6 (New York: G. P. Putnam's Sons, 1918).

18 Ward, *Applied Sociology*, 82.

19 Lester F. Ward, "The Purpose of Sociology. Contributions to Social Philosophy. IX," *American Journal of Sociology* 2:3 (1896): 446–60, 456–57, emphasis in original.

20 Scott, *Lester Frank Ward*, 162. Ironically, Frances Wright and Robert Dale Owen had opened halls of science seventy years earlier, to little avail.

21 Christian Smith (2003) provides an account of the secularization process in American sociology. Also see Cecil E. Greek, *The Religious Roots of American Sociology* (New York: Garland Publishing, 1992), 209–29; Susan E. Henking, "Protestant Religious Experience and the Rise of American Sociology: Evidence from the Bernard Papers," *Journal of the History of the Behavioral Sciences* 28:4 (1992): 325–39; "Sociological Christianity and Christian Sociology: The Paradox of Early American Sociology," *Religion and American Culture: A Journal of Interpretation* 3:1 (1993): 49–67; Arthur J. Vidich and Stanford M. Lyman,

American Sociology: Worldly Rejections of Religion and Their Directions (New Haven, CT: Yale University Press, 1985).

22 Vidich and Lyman, *American Sociology*, 35.

23 Cape, *Lester F. Ward; a Personal Sketch*, 121. Charlotte Perkins Gilman would later use Ward's framework to argue that, historically, religion has indeed been about *man's* thoughts and feelings. See Charlotte Perkins Gilman, *His Religion and Hers: A Study of the Faith of Our Fathers and the Work of Our Mothers* (New York: Century, 1923).

24 Lester F. Ward, "Spain and Ferrer," *Truth Seeker* 27:2 (1910): 17–18. Reprinted in *Glimpses of the Cosmos*, Vol. 6 (New York: G. P. Putnam's Sons, 1918), 348. An article reprinting one of Ward's lectures during the last year of his life provides a concise, summary statement of his position contra eugenics: Lester F. Ward, "Eugenics, Euthenics, and Eudemics," *American Journal of Sociology* 18:6 (1913): 737–54.

25 Ward's views on "race" remain ethnocentric and modernist, particularly in reference to Native Americans and other groups he labels as "savage." At the same time, relative to the intellectual climate he was working in, Ward's views of race are quite progressive, as he was adamant that any differences across racial groups were the product of environment and subjugation rather than heredity:

> It must be remembered that both races have descended from the same original stock, although they do not know it. There is therefore no essential difference in their general character. The superiority by which one was able to conquer the other may have been due to a variety of more or less accidental causes. It does not render them superior in other respects. (Lester F. Ward, "Evolution of Social Structures," *American Journal of Sociology* 10:5 [1905]: 589–605, 597)

26 Ward, *Dynamic Sociology*, vii.

27 Mitchell, "Some Recollections of Lester F. Ward and James Q. Dealey," 45.

28 Scott, *Lester Frank Ward*, 131, 135.

29 However, Ward does have a remarkably innovative and interesting general theory about the functions of religion that has gone almost completely unnoticed. See "The Essential Nature of Religion," *International Journal of Ethics* 8:2 (1898): 169–92.

30 It has been said that secularization theories are as "useless as a hotel elevator that only goes down" for examining religious revival or resurgence (Stark 1999: 269). For critical overviews of classical secularization perspectives, see Gorski and Altinordu (2008); Hadden (1987); Martin (1991); Swatos and Christiano (1999); Taylor (2007: 423–37). The most straightforward "rational choice" critique of secularization theories is laid out in Rodney Stark and Roger Finke, *Acts of Faith: Explaining the Human Side of Religion* (Berkeley: University of California Press, 2000). In effect, because classical secularization theories (at least implicitly) assume religion is irrational, economic theories provided a ready, and in many ways necessary, foil and corrective. The problem now becomes one of articulating

a framework for understanding religion that draws on the useful elements of both theories while avoiding their oversights, mistakes, and dogmatisms.

31 By setting religious economies in direct opposition to theories of secularization, rational choice perspectives end up with problems inverted from those of secularization. For instance, secularization theorists assume a declining demand for religion with the advance of modernity, leaving them in a difficult position to deal with revival movements (although see Casanova 1994; Martin 1969, 1991, 2005). Inversely, religious economies theories assume an innate demand for religious goods (Stark and Finke, *Acts of Faith*, 193), leaving such frameworks unable to deal with changes to religious consumption occurring absent restructurings of religious supply, as has been the case in the U.S. over the last three decades. Further, the strong emphasis of rational choice theories on religious suppliers, and their associated organizations, is ill suited for examining individuals, who by definition, are not "in the market" for religious goods and have no related organizations. Our training is in the intellectual lineage of market theories of religion, so we draw frequently from this school of thought, but our intimacy with rational choice preoccupations, such as privileging deductive theorizing, the de facto assumption of stable and innate religious demand, and the oversight of the integral role of emotions in religion make us acutely aware of the perspective's limitations. A full conception of meaning and identity is also decidedly missing from rational choice approaches.

32 For overviews of the different contemporary currents in the cultural study of religion, detailing how this approach offers an escape hatch from the stagnant secularization versus market debates, see Penny Edgell, "A Cultural Sociology of Religion: New Directions," *Annual Review of Sociology* 38 (2012): 247–65; David Smilde, "Beyond Cultural Autonomy in the Study of Religion," pp. 43–66 in *Religion on the Edge: Decentering and Recentering the Sociology of Religion*, edited by Courtney Bender, Wendy Cadge, Peggy Levitt, and David Smilde (New York: Oxford University Press, 2012).

33 William H. Sewell Jr., *The Logics of History: Social Theory and Social Transformation* (Chicago: University of Chicago Press, 2005), 152–74, which details of the multiple meanings and applications of the idea of "culture," is informative on this count and shapes the discussion here. Our use of the concept of culture also draws heavily on the work of Clifford Geertz, *The Interpretation of Cultures* (New York: Basic Books, 1973). Further, although her methodological strategy differs from our own, the work of Mary Douglas linking the contours of ideology to various types of social structure, and a person's position within such structures, is the theoretical vision closest to how we conceive of a reframed study of religiosity and secularity. See *Natural Symbols: Explorations in Cosmology* (New York: Pantheon Books, 1970); also James V. Spickard, "A Guide to Mary Douglas's Three Versions of Grid/Group Theory," *Sociological Analysis* 50:2 (1989): 151–70.

34 See Nancy Ammerman, *Sacred Stories, Spiritual Tribes: Locating Religion in Everyday Life* (New York: Oxford University Press, 2013), 291.

35 Penny Edgell defines schemas as "interpretive frameworks through which individuals . . . assess their own lives" (*Religion and Family in a Changing Society* [Princeton, NJ: Princeton University Press, 2005], 31).

36 Our theoretical perspective draws on Zerubavel's work on cognition and memory as collective endeavors. In short, he argues that seemingly internal (because they are mental) attributes are the products of inherently social processes. See Eviatar Zerubavel, *Social Mindscapes: An Invitation to Cognitive Sociology* (Cambridge, MA: Harvard University Press, 1997); and *Time Maps: Collective Memory and the Social Shape of the Past* (Chicago: University of Chicago Press, 2003). Zerubavel's arguments are similar to those set forth by other "social constructionists," such as Peter L. Berger and Thomas Luckmann, *The Social Construction of Reality: A Treatise in the Sociology of Knowledge* (New York: Anchor Books, 1966).

37 For critical reviews of the problems created by such approaches, see John Levi Martin, *The Explanation of Social Action* (New York: Oxford University Press, 2011), esp. chapters 3 and 4; Robert Wuthnow, *Meaning and Moral Order: Explorations in Cultural Analysis* (Princeton, NJ: Princeton University Press, 1987), 335–39.

38 For classical texts on the nature of selves and identities that provide the assumptions we use for thinking about these concepts, see Charles H. Cooley, *Social Organization: A Study of the Larger Mind* (New York: Charles Scribner's Sons, 1913), and Erving Goffman, *The Presentation of Self in Everyday Life*. (New York: Anchor Books, 1959). Despite the title of his seminal work, Goffman does not explicitly deal with the self as a concept—indeed, his work proceeds on the implicit assumption that the essentialist self is simultaneously a reality *and* a falsehood by showing all the ways presentations may be "inauthentic." This, however, assumes there is an authentic self, otherwise "inauthenticity" is a meaningless designation. On the dynamics of intersections between what he terms "self," "personal," "ego," and "social" identities, see Goffman, *Stigma: Notes on the Management of Spoiled Identity* (New York: Simon & Schuster, 1963). "A Reply to Denzin and Keller," *Contemporary Sociology* 10:1 (1981): 60–68, is also informative regarding Goffman's assumptions about the self: "If the result of my approach can be construed as 'decentering' the self, then I am happy to be in the vanguard, providing it is appreciated that this does not mean a lack of interest in the self, merely an effort to approach its figuring from additional directions" (62).

39 William I. Thomas and Dorothy Thomas, *The Child in America: Behavior Problems and Programs* (New York: Knopf, 1928), 572. For the interesting story of why the theorem is credited to W. I. Thomas to the exclusion of his coauthor, Dorothy Thomas, as well as the sociocognitive history of the theorem, see Robert K. Merton, "The Thomas Theorem and the Matthew Effect," *Social Forces* 72:2 (1995): 379–424.

40 The vast literature on differential association theory in criminology consistently demonstrates the impact of peers, parents, and siblings on delinquency and crime. Concerning the relationship between religious/political ideology

and networks, see Stephen Vaisey and Omar Lizardo, "Can Cultural Worldviews Influence Network Composition?" *Social Forces* 88:4 (2010): 1595–618.

41 In *Presentation of Self*, Goffman outlines the distinction between information "given" versus that "given off."

42 On the concept of a "master status" and commitment to a particular line of social action, see Howard S. Becker, "Notes on the Concept of Commitment," *American Journal of Sociology* 66:1 (1960): 32–40. As anyone who has occupied a marginalized status can attest, the distinction between a status an individual finds personally salient and one made salient by others is crucial. Regardless of personal salience, social recognition is integral, as "the individual can identify himself with a role only insofar as others have identified him with it" (Berger 1967: 37).

43 Zuckerman (2008, 2011).

44 Russell Hardin, *How Do You Know? The Economics of Ordinary Knowledge* (Princeton, NJ: Princeton University Press, 2009).

45 For general references on the demographics of religiosity and secularism, see Michael S. Hout, Andrew Greeley, and Melissa Wilde, "The Demographic Imperative in Religious Change in the United States," *American Journal of Sociology* 107:2 (2001): 468–500; Norris and Inglehart (2004: 231–41).

46 This line of thought is based on Pierre Bourdieu's notion of *habitus* from *Distinction: A Social Critique of the Judgement of Taste*, translated by Richard Nice (Cambridge, MA: Harvard University Press, 1984).

47 The now classic study of the role of social networks in conversion is John Lofland and Rodney Stark, "Becoming a World-Saver: A Theory of Conversion to a Deviant Perspective," *American Sociological Review* 30:6 (1965): 862–75; cf. David A. Snow and Cynthia L. Phillips, "The Lofland-Stark Conversion Model: A Critical Reassessment," *Social Problems* 27:4 (1980): 430–47. On the role played by mediated communication in identity maintenance in conjunction with social networks (but not as the sole source of conversion), see William S. Bainbridge, *The Sociology of Religious Movements* (New York: Routledge, 1997), 149–78; David Smilde, "A Qualitative Comparative Analysis of Conversion to Venezuelan Evangelicalism: How Networks Matter," *American Journal of Sociology* 111:3 (2005): 757–96.

48 Berger's (1967) notion of "taken-for-grantedness" regarding this process is apt. Our understanding of and theorizing about identity also builds on the work of Charles Taylor (1989) and Margaret Somers, "The Narrative Constitution of Identity: A Relational and Network Approach," *Theory and Society* 23:5 (1994): 605–49.

49 This concept is similar to the one that undergirds the idea of "cosmic war" outlined by Mark Juergensmeyer in *Terror in the Mind of God: The Global Rise of Religious Violence* (Berkeley: University of California Press, 2001). In effect, we have simply extended the concept to include expressions of secularity.

50 Philip Converse, "The Nature of Belief Systems in Mass Publics," pp. 206–61 in *Ideology and Discontent*, edited by David Apter (New York: Free Press, 1964), 207. For theoretical elaborations of the concept of belief systems, see James T. Borhek and Richard Curtis, *A Sociology of Belief* (New York: John Wiley and Sons, 1975). For mathematical measurements of belief system consensus and "constraint" and how these ideological elements are related to the structural hierarchy of power in groups, see John L. Martin, "Power, Authority, and the Constraint of Belief Systems," *American Journal of Sociology* 107:4 (2002): 861–904.

51 Some may be more assertive than others, hence the amusing bumper sticker "Militant agnostic: I don't know and you don't either."

52 Growing out of the understanding of making one's self an "object," the view of the self as an ongoing soliloquy is an excellent metaphor for this process; see Lonnie Athens, "The Self as a Soliloquy," *Sociological Quarterly* 35:3 (1994): 521–32; and "Dramatic Self Change," *Sociological Quarterly* 36:3 (1995): 571–86. In the broader sense, the diversity and efficacy of lines of action that are open to a given individual are determined by her relative social power. Those with greater levels of status have more possibilities of action available and can affect a greater number of people through the consequences of action. Agency can thus be stratified into interpersonal, organizational, and political economic power in ascending order of influence.

53 The study of social movements has recently come to a greater understanding of the role of belief systems by focusing on the importance of ideological framing and identity for collective action. See Robert D. Benford and David A. Snow, "Framing Processes and Social Movements: An Overview and Assessment," *Annual Review of Sociology* 26 (2000): 611–39.

54 The definitive statement on the reciprocal relationship between the ideological and the material is Berger and Luckmann's *Social Construction of Reality*. The most meticulous treatment of the topic is Bourdieu's *Distinction*. Although less well known, perhaps the most thorough and insightful treatment is Werner Stark, *The Sociology of Knowledge: Toward a Deeper Understanding of the History of Ideas* (New Brunswick, NJ: Transaction Publishers, [1958] 1991); see also Stark, *The Fundamental Forms of Social Thought* (New York: Fordham University Press, 1963). A more recent perspective that builds on Bourdieu's reflexive theory is John Levi Martin's field theory, which views perception as the cognitive processing of social objects embedded in relational fields. These objects can be anything from tools to people, but all are understood as the nexus of perceived social relations, although people may not recognize this to be the case. See John L. Martin, "What Is Field Theory?" *American Journal of Sociology* 109:1 (2003): 1–49; and *The Explanation of Social Action* (New York: Oxford University Press, 2011).

55 It is arguable that even for reactive cognition, preexisting belief systems may at least partially shape the reactive response. See Eliot R. Smith and Jamie DeCoster, "Dual-Process Models in Social and Cognitive Psychology: Conceptual Integration and Links to Underlying Memory Systems," *Personality and Social*

Psychology Review 4:2 (2000): 108–31. For an overview of the research on dual-process theories of cognition, see Jonathan St. B. T. Evans and Keith E. Stanovich, "Dual-Process Theories of Higher Cognition: Advancing the Debate," *Perspectives on Psychological Science* 8:3 (2013): 233–41.

CHAPTER 3. HISTORICAL FOUNDATIONS

1 Thomas Paine, *Age of Reason. Part the Second. Being an Investigation of True and Fabulous Theology* (London: Daniel Isaac Eaton, 1796), 79. The perception of religious identity as the outcome of personal decision rather than the result of obligatory familial or clan transmission is a central aspect of how secularity diffused into the wider public.

2 The parallels in the historical narratives related by philosopher Charles Taylor (2007) and historian James Turner (1985) are remarkably similar considering that neither acknowledges the work of the other. The differences between these accounts are primarily methodological. Taylor focuses on philosophical currents, while Turner focuses on a historical exploration of the development of nonbelief.

3 Taylor (2007).

4 Taylor (1989). Interpretations of secularity in the U.S. have come to play pivotal roles in debates about the connections between religion and modernity. If there is an inevitable relationship between modernity and secularity, as was the predominant thinking in Enlightenment-inspired theories, then the U.S. should be highly secular. Since it is not, the empirical viability of such theories is questionable. As a result, the "uniqueness" of the political history and longitudinal path of the U.S. has been invoked to both save and bury classical accounts of secularization; cf. Bruce (2002) and Stark (1999).

5 Porterfield (2012).

6 David Barton is a popular contemporary advocate of the belief that the U.S. is a "Christian nation." On public opinion about the U.S. as a Christian nation, see Jeremy B. Straughn and Scott L. Feld, "American as a 'Christian Nation'? Understanding Religious Boundaries of National Identity in the United States," *Sociology of Religion* 71:3 (2010): 280–306. On frontier religion, see Roger Finke and Rodney Stark, *The Churching of America, 1776–2005: Winners and Losers in Our Religious Economy*, revised edition (New Brunswick, NJ: Rutgers University Press, 2005), 25–54. For the now classic primers on American civil religion, see Robert Bellah, "Biblical Religion and Civil Religion in America," *Dædalus* 96:1 (1967): 1–21; and *The Broken Covenant: American Civil Religion in Time of Trial*, 2nd edition (Chicago: University of Chicago Press, 1992).

7 Morais ([1934] 1960: 17). Taylor (2007: chap. 6) details the integral role of aristocratic versions of deism in the development of exclusive humanisms and theistic disbelief. Walters's (1992) commentary accompanying original texts provides an excellent introduction to aristocratic and prophetic deism.

8 Grasso's (2008: 64) historical research provides a detailed account of the sensationalism and popularization of the Beadle tragedy by public figures, juxtaposed

with public responses to Allen's treatise. The examples show that even Allen, a folk hero, worked from a deficit to prove his morality absent a commitment to traditional religious precepts. On Allen's treatise, including the uncredited work of revolutionary Thomas Young as co-author, see Kolenda (2013). Young is also generally believed to be the author of a previous tract on natural religion, which was published under a pseudonym (see Aldridge 1997; Anderson 1937; cf. Stewart 2014).

9 In addition to the work of Bellah on the alignment of theological and political ideas of a divine covenant, see Michael W. Hughey, "The Political Covenant: Protestant Foundations of the American State," *State, Culture, and Society* 1:1 (1984): 113–56; Kenneth Wald and Allison Calhoun-Brown, *Religion and Politics in the United States*, 5th edition (Lanham, MD: Rowman & Littlefield, 2007), 39–64. On the patterns and prevalence of religious citations during the post–Revolutionary War period, see Donald S. Lutz, "The Relative Influence of European Writers on Late Eighteenth-Century American Thought," *American Political Science Review* 78 (1984): 189–97.

10 Derek H. Davis, "Separation, Integration, and Accommodation: Religion and State in America in a Nutshell," *Journal of Church and State* 43:1 (2001): 5–17, 8.

11 Grasso (2008: 65). Provisions against secularists holding public office remain on the books but unenforceable in many states.

12 Letter from Thomas Paine to Samuel Adams in 1803, emphasis in original, pp. 323–28 in *The Theological Works of Thomas Paine*, Vol. 3 (Boston: J. P. Mendum, 1859), 325. Nevertheless, Paine has since the publication of *Age of Reason* been declared an atheist, including famously by Theodore Roosevelt.

13 Morais ([1934] 1960); Koch ([1933] 1968).

14 Rogers (1968).

15 Porterfield (2012). On the role of religion and rhetoric thereof in the presidential campaign of 1800, see Edward J. Larson, *A Magnificent Catastrophe: The Tumultuous Election of 1800, America's First Presidential Campaign* (New York: Simon & Schuster, 2007), 138–63; also see Jon Butler, *Awash in a Sea of Faith: Christianizing the American People* (Cambridge, MA: Harvard University Press, 1990), 219.

16 Samuels (1987, 1990). On popular conspiracy theories linking freethought (and Paine and Jefferson) to Satanism, see W. Scott Poole, *Satan in America: The Devil We Know* (Lanham, MD: Rowan & Littlefield, 2009), 22–27, 94.

17 Much of the information presented on the deistic and freethought movement in the U.S. during this period is taken from its treatment by Post ([1943] 1974); also Grasso (2002). Koch ([1933] 1968: 168–84) and Walters (1992: 34) provide detail on the stagnation of the prophetic phase of the movement. An extensive bibliography compiled by J. Gordon Melton on the history of secularism, deism, and freethought is available at http://reason.sdsu.edu/index.html.

18 Butler, *Awash in a Sea of Faith*, 258–68. On the case of Massachusetts and disestablishment, see John D. Cushing, "Notes on Disestablishment in

Massachusetts, 1780–1833," *William and Mary Quarterly* 26:2 (1969): 169–90; Kelly Olds, "Privatizing the Church: Disestablishment in Connecticut and Massachusetts," *Journal of Political Economy* 102:2 (1994): 277–97.

19 Garver (1980).

20 Grasso (2002: 485).

21 Post ([1943] 1974: 104), emphasis in original. We added italics to the title of *The Bible of Reason* to clarify what is being referenced in the quote.

22 On the trials of Kneeland, see French (1980): 202–21. Kneeland's association with Frances Wright was openly used against him as part and parcel of his purported sexual licentiousness (see Levy 1973: xi).

23 Grasso (2002: 484).

24 Warren ([1943] 1966: 211).

25 Post ([1943] 1974: 231). This effort to create and sustain a viable "freethinker" movement parallels a time of great religious innovation.

26 Finke and Stark, *Churching of America*, 56. Similarly, Butler in *Awash in a Sea of Faith* describes the history of American religion as one of increasing "Christianization," with widespread indifference to organized religion combined with belief in an enchanted world full of magic, spirits, and the like in the colonial and revolutionary periods, followed by extensive religious pluralism and competition. The eras of the greatest expansion of Christian groups were after the Civil War and especially the early twentieth century, which corresponded with increased pluralism and an influx of immigrant Catholicism.

27 Jacoby (2004: 188); Putnam (1894: 500). Walters (1992) shares this assessment.

28 The gendering of God as masculine is purposeful here, designating the sexist assumptions that pervade, then as now, mainstream conceptions of the divine.

29 Multiple theorists and historians have traced the roots of modern secularism through religious discourse including Berger (1967), Campbell (1972), Taylor (2007), and Weber ([1922] 1991). Our discussion of this ideological sequencing draws most heavily on Turner (1985), because his account is the most grounded in available documentation.

30 Turner (1985: 182–191, 362).

31 Taylor (2007).

32 Turner (1985: 234). Buckley (1990), Taylor (2007: 232–34, 305–7), and Berger (1967: 53–80) also detail the pivotal role of Protestant theodicy in ideological secularization.

33 Warren ([1943] 1966: 75).

34 Turner (1985: 171–261).

35 Jacoby (2004: 149–85); cf. Warren ([1943] 1966), who argues that this period failed to produce substantial philosophical advances in freethought relative to the postrevolutionary period. This disjoint in evaluation stems from the differential judgment of the intellectualization of freethought in the earlier period and its popularization and diffusion in the latter period.

36 Warren ([1943] 1966: 166).

37 From Putnam's "To the Liberals of America," which appeared in *The Truth Seeker* on September 20, 1844, as quoted in Warren ([1943] 1966: 168).

38 Quotes are from Warren ([1943] 1966: 172, 175). For greater detail on the rise and fall of the American Secular Union, see Warren ([1943] 1966: chap. 7). Similar fates befell smaller secular organizations as well. Garver (1980) outlines how Czech American freethought groups declined as a result of restricted immigration, low levels of secular retention among second-generation immigrants, the undermining of utopian visions of positivist science upon which the ideology of the movement rested, and not least of all because Czechs seeking to more fully assimilate into U.S. citizenship began to downplay freethought traditions.

39 Warren ([1943] 1966: 229).

40 Jacoby (2004: 263); Robert T. Handy, "The American Religious Depression, 1925–1935," *Church History* 29:1 (1960): 3–16, 6.

41 For an exemplary historical narrative and summary of the Scopes trial, see Edward Larson, *Summer for the Gods: The Scopes Trial and America's Continuing Debate Over Science and Religion* (New York: Basic Books, 1997).

42 Handy, "The American Religious Depression."

43 Jacoby (2004: 268–85).

44 Smith (2003).

45 U.S. history is clearly neither wholly Christian nor secular. Instead, there was an earlier separation of church and state than had occurred elsewhere in the world, but simultaneously a long-standing Protestant establishment on state, local, and especially cultural levels. Practical disestablishment was a slow process that unfolded from the nation's founding until well after the Civil War. See Phillip Hammond, *Religion and Personal Autonomy: The Third Disestablishment in America* (Columbia: University of South Carolina Press, 1992); David Sehat, *The Myth of American Religious Freedom* (New York: Oxford University Press, 2011).

46 Warren ([1943] 1966: 173). The nine principles first appeared in the freethought periodical *The Index*, the official publication of the Free Religious Association, which represented "the spiritual descendants of the deists" and the (relatively) conservative wing of the freethought movement; see Warren ([1943] 1966: 96). The tenets were removal of tax exempt status for religious organizations; discontinuance of the employment of chaplains in public institutions, including the military; discontinuance of appropriations of public money for religious education and charities; discontinuance of the use of the Bible in public schools; discontinuance of appointments made at federal or state levels for "religious festivals and fasts"; abolition of judicial oaths and replacement with a simple affirmation; repeal of all blue laws; abolition of laws enforcing a "Christian morality"; and no governmental privilege for religions of any kind (a reiteration of separation). These demands became "the Bible of freethought secularism in America" (Warren [(1943) 1966]: 173).

47 Warren ([1943] 1966: 159).

48 As Taylor (2007: 258) summarizes, "this inward turn is also evident in religious life; indeed the whole turn was largely driven by religious motives."

49 Warren ([1943] 1966: 202).

50 For historical examples of religious responses to secularist movements, see Hughes (2013); Post ([1943] 1974: 199–225); Warren ([1943] 1966: 206–27).

51 We borrow the concept of "folk devils" from Stanley Cohen, *Folk Devils and Moral Panics: The Creation of the Mods and the Rockers*, 3rd edition (London: Routledge, 2002).

CHAPTER 4. THE GREAT ABDICATING

1 The first mention of what became "the pill" in the *New York Times* is in Emma Harrison, "Clerics in Debate on Birth Control" (November 21, 1957). Also see Nicholas Bakalar, "Birth Control Pills 1957," *New York Times* (October 25, 2010).

2 For detailed information on the 1957 CPS, see Samuel A. Mueller and Angela V. Lane, "Tabulations from the 1957 Current Population Survey on Religion: A Contribution to the Demography of American Religion," *Journal for the Scientific Study of Religion* 11:1 (1972): 76–98. Condran and Tamney (1985) use the data to analyze religious nones.

3 Women with school-age children are now much more likely to work. See "Women in the Labor Force: A Databook," U.S. Department of Labor Statistics Report 1049 (May 2014), available at http://www.bls.gov/cps/wlf-databook-2013.pdf. Also see Claudia Goldin, Lawrence F. Katz, and Ilyana Keziemko, "The Homecoming of College Women: The Reversal of the College Gender Gap," *Journal of Economic Perspectives* 20:4 (2006): 133–56.

4 For an exhaustive examination of GSS data on family structure and politics through 2006, see Tom W. Smith, "Changes in Family Structure, Family Values, and Politics, 1972–2006," GSS Social Change Report 53.

5 Wade Clark Roof and Robert Wuthnow provide some of the best overviews of changes to the U.S. religious landscape since World War II. See Wade Clark Roof, *A Generation of Seekers: The Spiritual Journeys of the Baby Boom Generation* (San Francisco: Harper San Francisco, 1993); Roof, *Spiritual Marketplace: Baby Boomers and the Remaking of American Religion* (Princeton, NJ: Princeton University Press, 1999); Robert Wuthnow, *The Restructuring of American Religion: Society and Faith since World War II* (Princeton, NJ: Princeton University Press, 1988); Wuthnow, "Restructuring of American Religion: Further Evidence," *Sociological Inquiry* 66:3 (1996): 303–29; Wuthnow, *After Heaven: Spirituality in America since the 1950s* (Berkeley: University of California Press, 1998). Robert Bellah et al., *Habits of the Heart: Individualism and Commitment in American Life* (Berkeley: University of California Press, 1985), remains the best examination of individualism. See Schwadel (2010) and Hout and Fischer (2002) on the "cohort effects" of the baby boomers as they relate to religious nones.

6 As political scientist James Morone summarizes, "the call to moral arms got organized and articulated in the Carter years (the late 1970s), gathered velocity with Reagan in the bully pulpit (1981–1989), and consolidated its power with the stunning midterm election of 1994" (*Hellfire Nation: The Politics of Sin in American History* [New Haven, CT: Yale University Press, 2003], 455).

7 Pew Forum (2012).

8 David Domke and Kevin Coe, *The God Strategy: How Religion Became a Political Weapon in America*, updated edition (New York: Oxford University Press, 2010).

9 See Chaves (2011: chapter 8); Andrew Greeley and Michael Hout, *The Truth about Conservative Christians* (Chicago: University of Chicago Press, 2006); Putnam and Campbell (2010: chap. 11). Thomas A. Hirschl, James G. Booth, and Leland G. Glenna, "The Link between Voter Choice and Religious Identity in Contemporary Society: Bringing Classical Theory Back In," *Social Science Quarterly* 90:4 (2009): 927–44, show how religious affiliation still reflects underlying differences of social location. For studies detailing the relationship between religious affiliation and ethnicity in the U.S. and the decline of Protestant hegemony in American civil religion in the mid-twentieth century, see Will Herberg, *Protestant, Catholic, Jew* (Garden City, NJ: Doubleday, 1955); Kevin M. Schultz, *Tri-Faith America: How Catholics and Jews Held Postwar America to Its Protestant Promise* (New York: Oxford University Press, 2011).

10 Changes within the Southern Baptist Convention, the largest Protestant denomination in the U.S., provide a microcosm of the broader political disputes in question. See Nancy T. Ammerman, *Baptist Battles: Social Change and Religious Conflict in the Southern Baptist Convention* (New Brunswick, NJ: Rutgers University Press, 1990); Arthur E. Farnsley, *Southern Baptist Politics: Authority and Power in the Restructuring of an American Denomination* (University Park: Penn State University Press, 1994). For a succinct summary of the political evolution of the religious Right, see Matthew C. Moen, "From Revolution to Evolution: The Changing Nature of the Christian Right," *Sociology of Religion* 55:3 (1994): 345–57.

11 Domke and Coe, *The God Strategy*, 42.

12 Ibid., 60–63.

13 Ibid., chapter 4.

14 Robert D. Loevy, *The Flawed Path to the Presidency in 1992* (Albany: SUNY Press, 1994), 182.

15 Video and text of the speech is available at http://www.americanrhetoric.com/speeches/patrickbuchanan1992rnc.htm. Quotations are taken from video of the speech at the convention rather than the written version.

16 Loevy, *The Flawed Path*; James M. Penning, "Pat Robertson and the GOP: 1988 and Beyond," *Sociology of Religion* 55:3 (1994): 327–44; Kyle Huckins, "Interest-Group Influence on the Media Agenda: A Case Study," *Journalism & Mass Communication Quarterly* 76:1 (1999): 76–86.

17 The full text of the platform is available at http://www.presidency.ucsb.edu/ws/?pid=25847.

18 Molly Ivins, "A Feast of Hate and Fear," *Newsweek* (August 31, 1992): 32. See Loevy, *The Flawed Path*, 181–87.

19 The political science literature on this shift is vast and consistent. See Alan I. Abramowitz, "It's Abortion Stupid: Policy Voting in the 1992 Presidential Campaign," *Journal of Politics* 57:1 (1995): 176–86; Laura W. Arnold and Herbert F. Weisberg, "Parenthood, Family Values, and the 1992 Presidential Election," *American Politics Research* 24:2 (1996): 194–220; Louis Bolce and Gerald De Maio, "A Prejudice for the Thinking Classes: Media Exposure, Political Sophistication, and the Anti-Christian Fundamentalist," *American Politics Research* 36:2 (2008): 155–85; Bolce and De Maio, "Religious Outlook, Culture War Politics, and Antipathy Toward Christian Fundamentalists," *Public Opinion Quarterly* 63:1 (1999): 29–61; Bolce and De Maio, "The Anti-Christian Fundamentalist Factor in Contemporary Politics," *Public Opinion Quarterly* 63:4 (1999): 508–42; Jo Freeman, "Feminism vs. Family Values: Women at the 1992 Democratic and Republican Conventions," *PS: Political Science and Politics* 26:1 (1993): 21–28; Phillip E. Hammond, Mark A. Shibley, and Peter M. Solow, "Religion and Family Values in Presidential Voting," *Sociology of Religion* 55:3 (1994): 277–90; Lyman A. Kellstedt, John C. Green, James L. Guth, and Corwin E. Schmidt, "Religious Voting Blocs in the 1992 Election: The Year of the Evangelical?" *Sociology of Religion* 55:3 (1994): 307–26; James A. McCann, "Electoral Choices and Core Value Change: The 1992 Presidential Campaign," *American Journal of Political Science* 41:2 (1997): 564–83.

20 Layman and his colleagues show how political activists have driven the increased polarization of party politics in the U.S., and influenced the views of the public over time. See "Religion and Political Behavior in the United States: The Impact of Beliefs, Affiliations, and Commitment from 1980 to 1994," *Public Opinion Quarterly* 61:2 (1997): 288–316, 299; "'Culture Wars' in the American Party System: Religious and Cultural Change among Partisan Activists since 1972," *American Politics Research* 27:1 (1999): 89–121; Geoffrey Layman, Thomas M. Carsey, John C. Green, Richard Herrera, and Rosalyn Cooperman, "Activists and Conflict Extension in American Party Politics," *American Political Science Review* 104:2 (2010): 324–46; also Douglas Usher, "Strategy, Rules, and Participation: Issue Activists in Republican National Convention Delegations," *Political Research Quarterly* 53:4 (2000): 887–903, 892. On how the "culture wars" narrative is salient only regarding specific policies such as abortion, and only to those voters who perceive these issues as paramount while being aware of partisan differences over them, see Geoffrey Layman and John C. Green, "Wars and Rumours of Wars: The Contexts of Cultural Conflict in American Political Behaviour," *British Journal of Political Science* 36:1 (2006): 61–89. For an evaluation of the relative impact of the Christian Right on Republican parties at the state level during the early 1990s, see John C. Green, James L. Guth, and Clyde Wilcox, "Less than Conquerors: The

Christian Right in State Republican Parties," pp. 117–35 in *Social Movements and American Political Institutions*, edited by Anne N. Costain and Andrew S. McFarland (Lanham, MD: Rowan & Littlefield, 1998).

21 To plot trends evenly in this chapter we combined the odd year spacing of the GSS in the following ways: 1972–1973 are combined and represented as 1972, 1974–1975 as 1974, 1976–1977 as 1976, 1982–1983 as 1982, 1984–1985 as 1984, 1986–1987 as 1986, 1988–1989 as 1988, and 1991–1993 as 1992. Thereafter the survey has been consistently biannual.

22 When calculated as coefficients of variation (CV)—the standard deviation divided by the mean, then multiplied by 100 to produce a standardized estimate of dispersion ranging from 0 (no dispersion) to 75 (maximum dispersion) in the case of a 1-to-7 censored variable with a reasonably large sample size—the lowest CV occurs in 1984 (30.8), while the highest CV occurs in 2010 (35.7). Another way of thinking about this is to say the dispersion for the political identity measure in 2010 was approximately 16% larger than it was for the same measure in 1984 ([35.7 – 30.8] / 30.8 = .159). For information about the parameters of sampling distributions for coefficients of variation with two basic examples, see Walter A. Hendricks and Kate W. Robey, "The Sampling Distribution of the Coefficient of Variation," *Annals of Mathematical Statistics* 7:3 (1936): 129–32.

23 Jeff Manza and Clem Brooks, "The Religious Factor in U.S. Presidential Elections, 1960–1992," *American Journal of Sociology* 103:1 (1997): 38–81. John Green and E. J. Dionne Jr. tracked changes to voting structure and patterns from 1944 until 2004 and found that the largest changes were a decline in the market share of mainline Protestants, an increase in seculars' market share, and the homogenization of conservative and liberal voting blocs among conservative Protestants and seculars; see "Religion and American Politics: More Secular, More Evangelical, or Both?" pp. 194–224 in *Red, Blue, and Purple America: The Future of Election Demographics*, edited by Ruy Teixeira (Washington, D.C.: Brookings Institution, 2008).

24 The overall vote share for each election was taken from the results published by the Federal Election Commission. The vote share for the nonaffiliated and white fundamentalists comes from results from the General Social Surveys and National Election Surveys, averaged together. The NES contains slightly less error in overall vote totals, but does not include the information necessary to classify white fundamentalists in the 1972 and 1976 elections. Fundamentalism was classified using self-identification to the FUND variable in the GSS and biblical literalism in the NES. For detail on cumulative NES data, see http://www.electionstudies.org/studypages/cdf/cdf.htm.

25 Tapper and Bingham (2012).

26 On the rise and fall of the Shakers, see Joseph J. Stein, *The Shaker Experience in America* (New Haven, CT: Yale University Press, 1994). On the success of Mormonism, see Rodney Stark, *The Rise of Mormonism*, edited by Reid Nelson (New York: Columbia University Press, 2005). Concerning the demographic

sources of religious change, see Kaufmann, Goujon, and Skirbekk (2012); Norris and Inglehart (2004); Sherkat (2001); Skirbekk, Kaufmann, and Goujon (2010).

27 See Wendy Cadge and Elaine H. Ecklund, "Religious Service Attendance among Immigrants: Evidence from the New Immigrant Survey–Pilot," *American Behavioral Scientist* 49:11 (2006): 1574–95; Frank van Tubergen, "Religious Affiliation and Attendance among Immigrants in Eight Western Countries: Individual and Contextual Effects," *Journal for the Scientific Study of Religion* 45:1 (2006): 1–22; Van Tubergen, "Religious Affiliation and Participation among Immigrants in a Secular Society: A Study of Immigrants in the Netherlands," *Journal of Ethnic and Migration Studies* 33:5 (2007): 747–65; Frank van Tubergen and Jórunn Í. Sindradóttir, "The Religiosity of Immigrants in Europe: A Cross-National Study," *Journal for the Scientific Study of Religion* 50:2 (2011): 272–88.

28 Not only do nones have fewer children, many children of secular parents end up with religious socialization anyway. Respondents to the 1991, 1998, and 2008 GSS were asked for their parents' religious affiliations, as well as whether they considered themselves as having been raised within a religion. Seventy-two percent of those whose fathers were religious nones still said they were raised in a religious tradition. The same was true for 46% of those whose mothers claimed no religion. Further, 33% of those who said both parents had no religion reported being raised within a religious tradition. Interestingly, nonaffiliated mothers without nonaffiliated fathers were extremely rare. Only 1% of respondents with a religiously affiliated father reported a nonaffiliated mother, compared to 7% of those with an affiliated mother who reported a nonaffiliated father.

29 Skirbekk, Kaufmann, and Goujon (2010) project that secularism will account for roughly 17% of the American population by 2043, but that secularism will continue to increase among whites, to over 25%.

CHAPTER 5. NONRELIGIOUS BELIEF SYSTEMS

1 The estimates for the proportion of secularists who never attend religious services or pray were taken from the 2010 GSS, while the other estimates from the GSS presented in this chapter were taken from the 2008 GSS because it contained an additional battery of questions about religion, as well as questions about attitudes toward science.

2 A national survey conducted by Pew assessing basic knowledge about world religions found atheists and agnostics to be the most knowledgeable, followed by Jews and Mormons. See Pew Forum, *U.S. Religious Knowledge Survey* (Washington, D.C., 2010), http://www.pewforum.org/files/2010/09/religious-knowledge-full-report.pdf.

3 The paranormal phenomenon attracting the highest rates of belief was extraterrestrials, with 46% of atheists and 47% of agnostics believing, although this likely reflects belief in the existence of ETs "out in the universe" more than it does UFO visitations. Belief in ESP was next (35% of atheists, 47% of agnostics), then ghosts (20% of atheists, 24% of agnostics), and finally Bigfoot (17% of atheists, 7% of

agnostics). The middle categories of nonaffiliated believers and the culturally religious have higher levels of paranormal belief, which matches the general pattern in which religious "dabblers" are more likely to believe in and experience the paranormal compared to both more committed secularists and religionists. See Christopher Bader, Joseph Baker, and Andrea Molle, "Countervailing Forces: Religiosity and Paranormal Belief in Italy," *Journal for the Scientific Study of Religion* 51:4 (2012): 705–20; Joseph Baker and Scott Draper, "Diverse Supernatural Portfolios: Certitude, Exclusivity, and the Curvilinear Relationship between Religiosity and Paranormal Beliefs," *Journal for the Scientific Study of Religion* 49:3 (2010): 412–24.

4 For instance, news stories often appear with headlines such as Matthew Brown's, "Religious Americans More Inclined to Have Upbeat Outlook," *Deseret News* (October 5, 2012). The academic literature on the relationship between religiosity and happiness is mixed. Many studies report no association. Examples include Leslie J. Francis, Hans-Georg Ziebertz, and Christopher A. Lewis, "The Relationship between Religion and Happiness among German Students," *Pastoral Psychology* 51:4 (2003): 273–81; Christopher A. Lewis, "Church Attendance and Happiness among Northern Irish Undergraduate Students: No Association," *Pastoral Psychology* 503 (2002): 191–95; Christopher A. Lewis, Stephen Joseph, and Kristy E. Noble, "Is Religiosity Associated with Life Satisfaction?" *Psychological Reports* 79:2 (1996): 429–30; Christopher A. Lewis, Ciaran Lanigan, Stephen Joseph, and Jan de Fockert, "Religiosity and Happiness: No Evidence for an Association among Undergraduates," *Personality and Individual Differences* 22:1 (1997): 119–21; Christopher A. Lewis, John Maltby, and Liz Day, "Religious Orientation, Religious Coping and Happiness among UK Adults," *Personality and Individual Differences* 38:5 (2005): 1193–202. However, there is a positive link between self-reported happiness and religious *practice*; see John Maltby, Christopher A. Lewis, and Liza Day, "Religious Orientation and Psychological Well-Being: The Role of the Frequency of Personal Prayer," *British Journal of Health Psychology* 4:4 (1999): 363–78; Rodney Stark and Jared Maier, "Faith and Happiness," *Review of Religious Research* 50:1 (2008): 120–25. Ultimately, how religiosity and happiness are measured has a strong influence on the relationships found; see Christopher A. Lewis and Sharon M. Cruise, "Religion and Happiness: Consensus, Contradictions, Comments and Concerns," *Mental Health, Religion & Culture* 9:3 (2006): 213–25. In general, it seems the impact of religiosity on happiness revolves around religious practice, likely due to the influence of private religious practice on coping and public religious practice on sense of belonging and the availability of social support. See Christopher G. Ellison, "Religious Involvement and Subjective Well-Being," *Journal of Health and Social Behavior* 32:1 (1991): 80–99; Sarah French and Stephen Joseph, "Religiosity and Its Association with Happiness, Purpose in Life, and Self-Actualisation," *Mental Health, Religion & Culture* 2:2 (1999): 117–20.

5 A prominent example of this narrative is that of Jews who cite the Holocaust as a reason for abandoning belief in God, such as Richard Rubenstein's *After*

Auschwitz: Radical Theology and Contemporary Judaism (Indianapolis: Bobbs-Merrill, 1966). Notably, for Rubenstein this did not necessarily mean abandoning religion, but rather a particular conception of the divine.

6 Hunsberger and Altemeyer (2006) found that atheists who were members of irreligious organizations scored relatively high on indices of dogmatic thinking.

7 The larger the sample size, the greater the statistical "power" and the likelihood of statistically significant results. Nonaffiliated believers and the culturally religious were the most likely to be dissatisfied according to this model. See the Data Analyses Appendix for the full model.

8 See Galen and Kloet (2011a, 2011b); Riley, Best, and Charlton (2005); Weber et al. (2012).

9 See Vargas (2012).

10 Palmer ([1801] 1992: 268).

11 Sam Harris, "Science Must Destroy Religion," *Huffington Post* (May 25, 2011), http://www.huffingtonpost.com/sam-harris/science-must-destroy-reli_b_13153.html.

12 Hunsberger and Altemeyer (2006); Baker (2012a); Cimino and Smith (2007: 417–19); Garneau (2012: 52–54); J. Smith (2011, 2013).

13 See Baker (2012b).

14 For an extensive treatment of the dimensions, strategies, and consequences of "passing" while possessing nonvisible but discreditable attributes, see Erving Goffman, *Stigma: Notes on the Management of Spoiled Identity* (New York: Simon & Schuster, 1963); Daniel G. Renfrow, "A Cartography of Passing in Everyday Life," *Symbolic Interaction* 27:4 (2004): 485–506.

15 The survey was collected May 29 to June 2, 2014, using Amazon's Mechanical Turk crowdsourcing system. Respondents were paid fifty cents to complete a short "human intelligence task." The data were collected through Calvin College's Center for Social Research, which uses Mechanical Turk to generate experimental survey data collected online through Qualtrics. Respondents were posed the battery of questions concerning their reasons for having no religious affiliation only if they said "none" to a religious preference question, so the data analyzed were from nonaffiliated atheists and agnostics, as well as nonaffiliated theistic believers. The sample consists of adults residing in the United States and included 489 religiously nonaffiliated atheists, 338 nonaffiliated agnostics, and 189 nonaffiliated believers, with a total sample size of 2,614. Overall, the sample is more educated and younger than nationally representative surveys, hence the higher levels of nontheists. Given that we are interested in the variation *within* secular categories, a nonparametric sample still adequately addresses questions about the most common reasons secular Americans give for not affiliating with a religion. For more information about the quality of the data generated by MTurk surveys compared to traditional methods, see Michael Buhrmester, Tracy Kwang, and Samuel D. Gosling, "Amazon's Mechanical Turk: A New Source of Inexpensive, yet High-Quality, Data?" *Perspectives on Psychological Science* 6:1 (2011): 3–5; Joseph K. Goodman,

Cynthia E. Cryder, and Amar Cheema, "Data Collection in a Flat World: The Strengths and Weaknesses of Mechanical Turk Samples," *Journal of Behavioral Decision Making* 26:3 (2013): 213–24; Winter Mason and Siddharth Suri, "Conducting Behavioral Research on Amazon's Mechanical Turk," *Behavioral Research Methods* 44:1 (2012): 1–23; and Jill D. Weinberg, Jeremy Freese, and David McElhattan, "Comparing Data Characteristics and Results of an Online Factorial Survey between a Population-Based and a Crowdsource-Recruited Sample," *Sociological Science* 1 (2014): 292–310.

16 We also factor analyzed these responses to see if certain reasons cluster together. Three factors emerged: the first and strongest was for having negative interactions with religious people, anti-clericalism, concern about theocracy, and the belief that religions have too many rules and dogmatisms; the second was the science versus religion narrative and the pluralism refuting religions option; the third was for personal suffering and social injustice, or what might be called concerns of theodicy.

17 J. Smith (2011). By starting with "questioning theism," this model assumes apostasy as the course of nonreligious identity rather than socialized secularity. Importantly, many people stop also at the first or second steps, effectively hiding their heretical beliefs from others who would disapprove.

18 For instance, we created a dataset that treats American states as cases (e.g., Alabama, Alaska, etc.). The correlation between the percentage in a state reporting a secular identity (on the Pew RLS) and the percentage who had internet access at home was $r = .57$. This was higher than the correlation with an index of educational attainment (.43) and other state-level measures such as the Human Development Index (.47).

19 Gervais and Norenzayan (2012a); Norenzayan and Gervais (2013); also see Pennycook et al. (2013, 2014).

20 Ecklund and Scheitle (2007); Larson and Witham, (1998). Interestingly, while many atheists enjoy reading "new atheist" authors, they often do not themselves identify with the antagonistic version of identity politics advocated (see Frost 2012).

21 Norenzayan, Gervais, and Trzesniewski (2012).

22 See Gervais (2011, 2013); Gervais and Norenzayan (2012b); Gervais, Shariff, and Norenzayan (2011).

CHAPTER 6. ETHNICITY, ASSIMILATION, AND SECULARITY

1 W. E. B. Du Bois, *Souls of Black Folk* (Chicago: A.C. McClurg, [1903] 1968), 240–41.

2 Du Bois's understanding of himself as a prophet is evident in recent historical and interpretive reappraisals of his supposed irreligion. See Edward J. Blum, *W. E. B. Du Bois: American Prophet* (Philadelphia: University of Pennsylvania Press, 2007); Jonathon S. Kahn, *Divine Discontent: The Religious Imagination of W. E. B. Du Bois* (New York: Oxford University Press, 2009). These works show how Du Bois's perspective on religion educes the deeper themes in his work.

3 On Wilkins's comments, see Charles Euchner, *Nobody Turn Me Around: A People's History of the 1963 March on Washington* (Boston: Beacon, 2010), 178–83; David Levering Lewis, *W. E. B. Du Bois: Biography of a Race, 1868–1919* (New York: Henry Holt, 1993), 1–3; Roy Wilkins, *Standing Fast: The Autobiography of Roy Wilkins* (New York: Da Capo Press, 1982), 293. Prior to the march, the Kennedy administration explicitly informed organizers that they should dissociate themselves with elements of communism (both real and perceived) in order to have a stronger impact on politicians.

4 W. E. B. Du Bois, *Autobiography of W. E. B. Du Bois: A Soliloquy on Viewing My Life from the Last Decade of Its First Century* (New York: International Publishers, 1968), 253. On the exclusion of Du Bois's thought and theory, see Dan S. Green and Edwin D. Driver, "W. E. B. DuBois: A Case in the Sociology of Sociological Negation," *Phylon* 37:4 (1976): 308–33; R. Charles Key, "Society and Sociology: The Dynamics of Black Sociological Negation," *Phylon* 39:1 (1978): 35–48; Reiland Rabaka, *Against Epistemic Apartheid: W. E. B. Du Bois and the Disciplinary Decadence of Sociology* (Lanham, MD: Lexington Books, 2010).

5 This dimension of Du Bois's exclusion from canonization is outlined by Charles Lemert, "A Classic from the Other Side of the Veil: Du Bois's *Souls of Black Folk*," *Sociological Quarterly* 35 (August 1994): 383–96.

6 Du Bois, *Autobiography*, 316.

7 Ibid., 323–24; see David Levering Lewis, *W. E. B. Du Bois, 1919–1963: The Fight for Equality and the American Century* (New York: Henry Holt, 2000), 493.

8 Du Bois, *Souls*, 3. Our reading of *Souls* draws heavily on the exegesis of Robert Gooding-Williams, *In the Shadow of Du Bois: Afro-Modern Political Thought in America* (Cambridge, MA: Harvard University Press, 2011).

9 Erving Goffman, *Stigma: Notes on the Management of Spoiled Identity* (New York: Simon & Schuster, 1963). For an assessment of the microsociological dynamics of interaction by race in the U.S., see Anne Warfield Rawls, "'Race' as an Interaction Order Phenomenon: W. E. B. Du Bois's 'Double Consciousness' Thesis Revisited," *Sociological Theory* 18:2 (2000): 241–74.

10 On the "in but not of" features of devalued status, see Eddie S. Glaude Jr., *Exodus! Religion, Race, and Nation in Early Nineteenth-Century Black America* (Chicago: University of Chicago Press, 2000), 33. Glaude replaces Du Bois's double consciousness with the "structure of ambivalence," a broader and more flexible concept. Also see Kahn, *Divine Discontent*, 55, on these points.

11 For an argument that Du Bois was "irreligious," see Zuckerman (2009b). It is clear that Du Bois's thought was not constrained by specific views of religious dogma or traditional authority; however, he did not abandon religious thought entirely, as is evident by his repeated and effective use of religious language, symbols, and ideas. See Kahn, *Divine Discontent*, 21–48.

12 From a letter in correspondence with Herbert Aptheker (ed.), *The Correspondence of W. E. B. Du Bois, Volume III: Selections, 1944–1963* (Amherst: University of Massachusetts Press, 1978), 395–96.

13 Phil Zuckerman, *Du Bois on Religion* (Walnut Creek, CA: AltaMira, 2000), 9.

14 On the use of "colored" Christs and other religious figures in the works of Du Bois, see Blum, *American Prophet*, 134–80; Kahn, *Divine Discontent*, 107–28. "Jesus Christ in Georgia," which first appeared in *The Crisis*, then later in *Darkwater* as "Jesus Christ in Texas," is perhaps the most exquisitely rendered work by Du Bois in this genre. Notably, *none* of Du Bois's stories of Christ end in physical resurrection. See W. E. B. Du Bois, *Darkwater: Voices from Within the Veil* (New York: Harcourt, Brace and Howe, 1920).

15 Du Bois, *Darkwater*, 1.

16 Blum, *American Prophet*.

17 Kahn, *Divine Discontent*.

18 The post–Reconstruction era until the early twentieth century has been referred to by historians as the "nadir" of race relations; e.g., Rayford W. Logan, *The Negro in American Life and Thought: The Nadir, 1877–1901* (New York: Dial Press, 1954).

19 Du Bois, *Souls*, 238. On the connections between "Of the Coming of John" and Wagner's opera, see Russell A. Berman, "Du Bois and Wagner: Race, Nation, and Culture between the United States and Germany," *German Quarterly* 70:2 (1997): 123–35; Gooding-Williams, *Shadow of Du Bois*, 120–25.

20 Gooding-Williams, *Shadow of Du Bois*, 119.

21 Du Bois, *Souls*, 242. The parallels between John's learning and the perils of eating of the tree of knowledge in the biblical account of Genesis are made apparent here; but in Du Bois's narrative, Adam is defiant and edified.

22 Ibid, 248–49.

23 Gooding-Williams, *Shadow of Du Bois*, 118.

24 Du Bois, *Souls*, 4.

25 Gooding-Williams, *Shadow of Du Bois*, 145.

26 For overviews of Du Bois's work on religion, see Zuckerman, *Du Bois on Religion*; and "The Sociology of Religion of W. E. B. Du Bois," *Sociology of Religion* 63:2 (2002): 239–53. Among Du Bois scholars, Arnold Rampersad most accurately recognized the in-but-not-of stance of Du Bois on religion, as well as his maintenance of a personalized sense of the religious even as he disengaged from organized religion. See Arnold Rampersad, *The Art and Imagination of W. E. B. Du Bois* (Cambridge, MA: Harvard University Press, 1976) 14, 41.

27 Du Bois, *Darkwater*, vii.

28 Christa Buschendorf and Cornel West, "A Figure of Our Times: An Interview with Cornel West on W. E. B. Du Bois," *Du Bois Review* 10 (2013): 261–78, 271–72.

29 Martin Luther King Jr., "Honoring Dr. Du Bois," pp. 20–28 in *W. E. B. Du Bois Speaks: Speeches and Addresses, 1890–1919*, edited by Philip S. Foner (New York: Pathfinder, 1970), 28, emphasis added.

30 Ange-Marie Hancock, "W. E. B. Du Bois: Intellectual Forefather of Intersectionality?" *Souls: A Critical Journal of Black Politics, Culture, and Society*

7:3–4 (2005): 74–84. Some feminist scholars highlight that Du Bois's work itself often fails to further the understanding of the intersectionality of gender domination by outlining an inherently masculinist perspective; see Hazel Carby, *Race Men* (Cambridge, MA: Harvard University Press, 1998); Patricia H. Collins, "Gender, Black Feminism, and Black Political Economy," *Annals of the American Academy of Political and Social Science* 568:1 (2000): 41–53; Farah J. Griffith, "Black Feminists and Du Bois: Respectability, Protection, and Beyond," *Annals of the American Academy of Political and Social Science* 568:1 (2000): 28–40; cf. Rabaka, *Against Epistemic Apartheid*, chapter 3.

31 For an empirical look at the intersectional effects of race and social class on policing and imprisonment, see Bruce Western, *Punishment and Inequality in America* (New York: Russell Sage, 2006).

32 Sociologist Patricia Hill Collins provides one of the most influential contemporary articulations of this perspective, noting that statuses are relational and best understood by examining "connections among and across these categories"; Patricia H. Collins, "The New Politics of Community," *American Sociological Review* 75:1 (2010): 7–30, 23. Although the framework of intersectionality is present in all of Collins's work, the most direct entry into it is *Black Feminist Thought*, 2nd edition (New York: Routledge, 2000).

33 On social class and civic engagement, see Robert D. Putnam, "Bowling Alone: America's Declining Social Capital," *Journal of Democracy* 6:1 (1995): 65–78; Evan Schofer and Marion Fourcade-Gourinchas, "The Structural Contexts of Civic Engagement: Voluntary Association Memberships in Comparative Perspective," *American Sociological Review* 66:6 (2001): 806–28. On the relationship between education level and public religiosity, see Michael J. McFarland, Bradley R. E. Wright and David Weakliem, "Educational Attainment and Religiosity: Exploring Variations by Religious Tradition," *Sociology of Religion* 72:2 (2011): 166–88.

34 The parenthetical addition of "Americans" to "white" references that conventional American society is "white." Whiteness operates as the default assumption for Americanness and descriptions of whites are typically not accompanied by modifications of the base designation of "American," as are descriptions of other(ed) racial and ethnic groups.

35 See Adam B. Cohen, Ariel Malka, Eric D. Hill, Felix Thoemmes, Peter C. Hill, and Jill M. Sundie, "Race as a Moderator of the Relationship between Religiosity and Political Alignment," *Personality and Social Psychology Bulletin* 35:3 (2009): 271–82.

36 This excerpt from the originally published version of Hughes's "A New Song" includes the controversial, direct references to Jesus that were removed for later publications. See Jean Wagner, *Black Poets of the United States: From Paul Laurence Dunbar to Langston Hughes* (Urbana: University of Illinois Press, 1973), 437–42.

37 Arnold Rampersad, *The Life of Langston Hughes, Volume I: 1902–1941, I, Too, Sing America* (New York: Oxford University Press, 1986); Rampersad, *The Life of*

Langston Hughes, Volume II: 1941–1967, I Dream a World (New York: Oxford University Press, 1988), 306.

38 Langston Hughes, "My Adventures as a Social Poet," *Phylon* 8 (1947): 205–12, 210–11.

39 Rampersad, *Life, Volume II*, 140; Claire A. Culleton, *Joyce and the G-Men: J. Edgar Hoover's Manipulation of Modernism* (New York: Palgrave Macmillan, 2004), 99–103.

40 See Rampersad, *Life, Volume II*, 189–222.

41 See Pinn (2004, 2012).

42 This finding is replicated in the Pew Asian American study, where 22% of first-generation respondents were secular (none, atheist, agnostic), compared to 32% of second-generation respondents, and 25% of third or later-generation respondents. For an ethnographic account of how supposedly secular Chinese Americans may continue to engage in "folk" religious practices centered around kinship, see Cheung (2012).

43 For census data on levels of education and income for Asian Americans and other racial and ethnic categories, see http://www.census.gov/newsroom/releases/pdf/cb13ff-09_asian.pdf.

44 Cavalcanti and Schleef (2005).

45 Excerpted from the interview with David Tamayo. Quotations within interview excerpts indicate our informant's best memory of others' and his own quotes and attitudes in recalling a scene, hypothetical or actual, of personal biography. The specificity of *narrative remembrance* is what the quotations signify.

46 The language of a "problem" echoes Du Bois's characterization of processes of stigmatization.

47 On identities and presentation of self in cyberspace, see Andrea Chester and Di Bretherton, "Impression Management and Identity Online," pp. 223–36 in *Oxford Handbook of Internet Psychology*, edited by Adam Joinson, Katelyn McKenna, Tom Postmes, and Ulf-Dietrich Reips (Oxford: Oxford University Press, 2007); John R. Suler, "Identity Management in Cyberspace," *Journal of Applied Psychoanalytic Studies* 4:4 (2002): 455–59; Zeynep Tufecki, "Can You See Me Now? Audience and Disclosure Regulation in Online Social Network Sites," *Bulletin of Science, Technology, and Society* 28:1 (2008): 20–36; Shanyang Zhao, Sherri Grasmuck, and Jason Martin, "Identity Construction on Facebook: Digital Empowerment in Anchored Relationships," *Computers in Human Behavior* 45:5 (2008): 1816–36. On cyber communities of secularists and the discourse that occurs in such forums, see Cimino and Smith (2011).

48 Du Bois, *Autobiography*, 422–23.

CHAPTER 7. GENDER AND SECULARITY

1 Frances Wright, *Parting Address* (New York: Office of *The Free Enquirer*, 1830), 11, emphasis in original.

2 For biographies of Wright, see Celia M. Eckhardt, *Fanny Wright: Rebel in America* (Cambridge, MA: Harvard University Press, 1984); A. J. G. Perkins and Theresa

Wolfson, *Frances Wright, Free Enquirer: The Study of a Temperament* (New York: Harper & Brothers, 1939); William R. Waterman, *Frances Wright* (New York: Columbia University Press, 1924).

3 Frances Wright, *A Few Days in Athens; Being the Translation of a Greek Manuscript Discovered in Heraculaneum* (Boston: J. P. Mendum, [1822] 1850), 199.

4 Eckhardt, *Rebel in America*, 12–23.

5 See "Frances Wright," *Monticello.org*, http://www.monticello.org/site/research-and-collections/frances-wright.

6 On Wright's efforts at the Nashoba commune, see O. B. Emerson, "Frances Wright and Her Nashoba Experiment," *Tennessee Historical Quarterly* 6 (1947): 291–315; Edd W. Parks, "Dreamer's Vision: Frances Wright at Nashoba (1825–30)," *Tennessee Historical Magazine* 2:2 (1932): 74–86.

7 The most interesting and comprehensive account of her role as the first woman to speak in the American public sphere is Robert J. Connors, "Frances Wright: First Female Civic Rhetor in America," *College English* 62:1 (1999): 30–57.

8 Horace Traubel, *With Walt Whitman in Camden (July 16, 1888—October 31, 1888)*, Vol. 2 (New York: Rowman & Littlefield [1907] 1961), 445, 499, 500. On the influence of Wright's thought on the works of Whitman, see David Goodale, "Some of Walt Whitman's Borrowings," *American Literature* 10:2 (1938): 202–13.

9 Eckhardt, *Rebel in America*, 187.

10 Ibid., 293.

11 Ibid., 191–94. William Godwin was a radical British philosopher. Percy Bysshe Shelley was a Romantic poet and husband of Godwin's daughter, pioneering feminist Mary Wollstonecraft Shelley, who advocated nonviolence and vegetarianism. Richard Carlile was a well-known advocate for freedom of the press, universal suffrage, and birth control. He was twice jailed for blasphemy and seditious libel in England, serving six years in prison for printing Paine's *Age of Reason*. See Joss Marsh, *Word Crimes: Blasphemy, Culture, and Literature in Nineteenth-Century England* (Chicago: University of Chicago Press, 1998), 60–77.

12 Susan Zaeske, "The 'Promiscuous Audience' Controversy and the Emergence of the Early Woman's Rights Movement," *Quarterly Journal of Speech* 81 (1995): 191–207, 192. On women reformers' use of moral suasion to gain a hearing in public, see Lori Ginzberg, *Women and the Work of Benevolence: Morality, Politics, and Class in the 19th-Century United States* (New Haven, CT: Yale University Press, 1990). On the role of equality in Wright's rhetoric, see Anthony Hillbruner, "Frances Wright: Egalitarian Reformer," *Southern Journal of Speech* 23:4 (1958): 193–203; Cary R. W. Voss and Robert C. Rowland, "Pre-Inception Rhetoric in the Creation of a Social Movement: The Case of Frances Wright," *Communication Studies* 51:1 (2000): 1–14. For a discussion of how Wright fails to fit the model of nineteenth-century female reformers, see Kathleen E. Kendall and Jeanne Y. Fisher, "Frances Wright on Women's Rights: Eloquence Versus Ethos," *Quarterly Journal of Speech* 60:1 (1974): 58–68; Molly A. Travis, "Frances Wright: The Other Woman of Early American Feminism," *Women's Studies* 22:3 (1993): 389–97.

13 Frances Wright, *Review of the Times* (New York: Office of *The Free Enquirer*, 1830), 16–17.
14 Frances Wright, "Address III: Opening of the Hall of Science," in *Course of Popular Lectures*, 6th edition (New York: G. W. & A. J. Matsell, [1829] 1836), 203.
15 Ibid., 205–6, emphasis in original.
16 Ibid., 220–21.
17 Ibid., 206.
18 Ibid., 219, emphasis in original.
19 Ibid., 223, emphasis in original.
20 Ibid., 210.
21 Ibid., 224. Wright's involvement with the (ironically named) Workingmen's Party was also an important source of political opposition to her ideas. On this aspect of her public life, see Eckhardt, *Rebel in America*, 216–22; Perkins and Wolfson, *Free Enquirer*, 250–62; Waterman, *Frances Wright*, 187–223.
22 The most thorough exposition of Wright's philosophical arguments and claims is Elizabeth A. Bartlett, *Liberty, Equality, Sorority* (Brooklyn, NY: Carlson Publishing, 1994). Regarding her emphasis on education, see especially Wright, *Course of Popular Lectures*.
23 The first wave of sociological literature empirically exploring the reasons for the relationship between gender and religiosity includes: David De Vaus, "Workforce Participation and Sex Differences in Church Attendance," *Review of Religious Research* 25:3 (1984): 247–56; David De Vaus and Ian Mcallister, "Gender Differences in Religion," *American Sociological Review* 54:2 (1987): 472–81; Ellen M. Gee, "Gender Differences in Church Attendance in Canada: The Role of Labor Force Participation," *Review of Religious Research* 32:3 (1991): 267–73; Jeffrey S. Levin, Robert J. Taylor, and Linda M. Chatters, "Race and Gender Differences in Religiosity among Older Adults: Findings from Four National Surveys," *Journal of Gerontology* 49:3 (1994): 137–45; Moniek Steggerda, "Religion and the Social Positions of Men and Women," *Social Compass* 40:1 (1993): 65–73; Antanas Suzoedelis and Raymond H. Potvin, "Sex Differences in Factors Affecting Religiousness among Catholic Adolescents," *Journal for the Scientific Study of Religion* 20:1 (1981): 38–51; Holley Ulbrich and Myles Wallace, "Women's Work Force Status and Church Attendance," *Journal for the Scientific Study of Religion* 23:4 (1984): 341–50. For summaries of research up until the shift toward "risk preference" as the dominant explanation, see Leslie J. Francis, "The Psychology of Gender Differences in Religion: A Review of Empirical Research," *Religion* 27:1 (1997): 81–96; Tony Walter and Grace Davie, "The Religiosity of Women in the Modern West," *British Journal of Sociology* 49:4 (1998): 640–60.
24 Alan S. Miller and John P. Hoffman, "Risk and Religion: An Explanation of Gender Differences in Religiosity," *Journal for the Scientific Study of Religion* 34:1 (1995): 63–75; Alan S. Miller and Rodney Stark, "Gender and Religiousness: Can Socialization Explanations be Saved?" *American Journal of Sociology* 107:6 (2002): 1399–423; Rodney Stark, "Physiology and Faith: Addressing the 'Universal'

Gender Difference in Religious Commitment," *Journal for the Scientific Study of Religion* 41:3 (2002): 495–507.

25 The largest discrepancies in the gender ratios between the two datasets were for the culturally religious (1.86 men per woman in the GSS compared to 2.29 men per woman in the Pew RLS) and agnostics (2.21 men per woman in the GSS compared to 1.88 men per woman in the Pew RLS). The difference in the culturally religious is likely a product of the "wider net" cast by our classification in the GSS, leading to greater gender parity. The difference for agnosticism may reflect lower public recognition or comfort with the label "agnostic" as compared to using a belief question about theism, which produced greater gender parity.

26 See, for example, Michael P. Carroll, "Give Me That Ol' Hormonal Religion," *Journal for the Scientific Study of Religion* 34:2 (2004): 275–78; Jeremy Freese, "Risk Preferences and Gender Differences in Religiousness: Evidence from the World Values Survey," *Review of Religious Research* 46:1 (2004): 88–91; Jeremy Freese and James D. Montgomery, "The Devil Made Her Do It: Evaluating Risk Preference as an Explanation of Sex Differences in Religiousness," *Advances in Group Processes* 24 (2007): 187–229; Louis M. Roth and Jeffrey C. Kroll, "Risky Business: Assessing Risk Preference Explanations for Gender Differences in Religiosity," *American Sociological Review* 72:2 (2007): 205–20; Paul D. Sullins, "Gender and Religion: Deconstructing Universality, Constructing Complexity," *American Journal of Sociology* 112:3 (2006): 838–80. Miller's own analysis of data from Eastern populations failed to support the universality of the relationship between gender and religiosity. See Alan S. Miller, "Going to Hell in Asia: The Relationship between Risk and Gender in a Cross-Cultural Setting," *Review of Religious Research* 42:1 (2000): 5–18.

27 Jessica L. Collett and Omar Lizardo, "A Power-Control Theory of Gender and Religiosity," *Journal for the Scientific Study of Religion* 48:2 (2009): 123–31. For a summary of the theoretical model of power-control theory, see John Hagan, A. R. Gillis, and John Simpson, "The Class Structure of Gender and Delinquency: Toward a Power-Control Theory of Common Delinquent Behavior," *American Journal of Sociology* 90:6 (1985): 1151–78. A recent study of elites in the U.S. problematizes the view that risk preference is driving the negative influence of high socioeconomic status on religiosity among women, instead showing the importance of education and the politics of religious expression. See Orestes Hastings and D. Michael Lindsay, "Rethinking Religious Gender Differences: The Case of Elite Women," *Sociology of Religion* 74:4 (2013): 471–95.

28 Although the figure shows only the "extremes" and moderates, all other lines between these, such as those "leaning" liberal or conservative, are mathematical functions falling between the categories shown. We show the "extremes" and midpoint in order to display the basic parameters of this relationship.

29 Marta Trzebiatowska and Steve Bruce, *Why Are Women More Religious than Men?* (Oxford: Oxford University Press, 2012).

30 Darren E. Sherkat, "Sexuality and Religious Commitment in the United States: An Empirical Examination," *Journal for the Scientific Study of Religion* 41 (2002): 313–23.

31 Leslie J. Francis and Carolyn Wilcox, "Religion and Gender Orientation," *Personality and Individual Differences* 20:1 (1996): 119–21; Francis and Wilcox, "Religiosity and Femininity: Do Women Really Hold a More Positive Attitude toward Christianity?" *Journal for the Scientific Study of Religion* 37:3 (1998): 462–69; Edward H. Thompson Jr., "Beneath the Status Characteristic: Gender Variations in Religiousness," *Journal for the Scientific Study of Religion* 30:4 (1991): 381–94; Edward H. Thompson Jr. and Kathryn R. Remmes, "Does Masculinity Thwart Being Religious? An Examination of Older Men's Religiousness," *Journal for the Scientific Study of Religion* 41:3 (2002): 521–32.

32 Sherkat, "Sexuality and Religious Commitment," 320.

33 Frances Wright, *Parting Address*, 18.

34 Ibid., 21.

35 Ibid., 20–21.

36 Ibid., 21–22.

37 Gerda Lerner, "Women's Rights and American Feminism," *American Scholar* 40:2 (1971): 235–48. In her final years, Wright came to see religion as an important element of human community, although her understanding of what constituted "religion" remained at odds with that of organized religion. See Eckhardt, *Rebel in America*, 275–80.

38 Frances Wright, "Explanatory Notes on Nashoba." *New-Harmony Gazette* (January 30, 1828).

39 Paul Baker (ed.), Introduction to *Views of Society and Manners in America* (Cambridge, MA: Harvard University Press, 1963); Eckhardt, *Rebel in America*, 186, 204, 217, 264; Wendy Martin, "Profile: Frances Wright, 1795–1852," *Women's Studies* 2 (1974): 273–78; Perkins and Wolfson, *Free Enquirer*, 213; Waterman, *Frances Wright*, 205.

40 Waterman, *Frances Wright*, 159.

41 Catharine Beecher, *Letters on the Difficulties of Religion* (Hartford, CT: Belknap & Hamersley, 1836), 22–23.

42 As quoted in Eckhardt, *Rebel in America*, 273.

43 Ibid., 290.

44 Traubel, *With Walt Whitman*, 204, 206, 445, 499.

45 On the connections between Wright and Rose, see Yuri Suhl, *Ernestine Rose and the Battle for Human Rights* (New York: Reynal, 1959).

46 On how Wright gets remembered by historians, when she is at all, see Gail Bederman, "Revisiting Nashoba: Slavery, Utopia, and Frances Wright, 1818–1826," *American Literary History* 17:3 (2005): 438–59.

47 Eckhardt, *Rebel in America*, 215.

CHAPTER 8. MARRIAGE, FAMILY, AND SOCIAL NETWORKS

1 See Helen R. Ebaugh and Janet S. Chafetz, *Religion and the New Immigrants: Continuities and Adaptations in Immigrant Congregations* (Walnut Creek, CA: AltaMira, 2000); Fenggang Yang and Helen R. Ebaugh, "Transformations in New Immigrant Religions and Their Global Implications," *American Sociological Review* 66:2 (2001): 269–88.

2 Stolzenberg, Blair-Loy, and Waite (1995).

3 Alicia Adsera, "Religion and Changes in Family-Size Norms in Developed Countries," *Review of Religious Research* 47:3 (2006): 271–86; Evelyn L. Lehrer, "Religion as a Determinant of Marital Fertility," *Journal of Population Economics* 9:2 (1996): 173–96.

4 For a good summary of interfaith marriage, see Naomi Schaefer Riley, *'Til Faith Do Us Part: How Interfaith Marriage Is Transforming America* (New York: Oxford University Press, 2013). Chaves (1994) argues that religious intermarriage is essentially a metric of secularization.

5 David Knox, Marty E. Zusman, and Vivian W. Daniels, "College Student Attitudes toward Interreligious Marriage," *College Student Journal* 36:1 (2002): 84–86.

6 Scott M. Myers, "Religious Homogamy and Marital Quality: Historical and Generational Patterns, 1980–1997," *Journal of Marriage and Family* 68:2 (2008): 292–304, 927.

7 For divorce, see Bernard Lazerwitz, "Jewish-Christian Marriages and Conversions," *Jewish Social Studies* 43:1 (1981): 31–46. On marital satisfaction, see Joshua G. Chinitz and Robert A. Brown, "Religious Homogamy, Marital Conflict, and Stability in Same-Faith and Interfaith Jewish Marriages," *Journal for the Scientific Study of Religion* 40:4 (2001): 723–33. For an overview, see Annette Mahoney, Kenneth I. Pargament, Nalini Tarakeshwar, and Aaron B. Swank, "Religion in the Home in the 1980s and 1990s: A Meta-Analytic Review and Conceptual Analysis of Links between Religion, Marriage, and Parenting," *Psychology of Religion and Spirituality* 15:4 (2001): 559–96.

8 See, e.g., Froma Walsh, "Spiritual Diversity: Multifaith Perspectives in Family Therapy," *Family Process* 49:3 (2010): 330–48; Mark Furlong and Abe W. Ata, "Observing Different Faiths, Learning about Ourselves: Practice with Inter-Married Muslims and Christians," *Australian Social Work* 59:3 (2006): 250–64. For a study of the impact on children, see Regine Froese, "One Family, Two Religions: Child Belief or Child Grief in Christian-Muslim Families?" *British Journal of Religious Education* 30:1 (2008): 37–47.

9 Patrick C. Hughes and Fran C. Dickson, "Communication, Marital Satisfaction, and Religious Orientation in Interfaith Marriages," *Journal of Family Communication* 51:1 (2005): 25–41, 37. People can also make the choice to modify their religious beliefs or practices to better fit their interreligious statuses, such as in the case of Jews who are going against traditional teachings that ban interfaith unions. See J. Alan Winter, "Consistency and Importance of Jewish Identity and

One's Own or One's Child's Intermarriage," *Review of Religious Research* 44:1 (2002): 38–57. On religious "distance" in interfaith marriages, see Darren E. Sherkat, "Religious Intermarriage in the United States: Trends, Patterns, and Predictors," *Social Science Research* 33:4 (2004): 606–25.

10 Martin Dribe and Christer Lundh, "Cultural Dissimilarity and Intermarriage: A Longitudinal Study of Immigrants in Sweden 1990–2005," *International Migration Review* 45:2 (2011): 297–324. Interreligious marriage is sometimes used as a proxy for assimilation among immigrant groups, such as in D. A. Coleman, "Trends in Fertility and Intermarriage among Immigrant Populations in Western Europe as Measures of Integration," *Journal of Biosocial Science* 26:1 (1994): 107–36.

11 Alan Booth, David R. Johnson, Ann Branaman, and Alan Sica, "Belief and Behavior: Does Religion Matter in Today's Marriage?" *Journal of Marriage and Family* 57:3 (1995): 661–71, 669; Kristen T. Curtis and Christopher G. Ellison, "Religious Heterogamy and Marital Conflict: Findings from the National Survey of Families and Households," *Journal of Family Issues* 23:4 (2002): 551–76; Christopher G. Ellison, Amy Burdette, and W. Bradford Wilcox, "The Couple that Prays Together: Race, Ethnicity, Religion, and Relationship Quality among Working-Age Adults," *Journal of Marriage and Family* 72:4 (2010): 963–75.

12 Randal D. Day and Alan Acock, "Marital Well-being and Religiousness as Mediated by Relational Virtue and Equality," *Journal of Marriage and Family* 75:1 (2013): 164–77; Christopher G. Ellison, Andrea K. Henderson, Norval D. Glenn, and Kristine E. Harkrider, "Sanctification, Stress, and Marital Quality," *Family Relations* 60:4 (2011): 404–20.

13 Myers, "Religious Homogamy and Marital Quality."

14 See James D. Davidson and Tracy Widman, "The Effect of Group Size on Interfaith Marriage among Catholics," *Journal for the Scientific Study of Religion* 41:3 (2002): 397–404.

15 In models assessing mediation, marital status accounts for 23% of the aging effects in the GSS for predicting religious nonaffiliation. Similarly, marital status mediates 25% of the aging effects for predicting atheism, agnosticism, or "nothing in particular" compared to affiliated belief in the Pew RLS data.

16 Similarly, interreligious relationships may be experienced differently by men and women, such as Daphna Hacker, "Inter-Religious Marriages in Israel: Gendered Implications for Conversion, Children, and Citizenship," *Israel Studies* 14:2 (2009): 178–97.

17 Sociologist Darren Sherkat has extensively mapped the predictors of religious "mobility." See Sherkat (1991, 2001); Sherkat and Wilson (1995). On interfaith socialization, see Hart M. Nelsen, "The Religious Identification of Children of Interfaith Marriages," *Review of Religious Research* 32:2 (1990): 122–34.

18 For instance, in the 2005 Baylor Religion Survey, 31% of respondents reported attending religious services weekly, compared to 49% who reported praying daily. See Joseph Baker, "A Sociological Investigation of Prayer Frequency and Content," *Sociology of Religion* 69:2 (2008): 169–85.

19 For an in-depth study of the socialization efforts of secular parents, see Manning (2013).

20 Unfortunately the RLS data do not differentiate between different Presbyterian denominations regarding socialization. We suspect that, consistent with other data on people raised in conservative versus more liberal denominations, those raised in the PCUSA have higher rates of secularity in adulthood compared to those raised in the PCA or other conservative Presbyterian churches.

21 For a summary of the findings from the Longitudinal Study of Generations in regard to religion, see Vern L. Bengtson, with Norella M. Putney and Susan Harris, *Families and Faith: How Religion Is Passed Down across Generations* (New York: Oxford University Press, 2013).

22 The pattern of the nonaffiliated being more likely not to know the religious affiliations of their parents is replicated in the 2006 Faith Matters Survey.

23 The GSS also asked the question about attendance at age twelve in 1991 and 1998. The rank order of secular type concerning a high level of religious socialization is the same in these waves as well. We report the results from 2008 in order to use more recent data and keep the analyses in the chapter confined to samples taken during a similar time frame.

24 Bengtson, *Families and Faith*, 142–43.

25 On falling rates of corporal punishment in the U.S., see Andrea J. Sedlak, Jane Mettenburg, Monica Basena, Ian Petta, Karla McPherson, Angela Green, and Spencer Li, *Fourth National Incidence Study of Child Abuse and Neglect (NIS-4)* (Washington, D.C.: U.S. Department of Health and Human Services, 2010); Adam J. Zolotor, Adrea D. Theodore, Desmond K. Runyan, Jen Jen Chang, and Antoinette L. Laskey, "Corporal Punishment and Physical Abuse: Population-Based Trends for Three- to Eleven-Year-Old Children in the United States," *Child Abuse Review* 20:1 (2011): 57–66.

26 Interestingly, Congregationalists do not have higher rates of atheist (0.3%) or agnostic (1%) partners, but rather a higher rate of culturally religious spouses (7%). Many Congregationalists' partners are affiliated believers, but with lower average levels of practice. In the case of Episcopalians, there are slightly higher rates of atheist or agnostic partners (2.2%). For some groups the difference seems to arise out of behavior, while for the others it is more an issue of theistic belief.

27 Baker and Smith (2009a).

28 Notably, this type of identity maintenance occurs throughout the life course. Especially with the most stigmatized category of atheism, research has shown that belonging to groups that are based on atheist identity can be an effective way to maintain secularity. See LeDrew (2013).

29 There are other interesting patterns: atheists and agnostics are the most likely to select "occupation," and atheists are most likely to select "region of the country" or "sexual orientation."

30 Bainbridge (2005) proposes network isolation as a potential root cause of atheism. Our analyses do not support this hypothesis.

CHAPTER 9. THE (EXPLICIT) POLITICS OF SECULARITY

1 Pew Research Center, "For 2016 Hopefuls, Washington Experience Could Do More Harm Than Good" (May 2014). Although "atheist" remains the most disliked attribute for a political candidate, the percentage saying this makes them less likely to vote for a candidate has declined in recent years. For example, a 2007 poll by Pew found that 63% of Americans said they would not vote for an atheist.

2 See Carla Marinucci, "Stark's Atheist Views Break Political Taboo," *San Francisco Chronicle*, (March 14, 2007). Available at http://www.sfgate.com/politics/article/Stark-s-atheist-views-break-political-taboo-2570270.php. Information on the religious affiliation of Congress was taken from the Pew Forum on Religion and Public Life's "Faith on the Hill: The Religious Composition of the 113th Congress" (Washington, D.C., 2012). Available at http://www.pewforum.org/2012/11/16/faith-on-the-hill-the-religious-composition-of-the-113th-congress.

3 Evidence for this conjecture is the fact that 10% of all members of Congress claimed to be generically Christian or to belong to an unidentified Christian denomination, in contrast to 5% of Americans generally who self-identified in these ways.

4 "About," *Bothwell's Blog*, http://bothwellsblog.wordpress.com/about, and "Who Am I?" *Cecil Bothwell for City Council/Blog*, http://cecilsblog.wordpress.com/2009/06/23/who-am-i.

5 See for instance, David Zucchino, "Councilman under Fire for Atheism," *Los Angeles Times* (December 20, 2009).

6 Quotations within interview excerpts again convey our informants' clearest memories of others' and their own quotes in recalling a scene.

7 Cecil Bothwell, *Pure Bunkum: The Life and Times of Buncombe County Sherriff Bobby Lee Medford* (Asheville, NC: Brave Ulysses Books, 2008). See *United States of America v. Bobby Lee Medford*, 4th Cir. No. 08–5030 (1:07-cr-00122-TSE-1, 2011). Available at http://www.ca4.uscourts.gov/Opinions/Published/085030.P.pdf.

8 See Jeffrey M. Jones, "Barack Obama, Hillary Clinton Again Top Most Admired List," *Gallup*, http://www.gallup.com/poll/151790/barack-obama-hillary-clinton-again-top-admired-list.aspx.

9 Cecil Bothwell, *Prince of War: Billy Graham's Crusade for a Wholly Christian Empire* (Asheville, NC: Brave Ulysses Books, 2007), 180.

10 The most relevant Supreme Court decision in a similar case is *Torcaso v. Watkins* (1961), which unanimously found a similar provision in Maryland unconstitutional based on the First and Fourteenth amendments.

11 Emphasis is ours.

12 This text was taken from one of the direct mailers used against Bothwell during his campaign for city council in 2009. Available at http://www.scribd.com/doc/21966512/Bothwell-Mailer.

13 On religious diversity within the general tradition of "conservative" Protestantism, see Robert Woodberry and Christian Smith, "Fundamentalism et al.:

Conservative Protestantism in America," *Annual Review of Sociology* 24 (1998): 25–56.

14 Regarding personal safety from crime and terrorism, atheists and agnostics reported feeling more secure, while actively religious and nonaffiliated believers felt less safe. Only 5% of agnostics were "very dissatisfied" with perceived personal safety in contrast to 13% of actively religious respondents. Overall, 80% of atheists, 85% of agnostics, 75% of nonaffiliated believers, 76% of the culturally religious, and 72% of actively religious Americans were satisfied with their level of safety. These patterns tangentially support Norris and Inglehart's (2004) "existential security" theory of religiosity.

15 On the connections between religiosity and support for the Iraq War, see Paul D. Froese and F. Carson Mencken, "A U.S. Holy War? The Effects of Religion on Iraq War Policy Issues," *Social Science Quarterly* 90:1 (2009): 103–16.

16 Mediation regression models indicate that religiosity, and by implication secularity, influences attitudes about the environment by virtue of a more general connection between religion and politics in the United States. See Stefano B. Longo and Joseph O. Baker, "Economy 'versus' Environment: The Influence of Political Identity and Economic Ideology on Perceived Threat of Eco-Catastrophe," *Sociological Quarterly* 55:2 (2014): 341–65.

17 Recent decades have seen a cultural coding of matters of sexual politics as issues of "morality" to the exclusion of other policies and issues, particularly economic, environmental, and criminal justice, which are also decidedly matters of morality and social justice. We refer to issues of sexual politics as "moral" to the exclusion of other matters because of this cultural coding, but do not mean to suggest that we agree with it.

18 For a discussion of state laws addressing homosexuality, as well as the mechanisms through which conservative religious groups influence such laws, see Christopher P. Scheitle and Bryanna B. Hahn, "From the Pews to Policy: Specifying Evangelical Protestantism's Influence on States' Sexual Orientation Policies," *Social Forces* 89:3 (2011): 913–33.

19 One caveat is that, as with religious attendance, social desirability bias affects survey responses concerning voting behavior. There are certain actions and beliefs that many respondents may want to exhibit for their interviewer, or even for themselves, that do not match actual behaviors (the opposite also occurs, of course, with deviant behaviors such as shoplifting or cheating). What may be especially misleading in the current case is that the same people who would overreport their religiosity would likely overreport their political engagement. To some extent, asking whether someone voted or attended church may be assessing the perception of how important or valued it is for a person to engage in these activities, instead of actually gauging whether s/he actually did it. Still, it is unlikely that systematic bias fully accounts for the voting gap found between religious and secular Americans.

20 The numbers for voting in general and votes cast were taken from the 2010 GSS. The numbers on voting patterns in the 2004 election were taken from the Pew Religious Landscape Survey. Those who were ineligible to vote at the time were excluded from analyses of voting rates. Regarding the percentage who voted for a specific candidate, the proportions were taken *only out of those who voted.* On the role of religion in the 2004 presidential election, see James L. Guth, Lyman Kellstedt, Corwin E. Schmidt, and John C. Green, "Religious Influences in the 2004 Presidential Election," *Presidential Studies Quarterly* 36:2 (2006): 223–42. On the mobilizing effects of state ballot initiatives on same-sex marriage for the conservatively religious, see David E. Campbell and J. Quin Monson, "The Religion Card: Gay Marriage and the 2004 Presidential Election," *Public Opinion Quarterly* 72:3 (2008): 399–419.

21 The PAC is relatively small, operating at or under $10,000 budget, even in the presidential election year of 2008.

22 The number of affiliated groups was taken from a count of those listed on the SSA website.

23 Quotations are taken from personal correspondence with August Brunsman IV.

24 See Jeff German, "Lipman Brown Vindicated in Legislative Prayer Battle," *Las Vegas Sun* (June 16, 1997), http://www.lasvegassun.com/news/1997/jun/03/columnist-jeff-german-lipman-brown-vindicated-in-l/.

25 E.g., Anspach, Coe, and Thurlow (2007); Steadman (2013).

26 On the implementation of Bush's faith-based initiatives, see Bob Wineburg, *Faith-Based Inefficiency: The Follies of Bush's Initiatives* (Westport, CT: Praeger, 2007).

27 Thomas Jefferson, *Notes on the State of Virginia*, edited by William Peden (Chapel Hill: University of North Carolina Press, [1785] 1955), 159. Notably, this statement "probably caused [Jefferson] more difficulty than anything else he said or did during his lifetime," 291.

28 Lipman Brown has written elsewhere about the issue of happiness and nontheism; see "Who's Unhappy?" pp. 161–64 in *50 Voices of Disbelief: Why We Are Atheists*, edited by Russell Blackford and Udo Schüklenk (Malden, MA: Wiley-Blackwell, 2009).

CONCLUSION

1 Pope Francis during morning Mass in Rome, May 22, 2013. Also see the pope's comments about atheists at Christmas later that year (Yardley 2013). The title of the conclusion is taken from a line in Ward, *Dynamic Sociology*, 15.

2 For instance, Father Thomas Rosica of Canada quickly clarified that people "cannot be saved who, knowing the Church as founded by Christ and necessary for salvation, would refuse to enter her or remain in her." Rosica's full note on the pope's comments is available at http://www.zenit.org/en/articles/

explanatory-note-on-the-meaning-of-salvation-in-francis-daily-homily-of-may-22. For an extended academic examination of the question of atheists in Catholic orthodoxy, see Bullivant (2012). For Speckhardt's comments, see Dan Merica, "Heaven for Atheists? Pope Sparks Debate," *CNN Belief Blog*, http://religion.blogs.cnn.com/2013/05/23/heaven-for-atheists-pope-sparks-debate/.

3 This tendency is evident in cross-national and psychological studies of anti-atheist prejudice (Gervais 2011, 2013).

4 We humbly suggest emphasizing social justice concerns over (a)theological disputations.

5 For overviews of the links between religion and ethnicity in Ireland, see John Coakley, "The Religious Roots of Irish Nationalism," *Social Compass* 58:1 (2011): 95–114; Claire Mitchell, *Religion, Identity and Politics in Northern Ireland* (Aldershot: Ashgate, 2006).

6 On Ireland and the U.S. as outliers of high religiosity in the Western world, see Norris and Inglehart (2004: 85). On falling rates of religiosity in Ireland among recent cohorts, see Karen Anderson, "Irish Secularisation of Religious Identities: Evidence of an Emerging New Catholic Habitus," *Social Compass* 57:1 (2010): 15–39; Jochen Hirschle, "From Religious to Consumption-Related Routine Activities? Analyzing Ireland's Economic Boom and the Decline in Church Attendance," *Journal for the Scientific Study of Religion* 49:4 (2010): 673–87; Tom Inglis, "Catholic Identity in Contemporary Ireland: Belief and Belonging to Tradition," *Journal of Contemporary Religion* 22:2 (2007): 205–20. Supernatural belief has also fallen in Northern Ireland over this time span. See Tom W. Smith, "Beliefs about God across Time and Countries," report for ISSP and GESIS, available at http://www.norc.org/PDFs/Beliefs_about_God_Report.pdf.

7 This point is made in Rodney Stark and Roger Finke, *Acts of Faith: Explaining the Human Side of Religion* (Berkeley: University of California Press, 2000), 239–43. The most prescient account of the coming decline in American levels of religiosity as linked to a decline in global hegemony is Smith (1986).

8 Norris and Inglehart (2004); Zuckerman (2008).

9 Countries included in the analysis were Algeria, Andorra, Argentina, Australia, Brazil, Burkina Faso, Canada, Chile, Columbia, Cyprus, Ecuador, Egypt, Estonia, Finland, France, Ghana, Guatemala, Hong Kong, India, Indonesia, Iran, Iraq, Italy, Japan, Lebanon, Libya, Malaysia, Mali, Mexico, Moldova, Morocco, Netherlands, New Zealand, Nigeria, Norway, Pakistan, Peru, Philippines, Rwanda, Singapore, Slovenia, South Africa, South Korea, Spain, Sweden, Switzerland, Taiwan, Thailand, Tunisia, Turkey, United Kingdom, Uruguay, United States, Zambia, and Zimbabwe. Communist or former communist countries included in the analysis of all countries, but excluded from the numbers presented in the main text of the chapter were Armenia, Azerbaijan, Belarus, Bulgaria, China, Ethiopia, Georgia, (East) Germany, Hungary, Kazakhstan, Kyrgyzstan, Poland, Romania, Russia, Serbia, Ukraine, Uzbekistan, Vietnam, and Yemen. The correlation between the full HDI variable including communist and former

communist countries with percentage either not religious or atheist is r =.61. To build this dataset, we aggregated data from Waves 5 and 6 of the WVS data and merged results with a cross-national dataset that contains political, social, health, and religious metrics at the national level. These data are publically available from the Association of Religion Data Archives at http://www.thearda.com/Archive/Files/Descriptions/INTL2008.asp.

10 Metrics for these correlative analyses were as follows: 2008 U.N. gender inequality index, 2009 Freedom House rule of law score, 2009 Freedom House civil liberties scale, 2005–2008 U.N. adult literacy rate, 2007 Marshall Religious Freedom Scale, 2010 U.N. gross national income per capita, and 2000–2010 U.N. average gini coefficient of income inequality. The relationship between HDI and secularity is also present *within* the American states. State level HDI positively correlates with the percentage in a state who self-identify as atheist, agnostic, or "nothing in particular" (r = .47), and negatively with the proportion who believe in God (r = -.69). Data for these analyses were created by aggregating the 2007 Pew Religious Landscape survey to the state level and merging it with HDI data from the Measure of America project. For a similar discussion, see Zuckerman (2008: 25–29).

11 Norris and Inglehart (2004).

12 On the case of the forced secularization of the Soviet Union, see Froese (2008).

13 The figure displays the R-squared statistic for the fit of a growth curve line, rather than a linear assessment. Linear Pearson correlations are reported in the main text.

14 Philip S. Brenner, "Exceptional Behavior or Exceptional Identity? Overreporting of Church Attendance in the U.S.," *Public Opinion Quarterly* 75:1 (2011): 19–41.

15 For sophisticated cross-cultural analyses of religiosity and secularity using the World Values Survey, see Tim Immerzeel and Frank van Tubergen, "Religion as Reassurance? Testing the Insecurity Theory in 26 European Countries," *European Sociological Review* 29:2 (2013): 359–72; Stijn Ruiter and Frank van Tubergen, "Religious Attendance in Cross-National Perspective: A Multilevel Analysis of 60 Countries," *American Journal of Sociology* 115:3 (2009): 863–95.

16 The comparative empirical study of religion has developed rapidly in the past twenty years. Exemplary studies include Norris and Inglehart's (2004) study, as well as Brian Grim and Roger Finke, *The Price of Freedom Denied: Religious Persecution and Conflict in the Twenty-First Century* (Cambridge, UK: Cambridge University Press, 2011); Jonathan Fox, *A World Survey of Religion and State* (Cambridge, UK: Cambridge University Press, 2008); and Robert Woodberry, "The Missionary Roots of Liberal Democracy," *American Political Science Review* 106:2 (2012): 244–74. These advancements should be mirrored by the development of comparative studies of secularity.

17 The liminality of these categories helps explain why it is relatively common for individuals to shift back and forth between different identifications (Lim, MacGregor, and Putnam 2010). For example, one could switch from atheist to agnostic without modifying any behaviors or public affiliations. Such shifts can be

due to changes across the life course, external changes such as death or tragedy, or internal, cognitive changes in sense of identity.

18 On the exclusion of nominal religiosity and the need for further study of this liminal category, see David Voas and Abby Day, "Recognizing Secular Christians: Toward an Unexcluded Middle in the Study of Religion," *ARDA Guiding Papers Series* (2010), available at http://www.thearda.com/rrh/papers/guidingpapers/voas.asp. On paranormalism, see Christopher Bader, F. Carson Mencken, and Joseph O. Baker, *Paranormal America: Ghost Encounters, UFO Sightings, Bigfoot Hunts, and Other Curiosities in Religion and Culture* (New York: NYU Press, 2010). On patterns of spiritual practice outside of institutionalized religious settings, see Nancy Ammerman, *Sacred Stories, Spiritual Tribes: Finding Religion in Everyday Life* (New York: Oxford University Press, 2013).

19 Asad (2003); Cannell (2010). Alternatively if by "rational" we mean analytic styles of cognition as outlined in dual process models of thinking, then rationality deters, but does not eliminate, religious thinking, making supernatural skepticism "more rational" than belief; but neither religion nor secularism can stake a monopolistic claim to rationality. Accordingly, researchers in this area stress "that present studies are silent on long-standing debates about the intrinsic value or rationality of religious beliefs" (Gervais and Norenzayan 2012a: 496). Also, see Pennycook et al. (2013, 2014).

20 One of the most insightful discussions of the differences between such definitions remains Peter Berger, "Some Second Thoughts on Substantive versus Functional Definitions of Religion," *Journal for the Scientific Study of Religion* 13:2 (1974): 125–33.

21 A recent example of the substantive definition is "religion consists of very general explanations of existence, including the terms of exchange with a god or gods" (Stark and Finke, *Acts of Faith*, 91).

22 Two of the most influential and insightful functionalist conceptualizations of religion are Emile Durkheim, *The Elementary Forms of Religious Life*, translated by Karen E. Fields (New York: Free Press, [1912] 1995); and Clifford Geertz, *The Interpretation of Cultures* (New York: Basic Books, 1973).

23 On the "flattening" of religion by functionalism, see Berger, "Some Second Thoughts," 128.

24 Attempts to reframe religion as "chains of memory" go a long way toward extricating the study of religion from self-imposed quandaries. Sociologist Danièle Hervieu-Léger suggested redefining religion as "an ideological, practical, and symbolic system through which consciousness, both individual and collective, of belonging to a particular chain of belief is constituted, maintained, developed and controlled" (*Religion as a Chain of Memory*, translated by Simon Lee [New Brunswick, NJ: Rutgers University Press, 2000], 82). Although a step in the right direction, this definition fails to distinguish belief systems focused on cosmological and existential questions from ideologies that do not address "ultimate" questions.

25 These categories are not mutually exclusive. For instance, some individuals may hold secular attitudes toward religion while believing in forms of paranormalism.

26 On how definitions are not true or false, only more or less useful, see Berger (1967: 175–77).

27 Because beliefs are necessarily social, the simplest way to approach studying both secularity and religiosity is to view each as a performed and achieved social status. In other words, belief is created out of and reinforced by social "location" relative to other people. Conceptualizing secularity and religiosity as beliefs rooted in social statuses highlights that individuals form and maintain identities through interaction with others. Cosmic beliefs are adopted from the cultural templates available and salient about what it means to be religious or secular, then reinforced (or sanctioned) by the reactions of those within one's social networks to performative expressions of belief. See Mary Douglas, *Natural Symbols: Explorations in Cosmology* (New York: Pantheon Books, 1970).

28 Social anthropologist Abby Day's in-depth examination of belief among contemporary Britons provides useful tools for pushing forward the study of both religion and secularity by outlining how belief operates as a marker of social group identification, as well as indicating where and in whom individuals place authority for (perceived) knowledge about the world. While Day's critical view of the utility of the concept of belief systems differs from our own, her work demonstrates the centrality of belief to both secular and religious ideologies, and also outlines some basic dimensions useful for assessing and comparing expressions of belief. Abby Day, *Believing in Belonging: Belief and Social Identity in the Modern World* (Oxford: Oxford University Press, 2011).

29 David Hume, *A Treatise on Human Nature*, edited by David F. Norton and Mary J. Norton (New York: Oxford University Press, [1738] 2001); cf. Alasdair MacIntyre, "Hume on 'Is' and "Ought,"" *Philosophical Review* 68:4 (1959): 451–68; John Searle, "How to Derive 'Ought' from 'Is,'" *Philosophical Review* 73:1 (1964): 43–58. On recent debates on this topic, see Shira Elqayam and Jonathan St. B. T. Evans, "Subtracting 'Ought' from 'Is': Descriptivism versus Normativism in the Study of Human Thinking," *Behavioral and Brain Sciences* 34:5 (2011): 233–90.

30 Max Weber, "Science as a Vocation," translated and edited by Hans H. Gerth and C. Wright Mills, pp. 129–56 in *From Max Weber: Essays in Sociology* (New York: Oxford University Press, [1918] 1946).

31 On this count, we endorse the stance of "methodological agnosticism" outlined in Douglas Porpora, "Methodological Atheism, Methodological Agnosticism and Religious Experience," *Journal for the Theory of Social Behaviour* 36:1 (2006): 57–75, rather than a stance of "methodological atheism," as outlined in Berger, "Some Second Thoughts."

32 Although the possibilities are vast, some areas of research immediately call for attention. As we have noted, ethnographies of secularities beyond public atheism are needed. See Lee (2012b) for a discussion of the potential research directions

and conceptual reformulations needed to accomplish this goal. Systematic textual analyses of how secularity is framed in popular discourse would deepen our understanding of the cultural frames commonly used by the public regarding secularism. On the quantitative side, narrowing the focus to analyses of specific types of secularity, or expanding focus to more macro, comparative analyses across cultural contexts are potentially fruitful strategies. Longitudinal data of all types will be useful for better understanding how individual narratives or discursive frames change over time.

33 As always, it is important to emphasize that these are general trends, and relative rather than absolute categories.

34 On the decline of liberal Protestantism, see Chaves (2011: 81–93); Michael Hout, Andrew Greeley, and Melissa J. Wilde, "The Demographic Imperative in Religious Change in the United States," *American Journal of Sociology* 107:2 (2001): 468–500.

35 Some theorists argue that this hemorrhaging of adherents is due precisely to the accommodation of secularism; for example, see Stark and Finke, *Acts of Faith*, 141–68. The best arguments for the role of strictness in organizational vitality are Laurence Iannaccone, "Why Strict Churches Are Strong," *American Journal of Sociology* 99:5 (1994): 1180–211; Dean M. Kelley, *Why Conservative Churches Are Growing* (Macon, GA: Mercer University Press, 1986). It could be argued that by being *so* liberal, the UUA has generated tension with its cultural environment by being more progressive than its surroundings. This is consistent with tension theory, but is not an option that any "strictness" theorists highlight, illustrating that "strictness" and "tension" are related, but distinct concepts in need of further refinement.

36 "Atheist and Agnostic People Welcome," *Unitarian Universalist Association*, http://www.uua.org/beliefs/welcome/atheism/index.shtml. See John C. Green, "A Liberal Dynamo: The Political Activism of the Unitarian-Universalist Clergy," *Journal for the Scientific Study of Religion* 42:4 (2003): 577–90. On the overrepresentation of the UUA relative to its membership in interfaith organizing efforts, see Brad Fulton and Richard L. Wood, "Interfaith Community Organizing: Emerging Theological and Organizational Challenges," *International Journal of Public Theology* 6:4 (2012): 398–420, 411.

37 Data are taken from the 1980, 1990, 2000, and 2010 Religious Congregational Membership Reports. All data are publically available from the Association of Religion Data Archives at http://www.thearda.com/rcms2010/index.asp. The categorization of denominations was based on the schema outlined in Brian Steensland, Jerry Z. Park, Mark D. Regnerus, Lynn D. Robinson, W. Bradford Wilcox, and Robert D. Woodberry, "The Measure of American Religion: Toward Improving the State of the Art," *Social Forces* 79:1 (2000): 291–318. The UUA was not classified as a liberal Protestant group, but rather a different type of religion based on its open embrace of multiple religious traditions, in spite of the history of its development rooted in liberal Protestantism. To be clear, the UUA still faces

the "public good" problem of having members who are less engaged on average than a group that maintains high levels of strictness. At the same time, Unitarians provide an instructive counterexample to the claim that organizations *must* be strict to grow. It seems that while strictness is often an engine for growth, there are also other ways to generate organizational vitality.

38 The Sunday Assembly, a "godless congregation" started by British comedians Sanderson Jones and Pippa Evans, is perhaps the best-known recent effort to create a quasi-religious organization based on secular ideology.

39 Preliminary research indicates that frequency of internet use correlates with secularity at the individual level; see Allen B. Downey, "Religious Affiliation, Education and Internet Use," *arXiv* 1403:5534 (2014). Also see Greg G. Armfield and R. Lance Holbert, "The Relationship between Religiosity and Internet Use," *Journal of Media and Religion* 2:3 (2003): 129–44. As we previously noted, there is also a high correlation between population rates of internet use and secularity in the U.S. at the state level (r = .57). We analyzed data from the Social Side of the Internet survey collected by Pew in 2010, and found a nonlinear pattern to the relationship between internet use and religious service attendance at the individual level. Those who used the internet at home multiple times a day attended less, as did those who used the internet infrequently. A quadratic (nonlinear) term for frequency of internet use was a stronger predictor of frequency of religious service attendance than education, income, race and ethnicity, gender, marital status, and urban/rural place of residence. Only political identity was a stronger predictor in the model. Much remains to be studied on this topic.

40 "2013 Year in Review," *Freedom from Religion Foundation*, http://ffrf.org/uploads/files/2013YIR.pdf.

41 Here we are applying the basic model of religious group growth outlined in Rodney Stark, "Why Religions Succeed or Fail: A Revised General Model," *Journal of Contemporary Religion* 11:2 (1996): 133–46.

42 The primary "competitors" for informal secularism are paranormalism and privatized spirituality, both of which have fared better in the Great Abdicating than more hardline forms of secularity.

DATA SOURCES APPENDIX

1 Michael Hout was added as a principal investigator in 2009.

2 Chaves (2011: 5).

3 For more detail on the collection methods of the GSS, see Peter V. Marsden and Tom W. Smith, "Appendix: The General Social Survey Project," pp. 369–78 in *Social Trends in American Life*, edited by Peter V. Marsden (Princeton, NJ: Princeton University Press, 2012). More in-depth information is available at http://www3.norc.org/GSS+Website.

4 Although relatively low, this overall response rate is consistent with the falling response rates to surveys and within acceptable parameters for RDD surveys,

which still produce reliable estimates of population parameters. See Scott Keeter, Courtney Kennedy, Michael Dimock, Jonathan Best, and Peyton Craighill, "Gauging the Impact of Growing Nonresponse on Estimates from a National RDD Telephone Survey," *Public Opinion Quarterly* 70:5 (2006): 759–79. Additionally, nonresponse is actually a relatively weak predictor of nonresponse bias. For a recent review of these matters, see Scott Keeter, Carolyn Miller, Andrew Kohut, Robert M. Groves, and Stanley Presser, "Consequences of Reducing Nonresponse in a National Telephone Survey," *Public Opinion Quarterly* 62:2 (2000): 125–48; Robert M. Groves and Emilia Peytcheva, "The Impact of Nonresponse Rates on Nonresponse Bias: A Meta-Analysis," *Public Opinion Quarterly* 72:2 (2008): 167–89.

5 Pew (2008: 114). For more detail on the Pew RLS, see the full report for the study, available at http://religions.pewforum.org/pdf/report-religious-landscape-study-full.pdf.

6 The full report from the survey, including further details on the collection procedures, is available at http://www.pewsocialtrends.org/files/2013/04/Asian-Americans-new-full-report-04-2013.pdf.

7 For more detail on the survey, see http://www.pewhispanic.org/files/2012/04/NSL_2011_hispanic_identity_topline.pdf.

8 For more detail on the survey, see the book *American Grace*, written by the study's principal investigators, political scientists Robert Putnam and David Campbell (2010: 557–61).

9 For more detail on the collection methods of the first two waves of the Baylor Religion Surveys, see Christopher Bader, F. Carson Mencken, and Paul Froese, "American Piety 2005: Methods and Select Findings from the Baylor Religion Survey," *Journal for the Scientific Study of Religion* 46:4 (2007): 447–63.

BIBLIOGRAPHY

Aiello, Thomas. 2005. "Constructing 'Godless Communism': Religion, Politics, and Popular Culture, 1954–1960." *Americana: The Journal of American Popular Culture* 4(1). http://www.americanpopularculture.com/journal/articles/spring_2005/aiello.htm.

Aldridge, A. Owen. 1997. "Natural Religion and Deism in America before Ethan Allen and Thomas Paine." *William and Mary Quarterly* 54(4): 835–48.

Allen, Ethan (and Thomas Young). [1784] 1854. *Reason, the Only Oracle of Man; Or a Compendious System of Natural Religion*. Boston: J. P. Mendum, Cornhill.

Anderson, George P. 1937. "Who Wrote 'Ethan Allen's Bible'?" *New England Quarterly* 10(4): 685–96.

Anspach, Whitney, Kevin Coe, and Crispin Thurlow. 2007. "The Other Closet?: Atheists, Homosexuals, and the Lateral Appropriation of Discursive Capital." *Critical Discourse Studies* 4(1): 95–119.

Arouet, François-Marie (Voltaire). [1764] 1972. *Philosophical Dictionary*. Edited and translated by T. Besterman. New York: Penguin.

Asad, Talal. 2003. *Formations of the Secular: Christianity, Islam, Modernity*. Stanford, CA: Stanford University Press.

Bainbridge, William S. 2005. "Atheism." *Interdisciplinary Journal of Research on Religion* 1(2): 1–24.

———. 2007. *Across the Secular Abyss: From Faith to Wisdom*. Lanham, MD: Lexington Books.

Baker, Joseph O. 2012a. "Perceptions of Science and American Secularism." *Sociological Perspectives* 55(1): 167–88.

———. 2012b. "Public Perceptions of Incompatibility between 'Religion and Science.'" *Public Understanding of Science* 21(3): 340–53.

Baker, Joseph O., and Buster G. Smith. 2009a. "The Nones: Social Characteristics of the Religiously Unaffiliated." *Social Forces* 87(3): 1251–64.

———. 2009b. "None Too Simple: Examining Issues of Religious Nonbelief and Nonbelonging in the United States." *Journal for the Scientific Study of Religion* 48(4): 719–33.

Bannister, Robert C. 1987. *Sociology and Scientism: The American Quest for Objectivity, 1880–1949*. Chapel Hill: University of North Carolina Press.

Bates, Stephen. 2004. "'Godless Communism' and Its Legacies." *Society* 41(3): 29–33.

Beit-Hallahmi, Benjamin. 2007. "Atheists: A Psychological Profile." Pp. 300–17 in *The Cambridge Companion to Atheism*, edited by Michael Martin. Cambridge, UK: Cambridge University Press.

Berger, Peter L. 1967. *The Sacred Canopy: Elements of Sociological Theory of Religion.* New York: Anchor Books.

Berger, Peter L., Grace Davie, and Effie Fokas. 2008. *Religious America, Secular Europe? A Theme and Variations.* Hampshire: Ashgate.

Bruce, Steve. 2001. "Christianity in Britain, R. I. P." *Sociology of Religion* 62(2): 191–203.

———. 2002. *God Is Dead: Secularization in the West.* Malden, MA: Blackwell.

———. 2008. *Fundamentalism.* 2nd edition. Cambridge, UK: Polity Press.

Bryson, Gladys. 1936. "Early English Positivists and the Religion of Humanity." *American Sociological Review* 1(3): 343–62.

Buckley, Michael J. 1990. *At the Origins of Modern Atheism.* New Haven, CT: Yale University Press.

Budd, Susan. 1977. *Varieties of Unbelief: Atheists and Agnostics in English Society, 1850–1960.* New York: Holmes & Meier.

Bullivant, Stephen. 2012. *The Salvation of Atheists and Catholic Dogmatic Theology.* Oxford: Oxford University Press.

Bullivant, Stephen, and Lois Lee. 2012. "Interdisciplinary Studies of Non-Religion and Secularity: The State of the Union." *Journal of Contemporary Religion* 27(1): 19–27.

Caldwell-Harris, Catherine, Angela L. Wilson, Elizabeth LoTempio, and Benjamin Beit-Hallahmi. 2011. "Exploring the Atheist Personality: Well-Being, Awe, and Magical Thinking in Atheists, Buddhists, and Christians." *Mental Health, Religion and Culture* 14(7): 659–72.

Calhoun, Craig, Mark Juergensmeyer, and Jonathan VanAntwerpen (eds.). 2011. *Rethinking Secularism.* New York: Oxford University Press.

Campbell, Colin. 1972. *Toward a Sociology of Irreligion.* New York: Herder and Herder.

Cannell, Fanella. 2010. "The Anthropology of Secularism." *Annual Review of Anthropology* 39: 85–100.

Casanova, José. 1994. *Public Religions in the Modern World.* Chicago: University of Chicago Press.

———. 2006. "Rethinking Secularization: A Global Comparative Perspective." *Hedgehog Review* 8(1–2): 7–22.

Cavalcanti, H. B., and Debra Schleef. 2005. "The Case for Secular Assimilation? The Latino Experience in Richmond, Virginia." *Journal for the Scientific Study of Religion* 44(4): 473–83.

Chaves, Mark. 1993. "Intraorganizational Power and Secularization in Protestant Denominations." *American Journal of Sociology* 99(1): 1–48.

——— 1994. "Secularization as Declining Religious Authority." *Social Forces* 72(3): 749–74.

———. 2011. *American Religion: Contemporary Trends.* Princeton, NJ: Princeton University Press.

Cheung, Russell. 2012. "Second-Generation Chinese Americans: The Familism of the Nonreligious." Pp. 197–221 in *Sustaining Faith Traditions: Race, Ethnicity, and Religion among the Latino and Asian American Second Generation*, edited by Russell Cheung and Carolyn Chen. New York: NYU Press.

Cimino, Richard, and Christopher Smith. 2007. "Secular Humanism and Atheism beyond Progressive Secularism." *Sociology of Religion* 68(4): 407–24.

———. 2011. "The New Atheism and the Formation of the Imagined Secularist Community." *Journal of Media and Religion* 10(1): 24–38.

Cockshut, A. O. J. 1964. *The Unbelievers: English Agnostic Thought, 1840–1890*. New York: NYU Press.

Commager, Henry S. 1935. "The Blasphemy of Abner Kneeland." *New England Quarterly* 8(1): 29–41.

Comte, Auguste. [1851] 1875. *System of Positive Polity or Treatise on Sociology*. London: Burt Franklin.

Condran, John G., and Joseph B. Tamney. 1985. "Religious 'Nones': 1957 to 1982." *Sociological Analysis* 46(4): 415–23.

Cragg, Gerald R. 1964. *The Church and the Age of Reason, 1648–1789*. Grand Rapids, MI: Wm. B. Eerdmans.

Cragun, Ryan T. 2007. *A Role Conflict Theory of Religious Change: An Explanation and Test*. Ph.D. dissertation, University of Cincinnati. https://etd.ohiolink.edu/ap/10?0:NO:10:P10_ACCESSION_NUM:ucin1179340860.

Crockett, Alasdair, and David Voas. 2006. "Generations of Decline: Religious Change in Twentieth-Century Britain." *Journal for the Scientific Study of Religion* 45(4): 567–84.

Davie, Grace. 1994. *Religion in Britain since 1945: Believing without Belonging*. Oxford: Blackwell.

———. 2000. *Religion in Modern Europe*. Oxford: Oxford University Press.

Demerath, N. J., III. 2000. "The Rise of 'Cultural Religion' in European Christianity: Learning from Poland, Northern Ireland, and Sweden." *Social Compass* 47(1): 127–39.

———. 2001. *Crossing the Gods: World Religions and Worldly Politics*. New Brunswick, NJ: Rutgers University Press.

———. 2007. "Secularization and Sacralization Deconstructed and Reconstructed." Pp. 57–80 in *The Sage Handbook of the Sociology of Religion*, edited by N. J. Demerath III and James A. Beckford. London: Sage Publications.

Dougherty, Kevin D., Byron R. Johnson, and Edward C. Polson. 2007. "Recovering the Lost: Remeasuring U.S. Religious Affiliation." *Journal for the Scientific Study of Religion* 46(4): 483–99.

Ecklund, Elaine H., and Kristen S. Lee. 2011. "Atheists and Agnostics Negotiate Religion and Family." *Journal for the Scientific Study of Religion* 50(4): 728–43.

Ecklund, Elaine H., Jerry Z. Park, and Phil T. Veliz. 2008. "Secularization and Religious Change among Elite Scientists." *Social Forces* 86(4): 1807–39.

Ecklund, Elaine H., and Christopher P. Scheitle. 2007. "Religion among Academic Scientists: Distinctions, Disciplines, and Demographics." *Social Problems* 54(2): 289–307.

Edgell, Penny, Joseph Gerteis, and Douglas Hartmann. 2007. "Atheists as 'Other': Cultural Boundaries and Cultural Membership in the United States." *American Sociological Review* 71(2): 211–34.

Evans, John H., and Michael S. Evans. 2008. "Religion and Science: Beyond the Epistemological Conflict Narrative." *Annual Review of Sociology* 34: 87–105.

Evans, Michael S. 2009. "Defining the Public, Defining Sociology: Hybrid Science—Public Relations and Boundary-Work in Early American Sociology." *Public Understanding of Science* 18(1): 5–22.

Ferraro, Kenneth F., and Jessica A. Kelley-Moore. 2001. "Religious Seeking among Affiliates and Non-Affiliates: Do Mental and Physical Health Problems Spur Religious Coping?" *Review of Religious Research* 42(3): 229–51.

Finke, Roger. 1992. "An Unsecular America." Pp. 145–69 in *Religion and Modernization: Sociologists and Historians Debate the Secularization Thesis*, edited by Steve Bruce. New York: Oxford University Press.

French, Roderick S. 1980. "Liberation from Man and God in Boston: Abner Kneeland's Free-Thought Campaign, 1830–1839." *American Quarterly* 32(2): 202–21.

Froese, Paul D. 2008. *The Plot to Kill God: Findings from the Soviet Experiment in Secularization*. Berkeley: University of California Press.

Frost, Jacqueline. 2012. "Atheist Scripts in a Nation of Religiosity: Identity Politics within the Atheist Movement." M.A. thesis, Portland State University. http://pdxscholar.library.pdx.edu/open_access_etds/549/.

Fuller, Robert C. 2001. *Spiritual, but Not Religious: Understanding Unchurched America*. New York: Oxford University Press.

Galen, Luke W., and James D. Kloet. 2011a. "Mental Well-Being in the Religious and the Non-Religious: Evidence for a Curvilinear Relationship." *Mental Health, Religion & Culture* 14(7): 673–89.

———. 2011b. "Personality and Social Integration Factors Distinguishing Nonreligious from Religious Groups: The Importance of Controlling for Attendance and Demographics." *Archive for the Psychology of Religion* 33(2): 205–28.

Gans, Herbert. 1994. "Symbolic Ethnicity and Symbolic Religiosity: Towards a Comparison of Ethnic and Religious Acculturation." *Ethnic and Racial Studies* 17(4): 577–92.

Garneau, Christopher R. H. 2012. *Perceived Stigma and Stigma Management of Midwest Seculars*. Ph.D. dissertation, University of Nebraska–Lincoln.

Garver, Bruce M. 1980. "Czech-American Freethinkers on the Great Plains." Pp. 147–69 in *Ethnicity on the Great Plains*, edited by Frederick C. Luebke. Lincoln: University of Nebraska Press.

Gervais, Will M. 2011. "Finding the Faithless: Perceived Atheist Prevalence Reduces Anti-Atheist Prejudice." *Personality and Social Psychology Bulletin* 37(4): 543–56.

———. 2013. "In Godlessness We Distrust: Using Social Psychology to Solve the Puzzle of Anti-Atheist Prejudice." *Social & Personality Psychology Compass* 7(6): 366–77.

———. 2014. "Everything Is Permitted? People Intuitively Judge Immorality as Representative of Atheists." *PLoS One* 9(4): 1–9.

Gervais, Will M., and Ara Norenzayan. 2012a. "Analytic Thinking Promotes Religious Disbelief." *Science* 336: 493–96.

———. 2012b. "Reminders of Secular Authority Reduce Believers' Distrust of Atheists." *Psychological Science* 23(5): 483–91.

Gervais, Will M., Azim F. Shariff, and Ara Norenzayan. 2011. "Do You Believe in Atheists? Distrust Is Central to Anti-Atheist Prejudice." *Journal of Personality and Social Psychology* 101(6): 1189–1206.

Glenn, Norval D. 1987. "The Trend in 'No Religion' Respondents to U.S. National Surveys, Late 1950s to Early 1980s." *Public Opinion Quarterly* 51(3): 293–314.

Gorski, Philp S., and Ateş Altinordu. 2008. "After Secularization?" *Annual Review of Sociology* 34: 55–85.

Grasso, Christopher. 2002. "Skepticism and American Faith: Infidels, Converts, and Religious Doubt in the Early Republic." *Journal of the Early Republic* 22(3): 465–508.

———. 2008. "Deist Monster: On Religious Common Sense in the Wake of the American Revolution." *Journal of American History* 95(1): 43–68.

Grossman, Cathy Lynn. 2009. "An Inaugural First: Obama Acknowledges 'Non-Believers.'" *USA Today*, January 20 (updated January 22). http://usatoday30.usatoday.com/news/religion/2009-01-20-obama-non-believers_N.htm.

Hadaway, C. Kirk, and Wade Clark Roof. 1979. "Those Who Stay Religious 'Nones' and Those Who Don't." *Journal for the Scientific Study of Religion* 18(2): 194–200.

Hadden, Jeffrey K. 1987. "Toward Desacralizing Secularization Theory." *Social Forces* 65(3): 587–611.

Hale, J. Russell. 1977. *The Unchurched: Who They Are and Why They Stay That Way*. San Francisco: Harper & Row.

Hayes, Bernadette C. 2000. "Religious Independents within Western Industrialized Nations: A Socio-Demographic Profile." *Sociology of Religion* 62(2): 191–210.

Hout, Michael, and Claude S. Fischer. 2002. "Why More Americans Have No Religious Preference: Politics and Generations." *American Sociological Review* 67(2): 165–90.

———. 2003. "O Be Some Other Name." *American Sociological Review* 68(2): 316–18.

Hughes, Patrick W. 2013. *Antidotes to Deism: A Reception History of Thomas Paine's* The Age of Reason, *1794–1809*. Ph.D. dissertation, University of Pittsburgh. http://d-scholarship.pitt.edu/18481/1/hughespw_etd_2013.pdf.

Hume, David. [1757] 1993. "The Natural History of Religion." Pp. 134–96 in *Dialogues and Natural History of Religion*, edited by J. C. A. Gaskin. New York: Oxford University Press.

Hunsberger, Bruce E., and Bob Altemeyer. 2006. *Atheists: A Groundbreaking Study of America's Nonbelievers*. Amherst, NY: Prometheus Books.

Hurd, Elizabeth S. 2011. "Suspension of (Dis)Belief: The Secular-Religious Binary and the Study of International Relations." Pp. 166–184 in *Rethinking Secularism*, edited by Craig Calhoun, Mark Juergensmeyer, and Jonathan VanAntwerpen. New York: Oxford University Press.

Hyman, Gavin. 2007. "Atheism in Modern History." Pp. 27–46 in *The Cambridge Companion to Atheism*, edited by Michael Martin. Cambridge, UK: Cambridge University Press.

Jacoby, Susan. 2004. *Freethinkers: A History of American Secularism*. New York: Metropolitan Books.

Kauffman, Eric, Anne Goujon, and Vegard Skirbekk. 2012. "The End of Secularization in Europe? A Socio-Demographic Perspective." *Sociology of Religion* 73(1): 69–91.

Ketchell, Aaron K. 2000. "Contesting Tradition and Combatting Intolerance: A History of Freethought in Kansas." *Great Plains Quarterly* 20(4): 281–95.

Koch, G. Adolf. [1933] 1968. *Religion of the American Enlightenment*. New York: Thomas Y. Crowell Co.

Kolenda, Benjamin. 2013. "Re-Discovering Ethan Allen and Thomas Young's *Reason, the Only Oracle of Man*: The Rise of Deism in Pre-Revolutionary America." M.A. thesis, Georgia State University.http://scholarworks.gsu.edu/cgi/viewcontent.cgi?article=1159&context=english_theses.

Kosmin, Barry A., and Ariela Keysar. 2006. *Religion in a Free Market: Religious and Non-Religious Americans: Who, What, Why, Where*. Ithaca, NY: Paramount Market Publishing.

Larson, Edward J., and Larry A. Witham. 1998. "Leading Scientists Still Reject God." *Nature* 394: 313.

LeDrew, Stephen. 2013. "Discovering Atheism: Heterogeneity in Trajectories to Atheist Identity and Activism." *Sociology of Religion* 74(4): 431–53.

Lee, Lois. 2012a. "Research Note: Talking about a Revolution: Terminology for the New Field of Non-Religion Studies." *Journal of Contemporary Religion* 27(1): 129–39.

———. 2012b. "Locating Nonreligion, in Mind, Body and Space: New Research Methods for a New Field." *Annual Review of the Sociology of Religion* 3: 135–57.

Lemert, Charles. 1979. "Science, Religion, and Secularization." *Sociological Quarterly* 20(4): 445–61.

Levy, Leonard. 1973. *Blasphemy in Massachusetts: Freedom of Conscience and the Abner Kneeland Case*. New York: Da Capo Press.

Lim, Chaeyoon, Carol A. MacGregor, and Robert D. Putnam. 2010. "Secular and Liminal: Discovering Heterogeneity among Religious Nones." *Journal for the Scientific Study of Religion* 49(4): 596–618.

Manning, Christel J. 2013. "Unaffiliated Parents and the Religious Training of Their Children." *Sociology of Religion* 74(2): 176–98.

Martin, David A. 1969. *The Religious and the Secular: Studies in Secularization*. New York: Schocken Books.

———. 1991. "The Secularization Issue: Prospect and Retrospect." *British Journal of Sociology* 42(3): 465–74.

———. 2005. *On Secularization: Towards a Revised General Theory*. Aldershot: Ashgate.

Marwell, Gerald, and N. J. Demerath III. 2003. "'Secularization' by Any Other Name." *American Sociological Review* 68(2): 314–16.

McLeod, Hugh. 2000. *Secularisation in Western Europe, 1848–1914*. Hampshire: Palgrave Macmillan.

Merino, Stephen M. 2012. "Irreligious Socialization? The Adult Religious Preferences of Individuals Raised with No Religion." *Secularism and Nonreligion* 1: 1–16.

Morais, Herbert M. [1934] 1960. *Deism in Eighteenth Century America*. New York: Russell and Russell.

Norris, Pippa, and Ronald Inglehart. 2004. *Sacred and Secular: Religion and Politics Worldwide*. Cambridge, UK: Cambridge University Press.

Norenzayan, Ara, and Will M. Gervais. 2013. "The Origins of Religious Disbelief." *Trends in Cognitive Sciences* 17(1): 20–25.

Norenzayan, Ara, Will M. Gervais, and Kali H. Trzesniewski. 2012. "Mentalizing Deficits Constrain Belief in a Personal God." *PLoS One* 7(5): 1–8.

Numbers, Ronald L. (ed.). 2009. *Galileo Goes to Jail and Other Myths about Science and Religion*. Cambridge, MA: Harvard University Press.

Paine, Thomas. [1794, 1795, 1807]. *The Age of Reason*, Parts I–III. http://www.ushistory.org/paine/reason/singlehtml.htm.

Palmer, Elihu. [1801] 1992. *Reason, the Glory of Our Nature*. Pp. 244–77 in *The American Deists: Voices of Reason and Dissent in the Early Republic*, edited by Kerry S. Walters. Lawrence: University of Kansas Press.

Paul, Gregory S. 2007. "Cross-National Correlations of Quantifiable Societal Health with Popular Religiosity and Secularism in the Prosperous Democracies." *Journal of Religion & Society* 7: 1–17.

———. 2010. "The Evolution of Popular Religiosity and Secularism: How First World Statistics Reveal Why Religion Exists, Why It has Been Popular, and Why the Most Successful Democracies Are the Most Secular." Pp. 149–208 in *Atheism and Secularity*, Vol. 1, edited by Phil Zuckerman. Santa Barbara, CA: Praeger.

Pennycook, Gordon, James A. Cheyne, Nathaniel Barr, Derek J. Koehler, and Jonathan A. Fugelsang. 2014. "Cognitive Style and Religiosity: The Role of Conflict Detection." *Memory & Cognition* 42(1): 1–10.

Pennycook, Gordon, James A. Cheyne, Derek J. Koehler, and Jonathan A. Fugelsang. 2013. "Belief Bias during Reasoning among Religious Believers and Skeptics." *Psychonomic Bulletin & Review* 20(4): 806–11.

Pew Forum on Religion and Public Life. 2007. *Changing Faiths: Latinos and the Transformation of American Religion*. Washington, D.C. http://www.pewhispanic.org/files/reports/75.pdf.

———. 2008. *U.S. Religious Landscape Survey: Religious Affiliation: Diverse and Dynamic*. Washington, D.C. http://religions.pewforum.org/pdf/report-religious-landscape-study-full.pdf.

———. 2009. *Faith in Flux: Changes in Religious Affiliation in the U.S.* Washington, D.C. http://pewforum.org/uploadedfiles/Topics/Religious_Affiliation/fullreport.pdf.

———. 2012. *'Nones' on the Rise: One-in-Five Adults Have No Religious Affiliation*. Washington, D.C. http://www.pewforum.org/uploadedFiles/Topics/Religious_Affiliation/Unaffiliated/NonesOnTheRise-full.pdf.

Pinn, Anthony B. 2004. *African American Humanist Principles: Living and Thinking Like the Children of Nimrod*. New York: Palgrave Macmillan.

———. 2012. *The End of God-Talk: An African American Humanist Theology*. New York: Oxford University Press.

Porterfield, Amanda. 2012. *Conceived in Doubt: Religion and Politics in the New American Nation*. Chicago: University of Chicago Press.

Post, Albert. [1943] 1974. *Popular Freethought in America, 1825–1850*. New York: Octagon Books.

Prochaska, Franklyn K. 1972. "Thomas Paine's *Age of Reason* Revisited." *Journal of the History of Ideas* 33(4): 561–76.

Proctor, James D. 2005. "In _________ We Trust: Science, Religion, and Authority." Pp. 87–108 in *Science, Religion, and the Human Experience*, edited by James D. Proctor. New York: Oxford University Press.

Putnam, Robert D., and David E. Campbell. 2010. *American Grace: How Religion Divides and Unites Us*. New York: Simon & Schuster.

Putnam, Samuel P. 1894. *400 Years of Freethought*. New York: Truth Seeker Company.

Riley, Jennifer, Sophia Best, and Bruce G. Charlton. 2005. "Religious Believers and Strong Atheists May Both Be Less Depressed than Existentially-Uncertain People." *QJM: An International Journal of Medicine* 98(11): 840.

Rogers, Richard S. 1968. "The Rhetoric of Militant Deism." *Quarterly Journal of Speech* 54(3): 247–51.

Roof, Wade Clark, and William McKinney. 1987. *American Mainline Religion: Its Changing Shape and Future*. New Brunswick, NJ: Rutgers University Press.

Samuels, Shirley. 1987. "Infidelity and Contagion: The Rhetoric of Revolution." *Early American Literature* 22(2): 183–91.

———. 1990. "*Wieland*: Alien and Infidel." *Early American Literature* 25(2): 46–66.

Saslow, Laura R., Robb Willer, Matthew Feinberg, Paul K. Piff, Katharine Clark, Dacher Keltner, and Sarina R. Saturn. 2012. "My Brother's Keeper?: Compassion Predicts Generosity More among Less Religious Individuals." *Social Psychological and Personality Science* 4(1): 31–38.

Schwadel, Philip. 2010. "Period and Cohort Effects on Religious Nonaffiliation and Religious Disaffiliation: A Research Note." *Journal for the Scientific Study of Religion* 49(2): 311–19.

Sherkat, Darren E. 1991. "Leaving the Faith: Testing Theories of Religious Switching Using Survival Models." *Social Science Research* 20(2): 171–87.

———. 2001. "Tracking the Restructuring of American Religion: Religious Affiliation and Patterns of Religious Mobility, 1973–1998." *Social Forces* 79(4): 1459–93.

———. 2008. "Beyond Belief: Atheism, Agnosticism, and Theistic Certainty in the United States." *Sociological Spectrum* 28(5): 438–59.

Sherkat, Darren E., and John Wilson. 1995. "Preferences, Constraints, and Choices in Religious Markets: An Examination of Religious Switching and Apostasy." *Social Forces* 73(3): 993–1026.

Shook, John R. 2010. *The God Debates: A 21st Century Guide for Atheists and Believers (and Everyone in Between)*. Chichester: Wiley.

Skirbekk, Vegard, Eric Kaufmann, and Anne Goujon. 2010. "Secularism, Fundamentalism, or Catholicism? The Religious Composition of the United States to 2043." *Journal for the Scientific Study of Religion* 49(2): 293–310.

Smith, Christian (ed.). 2003. *The Secular Revolution: Power, Interests, and Conflicts in the Secularization of American Public Life*. Berkeley: University of California Press.
Smith, Jesse M. 2011. "Becoming an Atheist in America: Constructing Identity and Meaning from the Rejection of Theism." *Sociology of Religion* 72(2): 215–37.
———. 2013. "Creating a Godless Community: The Collective Identity Work of Contemporary American Atheists." *Journal for the Scientific Study of Religion* 52(1): 80–99.
Smith, Peter. 1986. "Anglo-American Religion and Hegemonic Change in the World System." *British Journal of Sociology* 37(1): 88–105.
Smith, Tom W., and Seokho Kim. 2007. "Counting Religious Nones and Other Religious Measurement Issues: A Comparison of the Baylor Religion Survey and General Social Survey." *GSS Methodological Report No. 110*. http://publicdata.norc.org:41000/gss/documents/MTRT/MR110%20Counting%20Religious%20Nones%20and %20Other%20Religious%20Measurement%20Issues.pdf.
Smylie, James H. 1972–73. "Clerical Perspectives on Deism: Paine's *The Age of Reason* in Virginia." *Eighteenth-Century Studies* 6(2): 203–20.
Stark, Rodney. 1963. "On the Incompatibility of Religion and Science: A Survey of American Graduate Students." *Journal for the Scientific Study of Religion* 3(1): 3–20.
———. 1999. "Secularization, R.I.P." *Sociology of Religion* 60(3): 249–73.
Stark, Rodney, Laurence Iannaccone, and Roger Finke. 1996. "Religion, Science, and Rationality." *American Economic Review* 86(2): 433–37.
Steadman, Chris. 2013. "Atheism Is Not 'the New Gay Marriage' (or the New Anything Else)." Religion News Service, December 6. http://chrisstedman.religionnews.com/2013/12/06/atheism-new-gay-marriage-new-anything-else/.
Stewart, Matthew. 2014. *Nature's God: The Heretical Origins of the American Republic*. New York: W. W. Norton & Company.
Stolzenberg, Ross M., Mary Blair-Loy, and Linda J. Waite. 1995. "Religious Participation in Early Adulthood: Age and Family Life Cycle Effects on Church Membership." *American Sociological Review* 60(1): 84–103.
Storm, Ingrid. 2009. "Halfway to Heaven: Four Types of Fuzzy Fidelity in Europe." *Journal for the Scientific Study of Religion* 48(4): 702–18.
Swatos, William H. 1983. "The Faith of the Fathers: On the Christianity of Early American Sociology." *Sociological Analysis* 44(1): 33–52.
Swatos, William H., and Kevin J. Chistiano. 1999. "Secularization Theory: The Course of a Concept." *Sociology of Religion* 60(3): 209–28.
Tamney, Joseph, Shawn Powell, and Stephen D. Johnson. 1989. "Innovation Theory and Religious Nones." *Journal for the Scientific Study of Religion* 28(2): 216–29.
Tapper, Jake, and Amy Bingham. 2012. "Dems Quickly Switch to Include 'God,' 'Jerusalem.'" *ABC News*, September 5. http://abcnews.go.com/Politics/OTUS/democrats-rapidly-revise-platform-include-god/story?id=17164108.
Taylor, Charles. 1989. *Sources of the Self: The Making of the Modern Identity*. Cambridge, MA: Harvard University Press.
———. 2007. *A Secular Age*. Cambridge, MA: Harvard University Press.

Thomson, Ann. 2008. *Bodies of Thought: Science, Religion, and the Soul in the Early Enlightenment*. New York: Oxford University Press.

Tschannen, Oliver. 1991. "The Secularization Paradigm: A Systematization." *Journal for the Scientific Study of Religion* 30(4): 395–415.

Turner, James. 1984. "Natural Law, Morality, and Unbelief: Some Roots of Agnosticism." *Perspectives in American History: New Series* 1: 359–78.

———. 1985. *Without God, Without Creed: The Origins of Unbelief in America*. Baltimore: Johns Hopkins University Press.

Uecker, Jeremy, Mark Regnerus, and Margaret Vaaler. 2007. "Losing My Religion: The Social Sources of Religious Decline in Early Adulthood." *Social Forces* 85(4): 1667–92.

Vargas, Nicholas. 2012. "Retrospective Accounts of Religious Disaffiliation in the United States: Stressors, Skepticism, and Political Factors." *Sociology of Religion* 73(2): 200–23.

Vernon, Glenn M. 1968. "The Religious 'Nones': A Neglected Category." *Journal for the Scientific Study of Religion* 7(2): 219–29.

Voas, David. 2009. "The Rise and Fall of Fuzzy Fidelity in Europe." *European Sociological Review* 25(2): 155–68.

Voas, David, and Alasdair Crockett. 2005. "Religion in Britain: Neither Believing nor Belonging." *Sociology* 39(1): 11–28.

Walters, Kerry S. 1992. *American Deists: Voices of Reason and Dissent in the Early Republic*. Lawrence: University of Kansas Press.

Warner, R. Stephen. 1993. "Work in Progress toward a New Paradigm for the Sociological Study of Religion in the United States." *American Journal of Sociology* 96(5): 1044–93.

Warner, Rob. 2010. *Secularization and Its Discontents*. London: Continuum.

Warren, Sidney. [1943] 1966. *American Freethought: 1860–1914*. New York: Columbia University Press.

Weber, Max. [1922] 1991. *The Sociology of Religion*. Translated by Ephraim Fischoff. Boston: Beacon Press.

Weber, Samuel R., Kenneth I. Pargament, Mark E. Kunik, James W. Lomax II, and Melinda A. Stanley. 2012. "Psychological Distress among Religious Nonbelievers: A Systematic Review." *Journal of Religion and Health* 51(1): 72–86.

Williamson, David A., and George Yancey. 2013. *There Is No God: Atheists in America*. Lanham, MD: Rowman & Littlefield.

Wuthnow, Robert. 1989. *Communities of Discourse: Ideology and Social Structure in the Reformation, the Enlightenment, and European Socialism*. Cambridge, MA: Harvard University Press.

Yamane, David. 1997. "Secularization on Trial: In Defense of a Neosecularization Paradigm." *Journal for the Scientific Study of Religion* 36(1): 109–22.

Yardley, Jim. 2013. "Pope, Off Script, Nods to Atheists in Holiday Call for World Peace." *New York Times*, December 26, A4.

Zuckerman, Phil. 2007. "Atheism: Contemporary Numbers and Patterns." Pp. 47–65 in *The Cambridge Companion to Atheism*, edited by Michael Martin. Cambridge, UK: Cambridge University Press.

———. 2008. *Society without God: What the Least Religious Nations Can Tell Us about Contentment*. New York: NYU Press.
———. 2009a. "Atheism, Secularity, and Well-Being: How the Findings of Social Science Counter Negative Stereotypes and Assumptions." *Sociology Compass* 3(6): 949–71.
———. 2009b. "The Irreligiosity of W. E. B. Du Bois." Pp. 3–17 in *The Souls of W. E. B. Du Bois*, edited by Edward J. Blum and Jason R. Young. Macon, GA: Mercer University Press.
———. 2011. *Faith No More: Why People Reject Religion*. New York: Oxford University Press.

INDEX

Abingdon School District v. Schempp, 187
active religion, 18, 213–16; childhood socialization, 162; children, 158; educational attainment, 116–17; expansion of, 240n26; gender, 180–82; on government, 177–80; identity, 182–86; retention rate, 160; sexual orientation, 180–82; social networks, 165; social status, 20, 231n20; socioeconomic status, 116–17; spouse's religion, 163–64. *See also* religious affiliation/practice
Adams, Samuel, 239n12
affiliation. *See* nonaffiliated believers; nones/nonreligion; religious affiliation/practice
African Americans, 117–20. *See also* ethnicity/race
agency, social status, 42, 237n52
The Age of Reason (Paine), 49–50, 239n12, 254n11
agnosticism, 22–23, 66, 76–80; childhood socialization, 162; children, 158; cosmic belief systems, 89–105; cultural conflict, 98–99; defined, 15–19, 229n9, 230n19; educational attainment, 116–17; evolutionary, 54–58, 62; gender, 180–82, 256n25; on government, 177–80; happiness/satisfaction, 93–96; Humanism, 46; identity, 99–104, 182–86; Robert Ingersoll, 32, 54, 56, 58; in relation to religion, 89–93; religion/science conflict, 32, 232n16; scientific views, 96–98; scientism, 46; sexual orientation, 180–82; social networks, 165; social status, 116–17; socioeconomic status, 116–17
Allen, Ethan, 48, 58, 239n8; *Reason, the Only Oracle of Man*, 48, 239n8
American Atheists, 12, 187–88, 199
American Economic Association, 28
American Humanist Association, 12, 186–88, 199, 201
American Journal of Sociology (periodical), 28, 31
American Mosaic Survey, 4–5, 225n12
American Secular Union, 56–58, 62
American Sociological Society/Association, 28
Anthony, Susan B., 149
anti-federalism, 48–50
anti-fundamentalism, 74–75
apostates/apostasy, 18, 20; active religion, 160; identity, 102; secularity, 80–84
Applied Sociology (Ward), 31
Aptheker, Herbert, 110
aristocratic deism, 47–50, 62
Articles of Confederation, 48
Asian Americans, 120–22. *See also* ethnicity/race
assimilation: marriage, 259n10; secularity, 120–23
atheism, 1–3, 22–23, 49, 66, 76–80, 223n1, 239n12; acceptance of, 2–5, 167, 174, 225n12, 261n1; childhood socialization, 162; children, 158; cosmic belief systems, 89–105; cultural conflict, 98–99; cultural view of secularism, 103; defined, 15–19, 229n9, 230n19;

atheism (*cont.*)
educational attainment, 116–17; freethought, 53; gender, 180–82; on government, 177–80; happiness/satisfaction, 93–96; hard *vs.* soft, 15–16, 229n9; identity, 99–104, 182–86; morality, 100–101; organized secularism, 56; as pejorative term, 21–22, 230n19; political dimensions of, 11–12; presidential politics, 50; problematic definitions of, 6, 227n17; psychology of, 102–4; in relation to religion, 89–93; religion/science conflict, 32, 232n16; scientific views, 96–98; sexual orientation, 180–82; social networks, 165; social status, 116–17; socioeconomic status, 116–17
Augustine, Kathy, 190–91

Baptists, 53, 240n26; changes in Southern Baptist Convention, 243n10; disestablishment, 51
Baylor Religion Survey (BRS), 92–93, 97, 161–65, 222, 231n22, 259n18
Beacon (periodical), 51
Beadle, William, 47–48, 238n8
Beecher, Catharine, 148
Beecher, Henry Ward, 148
Beecher, Lyman, 148
belief systems. *See* cosmic belief systems; nonaffiliated believers; *specific type*
Bengston, Vern, 161–62
Bennett, D. M., 56, 63
Bennett, Mary, 56
Bentham, Jeremy, 134, 141
Bill of Rights, 48
binary classification of secularism, 14, 228n6
birth control, 53, 66, 73, 101, 149, 181
birth rates, 67; apostasy, 81; secularity, 84–85, 246n28
blasphemy trials of Abner Kneeland, 52–53
Boston Investigator (periodical), 51–52
Bothwell, Cecil, 11, 168–77, 206, 214
Brown, Lori Lipman, 12, 189–98, 206
Brown v. Board of Education, 66
BRS. *See* Baylor Religion Survey
Bryan, William Jennings, 59
Buchanan, Pat, 72–73
Bush, George H. W., 72, 74
Bush, George W., 70–71, 185; first inaugural of, 225n11; politicization of religion, 224n7; post-9/11 rhetoric of, 2

Calvinism, 63
Carlile, Richard, 135, 254n11
Carter, James, 71, 78–79, 243n6
Catholicism: apostasy, 81, 83; interfaith marriage, 154; political polarization, 70, 75; secularism, 47, 58–59, 65; U.S. Congress members, 167; voting patterns, 185
Census Bureau, 66
children: corporal punishment, 163; generational changes, 10; marriage, 154–57; religious socialization, 157–63; secularity, 154–63. *See also* birth rates; family structure
Christian Coalition, 73–74
Christianization. *See* religious affiliation/practice, expansion of; *specific denominations*
class. *See* social status; socioeconomic status
Clinton, Hillary, 72
Clinton, William Jefferson, 72, 225n11
Coe, Kevin, 69–71
cognition, reactive, 43, 237n55
cognitive dissonance, 43
cohabitation, 156–57
The Colbert Report, 189
Cold War, 60, 62, 66–68
Common Sense (Paine), 50
communism/socialism, 60, 66–69; W. E. B. Du Bois, 106; Langston Hughes,

118–19; March on Washington, 106, 250n3; space race, 66
Comte, Auguste, 29, 55, 139, 232n14
Congressional Record, 119
conservative Protestantism. *See* Protestantism; Religious Right; *specific denominations*
consolidation of identity, 39–40
Converse, Philip, 41; "The Nature of Belief Systems in Mass Publics," 228n21
conversion, social networks, 40
corporal punishment, 163
cosmic belief systems, 41–43; defined, 6, 8; inconsistency in, 41; meaning of experience, 42; nonreligious, 89–105; resources, 43, 237n54; socioeconomic status, 43, 237n54. *See also* nonaffiliated believers; *specific types*
cosmology, 39
counterculture, 60, 62, 67
The Crisis (Paine), 50
cultural diffusion, 45, 51, 56, 58–62
cultural religion, 17–18, 22–23, 229n14; childhood socialization, 162; children, 158; cosmic belief systems, 89–105; cultural conflict, 98–99; educational attainment, 116–17; gender, 180–82, 256n25; on government, 177–80; happiness/satisfaction, 93–96; identity, 182–86; in relation to religion, 89–93; scientific views, 96–98; sexual orientation, 180–82; social networks, 165; social status, 116–17; socioeconomic status, 116–17. *See also* religious affiliation/practice
cultural view of secularism, 10–11, 25, 34–37, 131–32, 210–12, 233n30–234n31; atheism, 103; conflict, 98–99; cosmic belief systems, 41–43; culture defined, 35, 234n33; identity, 36–40; perception, 36, 40; social status, 37–40
Current Population Survey, 66
Darrow, Clarence, 59
Darwin, Charles, 29
Darwinism, 54–55; social, 29
Data Analyses Appendix, 23
Davie, Grace, 229n12
Dawkins, Richard, 103
Declaration of Independence, 137
"definition of the situation," 37
deism, 27, 32, 45, 62; aristocratic, 47–50, 62; defined, 46; presidential politics, 50; prophetic, 49, 52, 62
Demerath, N. J., 17
Democratic Party. *See* party politics
Dilthey, Wilhelm, 107
disestablishment, 51
divorce, 20, 67, 84, 87, 153, 155–56
Dobson, James, 226n13
Domke, David, 69–71
Douglas, Mary, 234n33
Draper, John W., 32; *History of the Conflict between Religion Science*, 232n16
Du Bois, W. E. B., 8, 10, 106–15, 131, 206, 224n8; *The Negro Church*, 107; "Of the Coming of John," 111–13; *The Philadelphia Negro*, 107; religious affiliation/practice, 110–15, 231n1, 250n11, 251n14, 251n21, 251n26; *The Souls of Black Folk*, 109, 111, 113
Dynamic Sociology (Ward), 27–30

economic position. *See* social status
Edison, Thomas, 2
educational attainment: antifundamentalism, 75; ethnicity/race, 121–23; gender, 66; secularity, 10–11, 116–17, 143–44. *See also* social status
Eisenhower, Dwight, 66, 70
Enlightenment, 26, 31, 48, 238n4
Epicurus, 133
ethnicity/race, 32, 106–15, 233n25; acceptance of, 4–5, 225n12; *Brown v. Board of Education*, 66; educational attainment, 121–23;

ethnicity/race (*cont.*)
March on Washington, 106, 250n3; morality, 115; othering, 109; power, 10; secularity, 106–32; slavery, 101, 112–13, 134, 137, 140, 149; social status, 38, 109–10, 115–31. *See also* immigrants/immigration
evangelical freethought, 50–54, 62
evolutionary agnosticism, 54–58, 62
experience, meaning of, 42

Faith Matters Survey, 221–22
Falwell, Jerry, 41, 70
family structure, 67–68; children, 154–57; cohabitation, 156–57; gender, 155–57; gender of religious parent, 161–62; generational changes to, 10; religious views of, 39; secularity, 11, 37–39, 151–66. *See also* divorce; marriage
"A Feast of Hate and Fear" (Ivins), 74, 244n18
federalism, 48–50
A Few Days in Athens (Wright), 133–34
Ford, Gerald, 2–3, 70
foundational assumption of identity, 37
Fox News, 174
Francis, Pope, 201
Free Enquirer (periodical), 51, 134
Free Religion Association, 56
freethought, 9, 20–21, 27–28, 63; atheism, 53; defined, 46; evangelical, 50–54, 62; golden age of, 56–59; Hispanic American Freethinkers, 123–31; historical foundations of, 45–65
fundamentalism, 59, 74–75, 78–79, 245n24

Geertz, Clifford, *The Interpretation of Cultures*, 234n33
gender, 32, 66–67, 141–45, 251n30; children, 155–57; educational attainment, 66; family structure, 155–57; of God, 54, 240n28; marriage, 155–57; political views, 140–45; religiosity and secularity, 11; religious affiliation/practice, 140–45; of religious parent, 161–62; Religious Right, 67–75; secularism, 57; secularity, 133–50, 140–45, 180–82, 256n25; social status, 38, 66–68, 115, 251n30
General Social Surveys (GSS), 7, 16, 18, 22, 67, 76–78, 81–82, 89–90, 95, 97, 116, 141–46, 162, 180, 184, 219–20, 226n12, 229n14, 245n24, 245nn21–22, 246n1, 246n28, 256n25, 259n15, 260n23, 263n20
generational changes. *See* children
Glock, Charles Y., *Religion Society in Tension* (Glock and Stark), 228n7
"God strategy," 67–69, 75
Godwin, William, 135, 254n11
"Goodbye Christ" (Hughes), 118
Gooding-Williams, Robert, 112
Graham, Billy, 172–73, 177
Great Abdicating, 61–62, 66–88, 76–80; apostasy, 80–84; counterculture, 66; future of secularity, 84–86; political polarization, 66–80
Great Depression, 59–60, 69
"Great Disappointment," 20
Grimké, Angelina and Sarah, 136
GSS. *See* General Social Surveys

Haeckel, Ernst, 29
HAFree. *See* Hispanic American Freethinkers
"Halls of Science," 32, 52, 135, 137, 139
happiness, 93–96
hard atheism, 15–16, 229n9
Harris, Sam, 96
Hawkes, Albert, 119
Hicks, Elias, 149
Hispanic American Freethinkers (HAFree), 123–31, 188
Hispanic Americans, 122–23. *See also* ethnicity/race

History of the Conflict between Religion and Science (Draper), 232n16
History of the Warfare of Science with Theology in Christendom (White), 232n16
Hone, Philip, 148
Hoover, J. Edgar, 119
Hughes, Langston, 118–19; "Goodbye Christ," 118; "A New Song," 118, 252n36
Human Development Index, 203, 205
The Humanist (periodical), 186
humanitarianism, 46, 101
Hume, David, 209
Huxley, Thomas, 29, 55

The Iconoclast (periodical), 27, 30, 32
identity, 36–40; consolidation of, 39–40; media, 40; narrative, 40; othering, 101; political, 76, 78, 182–86; religious, perception of, 238n1; rhetorical form of, 40; secularity, 99–104, 182–86
immigrants/immigration: marriage, 259n10; power, 10; secularism, 52–53, 58, 65, 241n38; secularity, 115–31, 120–23. *See also* ethnicity/race
income. *See* social status; socioeconomic status
inconsistency in beliefs, 41
The Index (periodical), 56
Ingersoll, Robert, 32, 54, 56, 58, 225n8
interfaith marriage, 152–54, 259n10
The Interpretation of Cultures (Geertz), 234n33
irreligious, defined, 8
Ivins, Molly, 244n18

Jackson, Andrew, 53
Jackson, Stonewall, 27
James, William, 107
Jefferson, Thomas, 134, 196; deism, 50; secularism, 2
Judaism: apostasy, 81, 83; political polarization, 72, 75; secularism, 58–59, 189–98, 206; U.S. Congress members, 167; voting patterns, 185

Kennedy administration, 250n3
Kerry, John, 185
King, Martin Luther, Jr., 106, 115
Kneeland, Abner, 51–53, 240n22
Knowledge Networks, 230n20

Lafayette, Marquis de, 134
Latinos, 122–23. *See also* ethnicity/race
law of three stages, 231n6
Layman, Geoffrey, 75
Lincoln, Abraham, 27

March on Washington, 106, 250n3
marriage: assimilation, 259n10; children, 154–57; gender, 155–57; interfaith, 152–54, 259n10; rates of, 67–68; secularity, 151–66, 259n10; spouse's religion, 163–64. *See also* divorce; family structure
McCarthy, Joseph, 119
McPherson, Aimee Semple, 118–19
meaning of experience, 42
Medford, Bobby Lee, 172
media, identity and, 40
Mencken, H. L., 59
metaphysics, 39
Methodism, 53–54, 240n26
Miller, William, 20–21
minority status/minorities. *See* ethnicity/race; immigrants/immigration; social status
morality, 14; and atheism, 100–101; cultural connections to ethnicity/race, 115; and secularism, 45–46, 55
Moral Majority, 68, 70
Mott, Lucretia, 136
Mountain Xpress (periodical), 168
Murray v. Curlett, 187
Muslims, acceptance of, 4–5, 226n12
Myers, Scott, 154
Mylne, James, 133

Nader, Ralph, 185
narrative, 40
Nashoba commune, 134, 140, 147–49
National Association for the Advancement of Colored People, 106
National Election Surveys, 74–75, 245n24
National Liberal League, 57
National Liberal Reform League, 27
natural law, 45, 55
"The Nature of Belief Systems in Mass Publics" (Converse), 41, 228n21, 237n50
The Negro Church (Du Bois), 107
New Harmony Gazette (periodical), 134
newsletters. *See* organized secularism; *specific title*
"A New Song" (Hughes), 118, 252n36
Newsweek (periodical), 74
New York Times (periodical), 174
Nine Demands of Liberalism, 62–63, 241n46
Nixon, Richard, 70–71
nonaffiliated believers, 16, 18, 19–20, 22–23, 230n16, 231n22; childhood socialization, 162; cosmic belief systems, 89–105; cultural conflict, 98–99; educational attainment, 116–17; gender, 180–82; on government, 177–80; happiness/satisfaction, 93–96; identity, 99–104, 182–86; scientific views, 96–98; sexual orientation, 180–82; social networks, 165; social status, 116–17; socioeconomic status, 116–17
nonaffiliation. *See* nonaffiliated believers; nones/nonreligion
nones/nonreligion, 1–3, 14–15, 19–20, 22–23, 66–67, 69, 76–80, 84–87, 223n1, 223n3, 230n16, 231n22, 246n28; acceptance of, 4–5, 225n12; apostasy, 82; cosmic belief systems, 89–105; cultural conflict, 98–99; defined, 8; educational attainment, 143–44; gender, 143–44, 180–82; on government, 177–80; happiness/satisfaction, 93–96; identity, 99–104, 182–86; presidential politics, 2–4, 224nn7–8, 225n11; in relation to religion, 89–93; Religious Right, 69; scientific views, 96–98; sexual orientation, 180–82; social networks, 165; social status, 116–17; voting patterns among, 78–80, 245nn23–24
Norton, Charles Eliot, 56

Obama, Barack: first inaugural of, 2–4, 79, 223n4, 224n7, 225n11; nones/nonreligion, 79; party platform, 79
"Of the Coming of John" (Du Bois), 111–13
O'Hair, Madalyn Murray, 187
O'Reilly Factor, 189
organized secularism, 49, 51–60, 62–64, 213–16, 241n38, 241n46; atheism, 56; growth in, 186–98; history of, 7, 227n19
othering: ethnicity/race, 109; identity, 101; of nonreligious, 4–5, 225n12
Owen, Robert, 52, 134–35, 232n20

Paine, Thomas, 49–50, 57, 61, 135, 149, 239n12, 254n11; accusations of atheism, 239n12; *The Age of Reason*, 49–50, 239n12, 254n11; atheism, 49, 239n12; *Common Sense*, 50; *The Crisis*, 50; on deism, 45; freethought, 63; secularism, 2; Lester F. Ward, 26, 32
Palmer, Elihu, 49–50, 96; *Principles of Nature*, 49
paranormal phenomena, belief in, 92, 246n3
parents. *See* family structure; social networks
party politics, 68–80; party platform, 79–80; secularity, 182–86
peers. *See* social networks
perception: of identity, 36, 40, 238n1; of religious identity, 238n1

periodicals. *See* organized secularism; *specific title*
Pew Asian American and Latino/a Surveys, 122–23, 221, 253n42
Pew Religious Landscape Survey (RLS), 7, 18, 21–23, 81, 90–94, 91, 98, 116, 119–22, 141, 143, 155–59, 163, 177, 180–84, 220–21, 263n20, 265n10
The Philadelphia Negro (Du Bois), 107
political progressivism, 101, 143
political views: gender, 140–45; polarization of, 69–80; on secularity, 11, 167–77, 210–12; of seculars, 11, 177–86
politicization of religion: atheism, 11–12, 50; deism, 50; history of, 2–4, 224nn7–8, 225n11; Religious Right, 68–80; requirements of public office, 48–49, 239n11; secularism, 11–12, 48–49, 239n11. *See also* party politics; presidential politics
positivism, 29, 32
power, social status, 10, 115–17, 131–32, 251n30
practice. *See* religious affiliation/practice
presidential politics: atheism, 50; deism, 50; March on Washington, 106, 250n3; nonreligion, 2–4, 224nn7–8, 225n11; political polarization, 69–75; Religious Right, 68–80
Prince of War: Billy Graham's Crusade for a Wholly Christian Empire (Bothwell), 172
Principles of Nature (Palmer), 49
progressivism, political, 101, 143
Prohibition, 60
prophetic deism, 49, 52, 62
Prospect (periodical), 49
Protestantism: active religion, 160; apostasy, 81–83; political polarization, 69–75; secularism, 45–65, 69–75; U.S. Congress members, 167; voting patterns, 185. *See also* Religious Right; *specific denomination*
psychology of atheism, 102–4
Puritanism, 48
Putnam, Samuel, 54, 57, 62, 241n46

race. *See* ethnicity/race
Rachel Maddow Show, 174
Randolph, A. Philip, 2, 224n8
rational choice theories, 34, 44, 233n30–234n31
reactive cognition, 43, 237n55
Reagan, Ronald, 70–71, 74, 243n6; first inaugural of, 225n11; nones/nonreligion and, 78–79
reality, defining, 37–40
Reason, the Only Oracle of Man (Allen), 48, 239n8
Red Scare. *See* communism/socialism
Reed, Ralph, 73, 75
Reign of Terror, 49
relational social status, 6
religion. *See* active religion; cultural religion; religious affiliation/practice; religious function
Religion Society in Tension (Glock and Stark), 228n7
religious affiliation/practice, 14–15, 17–18, 66–69, 76–80, 110–15, 229n14; cultural conflict, 98–99; expansion of, 240n26; family, 39; gender, 140–45; secularity in relation to, 89–93; waning of (*see* Great Abdicating). *See also* active religion; cultural religion; *specific denominations*
religious function, 34, 233n29
Religious Right, 61–62; nones/nonreligion, 69; political polarization, 69–75
Religious Roundtable, 70
Republican Party. *See* party politics
resources, cosmic belief systems and, 43, 237n54
retention rate. *See* apostates/apostasy
rhetorical form of identity, 40
RLS. *See* Pew Religious Landscape Survey

Robertson, Pat, 72–73
Roe v. Wade, 68
Roosevelt, Franklin, 2, 70–71
Roosevelt, Theodore, 239n12
Rose, Ernestine, 149
Ross, E. A, 26

Sagan, Carl, 2, 41
Santayana, George, 107
satisfaction, 93–96
Schmoller, Gustav von, 107
science: religion/science conflict, 32, 232n16; views of, 96–98
scientism, 25, 46, 101–2. *See also* evolutionary agnosticism
Scopes trial, 59
Second Great Awakening, 26, 50, 62, 133
secular. *See* secularism; secularity/seculars; secularization
Secular Coalition for America, 12, 188–89, 195, 198
secularism, 1–3, 110–15, 223n1, 223n3, 250n11, 251n14, 251n21, 251n26; acceptance of, 4–5, 45, 225n12; categories of, 10; Catholicism and, 47, 58–59, 65; cultural view of (*see* cultural view of secularism); defined, 8, 13; federalism and, 48–50; historical foundations of, 45–65; historical themes of, 60–64, 241n45; immigration and, 52–53, 58, 65, 241n38; Judaism and, 58–59, 189–98, 206; morality and, 45–46, 55; organized (*see* organized secularism); outside the U.S., 202–4; political dimensions of, 11–12; problematic definitions of, 6, 227n17; Protestantism and, 45–65, 69–75; religious responses to, 7, 227n19; study of, 5–9. *See also* secularity/seculars
secularity/seculars, 21–23, 76–80, 84–87, 204–6, 230n19–231n22, 246n28; assimilation, 120–23; basic classifications of, 14–15; binary classification of, 14, 228n6; birth rates, 81, 84–85, 246n28; childhood socialization, 162; children, 154–63; classification of, 7–8, 227n20, 228n21; cosmic belief systems, 89–105; cultural conflict, 98–99; defined, 8, 13–24, 228n3, 228n6; educational attainment, 10–11, 116–17, 143–44; empirical account of, 14; ethnicity/race, 106–32, 115–31; family structure, 11, 37–39, 151–66; future of, 84–86; gender, 11, 38, 133–50, 140–45, 180–82, 256n25; on government, 177–80; historical dimensions of, 210–12; identity, 99–104, 182–86; immigrants/immigration, 115–31, 120–23; marriage, 151–66, 259n10; perception of religious identity, 238n4; political polarization, 69–80; political views of, 177–86, 210–12; political views on, 11, 167–99; power, 10; race, 38; in relation to religion, 89–93; sexual orientation, 11, 145–46; on sexual orientation, 180–82; socialized, 18, 157–63; social networks, 37–39, 165; social status, 37–40; socioeconomic status, 115–31, 116–17; sociological patterning of, 212–13; voting patterns among, 182–86. *See also* secularism
secularization: defined, 8; theories of, 34, 233n30
secular organizations. *See* organized secularism
Secular Student Alliance, 12, 188, 199
self/selves. *See* identity
separation of church and state, 46–47, 48–50, 239n11; disestablishment, 51
sexual orientation: acceptance of, 4–5; Religious Right and, 67–75; secularity, 11, 145–46, 180–82; Secular Student Alliance, 188
Shelley, Mary Wollstonecraft, 254n11
Shelley, Percy Bysshe, 135, 254n11

siblings. *See* family structure; social networks
Sinema, Krysten, 167
slavery, 101, 112–13, 134, 137, 140, 149
Small, Albion W., 27–28, 32
Smith, Adam, 133
social class. *See* social status; socioeconomic status
social Darwinism, 29
Social Gospel, 29
socialism. *See* communism/socialism
socialized seculars, 18, 157–63
social networks: conversion, 40; secularity, 37–39, 165. *See also* family structure
social status, 32; active religion, 20, 231n20; agency, 42, 237n52; cosmology, 39; ethnicity/race, 38, 109–10, 115–31; gender, 38, 66–68, 115, 251n30; metaphysics, 39; power, 10, 115–17, 131–32, 251n30; race, 38; relational, 6; secularity, 37–40; and socioeconomic status, 38. *See also* educational attainment; socioeconomic status
socioeconomic status: cosmic belief systems, 43, 237n54; immigrants/immigration, 121–23; power, 10; secularity, 115–31, 116–17; and social status, 38. *See also* social status
soft atheism, 15–16, 229n9
The Souls of Black Folk (Du Bois), 109, 111, 113
Southern Baptist Convention, 243n10
Speckhardt, Roy, 186–87, 201
Spencer, Herbert, 29, 55
spirituality, 10, 90, 104, 206, 208
spouses. *See* family structure; marriage; social networks
Stanton, Elizabeth Cady, 56, 149
Stark, Pete, 167
Stark, Rodney, 226n14; *Religion Society in Tension* (Glock and Stark), 228n7
Stowe, Harriet Beecher, 148
Sunday schools of secularism, 63
supernaturalism, 15, 45–46, 92, 103–5, 206–9; paranormal, 10, 92, 246n3; religious, 10, 92

Tamayo, David, 11, 123–31, 206
The Temple of Reason (periodical), 49
theistic belief, 15–17
theories: rational choice, 34, 44, 233n30–234n31; of religion, 6–7, 206–10, 223n29; of secularization, 34, 233n30; Thomas Theorem, 37, 40
Thomas, W. I., 37
Thomas Theorem, 37, 40
Trinitarianism, 51
Truman, Harry, 70
The Truth Seeker (periodical), 56, 63
Twain, Mark, 2, 225n8

Unitarianism, 51, 62, 63
Unitarian Universalist Association, 214–15
United States Constitution, 48, 137, 146
USA Today (periodical), 174

Vale, Gilbert, 52
Views of Society and Manners in America (Wright), 134
Villaraigosa, Antonio, 80
Voas, David, 229n12
Voltaire, 32

Ward, Justus, 26
Ward, Lester F., 8, 9, 26–34, 96, 107–8, 110, 206, 233n29, 233nn24–25; *Applied Sociology*, 31; Civil War, 27; *Dynamic Sociology*, 27–30; Enlightenment, 26, 31; freethought, 27–28; religion/science conflict, 32, 232n16; on religious function, 34, 233n29; social Darwinism, 29
Ward, Silence, 26
Weber, Max, 107
West, Cornel, 114

White, Andrew D., 32; *A History of the Warfare of Science with Theology in Christendom*, 232n16
white Americans, 117, 252n34. *See also* ethnicity/race
Whitman, Walt, 135, 149
Wilkins, Roy, 106
World Values Survey (WVS), 1–3, 203–5, 223n1, 223n3, 264n9, 265n15
Wright, Frances, 8, 11, 52, 133–42, 146–50, 206, 231n6, 232n20, 240n22, 255n21, 257n37; *Course of Popular Lectures*, 255n22; *A Few Days in Athens*, 133–34; *Views of Society and Manners in America*, 134
Wright, Jeremiah, 224n7

Zerubavel, Eviatar, 235n36
Zuckerman, Phil, 38, 110

ABOUT THE AUTHORS

Joseph O. Baker is Assistant Professor in the Department of Sociology and Anthropology at East Tennessee State University, and Senior Research Associate for the Association of Religion Data Archives. He is co-author of *Paranormal America* (NYU Press).

Buster G. Smith is Assistant Professor in the Department of Sociology at Catawba College. He received his Ph.D. from Baylor University in the sociology of religion and performed his undergraduate work at Middlebury College.